NWi5D5i

KT-214-927

PRINCIPLES OF COGNITIVE PSYCHOLOGY

WITHDRAWN

N 0111710 6

THE PRINCIPLES OF PSYCHOLOGY SERIES

The books in this series are ideal for students with little prior knowledge of psychology. Together they are intended to cover all the major areas of psychology studied today. They will be suitable for all students beginning psychology courses, for those studying psychology as a supplement to other applied courses, and for all those requiring a general and up-to-date overview of the major concerns and issues in psychology. The following titles are available:

PERSPECTIVES ON PSYCHOLOGY
MICHAEL W. EYSENCK (Royal Holloway University of London)
0-86377-254-4 hbk / 0-86377-255-2 pbk 1994 192pp.

PRINCIPLES OF DEVELOPMENTAL PSYCHOLOGY
GEORGE BUTTERWORTH (University of Sussex)
MARGARET HARRIS (Royal Holloway University of London)
0-86377-279-X hbk / 0-86377-280-3 pbk 1994 288pp.

PRINCIPLES OF COGNITIVE PSYCHOLOGY, Second Edition
MICHAEL W. EYSENCK (Royal Holloway University of London)
1-84169-259-X hbk / 1-84169-260-3 pbk 2001 400pp.

PRINCIPLES OF BIOPSYCHOLOGY
SIMON GREEN (Birkbeck College, London)
0-86377-281-1 hbk / 0-86377-282-X pbk 1994 224pp.

PRINCIPLES OF SOCIAL PSYCHOLOGY
NICKY HAYES (University of Huddersfield)
0-86377-258-7 hbk / 0-86377-259-5 pbk 1993 176pp.

PRINCIPLES OF COMPARATIVE PSYCHOLOGY
NICKY HAYES (University of Huddersfield)
0-86377-292-7 hbk / 0-86377-293-5 pbk 1994 256pp.

INDIVIDUAL DIFFERENCES: NORMAL AND ABNORMAL
MICHAEL W. EYSENCK (Royal Holloway University of London)
0-86377-256-0 hbk / 0-86377-257-9 pbk 1994 208pp.

PRINCIPLES OF ABILITIES AND HUMAN LEARNING
MICHAEL J.A. HOWE (University of Exeter)
0-86377-532-2 hbk / 0-86377-533-0 pbk 1998 160pp.

TEACHING INTRODUCTORY PSYCHOLOGY
ROZ BRODY and NICKY HAYES
0-86377-373-7 pbk 1995 160pp.

Principles of Cognitive Psychology

Second Edition

Michael W. Eysenck

A volume in the series
Principles of Psychology

Series Editors
Michael W. Eysenck
Simon Green
Nicky Hayes

PSYCHOLOGY PRESS
· Taylor & Francis Group ·

First published 2001 by Psychology Press Ltd
27 Church Road, Hove, East Sussex, BN3 2FA, UK

www.psypress.co.uk

Simultaneously published in the USA and Canada
by Taylor & Francis Inc
325 Chestnut Street, Suite 800, Philadelphia, PA 19106, USA

Psychology Press is part of the Taylor & Francis Group

© 2001 by Psychology Press Ltd

All rights reserved. No part of this book may be reprinted or
reproduced or utilised in any form or by any electronic,
mechanical, or other means, now known or hereafter invented,
including photocopying and recording, or in any information
storage or retrieval system, without permission in writing from
the publishers.

NEWMAN COLLEGE
BARTLEY GREEN
BIRMINGHAM B32 3NT
CLASS 155.413
BARCODE 01117106
AUTHOR Eys

British Library Cataloguing in Publication Data
A catalogue record for this book is available from the British Library

Library of Congress Cataloging-in-Publication Data
Eysenck, Michael W.
    Principles of cognitive psychology / Michael W. Eysenck – 2nd ed.
        p. cm. – (Principles of psychology, ISSN 0965-9706)
    Includes bibliographical references and indexes.
    ISBN 1-84169-259-X – ISBN 1-84169-260-3 (Pbk.)
    1. Cognitive psychology. I. Title. II. Series.

BF201 .E97 2001
153–dc21

                                        00–065313

    ISBN 1-84169-259-X (Hbk)
    ISBN 1-84169-260-3 (Pbk)
    ISSN 0965-9706

Cover design by Sandra Heath
Typeset in the UK by Mayhew Typesetting, Rhayader, Powys
Printed and bound in the UK by TJ International Ltd, Padstow, Cornwall

To my daughter Fleur with love

The secret of science is to ask the right question.
(Henry Tizard, 1885–1959, British scientist)

Contents

About the Author

Michael W. Eysenck is one of the best-known British psychologists. He is Professor of Psychology and Head of the Psychology Department at Royal Holloway University of London, which is one of the leading departments in the United Kingdom. His academic interests lie mainly in cognitive psychology, with much of his research focusing on the role of cognitive factors in anxiety in normal and clinical populations.

He is the author of many titles, and his previous textbooks published by Psychology Press include *Simply Psychology* (1996), *Perspectives on Psychology* (1994), *Individual Differences: Normal and Abnormal* (1994), *Psychology: A Student's Handbook* (2000), *Cognitive Psychology: A Student's Handbook*, 4th Edition (2000, with Mark Keane), *Psychology for AS Level* (2000, with Cara Flanagan) and *Psychology for A2 Level* (2001, with Cara Flanagan). He has also written the research monographs *Anxiety and Cognition: A Unified Theory* (1997) and *Anxiety: The Cognitive Perspectives* (1992), along with the popular title *Happiness: Facts and Myths* (1990).

Preface

Cognitive psychology is perhaps the most successful branch of psychology. This can be seen in the fact that our knowledge of topics such as attention, perception, learning, memory, problem solving, and reasoning has increased substantially in recent years. This has happened in part because cognitive psychologists are making more and more use of a wide range of approaches to the subject of human cognition. For example, technological advances such as PET scans and functional magnetic resonance imaging have allowed us to observe the brain in action more directly than was possible before. In addition, there are more attempts to use computer modelling to simulate human cognition, and the study of brain-damaged patients is shedding much light on normal cognition. All of these approaches are now used extensively, and the traditional, laboratory-based approach also remains popular.

I know from many years of teaching that students often find cognitive psychology complicated and of less appeal than some other areas of psychology. I have attempted in this introductory book to make cognitive psychology accessible to students who have never studied it before, while maintaining a critical perspective on the theories and research that are discussed. Those students who find areas such as social, developmental, or abnormal psychology more to their taste than cognitive psychology should perhaps bear in mind that advances in all of these areas depend increasingly on the insights and research of cognitive psychologists. For example, cognitive and cognitive-behavioural therapy are becoming the dominant forms of treatment for anxiety and depression.

I am very grateful to several people for reading an entire draft of this book, and for offering valuable advice on how it could be improved. They include Gerry Quinn, Ian S. Robertson, Jane Willson and an anonymous reviewer. I would also like to thank my family for their support both throughout the writing of this book and over the years. This book is dedicated to dear Fleur, who is all one would hope for in a daughter.

Michael W. Eysenck
Rio de Janeiro

Approaches to cognitive psychology 1

Introduction

As this entire book is devoted to cognitive psychology, it is only right and proper to set the scene by describing in some detail exactly what we mean by cognitive psychology. This is easier said than done. Cognitive psychologists favour different theoretical approaches and study a wide range of phenemona, and it is hard to describe their endeavours in a coherent way. Despite this, we will try to impose a structure on the discipline of cognitive psychology.

Most cognitive psychologists agree that the subject matter of cognitive psychology consists of the main internal psychological processes that are involved in making sense of the environment and deciding what action might be appropriate. These processes include attention, perception, learning, memory, language, problem solving, reasoning, and thinking.

It is important to note that cognitive psychology has become increasingly important in several other areas of psychology. For example, consider the areas of developmental psychology, social psychology, and abnormal psychology. In order to understand how infants develop into adolescents and adults, it is essential to consider the massive cognitive changes that occur during the years of childhood. In order to understand how individuals interact with each other in social situations, we need to take account of the knowledge of themselves and of each other they have stored in memory, their interpretations of the current social situation, and so on. In order to understand patients suffering from anxiety disorders or depression, it is important to focus on their biased interpretations of themselves and of their current and future prospects.

Information-processing approach

Historically, most cognitive psychologists have adopted what is often referred to as the information-processing approach (see Lachman, Lachman, & Butterfield, 1979). Some of the main assumptions of this approach are as follows:

- Information made available by the environment is processed by a series of processing systems (e.g., attention, perception, short-term memory).
- These processing systems transform or alter the information in various systematic ways (e.g., three connected lines are presented to our eyes, but we see a triangle).
- The major goal of research is to specify the processes and structures (e.g., long-term memory) that underlie cognitive performance.
- Information processing in people resembles that in computers.

A version of the information-processing approach that was popular about 30 years ago is shown in Figure 1.1. According to this version, a stimulus (an environmental event such as a problem or task) is presented to the participant, and this stimulus causes certain internal cognitive processes to occur. These processes finally produce the required response or answer. Processing directly affected by the stimulus input is usually described as *bottom-up processing*. In addition, it was assumed within this version of information-processing theory that only one process occurs at any moment in time. This is known as *serial processing*, and means that one process is completed before the next begins.

Unfortunately for the type of information-processing theory we have been discussing, there are numerous situations in which processing is neither exclusively bottom-up nor serial. There is also *top-down processing*, which is processing that is influenced by the individual's expectations and knowledge rather than simply by the stimulus itself. Look at the triangle in Figure 1.2, and read what it says. Unless you are familiar with this trick, you will probably have read it as "Paris in the spring". Look again, and you will see that the word "the" is repeated. Your expectation that it is the well-known phrase (i.e., top-down processing) dominated the information actually available in the stimulus (i.e., bottom-up processing).

It is now widely accepted that most cognition involves a mixture of bottom-up and top-down processing. An especially clear

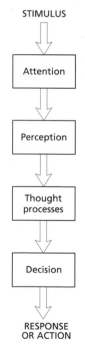

Figure 1.1. An early version of the information-processing approach.

Figure 1.2. Diagram to demonstrate top-down processing.

PARIS

IN THE

THE SPRING

demonstration of this comes from a study by Bruner, Postman, and Rodrigues (1951), in which the participants expected to see conventional playing cards presented very briefly. When black hearts were presented, some of the participants claimed to have seen purple or brown hearts. Here we have an almost literal blending of the black colour stemming from bottom-up processing and of the red colour stemming from top-down processing due to the expectation that hearts will be red.

Processing in which some or all of the processes involved in a cognitive task occur at the same time is known as *parallel processing*. It is often hard to know whether a particular task is being processed in a serial or a parallel fashion. However, the amount of practice an individual has had on a given task is of great importance. As we will see in Chapter 4, parallel processing occurs much more often when someone is highly skilled than when they are starting to master a skill. For example, someone who is just starting to learn to drive finds it very hard to change gear and to steer accurately at the same time. In contrast, an experienced driver finds it easy, and can even hold a conversation while changing gear and steering.

Four major approaches

As you can perhaps imagine, it is very difficult to study cognitive processes. These processes often occur very rapidly, and they are occurring inside the head so that they cannot be observed directly. The responses that participants make when given some task to perform can tell us something about the internal cognitive processes that have occurred, but they typically only provide an indirect reflection of those processes. How have cognitive psychologists responded to this challenge? In essence, they have developed four major approaches to the study of human cognition (discussed below), and have argued that combining information from all of these approaches will allow us to develop a full understanding of cognitive processes and structures.

The four major approaches are as follows:

- *Experimental cognitive psychology*: This approach involves carrying out experiments on normal individuals, typically under laboratory conditions.
- *Cognitive neuropsychology*: This approach involves studying patterns of cognitive impairment shown by brain-damaged patients in order to understand normal human cognition.
- *Cognitive science*: This approach involves developing computational models to understand human cognition.
- *Cognitive neuroscience*: This approach involves using several techniques for studying brain functioning (e.g., brain scans) in order to identify the processes and structures used in cognition.

The above distinctions are less neat and tidy in reality than has been implied. Terms such as cognitive science and cognitive neuroscience are sometimes used in a broader and more inclusive way than has been done here. In addition, some of the distinctions have become somewhat blurred, because there has been a rapid increase in studies combining elements of more than one approach. For example, there is what might be called "connectionist neuropsychology", in which connectionist networks are "lesioned" or damaged in order to see whether the resulting pattern of performance resembles that of brain-damaged patients (e.g., Plaut & Shallice, 1993). This approach combines cognitive science and cognitive neuropsychology.

Experimental cognitive psychology

For many years, nearly all research in cognitive psychology involved carrying out experiments on normal individuals under laboratory conditions. Experiments carried out under such conditions are typically tightly controlled and "scientific". This approach has proved very useful, and the data thus obtained have played a major role in the development and subsequent testing of most theories in cognitive psychology. However, there are two major potential problems with the use of such data:

(1) Measures of the speed and accuracy of performance provide only *indirect* evidence about the internal processes involved in cognition.

(2) There is a danger that the ways in which people behave in the laboratory may differ greatly from the ways they behave in everyday life. This criticism was expressed forcefully by Heather (1976, p. 33): "The main kind of knowledge gleaned from years of experimentation with human subjects is information about how strangers interact in the highly artificial and unusual social setting of the psychological experiment."

Problems concerning the artificiality of laboratory research have often been expressed by claiming that such research lacks ecological validity. According to Kvavilashvili and Ellis (in press), *ecological validity* consists of two aspects that are frequently confused: (1) *representativeness*; and (2) *generalisability*. Representativeness refers to the naturalness of the experimental situation, stimuli, and task, whereas generalisability refers to the extent to which the findings of a study are applicable to the real world. There are several examples in this book of the increased representativeness of experimental research. For example, memory researchers have become more interested in memory for faces, which are very significant stimuli in everyday life (see Chapter 6). However, generalisability is more important than representativeness, and it has proved hard to assess.

Cognitive neuropsychology

One way of trying to understand normal human cognition is by studying brain-damaged patients, as happens within cognitive neuropsychology. Cognitive neuropsychologists assume that the cognitive system consists of several *modules* or cognitive processors within the brain. These modules operate relatively independently of each other, so that brain damage can impair the functioning of some modules while leaving others intact. Thus, for example, the modules or processors involved in understanding speech are presumably rather different from those involved in actually speaking. As a result, there are some brain-damaged patients who are good at language comprehension and poor at speaking, and others who show the opposite pattern.

Cognitive neuropsychologists try to understand how the cognitive system works by looking for dissociations. A dissociation occurs when a patient performs at a normal level on one task but is severely impaired on a second task. For example, amnesic patients perform well on tasks involving short-term memory but exhibit very poor performance on most long-term memory tasks (see Chapter 5). This suggests that short-term memory and long-term memory involve separate modules. However, it could be argued that brain damage reduces the ability to perform difficult (but not easy) tasks, and that long-term memory tasks are harder than short-term memory tasks. This explanation is most unlikely to explain the findings, because some brain-damaged patients have good long-term memory but impaired short-term memory.

The memory research that has just been discussed illustrates a double dissociation. A *double dissociation* between two tasks occurs when some patients perform task A normally but are impaired on task B, whereas other patients perform task B normally but are impaired on task A. It is generally agreed that double dissociations provide the strongest evidence for the existence of separate modules. As we will see later in the book, numerous double dissociations have been found in various areas of cognitive psychology.

Limitations

What are the limitations of the cognitive neuropsychological approach? First, it is assumed that the cognitive performance of brain-damaged patients provides *direct* evidence of the impact of brain damage on previously normal cognitive systems. However, some brain-damaged patients may have had somewhat unusual cognitive systems prior to brain damage. In addition, some of the impact of brain damage on cognitive functioning may be camouflaged because patients develop *compensatory strategies* to help them cope with their brain damage.

Second, the whole cognitive neuropsychological approach is very complex, because there are often large differences among individuals having broadly similar brain damage. As Banich (1997, p. 55) pointed out, such individuals "typically vary widely in age, socioeconomic status, and educational background. Prior to brain damage, these individuals may have had diverse life experiences. Afterward, their life experiences likely vary too, depending on the type of rehabilitation they receive, their attitudes toward therapy and recovery and their social support network."

Third, the modular approach may exaggerate the extent to which cognitive functions are localised within the brain (Farah, 1994). As Banich (1997, p. 52) noted, "the brain is comprised of about 50 billion *interconnected* neurons. Therefore, even complex cognitive functions for which a modular description seems apt rely on a number of interconnected brain regions or systems."

Fourth, the study of brain-damaged patients can lead to *under-estimates* of the brain areas involved in performing any given cognitive function. The lesion method generally only permits identi-fication of those brain areas of crucial importance to a cognitive function, but not of those that may be partially involved.

Fifth, the study of brain-damaged patients can lead to *overestimates* of the areas of the brain directly involved in certain aspects of cognitive functioning. This can happen when the damaged region contains axons known as fibres of passage, which connect the brain areas crucially involved in performing a certain cognitive function.

Cognitive science

Cognitive scientists develop computational models to understand human cognition. A good computational model can show us how a given theory can be specified in detail, and allows us to predict behaviour in new situations. This is a clear advantage over many previous theories in cognitive psychology, which were expressed so vaguely that it was not clear exactly what predictions were supposed to follow from them.

Three of the main types of computational model are semantic networks, production systems, and connectionist networks. In recent years, however, the focus has increasingly been on connectionist networks. *Connectionist networks* typically consist of elementary or neuron-like units or nodes connected together. Most networks have different structures or layers, often consisting of a layer of input links, intermediate layers (of so-called "hidden units"), and a layer of output units. Within such networks, memories are distributed over the network rather than being in a single location.

Why have connectionist models become so popular? There are various reasons. First, at least superficially, the numerous elementary units within a connectionist network seem to resemble the neurons within the brain. Second, connectionist networks differ from most previous computational models in that they can to some extent program themselves. Thus, they can "learn" to produce specific outputs when certain inputs are given to them. Third, connectionist models also differ from earlier computational models in that they engage in parallel processing. This is an advantage, because most human information processing occurs in a parallel rather than serial fashion.

Limitations

What are the limitations of cognitive science? First, computational models are rarely used to make predictions; they are produced as a prop for a theory, but often have no real predictive function. For any given theory, there are a huge number of possible models (probably an infinite number), and these variations are rarely explored. To quote Gazzaniga, Ivry, and Mangun (1998, p. 102), "Unlike experimental work which by its nature is cumulative, modelling research tends to occur in isolation. There may be lots of ways to model a particular phenomenon, but less effort has been devoted to devising critical tests that pit one theory against another."

Second, connectionist models that are claimed to have neuronal plausibility do not really resemble the human brain. Connectionist models typically use thousands or tens of thousands of connected units to model a cognitive task that might be performed by tens of millions of neurons in the brain.

Third, numerous models can generally be found to "explain" any set of findings. As Carey and Milner (1994, p. 66) pointed out, "any neural net which produces a desired output from a specified input is hugely under-constrained; an infinitely large number of solutions can be found for each problem addressed."

Fourth, Ellis and Humphreys (1999) pointed out that most computational models have been designed to simulate human performance on single tasks. That obviously limits what they can tell us about human cognition. It is also limiting in less obvious ways, as was pointed out by Ellis and Humphreys (1999, p. 623): "Double dissociations [discussed under cognitive neuropsychology] based on evidence from different tasks . . . cannot be captured in models that perform only single tasks. To begin to address such evidence, multi-task models are needed."

Cognitive neuroscience

There have been several technological advances in recent years in methods for studying the brain directly. In principle, it is possible to establish *where* in the brain certain cognitive processes occur, and *when* these processes occur. Such information can allow us to determine the order in which different parts of the brain become active when someone is performing a task. It also allows us to find out whether two tasks involve the same parts of the brain in the same way, or whether there are important differences. This can tell us whether the two tasks make use of the same, or different, processes.

A few of the main techniques are as follows:

- *Event-related potentials* (ERPs): Electroencephalograms (EEGs) based on recordings of electrical brain activity measured at the surface of scalp are obtained several times to repeated presentation of a stimulus, and then averaged. ERPs have excellent temporal resolution but very poor spatial resolution; they are mainly of value when the stimuli are simple, and so can be repeated without influencing the way in which they are processed.
- *Positron emission tomography* (PET): This is a brain-scanning technique based on the detection of positrons, which are the atomic particles emitted by some radioactive substances. PET has reasonable spatial resolution but poor temporal resolution. PET provides only an *indirect* measure of neural activity, because PET signals reflect blood flow, which is assumed to reflect neural activity.
- *Magnetic resonance imaging* (MRI and fMRI): Radio waves are used to excite atoms in the brain, and this produces magnetic changes that are detected by an 11-ton magnet surrounding the individual. MRI provides information about brain structure, and is useful in detecting very small brain tumours. fMRI provides information about brain activity; it is more useful than PET, because it provides more precise spatial information, and shows changes over shorter periods of time. It provides only an *indirect* measure of neural activity, because fMRI signals reflect blood flow, which is assumed to reflect neural activity.
- *Magneto-encephalography* (MEG): This involves using a superconducting quantum interference device (SQUID), which measures the magnetic fields produced by electrical brain activity. MEG assesses neural activity reasonably directly, and supplies fairly detailed information at the millisecond level about the time course of cognitive processes. It is very hard to prevent irrelevant sources of magnetism from interfering with the measurement of brain activity.

As we have seen, techniques for studying brain functioning have their own strengths and limitations. Of particular significance, they differ in their spatial and temporal resolution. Some techniques provide information at the single-cell level, whereas others tell us about activity over much larger areas of the brain. In similar fashion,

Figure 1.3. The spatial and temporal ranges of some techniques used to study brain functioning. Adapted from Churchland and Sejnowski (1991).

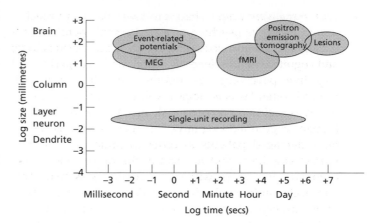

some techniques provide information about brain activity on a millisecond-by-millisecond basis, whereas others indicate brain activity only over much longer time periods such as minutes or hours. The spatial and temporal resolutions of the major techniques (including some not discussed here) are shown in Figure 1.3. *Draw*

The techniques used within cognitive neuroscience are most useful when applied to areas of the brain that are organised neatly and tidily or in functionally discrete ways (S. Anderson, pers. comm.). This seems to be the case for various aspects of perception (see Chapter 2). However, it is much less clear that higher-order cognitive functions (e.g., reasoning, decision making) are organised neatly and tidily. Thus, the various techniques may prove less informative when applied to such functions.

Summary: Approaches to cognitive psychology

- *Introduction*: According to the information-processing approach, information processing in people resembles that in computers, and the major goal of research is to specify the processes and structures underlying cognitive performance. Early versions of this approach emphasised bottom-up and serial processing, whereas later versions allowed for more top-down and parallel processing.

- *Four major approaches*: There are four major approaches within cognitive psychology: experimental cognitive psychology; cognitive science; cognitive neuropsychology; and cognitive neuroscience. Research within experimental cognitive psychology is tightly controlled, but such research often lacks ecological validity. Cognitive science involves using computational models to understand human cognition. Cognitive neuropsychologists study brain-damaged patients in order to understand normal human cognition, and to identify the major modules or cognitive processors within the cognitive system. This approach can be misleading if patients develop compensatory strategies to cope with the effects of brain damage, and it may exaggerate the extent to which cognitive functions are localised within the brain. Cognitive science involves using computational models to understand human cognition. Connectionist networks consist of interconnected neuron-like units arranged in layers. These networks can to some extent program themselves, and they use parallel processing. Computational models are rarely used to make predictions, and they are generally designed to simulate human performance on only a single task. Cognitive neuroscience makes use of technological advances to establish where and when cognitive processes occur within the brain. Most of the techniques used are limited in either spatial or temporal resolution, and they are of most value when applied to areas of the brain that are organised neatly and tidily.

Essay question

(1) Describe and evaluate the major approaches to the study of human cognition.

Further reading

Eysenck, M.W., & Keane, M.T. (2000). *Cognitive psychology: A student's handbook* (4th ed.). Hove, UK: Psychology Press. The first and last chapters of this book provide more detailed evaluation of the four major approaches to cognitive psychology than has been possible here.

Gazzaniga, M.S., Ivry, R.B., & Mangun, G.R. (1998). *Cognitive neuroscience: The biology of the mind*. New York: W.W. Norton. The cognitive neuroscience approach to the major areas of cognitive psychology is considered in detail, but the other main approaches are also discussed.

Parkin, A.J. (1996). *Explorations in cognitive neuropsychology*. Oxford: Blackwell. This book contains an authoritative account of what is known about some of the main types of cognitive disorder.

Major perceptual processes 2

This chapter and the next are concerned with visual perception. This chapter deals with the visual system and some of the basic ways in which visual perception is organised. In addition, it deals with very general approaches to visual perception (e.g., the constructivist and direct approaches). The next chapter focuses on the processes involved in object recognition. More specifically, how do we recognise or identify the two- and three-dimensional stimuli we encounter?

The visual system

Far more of the cortex is devoted to vision than to any other sense modality. Why is that so? There are two main reasons. First, vision is of enormous importance in our lives, and is perhaps even more important than our other senses. Second, the human visual system carries out complex processing activities. In the words of Pinel (1997, p. 151), "From the tiny, distorted, upside-down, two-dimensional retinal images projected upon the visual receptors lining the backs of our eyes, the visual system creates an accurate, richly detailed, three-dimensional perception."

Light waves from objects in the environment pass through the transparent cornea at the front of the eye and proceed to the iris (see Figure 2.1). It is just behind the cornea and it gives the eye its distinctive colour. The amount of light entering the eye is determined by the pupil, which is an opening in the iris. This is achieved by the pupil becoming smaller when the lighting is very bright, and larger when there is relatively little light. The lens focuses light onto the retina at the back of the eye. Each lens adjusts in shape by a process of *accommodation* to bring images into focus on the retina.

The retina itself is complex. It consists of five different layers of cells: receptors; horizontal cells; bipolar cells; amacrine cells; and

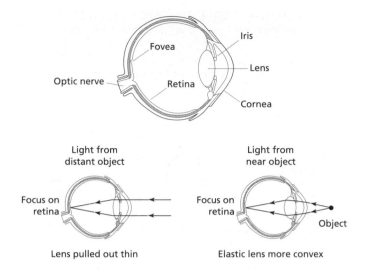

Figure 2.1. The visual system and accommodation.

Fovea

Iris

Lens

Optic nerve

Retina

Cornea

Light from distant object

Light from near object

Focus on retina

Focus on retina

Object

Lens pulled out thin

Elastic lens more convex

retinal ganglion cells. The arrangement of these cells is slightly odd. Light from the lens goes through all of the layers of cells until it reaches the receptor cells at the back, after which the neural message goes back through the layers. Impulses from the retina leave the eye via the optic nerve, which is at the front of the retina. There are two types of receptors in the retina: rods and cones. These receptors are discussed later in the section on colour vision.

Why do we have two eyes? A key reason is because this produces *binocular disparity*, which means that the image of any given object is slightly different on the two retinas. Binocular disparity provides useful information for the task of constructing a three-dimensional world out of two-dimensional retinal images (see later in chapter).

Pathways from eye to cortex

The main pathway between the eye and the cortex is the retina–geniculate–striate pathway. This transmits information from the retina to the primary visual cortex or striate cortex via the lateral geniculate nuclei of the thalamus. The entire retinal–geniculate–striate system is organised in a similar way to the retinal information. Thus, for example, two stimuli that are adjacent to each other in the retinal image will also be adjacent to each other at higher levels within that system. When the primary visual cortex of blind patients is stimulated by electrodes forming a given shape, they report "seeing" that shape (Dobelle et al., 1974).

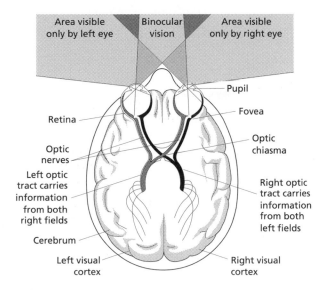

Figure 2.2. Route of visual signals.

Route of visual signals
Note that all light from the fields left of centre of both eyes falls on the right sides of the two retinas; and information about these fields goes to the right visual cortex. Information about the right fields of vision goes to the left cortex. Data about binocular vision go to both cortices.

Each eye has its own optic nerve, and the two optic nerves meet at the optic chiasma. At this point, the axons from the outer halves of each retina proceed to the hemisphere on the same side, whereas the axons from the inner halves cross over and go to the other hemisphere. Signals then proceed along two optic tracts within the brain. One tract contains signals from the left half of each eye, and the other signals from the right half of each eye (see Figure 2.2).

After the optic chiasma, the optic tract proceeds to the lateral geniculate nucleus, which is part of the thalamus. Nerve impulses finally reach the primary visual cortex within the occipital lobe before speading out to nearby secondary visual cortical areas.

There is another important feature of the retina–geniculate–striate system. There are two independent channels within this system:

(1) *The parvocellular (or P) pathway*: This pathway is most sensitive to colour and to fine detail; most of its input comes from cones.
(2) *The magnocellular (or M) pathway*: This pathway is most sensitive to information about movement; most of its input comes from rods.

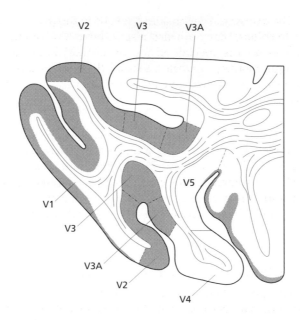

Figure 2.3. Cross-section of the visual cortex of the macaque monkey (Zeki, 1992).

Processing in the cortex

According to Zeki's (1992, 1993) functional specialisation theory, different parts of the cortex are specialised for different visual functions. This theory differs from the traditional view, according to which there is a unitary visual processing system.

An oversimplified view of the main cortical areas involved in visual processing is shown in Figure 2.3. The retina connects primarily to what is known as the primary visual cortex or area V1. The importance of area V1 is shown by the fact that lesions at any point along the pathway to it from the retina lead to total blindness within the affected part of V1. Areas V2 to V5 are also of major significance in visual perception. Here are the main functions that Zeki (1992, 1993) ascribed to these areas:

- *V1 and V2*: These areas are involved at an early stage of visual perception. They contain different groups of cells responsive to colour and form.
- *V3 and V3A*: Cells in these areas are responsive to form (especially the shapes of objects in motion) but not to colour.

- *V4*: The overwhelming majority of cells in this area are responsive to colour; many are also responsive to line orientation.
- *V5*: This area is specialised for visual motion. Studies using macaque monkeys revealed that all the cells in this area are responsive to motion, but are not responsive to colour (see Zeki, 1993).

A central assumption made by Zeki (1992, 1993) was that colour, form, and motion are processed in anatomically separate parts of the visual cortex. Much of the original evidence came from studies of monkeys. However, there is now considerable evidence from humans that Zeki's assumption is broadly correct, although form processing occurs in several different areas. Some of this evidence is considered shortly.

Edge perception and simultaneous contrast

As Pinel (1997) pointed out, "Edges are the most informative features of any visual display because they define the extent and position of the various objects in it" (p. 163). What are edges? They are the meeting place of two adjacent areas of the visual field.

In order to perceive an edge, there needs to be some kind of *contrast* between two adjacent areas. Suppose that you look at two adjacent columns, one of which is brighter than the other. What happens in the area around the dividing line or edge between them is that the brighter column looks brighter than it actually is, whereas the darker column looks darker than it is. These illusory stripes are sometimes called *Mach bands*.

The contrast effect associated with Mach bands is very similar to another phenomenon. It has been known for a long time that a grey patch looks lighter when it is presented on a black rather than a white background. This illustrates what is known as *simultaneous contrast*. Wallach (1948) studied simultaneous contrast, and found that the apparent lightness of an object is given by the ratio of its luminance or brightness to that of the surrounding area. This is a reasonable generalisation, but there are various exceptions to it (Sekuler & Blake, 1994).

Mach bands and simultaneous contrast are caused by *lateral inhibition* (inhibition exerted sideways) in which receptor cells in the visual system inhibit each other. Let us consider a simple situation in which receptor cell A in the retina is stimulated by a light part of a visual display, and so is in a state of intense excitation. A neighbouring receptor cell B is stimulated by a darker part of the display, and so is in a state of relatively low excitation. Excitation from these cells is passed on to other cells. However, some of the excitation from cell B does not proceed through the visual system. The reason is that excitation from cell A excites other cells, some of which exert an inhibitory effect on excitation proceeding onwards from cell B. This creates lateral inhibition, and so the dark part of the display appears darker than it is.

Dark adaptation

When you go to the cinema, you probably find it hard at first to find the way to your seat because of the darkness. However, after a few minutes, your eyes adjust to the darkness, and you can see the layout of the cinema and the faces of other people reasonably well. The term *dark adaptation* is used to refer to the increase in visual sensitivity that occurs over time in darkened conditions following exposure to light.

Dark adaptation has been studied under laboratory conditions. Initially the participant is presented with a strong light known as the adaptation stimulus. After that, the participant is given the task of detecting a very faint flashing light (the test stimulus). The intensity of the light gradually increases until it is detected. After that, the light intensity decreases rapidly and then slowly increases until it is detected once more. Studies of this sort indicate that sensitivity to light can increase by a factor of 100,000 during the course of dark adaptation (Sekuler & Blake, 1994).

What factors are responsible for dark adaptation? One minor factor relates to changes in the pupil. It dilates in darkness, and this allows more light into the eye. Far more important are changes in the sensitivity of the rods and cones in the retina of the eye. In order to assess dark adaptation in the cones (the photopic system), what is done is to present the test stimulus to the fovea or central area of the retina. In similar fashion, dark adaptation in the rods (the scotopic system) can be measured by presenting the test stimulus to the periphery of the retina. The photopic or cone-based system is initially more sensitive to light than the scotopic or rod-based system. However, sensitivity increases more rapidly over time in the scotopic system, so that after about 8 minutes in darkness the scotopic system becomes more sensitive to light than the photopic system. As would be expected, dark adaptation to test stimuli that are presented to both rods and cones is determined by the joint effects of the photopic and scotopic systems.

Colour processing

The notion that different areas of the cortex are involved in colour and motion processing received support in a study by Cavanaugh, Tyler, and Favreau (1984). They presented a moving grating consisting of alternating red and green bars of equal brightness. The observers reported either that the bars did not seem to be moving, or there was only a modest impression of movement. Cavanaugh et al. (1984) found that the moving display only affected the colour-processing system. It did not stimulate the motion-processing system, because that system responds only to differences in brightness.

Evidence that area V4 is specialised for colour processing was reported by Lueck et al. (1989). They presented coloured or grey squares and rectangles to observers. PET scans indicated that there was about 13% more blood flow within area V4 with the coloured stimuli, but other areas were not more affected by colour.

If area V4 is specialised for colour processing, then patients with damage mostly limited to that area should show little or no colour perception, combined with fairly normal form and motion perception. This is the case in some patients with *achromatopsia*. However, many of them do have problems with object recognition as well as an inability to identify colours by name.

In spite of the fact that patients with achromatopsia complain that the world seems devoid of colour, some aspects of colour processing are preserved. Heywood, Cowey, and Newcombe (1994) studied M.S., a patient with achromatopsia. He performed well on a task on which he had to select the odd form out of a set of stimuli. This task could only be performed accurately by using colour information, but did not require conscious access to that information. As Köhler and Moscovitch (1997, p. 326) concluded, "M.S. is able to process information about colour implicitly when the actual perceptual judgement concerns form, but is unable to use this information explicitly when the judgement concerns colour."

Motion processing

There is convincing evidence from cognitive neuroscience that area V5 is involved in motion processsing. For example, Anderson et al. (1996) used magneto-encephalography (MEG) and MRI to assess brain activity in response to motion stimuli (see Chapter 1). They reported that "human V5 is located near the occipito-temporal border in a minor sulcus [groove] immediately below the superior temporal sulcus" (Anderson et al., 1996, p. 428).

Additional evidence about the importance of area V5 in motion processing comes from studies on brain-damaged patients with *akinetopsia*. In this condition, stationary objects can generally be perceived fairly normally, but objects in motion become invisible. Zihl, von Cramon, and Mai (1983) studied L.M., a woman with akinetopsia who had suffered brain damage in both hemispheres. A subsequent high-resolution MRI scan revealed that L.M. has bilateral damage to V5 (Shipp et al., 1994). She was good at locating stationary objects by sight, she had good colour discrimination, and her binocular visual functions (e.g., stereoscopic depth perception) were normal. However, her motion perception was grossly deficient. According to Zihl et al. (1983):

> She had difficulty . . . in pouring tea or coffee into a cup because the fluid appeared to be frozen, like a glacier. In addition, she could not stop pouring at the right time since she was unable to perceive the movement in the cup (or a pot) when the fluid rose.

L.M.'s condition did not improve over time. However, she developed various ways of coping with her lack of motion perception. For example, she stopped looking at people who were talking to her, because she found it disturbing that their lips did not seem to move (Zihl et al., 1991).

Striking evidence of the involvement of V5 in motion perception was reported by Beckers and Zeki (1995). They used transcranial magnetic stimulation to produce temporary inactivation of V5. This produced a short-lasting (but complete) akinetopsia.

Perceptual organisation

It is important to account for perceptual segregation, i.e., our ability to work out which parts of the visual information presented to us belong together and thus form separate objects. One of the first systematic attempts to study perceptual segregation and the perceptual organisation to which it gives rise was made by the Gestaltists. They were a group of German psychologists (including Koffka, Köhler, and Wertheimer) who emigrated to the United States between the two World Wars. Their fundamental principle of

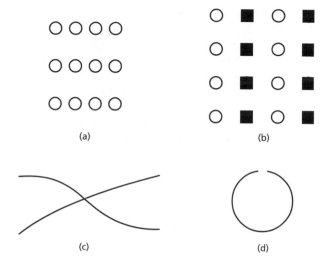

Figure 2.4. The law of Prägnanz.

(a)

(b)

(c)

(d)

perceptual organisation was the law of Prägnanz: "Of several geometrically possible organisations that one will actually occur which possesses the best, simplest and most stable shape" (Koffka, 1935, p. 138).

Although the law of Prägnanz was their key organisational principle, the Gestaltists put forward several other laws. Most of these laws (see Figure 2.4) can be subsumed under the law of Prägnanz. The fact that three horizontal arrays of dots rather than vertical groups are perceived in Figure 2.4(a) indicates that visual elements tend to be grouped together if they are close to each other (the law of proximity). Figure 2.4(b) illustrates the law of similarity, which states that elements will be grouped together perceptually if they are similar to each other. Vertical columns rather than horizontal rows are seen because the elements in the vertical columns are the same, whereas those in the horizontal rows are not. We see two crossing lines in Figure 2.4(c), because according to the law of good continuation we group together those elements requiring the fewest changes or interruptions in straight or smoothly curving lines. Figure 2.4(d) illustrates the law of closure, according to which missing parts of a figure are filled in to complete the figure. Thus, a circle is seen even though it is incomplete.

The Gestaltists emphasised the importance of *figure–ground organisation* in perceptual organisation. One object or part of the visual field is identified as the figure, whereas the rest of the visual field is of less

Figure 2.5. The faces–goblet ambiguous figure.

significance and so forms the ground. The laws of perceptual organisation permit this segregation into figure and ground to happen. The figure is perceived as having a distinct form or shape, whereas the ground lacks form. In addition, the figure is perceived as being in *front* of the ground, and the contour separating the figure from the ground is seen as belonging to the figure.

You can check the validity of these claims about figure and ground by looking at reversible figures such as the faces–goblet figure (see Figure 2.5). When the goblet is the figure, it seems to be in front of a black background, whereas the faces are in front of a white background when they form the figure.

Evidence that there is more attention to, and processing of, the figure than of the ground was reported by Weisstein and Wong (1986). They flashed vertical lines and slightly tilted lines onto the faces–goblet figure, and gave their participants the task of deciding whether the line was vertical. Performance on this task was three times better when the line was presented to what the participants perceived as the figure rather than to the ground.

The Gestaltists tried to explain their laws of perceptual organisation by their doctrine of *isomorphism*. According to this doctrine, the experience of visual organisation is mirrored by a precisely corresponding process in the brain. It was assumed that there are electrical "field forces" in the brain that help to produce the experience of a stable perceptual organisation when we look at our visual environment.

The Gestaltists' pseudo-physiological ideas have not survived. Much damage was done to the theory by Lashley, Chow, and Semmes (1951) in a study on two chimpanzees. They placed four gold foil "conductors" in the visual area of one of the chimpanzees, and 23 gold pins vertically through the cortex of the other chimpanzee. Lashley et al. (1951) argued persuasively that the unpleasant things they had done to these chimpanzees would have severely disrupted any electrical field forces. In fact, the perceptual abilities of their chimpanzees were hardly affected. This suggests that electrical field forces are of much less significance than the Gestaltists claimed.

Evaluation

The Gestalt approach led to the discovery of several important aspects of perceptual organisation. As Rock and Palmer (1990, p. 50) pointed out, "the laws of grouping have withstood the test of time. In fact, not one of them has been refuted."

The Gestaltists relied heavily on introspective reports, or the "look at the figure and see for yourself" method. More convincing evidence was provided by Pomerantz and Garner (1973), who gave participants the task of sorting displays into two piles as rapidly as possible. Their key finding was that distracting stimuli within the display could not be ignored when they were similar to (or close to) the task-relevant stimuli. Thus, the performance of the participants was influenced by the laws of proximity and similarity.

The Gestaltists produced *descriptions* of interesting perceptual phenomena, but failed to provide adequate *explanations*. They assumed that observers use the various laws of perceptual grouping without the need for relevant perceptual learning. However, they did not provide any supporting evidence.

The Gestaltists argued that grouping of perceptual elements occurs *early* in visual processing. This assumption was tested by Rock and Palmer (1990). They presented luminous beads on parallel strings in the dark. The beads were closer to each other in the vertical direction than the horizontal one. As the law of proximity predicts, the beads were perceived as forming columns. When the display was tilted backwards, the beads were closer to each other horizontally than vertically in the two-dimensional retinal image, but remained closer to each other vertically in three-dimensional space.

What did the observers report? They saw the beads organised in vertical columns. As Rock and Palmer (1990, p. 51) concluded, "Grouping was based on perceived proximity in three-dimensional space rather than on actual proximity on the retina. Grouping by proximity must therefore occur after depth perception." Thus, grouping happens later in processing than was assumed by the Gestaltists.

According to the Gestaltists, the various laws of grouping operate

Figure 2.6.
Overlapping
transparent letters of
the type used by
Vecera and Farah
(1997).

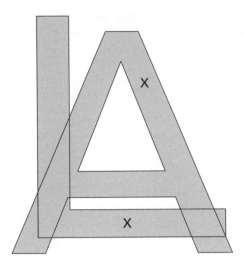

in a bottom-up way to produce perceptual organisation. According to this position, information about objects in the visual field is *not* used to determine how the visual field is segmented. Contrary evidence was reported by Vecera and Farah (1997). They presented two overlapping transparent letters (see Figure 2.6). The participants' task was to decide as rapidly as possible whether two x's in the figure were on the same shape. The key manipulation was whether the letters were presented in the upright position or upside down.

Performance was significantly faster with upright letters than with upside-down ones. This occurred because the two shapes to be segmented were much more familiar in the upright condition. Thus, as Vecera and Farah (1997, p. 1293) concluded, "top-down activation can partly guide the segmentation process." The implication is that the Gestaltists exaggerated the role of bottom-up processes in segmentation.

Subsequent theories

The Gestaltists emphasised the importance of the law of Prägnanz, according to which the perceptual world is organised into the simplest and best shape. However, they lacked any effective means of assessing what shape is the simplest and best. Restle (1979) proposed an interesting way of clarifying the notion of simplicity. He studied the ways in which dots moving across a display are perceived. The most complicated approach would be to treat each dot as completely separate from all the others, and to calculate its starting position, speed, and direction of movement, and so on. In contrast, it is possible to treat the moving dots as belonging to groups, especially if they move together in the same direction and at the same speed. Restle (1979) was able to calculate how much processing would be involved in each approach. Whatever grouping of moving dots in a display involved the least calculation generally corresponded to what was actually perceived.

There are other ways in which we could decide which perceptual organisation is the simplest. For example, there is Kolmogorov complexity theory, according to which the complexity of an object is defined as "the length of the shortest description that uniquely specifies that object. The idea is that simple things have short descriptions; complex things have long descriptions" (Chater, 1997, pp. 495–496). This approach could usefully be applied to issues of perceptual organisation. However, limitations of human processing probably mean that we often fail to achieve the simplest possible perceptual organisation of the visual environment. Chater (1997, p. 496) proposed that the following is what actually happens: "The cognitive system cannot find the shortest possible description for an object; but it can choose the shortest description *that it can find.*"

The Gestaltists de-emphasised the complexities involved when laws of grouping are in conflict. This issue was addressed by Quinlan and Wilton (1998). For example, they presented a display such as the one shown in Figure 2.7(a), in which there is a conflict between proximity and similarity. About half the participants grouped the stimuli by proximity and half by similarity. Quinlan and Wilton (1998) also used more complex displays like those in Figure 2.7(b) and (c). Their findings led them to propose the following notions:

- The visual elements in a display are initially grouped or clustered on the basis of proximity.

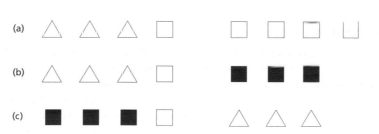

Figure 2.7. (a) Display involving a conflict between proximity and similarity. (b) Display with a conflict between shape and colour. (c) A different display with a conflict between shape and colour. Adapted from Quinlan and Wilton (1998).

- Additional processes are used if elements that have provisionally been clustered together differ in one or more features (within-cluster mismatch).
- If there is a within-cluster mismatch on features but a between-cluster match (e.g., Figure 2.7(a)), then participants choose between groupings based on proximity and on similarity.
- If there are within-cluster and between-cluster mismatches, then proximity is ignored, and grouping is often based on colour. In the case of the displays shown in Figure 2.7(b) and (c), most participants grouped on the basis of common colour rather than common shape.

In sum, there has been progress in developing theories that overcome some of the limitations in the Gestaltist approach. However, much remains to be done. For example, while Quinlan and Wilton (1998) described the ways in which certain complex visual displays are perceived, they did not provide an account of the underlying processes.

General approaches to perception

Visual perception obviously depends crucially on the information that is presented to the retina of the eye. In the terms introduced in Chapter 1, visual perception involves *bottom-up processing* driven by the stimulus. In addition, visual perception depends in part on the knowledge and expectations of the observer. These factors influence visual perception by means of *top-down processing* (Chapter 1). There has been some theoretical controversy about the relative importance of these two types of processing in perception. Constructivist theorists emphasise the role of top-down processes in visual perception, whereas direct theorists emphasise bottom-up processes and the richness of the information contained within the stimulus. We will consider these two approaches, and then we will focus on attempts to produce a reconciliation between them.

Constructivist approach

Constructivist theorists such as Bruner (1957), Neisser (1967), and Gregory (1972, 1980) all subscribe to the following assumptions:

- Perception is an active and constructive process.
- Perception occurs as the end-product of the interactive influences of the presented stimulus and internal hypotheses, expectations, and knowledge, as well as motivational and emotional factors.
- Perception is influenced by hypotheses and expectations that are prone to error.

Gregory (1972) claimed that perceptions are constructions "from floating fragmentary scraps of data signalled by the senses and drawn from the brain memory banks, themselves constructions from the snippets of the past." Thus, the frequently inadequate information supplied to the sense organs is used as the basis for making inferences or forming hypotheses about the external environment.

Contextual information can be used in making inferences about a visual stimulus. Palmer (1975) presented a scene (e.g., a kitchen) in pictorial form, followed by the very brief presentation of the picture of an object. This object was appropriate to the context (e.g., loaf) or inappropriate (e.g., mailbox). There was also a further condition in which no contextual scene was presented. The probability of identifying the object correctly was greatest when it was appropriate to the context, intermediate when there was no context, and lowest when it was inappropriate.

According to constructivist theorists, the formation of incorrect hypotheses or expectations leads to perceptual errors. Ittelson (1952) argued that the perceptual hypotheses formed may be very inaccurate if a visual display appears familiar but is actually novel. An example of this is the well-known Ames distorted room. The room is actually of a peculiar shape, but when viewed from a particular point it gives rise to the same retinal image as a conventional rectangular room.

It is perhaps not surprising that observers decide that the room is like a normal one. However, what is puzzling is that they maintain this belief even when someone inside the room walks backwards and forwards along the rear wall, apparently growing and shrinking as he or she proceeds! The reason for the apparent size changes is that the rear wall is not at right angles to the viewing point: one corner is actually much further away from the observer than the other corner.

Motivation and emotion

A central assumption of the constructivist approach is that perception is not determined entirely by external stimuli. It is assumed that current motivational and emotional states may influence people's perceptual hypotheses and thus their visual perception. Consider, for example, a study by Schafer and Murphy (1943). They prepared drawings consisting of an irregular line drawn vertically through a circle so that either half of the circle could be seen as the profile of a face. During initial training, each face was presented separately. One face in each pair was associated with financial reward, whereas the other face was associated with financial punishment. When the original combined drawings were then presented briefly, participants typically reported perceiving the previously rewarded face. In similar fashion, Smith and Hochberg (1954) found that delivering a shock when one of the two profile faces was presented decreased its tendency to be perceived later.

Bruner and Goodman (1947) studied motivational factors by asking rich and poor children to estimate the sizes of coins. The poor children overestimated the size of every coin more than did the rich children. Although this finding may reflect the greater value of money to poor children, a simpler explanation is that the rich children had more familiarity with coins, and so were more accurate in their size estimates. Ashley, Harper, and Runyon (1951) eliminated this explanation by hypnotising adult participants into believing they were rich or poor. The size estimates of coins were consistently larger when the participants were in the "poor" state.

Several other studies seem to show effects of motivation and emotion on perception. However, it is difficult to interpret the various findings. It is possible that motivation and emotion influenced participants' *responses*, but had little or no effect on their actual visual perception.

Evaluation

The constructivist approach has led to the discovery of a wide range of interesting perceptual phenomena. Processes resembling those postulated by constructivist theorists probably underlie most of these phenemona. However, many theorists disagree strongly with the constructivist viewpoint. Some of the major problems for the constructivist approach will now be discussed.

First, this approach predicts that perception will often be in error, whereas in fact perception is typically accurate. If we are constantly using hypotheses and expectations to interpret sensory data, why is it that these hypotheses and expectations are correct nearly all the time? Presumably the environment provides much more information than the "fragmentary scraps" assumed by constructivist theorists.

Second, many of the experiments carried out by constructivist theorists involve artificial stimuli. For example, many studies supporting the constructivist approach (e.g., Bruner et al., 1951; Palmer, 1975) involved presenting visual stimuli very briefly. Brief presentation reduces the impact of bottom-up processes, allowing more scope for top-down processes (e.g., hypotheses) to operate.

Third, it is not always clear what hypotheses would be formed by observers. Let us return to the study (Ittelson, 1951) in which someone walks backwards and forwards along the rear wall of the Ames room. Observers could interpret what they are seeing by hypothesising that the room is distorted and the person remains the same size, or by assuming that the room is normal but the person grows and shrinks. The former hypothesis seems more plausible, but most observers favour the latter.

Direct perception

Gibson's direct perception approach can be regarded as a bottom-up theory: he claimed there is much more information potentially available in sensory stimulation than is generally realised. However, he emphasised the role played in perception by movement of the individual within his or her environment, so his is not a bottom-up theory in the sense of an observer passively receiving sensory stimulation.

Some of Gibson's main theoretical assumptions are as follows:

- The pattern of light reaching the eye is an *optic array*; this structured light contains all the visual information from the environment striking the eye.
- The optic array provides unambiguous or invariant information about the layout of objects in space. This information comes in many forms, including texture gradients, optic flow patterns, and affordances (all described later).
- Perception involves "picking up" the rich information provided by the optic array directly via resonance with little or no information processing being involved.

Gibson (1950) wondered what information pilots have available to them while taking off and landing. There is an *optic flow pattern*, which can be illustrated by considering a pilot approaching the landing strip. The point towards which the pilot is moving (the *focus of expansion* or pole) appears motionless, with the rest of the visual environment apparently moving away from that point. The further away any part of the landing strip is from that point, the greater is its apparent speed of movement. A shift in the centre of the outflow reflects a change in the direction of the plane.

According to Gibson (1950), optic flow fields provide pilots with unambiguous information about their direction, speed, and altitude. Gibson then devoted himself to an analysis of the kinds of information available in sensory data under other conditions. For example, he argued that texture gradients provide very useful information. Objects slanting away from you have a gradient (rate of change) of texture density as you look from the near edge to the far edge. Gibson (1966, 1979) claimed that observers "pick up" this information directly from the optic array.

The optic flow pattern and texture density illustrate some of the information providing observers with an unambiguous spatial layout of the environment. More generally, Gibson (1966, 1979) argued that certain higher-order characteristics of the visual array (invariants) remain unaltered when observers move around their environment. The fact that they remain the same over different viewing angles makes invariants of particular importance. The lack of apparent movement of the point towards which we are moving is one invariant feature of the optic array. Another invariant is useful in terms of maintaining size constancy: the ratio of an object's height to the distance between its base and the horizon is invariant regardless of its distance from the viewer. This invariant is known as the horizon ratio relation.

Meaning: Affordances

Gibson (1979) claimed that all the potential uses of objects (their *affordances*) are directly perceivable. For example, a chair "affords" sitting, and a ladder "affords" ascent or descent. We have to learn which affordances will satisfy particular goals, and we need to learn to attend to the appropriate aspects of the visual environment. According to Gibson's theory (Gordon, 1989, p. 161), "The most important contribution of learning to perception is to educate attention."

Resonance

How do human perceivers manage to "pick up" the invariant information supplied by the visual world? According to Gibson, there is a process of *resonance*, which he explained by analogy to the workings of a radio. When a radio set is turned on, there may be only a hissing sound. However, if it is tuned properly, speech or music will be clearly audible. In Gibson's terms, the radio is now resonating with the information contained in the electromagnetic radiation.

This analogy suggests that perceivers can pick up information from the environment relatively automatically if they are attuned to it. The radio operates in a holistic or integrated way, in the sense that damage to any part of its circuitry would prevent it working. Gibson assumed that the nervous system works in a holistic way when perceiving.

Evaluation

The direct approach has proved successful in some ways. First, Gibson was right that the visual environment provides much more information than had previously been thought to be the case. Traditional laboratory research had generally involved static observers looking at impoverished visual displays, often with chin rests being used to prevent head movements. In contrast, Gibson correctly emphasised that we spend much of our time in motion, and that the consequent moment-by-moment changes in the optic array provide useful information.

Second, Gibson was correct that inaccurate perception often depends on the use of very artificial stimuli (e.g., most visual illusions). However, there are some exceptions. Consider, for example, the vertical–horizontal illusion shown in Figure 2.8. The two lines are actually the same length, but the vertical line appears longer than the horizontal one. This tendency to overestimate vertical extents relative to horizontal ones can readily be shown with real objects by taking a teacup, saucer, and two similar spoons. Place one spoon horizontally in the saucer and the other spoon vertically in the cup, and you should find that the vertical spoon looks much longer.

On the negative side, Gibson's direct theory of perception has attracted many criticisms. First, perceptual processes are much more complicated than was implied by Gibson. In the words of Marr (1982, p. 30), the major shortcoming of Gibson's analysis

> results from a failure to realise two things. First, the detection of physical invariants, like image surfaces, is exactly and precisely an information-processing problem, in modern terminology. And second, he vastly under-rated the sheer difficulty of such detection.

Second, Gibson's theoretical approach applies much more to some aspects of perception than to others. The distinction between "seeing"

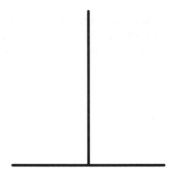

Figure 2.8. The vertical–horizontal illusion.

and "seeing as" (Fodor & Pylyshyn, 1981) is useful here (Bruce et al., 1996). "Seeing" refers to basic visual perception, whereas "seeing as" refers to the perceived significance or meaning of a stimulus. Fodor and Pylyshyn (1981) illustrated the distinction by considering someone called Smith who is lost at sea. Smith sees the Pole Star, but what matters for his survival is whether he sees it as the Pole Star or as simply an ordinary star. If it is the former, then this will be useful for navigational purposes; if it is the latter, then he remains as lost as ever. Gibson's approach is relevant to "seeing", but has little to say about "seeing as".

Third, Gibson's argument that there is no need to postulate internal representations (e.g., memories; 2½-D sketches) to understand perception is flawed. Bruce, Green and Georgeson (1996) cited the work of Menzel (1978) as an example of the problems flowing from Gibson's argument. Chimpanzees were carried around a field, and shown the locations of 20 pieces of food buried in the ground. When each chimpanzee was released, it moved around the field efficiently picking up the pieces of food. As there was no information in the light reaching the chimpanzees to guide their search, they must have made use of memorial representations of the locations of the pieces of food.

Theoretical integration

Top-down processes in perception are emphasised by constructivist theorists, whereas Gibson argued that bottom-up processes are of paramount importance. In fact, however, the relative importance of top-down and bottom-up processes depends on various factors. Visual perception may be largely determined by bottom-up processes when the viewing conditions are good, but involves top-down processes as the viewing conditions deteriorate because of very brief presentation times or lack of stimulus clarity. In line with this analysis, Gibson focused on visual perception under optimal viewing conditions, whereas constructivist theorists often use suboptimal viewing conditions.

Indirect versus direct theories

The distinction between the constructivist and direct approaches is an important one, but of even greater significance is the related distinction between indirect and direct theories of perception. Most of the approaches to perception discussed in this book (e.g., the constructivist approach; the theories of Marr and Biederman) are indirect theories, whereas Gibson put forward a direct theory. According to Bruce et al. (1996), the following differences between indirect and direct theories are central:

- Indirect theorists argue that perception involves the formation of an internal representation, whereas Gibson argued this is not necessary.
- Indirect theorists assume that memory in the form of stored knowledge of the world is of central importance to perception, but Gibson denied this.
- Most indirect theorists argue that we need to understand the *interrelationships* of perceptual processing at different levels. In contrast, Gibson argued there are separate ecological and physiological levels of explanation, and he focused almost exclusively on the ecological level.

There are clear similarities between the indirect and constructivist approaches, and constructivist theorists accept most (or all) of the assumptions of the indirect approach. However, there is one important difference. Constructivist theorists attach considerable significance to the hypotheses and expectations that allegedly influence perception. In contrast, many indirect theorists (e.g., Marr, Biederman; see Chapter 3) have argued that hypotheses and expectations play only a minor role in visual perception, even though they assume that stored knowledge is of crucial importance.

The indirect approach is more generally applicable than the direct approach to most human visual perception. According to Bruce et al. (1996, p. 374), "Perception of other people, familiar objects, and almost everything we perceive . . . requires additional kinds of representation of the perceived object." Gibson's assumption that stored knowledge is not involved in visual perception is highly dubious. An illustration of the problems associated with Gibson's assumption was provided by Bruce et al. (1996, p. 377): "We find it unconvincing to explain to a person returning after 10 years to their grandparents' home and seeing that a tree has been cut down as having detected directly an event specified by a transformation in the optic array."

Reconciliation

A key reason why the indirect and direct theories differ so much is because the theorists concerned have been pursuing very different goals. Consider the distinction between perception for recognition (in which objects are recognised and identified) and perception for action (in which the precise location of visual stimuli is determined). This distinction, which was proposed by Milner and Goodale (1995, 1998), is supported by evidence from cognitive neuroscience and from cognitive neuropsychology. There is a ventral stream of processing more involved in perception for recognition and a dorsal stream more involved in perception for action, although perception for most purposes is typically based on both streams of processing. Most perception theorists (including Gregory, Marr, and Biederman) have focused on perception for recognition, whereas Gibson emphasised perception for action.

Some of the strongest evidence that there are rather different systems involved in perception for recognition and perception for action comes from certain patients suffering from *visual agnosia*. This is a condition in which patients have severe difficulties in recognising objects (see Chapter 3). Goodale et al. (1991) studied a visual agnosic, D.F., who could not recognise objects or even describe their shape, size, or orientation. However, when D.F. was asked to pick up a block, she adjusted her grasping movements so that they were appropriate to the size of the block. In a second study by Goodale et al. (1991), D.F. was asked to place a card in a slot. She was as accurate as normal individuals in her ability to orientate her hand to match the slot.

The findings from D.F. suggest that she had good perception-for-action abilities but very poor perception-for-recognition abilities. Such findings are consistent with the notion of a separate action-based perceptual system. However, it is important not to exaggerate D.F.'s ability to use perceptual information to control action. Carey, Harvey, and Milner (1996) found that D.F. did not show normal grasping behaviour when trying to pick up complex objects (e.g., crosses) in which two different orientations were present together. It may be that the perception-for-recognition system is needed to assist in the control of action with relatively complex stimuli.

If the distinction between perception for recognition and perception for action is of major importance, then it should probably be possible to find patients showing the opposite pattern of good perception for recognition but poor perception for action. The existence of such opposing patterns is known as a *double dissociation.* Patients suffering from *optic ataxia* show this pattern. According to Georgopoulos (1997, p. 142), "such patients do not usually have impaired vision or impaired hand or arm movements, but show a severe impairment in visually guided reaching in the absence of perceptual disturbance in estimating distance." For example, Perenin and Vighetto (1988) found that patients with optic ataxia experienced great difficulty in rotating their hands appropriately when given the task of reaching towards and into a large oriented slot in front of them.

Goodale and Humphrey (1998, pp. 201–202) provided a detailed account of the relevance of the distinction between dorsal (action) and ventral (recognition) streams of visual processing to major theoretical positions: "The preoccupation with visually guided actions that characterises behaviourist approaches to vision [and Gibson's approach] has meant that most of the visual mechanisms that are being studied are those found in the dorsal stream. In contrast, the reconstructive approach (e.g., Marr, 1982) [discussed in Chapter 3] . . . is a 'passive' approach in which the representation is central and the external behaviour of the external world is largely ignored. Reconstruction of the external world is exactly the kind of activity which we believe is carried out by the ventral stream."

Where does that leave the relationship between these major approaches? According to Goodale and Humphrey (1998, p. 181), "Marrian or 'reconstructive' approaches and Gibsonian or 'purposive–animate–behaviourist' approaches need not be seen as mutually exclusive, but rather as complementary in their emphasis on different aspects of visual function."

There are two important final points. First, the two processing systems are interconnected and there is generally extensive communication and cooperation between them. Second, the descriptions by Milner and Goodale (1995, 1998) of the processing occurring within the dorsal and ventral streams are undoubtedly oversimplified.

Visual illusions

There are numerous well-known visual illusions, some of which are claimed to provide support for constructivist or indirect theories of perception rather than for Gibson's direct theory. Before proceeding, it should be noted that visual illusions fall into various categories. Gregory (1996) argued that there are four main categories:

(1) Illusions based on physiological signals (e.g., Mach bands and simultaneous contrast discussed earlier).
(2) Illusions based on top-down knowledge (e.g., the faces–goblet illusion discussed earlier).
(3) Illusions based on physical input (e.g., a straight stick placed half in water appears bent).
(4) Illusions based on sideways or organising rules, including the Gestalt laws (e.g., most of the well-known illusions such as the Müller–Lyer and Ponzo discussed below).

We will focus on illusions depending on sideways rules for two reasons. First, it has often been assumed that such illusions provide support for constructivist or indirect theories of perception rather than for Gibson's direct theory. Second, many of the most studied visual illusions seem to depend on sideways rules, and our knowledge of them is greater than for most other illusions.

According to Gregory (1970, 1980), many classic visual illusions can be explained in a constructivist way by assuming that rules derived from the perception of three-dimensional objects are applied inappropriately to the perception of two-dimensional figures. For example, people typically see a given object as having a constant size by taking account of its apparent distance. *Size constancy* means that an object is perceived as having the same size whether it is looked at from a short or a long distance away (see later in this chapter). This constancy contrasts with the size of the retinal image, which becomes progressively smaller as an object recedes into the distance. Gregory's (1970, 1980) misapplied size-constancy theory argues that this kind of perceptual processing is applied wrongly to produce several illusions.

The basic ideas in the theory can be understood with reference to the Ponzo illusion (see Figure 2.9). The long lines look like railway lines or the edges of a road receding into the distance. Thus, the top horizontal line can be seen as further away from us than the bottom horizontal line. As rectangles A and B are the same size in the retinal image, the more distant rectangle (A) must actually be larger.

Misapplied size-constancy theory can also explain the Müller–Lyer illusion; see Figure 2.10). The vertical lines in the two figures are the same length. However, the vertical line on the left looks longer

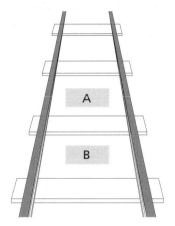

Figure 2.9. The Ponzo illusion.

The Ponzo illusion

Figure 2.10. The Müller–Lyer illusion.

The Muller-Lyer illusion

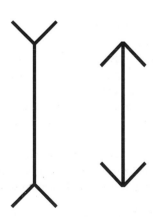

than the one in the figure on the right. According to Gregory (1970), the Müller–Lyer figures can be regarded as simple perspective drawings of three-dimensional objects. The left figure looks like the inside corners of a room, whereas the right figure is like the outside corners of a building. Thus, the vertical line in the left figure is further away from us than its fins, whereas the vertical line in the right figure is closer to us than its fins. Since the size of the retinal image is the

Figure 2.11. The spine of the middle book is closer to the spine of which other book? Now check your answer with a ruler.

same for both vertical lines, the principle of size constancy tells us that the line that is further away (i.e., the one in the left figure) must be longer. This is precisely the Müller–Lyer illusion. However, this explanation only works on the assumption that all fin tips of both figures are in the same plane, and it is not clear why perceivers would make this assumption (Georgeson, pers. comm.).

Gregory argued that figures such as the Ponzo and the Müller–Lyer are treated in many ways as three-dimensional objects. Why, then, do they seem flat and two-dimensional? According to Gregory, cues to depth are used *automatically* whether or not the figures are seen to be lying on a flat surface. As Gregory predicted, the two-dimensional Müller–Lyer figures appear three-dimensional when presented as luminous models in a darkened room. However, they are not seen three-dimensionally by everyone.

Matlin and Foley (1997) proposed the *incorrect comparison theory*, according to which our perception of visual illusions is influenced by parts of the figure not being judged. Evidence in line with this theory was reported by Coren and Girgus (1972). The size of the Müller–Lyer illusion was greatly reduced when the fins were in a different colour from the vertical lines. Presumably this made it easier to ignore the fins.

DeLucia and Hochberg (1991) obtained convincing evidence that Gregory's theory is incomplete. They used a three-dimensional display consisting of three 2-foot high fins on the floor. It was obvious that all the fins were at the same distance from the viewer, but the typical Müller–Lyer effect was obtained. You can check this out by placing three open books in a line so that the ones on the left and the right are open to the right and the one in the middle is open to the left (see Figure 2.11). The spine of the book in the middle should be the same distance from the spines of each of the other two books. In spite of this, the distance between the spine of the middle book and the spine of the book of the right should look longer.

Disappearing illusions: Action

It will be remembered that Gibson emphasised the notion that there is a very close link between perception and action. As he might have predicted, many visual illusions seem to be reduced or eliminated when the participants have to take some form of appropriate action

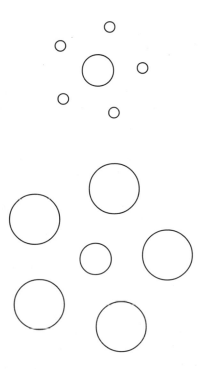

Figure 2.12. The Ebbinghaus illusion.

with respect to the figure rather than just observe it (see Milner and Goodale, 1998). For example, consider a study by Aglioti, De Souza, and Goodale (1995) with the Ebbinghaus illusion (see Figure 2.12). In this illusion, the central circle surrounded by smaller circles looks larger than a central circle of the same size surrounded by larger circles. Aglioti et al. (1995) constructed a three-dimensional version of this illusion, and obtained the usual illusion effect. More interestingly, when the participants reached to pick up one of the central discs, the maximum grip aperture of their reaching hand was almost entirely determined by the actual size of the disc. Thus, no illusion was apparent in the size of the hand grip.

Caution is required in interpreting the above findings. Franz et al. (2000) pointed out that the perceptual task used by Aglioti et al. (1995) involved a direct comparison of the two central discs, whereas the grasping task involved reaching out for only one of the discs. Franz et al. (2000) carefully matched the two tasks, and found that the size of the Ebbinghaus illusion was similar in visual and in grasping conditions.

Evidence supporting the hypothesis that visual illusions can be reduced when action towards the figure is required was reported by

Wraga, Creem, and Proffitt (2000). They presented one part of the Müller–Lyer figure on the floor on each trial. The participants either provided a verbal estimate of the length of the line or they walked its length while blindfolded. There was a highly significant visual illusion effect with the verbal estimation task, but there was no illusion effect at all with blind-walking. These findings are especially impressive because the verbal and motor tasks were carefully matched.

Evaluation

It has proved very difficult to provide an adequate explanation for the visual illusions that allegedly depend on sideways rules. One reason may be that the factors responsible vary from illusion to illusion. It is likely that misapplied size constancy plays a role with some illusions, but simpler explanations (e.g., incorrect comparison) often seem plausible.

It is noteworthy that some visual illusions disappear when observers respond to illusion figures with action rather than simply perception. In general terms, visual illusions clearly present when the task involves the perception-for-recognition (or ventral) system are sometimes reduced when the task involves the perception-for-action (or dorsal) system (e.g., Wraga et al., 2000). Indirect or constructivist theories may be more applicable in the former case, whereas direct theories are more applicable in the latter case.

Colour perception

Why has colour vision developed? After all, if you see an old black-and-white film on television, it is perfectly easy to make sense of the moving images presented to your eyes. There are two main reasons why colour vision is of value to us (Sekuler & Blake, 1994):

- *Detection*: Colour vision helps us to distinguish between an object and its background.
- *Discrimination*: Colour vision makes it easier for us to make fine discriminations among objects (e.g., between ripe and unripe fruit).

There are two types of visual receptor cells in the retina: cones and rods. There are about six million cones, and they are mostly found in the fovea or central part of the retina. The cones are specialised for colour vision and for sharpness of vision. There are about 125 million rods, and they are concentrated in the outer regions of the retina. Rods are specialised for vision in dim light and for the detection of movement. Many of these differences stem from the fact that a retinal ganglion cell receives input from only a few cones but from hundreds of rods. Thus, only rods produce much activity in retinal ganglion cells in poor lighting conditions.

Young–Helmholtz theory

Cone receptors contain light-sensitive photopigment, which allows them to respond to light. According to the component or trichromatic theory put forward by Thomas Young and developed by Hermann von Helmholtz, there are "three distinct sets of nervous fibres" differing in the light wavelengths to which they respond most strongly. Subsequent research led to these sets of fibres becoming identified with cone receptors. One type of cone receptor is most sensitive to short-wavelength light, and has the greatest response to stimuli that are perceived as blue. A second type of cone receptor is most sensitive to medium-wavelength light, and responds greatly to stimuli that are seen as green. The third type of cone receptor responds most to long-wavelength light such as that coming from stimuli distinguished as red.

How do we see other colours? According to the theory, many stimuli activate two or even all three cone types. The perception of yellow is based on the second and third cone types, and white light involves the activation of all three cone types.

Dartnall, Bowmaker, and Mollon (1983) obtained support for this theory using a technique known as *microspectrophotometry*. This revealed that there are three types of cones or receptors responding maximally to different wavelengths of light (see Figure 2.13). Each cone type absorbs a wide range of wavelengths, and so it would be wrong to equate one cone type with perception of blue, one with green, and one with red. Cicerone and Nerger (1989) found there are about four million long-wavelength cones, over two million medium-wavelength cones, and under one million short-wavelength cones.

Most individuals suffering from colour deficiency are not completely colour-blind. The most common type of colour blindness is *red–green deficiency*, in which blue and yellow can be seen but red and green cannot. There are other, rarer forms of colour deficiency,

Figure 2.13. The three types of cone.

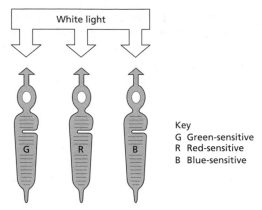

White light

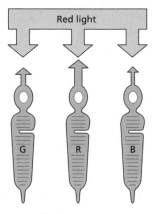

G

R

B

Key
G Green-sensitive
R Red-sensitive
B Blue-sensitive

Response to white light
White light consists of a mixture of all wavelengths (colours), so it stimulates all three classes of cone to signal equally. This pattern of response produces the sensation of whiteness in the brain.

Red light

G

R

B

Response to red light
Light with a long wavelength (red light) produces a strong response from red-sensitive cones, a weak response from blue-sensitive cones, and an intermediate response from green-sensitive cones. This pattern of signalling is interpreted as the colour red in the brain.

such as an inability to perceive blue or yellow, combined with the ability to see red and green. According to the Young–Helmholtz theory, we can explain the fact that red–green deficiency is the commonest form of colour blindness by arguing that the medium-

and long-wavelength cone types are more likely to be damaged or missing than are the short-wavelength cones. That is actually the case (Sekuler & Blake, 1994). There are rarer cases in which the short-wavelength cones are missing, and this disrupts perception of blue and yellow. However, this is an incomplete account of colour deficiency. For example, the Young–Helmholtz theory fails to explain what is known as the *negative afterimage*. If you stare at a square of a given colour for several seconds, and then shift your gaze to a white surface, you will see a negative afterimage in the complementary colour. For example, a green square produces a red afterimage, whereas a blue square produces a yellow afterimage.

Opponent-process theory

Ewald Hering (1878) put forward an opponent-process theory that handles some findings that cannot be explained by the Young–Helmholtz theory. Hering's key assumption was that there are three types of opponent processes in the visual system. One type of process produces perception of green when it responds in one way and of red when it responds in the opposite way. A second type of process produces perception of blue or yellow in the same fashion. The third type of process produces the perception of white at one extreme and of black at the other.

Evidence consistent with opponent-process theory was reported by Abramov and Gordon (1994). They presented observers with single wavelengths, and asked them to indicate the percentage of blue, green, yellow, and red they perceived. According to Hering's theory, we cannot see blue and yellow together or red and green together, but the other colour combinations are possible. That is what Abramov and Gordon (1994) found.

Opponent-process theory helps to explain colour deficiency and negative afterimages. Red–green deficiency occurs when the high- or medium-wavelength cones are damaged or missing, and so the red–green channel cannot be used. Individuals lacking the short-wavelength cones cannot make effective use of the yellow–blue channel, and so their perception of these colours is disrupted. Negative afterimages can be explained by assuming that prolonged viewing of a given colour (e.g., red) produces one extreme of activity in the relevant opponent processes. When attention is then directed to a white surface, the opponent process moves to its other extreme, and this produces the negative afterimage.

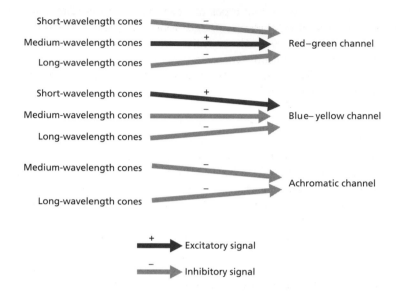

Figure 2.14. Two-stage theory of colour vision.

DeValois and DeValois (1975) discovered what they called opponent cells in monkeys. These cells are located in the lateral geniculate nucleus and show increased activity to some wavelengths of light but decreased activity to others. For some cells, the transition point between increased and decreased activity occurred between the green and the red parts of the spectrum. As a result, they were called red–green cells. Other cells had a transition point between the yellow and blue parts of the sprectrum, and so they were called blue–yellow cells.

Synthesis

The Young–Helmholtz and Hering theories are both partially correct. Hurvich (1981; see Atkinson et al., 1993) argued that we can combine the two theories. According to this two-stage theory, signals from the three cone types identified by the Young–Helmholtz theory are sent to the opponent cells described within the opponent-process theory (see Figure 2.14). The short-wavelength cones send excitatory signals to the blue–yellow opponent cells, and the long-wavelength cones send inhibitory signals. If the strength of the excitatory signals is greater than that of the inhibitory ones, blue is seen; if the opposite is the case, then yellow is seen.

The medium-wavelength cones send excitatory signals to the green–red opponent cells, and the long-wavelength cones send inhibitory signals. Green is seen if the excitatory signals are stronger than the inhibitory ones, and red is seen otherwise. There is support for the theory from individuals suffering from the various forms of deficient colour perception discussed earlier.

Colour constancy

Colour constancy is the tendency for a surface or object to appear to have the same colour when the illumination varies. Colour constancy indicates that colour vision does not depend *only* on the wavelengths of the light reflected from objects. If that were the case, then the same object would appear redder in artificial light than in natural light. In fact, we generally show reasonable colour constancy in such circumstances.

Why do we show colour constancy? One factor is *chromatic adaptation*, in which sensitivity to light of any given colour decreases over time. For example, if you are standing outside after dark, you may be struck by the yellowness of the artificial lights in people's houses. However, if you have been in a room illuminated by artificial light for some time, the light does not seem yellow. Chromatic adaptation reduces the distorting effects of any given illumination on colour constancy.

One reason why we show colour constancy is because of familiarity. We know that pillar boxes are bright red, and so they look the same colour whether they are illuminated by the sun or by artificial street lighting. Delk and Fillenbaum (1965) presented various shapes cut out of the same orange-red cardboard. The shapes of objects that are typically red (e.g., heart, apple) were perceived as slightly redder than the shapes of other objects (e.g., mushrooms). However, it is hard with such evidence to distinguish between genuine perceptual effects and response or reporting bias.

How can we explain colour constancy for unfamiliar objects? Some insight into the factors involved was obtained by Land (1977). He presented participants with two displays (known as Mondrians) consisting of rectangular shapes of different colours. He then adjusted the lighting of the displays so that two differently coloured rectangles (one from each display) reflected exactly the same wavelengths of light. The two rectangles were seen in their actual colours, showing strong evidence of colour constancy in the absence of familiarity. Finally, Land (1977) found that the two rectangles looked exactly the same (and so colour constancy broke down) when everything else in the two displays was blocked out.

What was happening in Land's study? According to Land's (1977, 1986) retinex theory, we decide the colour of a surface by *comparing* its ability to reflect short, medium, and long wavelengths against that of adjacent surfaces. Colour constancy breaks down when such comparisons cannot be made.

Zeki (1983) identified part of the physiological system involved in colour constancy. He found in a study on monkeys that certain cells in area V4 (colour-processing area) responded strongly to a red patch in a multi-coloured display illuminated mainly by red light. However, these cells did not respond when the red patch was replaced by a green, blue, or white patch, even when the dominant reflected wavelength was red. Thus, these cells seem to respond to the *actual* colour of a surface rather than simply to the wavelengths reflected from it.

Evaluation

As is predicted by retinex theory, the perception of an object's colour depends on some kind of *comparison* of the wavelengths of light reflected from that object and from other objects in the visual field. However, retinex theory does not provide a complete account of colour perception and colour constancy. It does not indicate the precise ways in which neurons such as colour-opponent cells might be involved in colour perception. In addition, it does not directly address the role of familiar colour in influencing colour constancy.

According to retinex theory, colour constancy should be complete provided that observers can see the surroundings of a shape or object. However, that is often not the case. The extent to which colour constancy is obtained varies across studies from about 20% to 130% (Bramwell & Hurlbert, 1996). One reason why colour constancy is often far from complete is because of limitations in the method of asymmetric matching by adjustment that is generally used. With this method, participants view two scenes under different lighting conditions, and adjust the colour of part of one scene to match that of the other scene. In everyday life, in contrast, we tend simply to decide whether a colour is the same as, or different from, that seen under different lighting conditions. Bramwell and Hurlbert (1996) devised a more natural task, and found greater colour constancy. However, it was far from perfect.

Further evidence that retinex theory provides an incomplete account of colour constancy was produced by Jakobsson et al. (1997). Participants viewed a complex two-dimensional visual display that was seen as three-dimensional. There was only one display. However, it could be perceived in two different ways, with parts of the display appearing to be angled differently depending on the perceptual interpretation. One way in which the display could be perceived gave rise to almost complete colour constancy, whereas the other produced no colour constancy. Land's (1977, 1986) retinex theory cannot account for the findings. According to that theory, the observers had adequate information to show colour constancy. However, retinex theory is a 2-D model, and so it is perhaps unsurprising that it cannot handle some of the findings when more complex 3-D factors are considered.

Movement perception

Historically, most research on visual perception involved a motionless observer viewing one or more static objects. Such research lacked *ecological validity* or relevance to our everyday experiences. We reach for objects, and we walk, run, or drive through the environment. At other times, we are stationary, but other living creatures or objects in the environment are in movement relative to us.

Gibson's theorising increased interest in issues such as visually guided action and the perception of movement. In the words of Greeno (1994, p. 341), Gibson believed that "perception is a system that picks up information that supports coordination of the agent's actions with the systems that the environment provides."

We will start with the role of eye movements in visual perception. We are generally very efficient at deciding whether changes in the retinal image reflect movements made by ourselves or by objects in the environment, or whether they simply reflect eye movements. After that, we consider how we perceive object motion.

An important issue is whether Gibson (1979) was correct in assuming that we interact directly with the environment making use of invariant information. Directly available information (e.g., about optic flow patterns) is used in some of our interactions with the environment, but it remains controversial whether this is generally the case.

Eye movements

Our eyes move about three or four times a second, and these eye movements generally produce substantial effects on the retinal image. However, we normally perceive the environment as stable and unmoving. How does our visual system achieve this stability? Helmholtz (1866) proposed an outflow theory, in which movement of the retinal image is interpreted by using information about intended movement sent to the eye muscles. The fact that the visual world appears to move when the side of the eyeball is pressed supports this theory. There is movement within the retinal image unaccompanied by commands to the eye muscles, and so it is perceived as genuine. Sekuler and Blake (1994, p. 267) spelled out some of the details: "Perceived direction [of an object] develops from a comparison between two quantities, the command signals to the extraocular [outside the eye] muscles and the accompanying retinal image motion. To derive perceived direction, simply subtract the retinal image motion from the command signal." As predicted, when the eyeball is pressed in one direction, the visual environment seems to move in the opposite direction.

Evidence for Helmholtz's theory was reported by Duhamel, Colby, and Goldberg (1992). They found that the parietal cortex in the monkey brain is of major importance to an understanding of how the visual system handles eye movements. Duhamel et al. (1992, p. 91) concluded as follows: "At the time a saccade [rapid, jerky eye movement] is planned, the parietal representation of the visual world undergoes a shift analogous to the shift of the image on the retina." Thus, visual processing in the parietal cortex *anticipates* the next eye movement in the period between its planning and execution.

In spite of the successes of outflow theory, it cannot be the whole story. As Tresilian (1994, p. 336) remarked, outflow theory "predicts that if the eyes are stationary in the head, as the head rotates, the resulting image motion will be interpreted as motion of the environment, yet everyone knows that this does not happen." Thus, we do not rely exclusively on information about intended eye movements in order to perceive a stable environment. Movement of the entire retinal image is probably attributed to movement of the head or eye, whereas movement of part of the retinal image is interpreted as movement of an external object.

Time to contact

Imagine that an object (e.g., a car) is approaching you at constant velocity or speed. How do we work out the time to contact? One possibility is that we estimate the speed of the object and its distance from us, and combine information from the two estimates. According to various theorists (e.g., Lee, 1980), time to contact can be calculated using only *one* variable, namely, the rate of expansion of the object's retinal image: the faster the image is expanding, the less time there is to contact. Lee (1980) proposed a measure of time to contact called *T* or tau, which is defined as the inverse of the rate of expansion of the retinal image of the object: $T = 1/$(rate of expansion of object's retinal image). This theory is in general agreement with Gibson's approach, because it is assumed that information about time to contact is directly available.

Lee (1980) assumed that the rate of expansion of an object's retinal image is the crucial factor influencing judgements of time to contact. It would thus be valuable to manipulate the rate of expansion as directly as possible. Savelsbergh, Pijpers, and van Santvoord (1993) achieved this by asking participants to catch a deflating or non-deflating ball swinging towards them on a pendulum. The rate of expansion of the retinal image is less for a deflating than for a non-deflating ball. Thus, on Lee's theory, participants should assume that the deflating ball would take longer to reach them than was actually the case. The peak grasp closure was 30 ms later with the deflating ball than with the non-deflating one, which is in line with prediction.

Wann (1996) argued that the findings of Savelsbergh et al. (1993) do *not* show that tau is the only factor involved in judging time to contact. Strict application of the tau hypothesis to their findings revealed that the peak grasp closure should have occurred about 230 ms later to the deflating ball than to the non-deflating ball rather than the actual 30 ms. As Wann (1996, p. 1043) concluded, "The results of Savelsbergh et al. point to it [tau] being only one component in a multiple-source evaluation process."

Wann and Rushton (1995) used a virtual reality setup, which allowed them to manipulate both tau and *binocular disparity* (slight differences in the images projected on the two retinas). The participants' task was to grasp a moving virtual ball with their hand. Tau and binocular disparity were both used to determine the timing of the participants' grasping movements. Whichever variable predicted an earlier arrival of the ball had more influence on grasping behaviour.

Evaluation
Tau is often taken into account when deciding on the time to contact. However, it is clearly not the *only* source of information used by observers. Tau may be the most important variable, but familiar size, binocular disparity, angular position, and velocity of the object relative to the observer are other important variables (Tresilian, 1995).

Biological movement

Most people are very good at interpreting the movements of other people. How successful would we be at interpreting biological movement if the visual information available to us were greatly reduced? Johansson (1975) addressed this issue by attaching lights to actors' joints (e.g., wrists, knees, ankles). The actors were dressed entirely in black so that only the lights were visible, and they were then filmed as they moved around. Reasonably accurate perception of a moving person could be achieved even with only six lights and a short segment of film. Most observers could describe accurately the posture and movements of the actors, and it almost seemed as if their arms and legs could be seen.

Some of the most interesting findings with point-light displays were reported by Runeson and Frykholm (1983). They filmed actors as they carried out a sequence of actions naturally or as if they were a member of the opposite sex. Observers guessed the gender of the actor correctly 85.5% of the time when he or she acted naturally, and there was only a modest reduction to 75.5% correct in the deception condition.

Theoretical accounts

Does our ability to perceive biological motion accurately involve complex cognitive processes? Much of the evidence suggests that it does not. For example, Fox and McDaniel (1982) presented two different motion displays side by side to infants. One display consisted of dots representing someone running on the spot, and the other showed the same activity but presented upside down. Infants 4 months of age spent most of their time looking at the display that was the right way up, suggesting that they were able to detect biological motion.

The findings of Fox and McDaniel (1982) are consistent with Johansson's (1975) view that the ability to perceive biological motion is innate. However, 4-month-old infants may have learned to perceive biological motion. Runeson and Frykholm (1983) argued for a Gibsonian position, according to which aspects of biological motion provide invariant information, and these invariants can be perceived with the impoverished information available from point-light displays.

There have been various attempts to identify the invariant or invariants that might be used by observers to make accurate sex judgements. Cutting, Proffitt, and Kozlowski (1978) pointed out that men tend to show relatively greater side-to-side motion (or swing) of the shoulders than of the hips, whereas women show the opposite. The reason for this is that men typically have broad shoulders and narrow hips in comparison to women. The shoulders and hips move in opposition to each other; that is, when the right shoulder is forward, the left hip is forward. One can identify the *centre of moment* in the upper body, which is the neutral reference point around which the shoulders and hips swing. The position of the centre of moment is determined by the relative sizes of the shoulders and hips, and is typically lower in men than in women. Cutting et al. (1978) found that the centre of moment correlated well with the sex judgements made by observers.

Mather and Murdoch (1994) used artifical point-light displays (i.e., the lights were *not* attached to people). Most previous studies had involved movement across the line of sight, but the "walkers" in their displays appeared to be walking either towards or away from the camera. There are two correlated cues that may be used by observers to decide whether they are looking at a man or a woman in point-light displays:

(1) Structural cues based on the tendency of men to have broad shoulders and narrow hips, whereas women have the opposite tendency; these structural cues form the basis of the centre of moment.
(2) Dynamic cues based on the tendency for men to show relatively greater body sway with the upper body than with the hips when walking, whereas woman show the opposite.

Sex judgements were based much more on dynamic cues than on structural ones when the two cues were in conflict. Thus, the centre of moment may be less important than was assumed by Cutting (e.g., 1978).

Evaluation
We are very good at detecting and interpreting biological movement even when the visual information available is fairly impoverished. This ability seems to depend at least in part on the detection of invariant types of information (e.g., centre of moment). What remains unclear is whether our ability to perceive biological motion is innate or whether it depends on certain kinds of learning experiences.

Space or depth perception

In visual perception, the two-dimensional retinal image is transformed into perception of a three-dimensional world. In everyday life, cues to depth are often provided by movement either of the observer or of objects in the visual environment. However, the emphasis here will be on depth cues that are available even if the observer and the objects in the environment are static. *Monocular cues* require the use of only one eye, but can also be used when someone has both eyes open. Such cues clearly exist, because the world still retains a sense of depth with one eye closed. *Binocular cues* involve both eyes being used together. Finally, *oculomotor cues* are kinaesthetic, depending on sensations of muscular contraction of the muscles around the eye.

Monocular cues

There are various monocular cues to depth. They are sometimes known as pictorial cues, because they are used by artists trying to create the impression of three-dimensional scenes. One such cue is *linear perspective*. Parallel lines pointing directly away from us seem closer together as they recede into the distance (e.g., railway tracks). This convergence of lines can create a powerful impression of depth in a two-dimensional drawing.

Another aspect of perspective is known as aerial perspective. Light is scattered as it travels through the atmosphere, especially if the atmosphere is dusty. As a result, more distant objects lose contrast and seem somewhat hazy.

Another cue related to perspective is texture. Most objects possess texture, and textured objects slanting away from us have what Gibson (1979) called a texture gradient. This is an increased gradient (rate of change) of texture density as you look from the front to the back of a slanting object. For example, if you look at a large patterned carpet, the details towards its far end are less clear than those towards its near end.

A further cue is *interposition*, in which a nearer object hides part of a more distant object. Evidence of the power of interposition is provided by Kanizsa's (1976) illusory square (see Figure 2.15). There is a strong subjective impression of a white square in front of four black circles. We make sense of the four sectored black discs by perceiving an illusory interposed white square.

Another cue to depth is provided by shading, or the pattern of light and dark on and around an object. Flat, two-dimensional

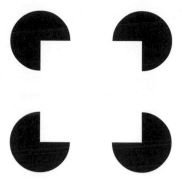

Figure 2.15.
Kanizsa's illusory
square.

Kanizsa's illusory square

surfaces do not cause shadows, and so shading provides good evidence for the presence of a three-dimensional object.

Another cue to depth is familiar size. If we know an object's actual size, then we can use its retinal image size to provide an estimate of its distance. When participants looked at playing cards through a peephole, unusually large ones looked further away than they actually were, whereas undersized playing cards looked closer than was the case (Ittelson, 1951).

The final monocular cue is *motion parallax*. This is based on the movement of an object's image over the retina. Consider, for example, two objects moving left to right across the line of vision at the same speed, but one object is much further away from the observer than is the other. In that case, the image cast by the nearer object would move much faster across the retina.

Binocular and oculomotor cues

There are three other depth cues. However, these cues (itemised below) lose any effectiveness they may have when objects are more than a short distance away:

(1) *Convergence*: The eyes turn inwards to focus on an object to a greater extent when the object is very close.
(2) *Accommodation*: The thickening of the lens of the eye when focusing on a close object.

(3) *Stereopsis*: Stereoscopic vision depends on the disparity in the images projected on the retinas of the two eyes; this is the only true binocular cue.

There has been controversy about the value of convergence as a cue to distance. The findings have tended to be negative when real objects are used. Accommodation is also of very little use. Its potential value as a depth cue is limited to the region of space immediately in front of you. However, distance judgements based on accommodation are inaccurate, even when the object is at close range (Kunnapas, 1968).

The importance of stereopsis was shown by Wheatstone (1838), who was the inventor of the stereoscope. In a stereoscope, separate pictures or drawings are presented to the observer so that each eye receives the information it would receive if the objects depicted were actually presented. Stereoscopic vision produces a strong depth effect.

Combining information from cues

So far, we have considered depth cues one at a time. In the real world, however, we generally have access to several depth cues at the same time, and so we need to know how information from various cues is combined and integrated. Bruno and Cutting (1988) identified three strategies that might be used by observers who had information available from two or more depth cues:

(1) *Additivity*: All the information from different cues is simply added together.
(2) *Selection*: Information from one cue is used, with information from the other cue or cues being ignored.
(3) *Multiplication*: Information from different cues interacts in a multiplicative way.

Bruno and Cutting (1988) presented three untextured parallel flat surfaces in depth. The observers viewed the displays monocularly, and there were four sources of depth information: relative size; height in the projection plane; interposition; and motion parallax. The findings supported the additivity notion. However, the visual system probably often makes use of weighted addition. Thus, information from different depth cues is combined, but more weight is attached to some cues than to others.

It generally makes sense to combine information from depth cues in an additive fashion. Most depth cues sometimes provide inaccurate information, and so relying totally on one cue would often lead to error. In contrast, taking account of all of the available information is usually the best way to make sure that depth perception is accurate. However, the selection strategy is used occasionally. Woodworth and Schlosberg (1954) discussed a study in which two normal playing cards of the same size were attached to stands, with one card being closer to the observer. The observers viewed the two cards monocularly, and the further card looked more distant. In the next, crucial phase of the study, part of the nearer card around the corner was clipped, and the two cards were arranged so that the edges of the more distant card seemed to fit exactly the cut-out edges of the nearer card. With monocular vision, the more distant card seemed to be in front of, and partially obscuring, the nearer card. In this case, the cue of interposition overwhelmed the cue of familiar size.

Size constancy

Judgements of the size of an object depend in part on judgements of its distance away from us. Thus, depth cues help us to make accurate judgements about objects' sizes. In this section, we will focus on *size constancy*, which is the tendency for any given object to appear the same size whether its size in the retinal image is large or small. For example, if you see someone walking towards you, their retinal image increases progressively, but their size seems to remain the same. Reasonable or high levels of size constancy have been obtained in numerous studies (see Goldstein, 1996).

Why do we show size constancy? A key reason is that we take account of an object's apparent distance when judging its size. For example, an object may be judged to be large even though its retinal image is very small if it is perceived to be a long way away. The fact that size constancy is often not shown when we look at objects on the ground from the top of a tall building or from a plane may occur because it is hard to judge distance accurately. These ideas are incorporated into the size–distance invariance hypothesis (Kilpatrick & Ittelson, 1953), according to which for a given size of retinal image the perceived size of an object is proportional to its perceived distance.

Evidence consistent with the size–distance invariance hypothesis was reported by Holway and Boring (1941). Participants sat at the intersection of two hallways. The test circle was presented in one hallway, and the comparison circle was presented in the other one.

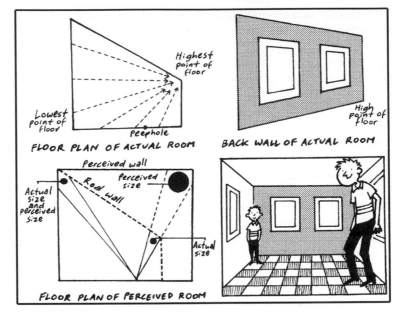

The test circle could be of various sizes and at various distances, and the participants' task was to adjust the comparison circle so that it was the same size as the test circle. Their performance was very good when depth cues were available. However, it became poor when depth cues were removed by placing curtains in the hallway and requiring the participants to look through a peephole. Lichten and Lurie (1950) went a step further and removed all depth cues by using screens that only allowed the observers to see the test circles. In those circumstances, the participants relied totally on retinal image size in their judgements of object size.

If size judgements depend on perceived distance, then size constancy should not be found when the perceived distance of an object is very different from its actual distance. The Ames room, which was discussed earlier in the chapter, provides a good example (see Figure 2.16). It has a peculiar shape: the floor slopes, and the rear wall is not at right angles to the adjoining walls. In spite of this, the Ames room creates the same retinal image as a normal rectangular room when viewed through a peephole. The fact that one end of the rear wall is much further from the viewer is disguised by making it much higher. The cues suggesting that the rear wall is at right angles to the viewer are so strong that observers mistakenly assume that two adults standing in the corners by the rear wall are at the same distance from them. This leads them to estimate the size of the nearer adult as being much greater than that of the adult who is further away.

Evaluation

Perceived size and size constancy do typically depend in part on perceived distance. However, the relationship between perceived distance and perceived size is influenced by the kind of size judgements that observers are asked to make. Kaneko and Uchikawa (1997) argued that the instructions given to observers in previous studies were not always clear. They distinguished between perceived linear size (what the *actual* size of the object seems to be) and perceived angular size (the *apparent* retinal size of the object). Kaneko and Uchikawa (1997) manipulated various depth cues. Overall, they found much more evidence for size constancy with linear-size instructions than with angular-size instructions. There was a closer approximation to size constancy with linear-size instructions when depth was reasonably easy to judge accurately, but this was less so with angular-size instructions. Thus, the size–distance invariance hypothesis is more applicable to judgements of linear size than of angular size.

Size judgements also depend on information about familiar size. Schiffman (1967) asked observers to view familiar objects at various distances in the presence or absence of depth cues. Their size estimates were accurate even when depth cues were not available, because they used their knowledge of familiar size.

The horizon is sometimes used in size estimation. When the horizon is a long way away, an object that is on the line between a standing observer and the horizon is about 1.50–1.75 m tall. Bertamini, Yang, and Proffitt (1998) obtained size judgements from standing and sitting observers. These judgements were most accurate when the objects being judged were at about eye-level height, suggesting that the horizon can be used as a reference point for size estimation.

In sum, size constancy depends on various factors including perceived distance, size familiarity, the horizon, and so on. As yet, we do not have a theory providing a coherent account of how these factors combine to produce size judgements.

Perception without awareness

When we think about visual perception, we typically regard it as a conscious process, at least in the sense that we are consciously aware of the objects or objects at which we are looking. However, there have been numerous attempts to demonstrate what is known as *subliminal perception*, which is perception occurring below the level of conscious awareness. We will consider some of the evidence on subliminal perception in normals. After that, we will discuss evidence from brain-damaged patients with *blindsight*, who can apparently respond appropriately to visual stimuli in the absence of conscious awareness of those stimuli.

Subliminal perception

Americans first became interested in subliminal perception in 1957. James Vicary, who was running a failing marketing business, claimed to have flashed the words EAT POPCORN and DRINK COCA-COLA for 1/300th of a second numerous times during the showing of a film in a cinema. This subliminal advertising continued for 6 weeks, and allegedly led to an 18% increase in the cinema sales of Coca-Cola and a 58% increase in the sales of popcorn. However, the film that was showing (*Picnic*) contained scenes of eating and drinking, and it is unclear whether it was the subliminal advertising or the film itself that caused the increased sales. More worryingly, there are indications that James Vicary made up the whole study to prop up his business (Weir, 1984). In fact, there is little or no evidence that subliminal advertising is effective in the more than 200 studies that have been carried out (Pratkanis & Aronson, 1992).

The main issue in evaluating laboratory research on subliminal perception concerns the threshold or criterion to be used to define conscious awareness of visual stimuli. Cheesman and Merikle (1985) made an important distinction between two thresholds:

(1) *Subjective threshold*: This is defined in terms of the participant's failure to report conscious awareness of the stimulus.
(2) *Objective threshold*: This is defined in terms of the participant's inability to make a voluntary discriminative response to a stimulus (e.g., guess at above chance level whether it is a word or not).

As Cheesman and Merikle (1985) pointed out, people often show "awareness" of a stimulus as assessed by the objective threshold, even though the stimulus does not exceed the subjective threshold. Thus, what appears to be subliminal perception using the subjective threshold is often no longer subliminal when the objective threshold is used.

Holender (1986) considered research on subliminal perception, focusing mainly on the objective threshold. He argued that the strongest evidence for subliminal perception comes from studies in which a stimulus was presented very briefly and replaced by a pattern mask. For example, Marcel (1983) found on a lexical decision task that the decision that a string of letters formed a word (e.g., "doctor") was made faster when preceded by a relevant masked stimulus (e.g., "nurse") that the participants could not detect at the conscious level. The implication is that the meaning of the masked (and subliminal) words was processed, and this enhanced performance on the lexical decision task.

Holender (1986) argued that there were inadequacies in studies such as that of Marcel (1983). For example, Marcel (1983) adjusted the time interval between the initial word and the pattern mask at the start of the experiment until the participants detected its presence on under 60% of occasions when they were asked to guess whether or not a word had been presented. The threshold of awareness may vary over time, and so awareness checks should have been made at various points during the experiment. As a result of such omissions, Holender (1986) was unconvinced of the existence of subliminal perception.

Several studies using the emotional Stroop task in groups high and low in anxiety seem to provide reasonable evidence for subliminal perception (see Eysenck, 1997). In essence, anxiety-relevant, neutral words, and non-words are presented subliminally, and the participants have to name the colours presented with the words as rapidly as possible. The key finding is that anxious individuals are slowed down more than non-anxious individuals in their colour naming when anxiety-relevant words are presented, presumably because they process these words more thoroughly and this interferes with colour naming. In studies by MacLeod and Rutherford (1992) and MacLeod and Hagan (1992), each word was presented for only 20 ms before being followed by a pattern mask. There were regular awareness checks in both studies. These checks involved a lexical decision task on which the participants had to decide whether the subliminal stimuli were words or non words, indicating that the more objective threshold for detection of conscious awareness was not exceeded.

Blindsight

According to Zeki (1992, 1993), area V1 (the primary visual cortex) plays a central role in visual perception. Nearly all signals from the retina pass through this area before proceeding to the other areas specialised for different aspects of visual processing. Patients with partial or total damage to this area have a loss of vision in part or all of the visual field. However, in spite of this loss of conscious vision, some of these patients can make accurate judgements and discriminations about visual stimuli presented to the "blind" area. Such patients are said to show blindsight.

The most thoroughly studied patient with blindsight was D.B., who was tested by Weiskrantz (e.g., 1986). Following an operation, D.B. was left with an area of blindness in the lower left quadrant of the visual field. However, he guessed with above-chance accuracy whether or not a visual stimulus had been presented to the blind area, and he could also identify its location.

In spite of D.B.'s performance, he seemed to have no conscious visual experience. According to Weiskrantz et al. (1974, p. 721), "When he was shown a video film of his reaching and judging orientation of lines, he was openly astonished." However, it is hard to be sure that D.B. had no conscious visual experience. Weiskrantz, Barbur, and Sahraie (1995) argued that any residual conscious vision in blindsight patients is very different from conscious vision in normal individuals. It is characterised by "a contentless kind of awareness, a feeling of something happening, albeit not normal seeing" (Weiskrantz et al., 1995, p. 6122).

Evidence that blindsight does not depend on conscious visual experience was reported by Rafal et al. (1990). Blindsight patients performed at chance level when given the task of detecting a light presented to the blind area of the visual field. However, their speed of reaction to a light presented to the intact part of the visual field was slowed down when a light was presented to the blind area at the same time. Thus, a light that did not produce any conscious awareness nevertheless received sufficient processing to disrupt visual performance on another task.

Brain systems

What brain systems underlie blindsight? Köhler and Moscovitch (1997) discussed findings from several patients who had had an entire cerebral hemisphere removed. These patients showed evidence of blindsight for stimulus detection, stimulus localisation, form discrimination, and motion detection. These findings led Köhler and Moscovitch (1997, p. 322) to conclude: "The results . . . suggest that subcortical rather than cortical regions may mediate blindsight on tasks that involve these visual functions."

Another possibility is that there is a "fast" pathway that proceeds directly to V5 (motion processing) without passing through V1 (primary visual cortex). Evidence supporting this view was reported by ffytche, Guy, and Zeki (1995). They obtained visual event-related potentials when moving stimuli were presented, and found that V5 became active before, or at the same time as, V1. Blindsight patients may use this pathway even if V1 is totally destroyed.

Evaluation

It is very difficult to be certain that perception without conscious awareness has occurred. However, laboratory studies on subliminal perception have become increasingly sophisticated, and there continue to be regular positive findings. In addition, the most natural interpretation of studies on blindsight is that perception without awareness is involved. This does not imply that the unconscious is as complicated as was proposed by Sigmund Freud. All that is implied is that some basic perceptual processing can occur outside of awareness. More specifically, as Greenwald (1992) pointed out, the main achievement of subliminal perception is probably the partial processing of the meaning of individual words.

Summary: Major perceptual processes

- *The visual system*: The main pathway between the eye and the cortex is the retina–geniculate–striate system. There are two essentially independent channels within this system: the parvocellular or P pathway and the magno-cellular or M pathway. Different parts of the visual cortex are specialised for different functions. Lateral inhibition is involved in edge perception and the phenomenon of simultaneous contrast. Dark adaptation depends mainly on changes in the sensitivity of the rods and cones, but also in part on pupil dilation. There is evidence from neuroimaging and from brain-damaged patients that area V4 is specialised for colour processing, whereas area V5 is specialised for motion processing.
- *Perceptual organisation*: According to the Gestaltists, perceptual segregation and organisation depend on several laws of grouping (e.g., law of proximity, law of similarity). There is segregation into figure and ground, with only the figure being perceived as having a distinct form or shape.

The Gestaltists tried unsuccessfully to explain their laws of grouping by the doctrine of isomorphism. The Gestaltists assumed wrongly that the grouping of perceptual elements occurs early in visual processing in a bottom-up way. They also minimised the complexities involved when laws of grouping are in conflict.

- *General approaches to perception*: According to constructivist theorists, perception is an active and constructive process that is influenced by the observer's hypotheses, expectations, and knowledge. The constructivist approach predicts that perception will often be in error, but it is typically accurate. Many of the visual illusions studied by constructivist theorists are artificial and contrived. According to Gibson's direct theory, there is much more information available in sensory stimulation than is generally realised, especially when the observer is in motion. Perceptual processing and the attachment of meaning to visual stimuli are both much more complicated than was assumed by Gibson. Constructivist and indirect theorists focus on perception for recognition, whereas Gibson emphasised perception for action. Several visual illusions can apparently be explained in terms of misapplied size constancy. However, the fact that some visual illusions are greatly reduced when the observer makes some form of appropriate action towards them suggests that the direct and indirect approaches may both be relevant to an understanding of visual illusions.

- *Colour perception*: The Young–Helmholtz theory led to the assumption that there are three types of cone receptors differing in the wavelengths of light to which they are most sensitive. This theory cannot explain negative afterimages. According to Hering's opponent-process theory, there are three types of opponent processes: red–green; blue–yellow; and black–white. This theory helps to explain the patterns of colour deficiency and of negative afterimages. The two theories can be combined on the assumption that signals from the three cone types of the Young–Helmholtz theory are sent to the opponent cells of Hering's theory. Colour constancy depends on chromatic adaptation, object familiarity, and comparisons of the light reflected from adjacent surfaces. Retinex theory explains many of the findings on colour constancy, but seems to predict greater colour constancy than is generally found. It is a 2-D model, and cannot account for some of the findings when 3-D factors are involved.

- *Movement perception*: According to Helmholtz's outflow theory, our ability to perceive the world as stable depends on using information about intended eye movements. In addition, movement of the entire retinal image is attributed to movement of the head or eye. Judgements of the time to contact of an object depend in part on the rate of expansion of the retinal image of the object. However, other factors (e.g., binocular disparity) are also important. Judgements of biological movement are very accurate even when only minimal visual information is available. Observers' ability to make accurate sex judgements when viewing point-light displays may depend on the centre of moment and on more dynamic cues.

- *Space or depth perception*: There are monocular, binocular, and oculomotor cues to depth. The monocular cues include linear perspective, aerial perspective, texture, interposition, shading, familiar size, and motion parallax. The binocular and oculomotor cues are convergence, accommodation, and stereopsis. These cues are only effective when objects are close to the observer. Information from different cues is generally combined in an additive way. A major reason for size constancy is that we take account of an object's apparent distance when judging its size. In addition, size judgements depend on information about familiar size, on the instructions given to observers, and on the line between the observer's eyes and the horizon.

- *Perception without awareness*: Studies of subliminal advertising have failed to produce convincing evidence of its effectiveness. However, there is evidence of subliminal perception in numerous laboratory studies, especially when the subjective threshold rather than the objective threshold is used. Patients with blindsight provide good evidence for perception without awareness. Blindsight may depend on subcortical processes and/or a direct pathway to area V5, which is involved in motion processing.

Essay questions

(1) Describe the main features of the human visual system.
(2) What are the strengths and limitations of the Gestalt approach to visual perception?
(3) Compare and contrast the constructivist and direct approaches to perception.
(4) Consider evidence for the view that there are separate systems involved in perception for recognition and perception for action.
(5) What factors are involved in colour constancy?
(6) What are the main cues that are used in depth perception?
(7) Does subliminal perception exist?

Further reading

Bruce, V., Green, P.R., & Georgeson, M.A. (1996). *Visual perception: Physiology, psychology, and ecology* (3rd ed.). Hove, UK: Psychology Press. Several chapters of this book (especially Chapter 17) are relevant to the topics dealt with in this chapter.

Gazzaniga, M.S., Ivry, R.B., & Mangun, G.R. (1998). *Cognitive neuroscience: The biology of the mind*. New York: W.W. Norton. Several of the topics discussed in this chapter are considered in detail in Chapters 4 and 5 of this book.

Goldstein, E.B. (1996). *Sensation and perception* (4th ed.). New York: Brooks/Cole. There is good basic coverage of visual perception in this textbook.

Object recognition 3

Introduction

As a result of visual perception, we can recognise or identify the two-dimensional and three-dimensional stimuli that we encounter constantly during our waking lives. The fact that we rarely have problems in recognising objects indicates that the processes involved in recognition of three-dimensional objects generally function very effectively. However, these processes are more complex than might be imagined. First, there are typically numerous overlapping objects in the visual environment, and we have to decide where one object ends and the next starts. Second, objects can be recognised accurately over a wide range of viewing distances and orientations, even though the retinal image changes considerably. Third, we recognise that an object is, say, a chair without any apparent difficulty. However, chairs (and many other objects) vary enormously in their visual properties (e.g., colour, size, shape), and it is not immediately clear how we manage to allocate such diverse visual stimuli to the same category.

In this chapter, we will focus initially on the processes involved in the recognition of two-dimensional stimuli, followed by a consideration of object recognition. Faces are a particularly important type of object, and face recognition seems to differ in some ways from normal object recognition. Accordingly, a section of the chapter is devoted to face recognition. Finally, we consider object recognition and other aspects of visual perception from the developmental perspective. We will consider attempts to understand *how* and *when* visual abilities develop in infants and young children.

Pattern recognition

Given the complexities in recognising three-dimensional objects, it is sensible to start by considering the processes involved in the *pattern recognition* (identification or categorisation) of two-dimensional patterns. Much of this research has addressed the question of how alphanumeric patterns (alphabetical and numerical symbols) are recognised. A key issue here is the flexibility of the human perceptual system. For example, we can recognise the letter "A" rapidly and accurately across considerable variations in orientation, in typeface, in size, and in writing style. Why is pattern recognition so successful? Advocates of template and feature theories have proposed different answers to this question. However, pattern recognition clearly involves matching information from the visual stimulus with information stored in memory.

Template theories

The basic idea behind template theories is that there is a miniature copy or template stored in long-term memory corresponding to each of the visual patterns we know. A pattern is recognised on the basis of the template providing the closest match to the stimulus input. Template matching is basically the system used by banks. They have machines using a system of template matching to "read" your bank account number from your cheques. This is a very simple situation, because the digits on cheques are in a standard shape and are in standard locations on the cheque. It is *not* representative of everyday life, because there are generally enormous variations in the visual stimuli allegedly matching any given template.

One modest improvement in the basic template theory is to assume that the visual stimulus undergoes a normalisation process (i.e., producing an internal representation in a standard position, size, and so on) before the search for a matching template begins. Normalisation would help pattern recognition for letters and digits, but it is improbable that it would consistently produce matching with the appropriate template.

Another way of trying to improve template theory would be to assume that there is more than one template for each letter and numeral. This would permit accurate matching of stimulus and template across a wider range of stimuli, but only at the cost of making the theory much more unwieldy.

How effective at pattern recognition are template theories that incorporate the various kinds of improvements indicated above? Larsen and Bundesen (1992) tried to answer this question by studying machine recognition of digits handwritten by various people. The stimuli were normalised for orientation and size, and several templates were stored for each of the 10 digits. The machine then found the single best match between the presented digit and the stored templates. Pattern recognition occurred on 69% of trials when 5 templates were stored for each digit, and this improved to 77% when 10 templates were stored, and to 89% when 60 templates were stored. Thus, the number of stored templates did have a significant influence on performance. However, human participants averaged 97% on this task, so machine recognition was well below human recognition.

Most template theories are limited, in that pattern recognition depends solely on the *one* template producing the best match with the visual stimulus. Thus, information concerning the level of match with all the other templates is totally ignored. Larsen and Bundesen (1996) argued that it would be possible to devise an improved template theory by avoiding that limitation. This led them to produce a theory that was a combination of a template theory and a feature theory (see next section). The theory is a general one, but they applied it to pattern recognition of digits:

(1) There are several stored templates for each digit.
(2) Feature analysers or demons determine the degree of match between each stored template and the visual stimulus.
(3) There are cognitive demons above the feature analysers or demons, one for each digit. Each cognitive demon becomes activated on the basis of degrees of match of its associated feature demons. Thus, information from *all* templates is taken into account.
(4) At the top level of analysis, the decision demon classifies the visual stimulus on the basis of the most activated cognitive demon.

Larsen and Bundesen (1996) found machine recognition for digits based on this theory was 95.3% accurate with an average of 37 templates per type of digit. This level of performance is clearly superior to the levels reported by Larsen and Bundesen (1992), and it is only 2–3% below that of human participants.

Evaluation
Template theories can provide a reasonable account of pattern recognition for simple stimuli, especially if there are normalisation processes and multiple templates for each category of stimuli. In addition, template theories are more effective when they take account

of information from *all* the templates rather than simply the *one* producing the closest match to the input stimulus.

Template theories have mostly been applied to relatively simple stimuli such as letters and digits. Such theories are less useful when stimuli belong to ill-defined categories for which no single template could possibly suffice (e.g., buildings). Furthermore, template theories do not usually take context effects into account. For example, Palmer (1975) found that briefly presented pictures (e.g., a loaf) could be identified more accurately when they were preceded by a picture of an appropriate context (e.g., a kitchen) than by no context. Such findings cannot readily be explained by template theories.

Feature theories

According to feature theories, a pattern consists of a set of specific features or attributes. For example, a face could be said to possess various features: a nose, two eyes, a mouth, a chin, and so on. Pattern recognition begins with the extraction of the features from the presented visual stimulus. This set of features is then combined, and compared against information stored in memory.

Consider an alphanumeric pattern such as "A". Feature theorists might argue that its crucial features are two straight lines and a connecting cross-bar. This kind of theoretical approach has the advantage that visual stimuli varying greatly in size, orientation, and minor details may nevertheless be identifiable as instances of the same pattern.

Experimental evidence

The feature-theory approach has received support in studies of visual search, in which a target letter has to be identified as rapidly as possible (see also Chapter 5). Neisser (1964) compared the time taken to detect the letter "Z" when the distractor letters consisted of straight lines (e.g, W, V) or contained rounded features (e.g., O, G) (see Figure 3.1). Performance was faster in the latter condition, presumably because the distractors shared fewer features with the target letter Z.

Feature theories are based on the assumption that visual processing proceeds from a detailed analysis of a pattern or object to a global or general analysis. However, global processing often precedes more specific processing. Navon (1977) presented his participants with stimuli such as the one shown in Figure 3.2. In one of his studies, participants on some trials had to decide as rapidly as possible whether the large letter was an "H" or an "S"; on other trials,

Example of arrangement of letters	
List 1	**List 2**
IMVXEW	ODUGQR
WVMEIX	GRODUQ
VXWIEM	DUROQG
MIEWVX	RGOUDQ
IWVXEM	UGQDRO
IXEZVW	GUQZOR
VWEMXI	ODGRUQ
MIVEWX	DRUQGO
WXEIMV	UQGORD

Figure 3.1. Neisser used stimuli like these to measure the time it took for people to detect the letter Z. He found that they took less time to find it in the block of rounded letters than in the block of "straight-line" letters.

```
S                      S
S                      S
S                      S
S                      S
S                      S
SSSSSSSSSSSSS
S                      S
S                      S
S                      S
S                      S
S                      S
```

Figure 3.2. Example of stimulus designed by Navon.

they had to decide whether the small letters were H's or S's. Performance speed with the small letters was greatly slowed when the large letter differed from the small letters. In contrast, decision speed with the large letter was unaffected by the nature of the small letters. According to Navon (1977, p. 354), these findings indicate that, "perceptual processes are temporally organised so that they proceed from global structuring towards more and more fine-grained analysis."

Some evidence is inconsistent with Navon's conclusion. Kinchla and Wolfe (1979) used similar stimuli to those of Navon (1977), but of variable size. When the large letter was very large, processing of the small letters preceded that of the large letter. They argued that global processing occurs prior to more detailed processing only when the global structure of a pattern or object can be ascertained by a single eye fixation.

Cognitive neuroscience

Cognitive neuroscientists have obtained evidence of relevance to feature theories. If the presentation of a visual stimulus leads initially to detailed processing of its basic features, then we might be able to identify cells in the cortex involved in such processing. However, while the existence of cells specialised for responding to specific aspects of visual stimuli may be consistent with feature theories, it does *not* demonstrate that they are correct for reasons to be discussed shortly.

Hubel and Wiesel (e.g., 1979), used single-unit recordings to study individual neurons (see Chapter 1). They found that many cells responded in two different ways to a spot of light depending on which part of the cell was affected:

(1) An "on" response, with an increased rate of firing while the light was on.
(2) An "off" response, with the light causing a decreased rate of firing.

Many retinal ganglion cells, lateral geniculate cells, and layer IV primary visual cortex cells can be divided into on-centre cells and off-centre cells. On-centre cells produce the on-response to a light in the centre of their receptive field and an off-response to a light in the periphery; the opposite is the case with off-centre cells.

Hubel and Wiesel (e.g., 1979) discovered the existence of two types of neurons in the receptive fields of the primary visual cortex: simple cells and complex cells. Simple cells have "on" and "off" regions, with each region being rectangular in shape. These cells play an important role in detection. They respond most to dark bars in a light field, light bars in a dark field, or to straight edges between areas of light and dark. Any given simple cell only responds strongly to stimuli of a particular orientation, and so the responses of these cells could be relevant to feature detection.

There are many more complex cells than simple cells. They resemble simple cells in that they respond maximally to straight-line stimuli in a particular orientation. However, there are significant differences:

(1) Complex cells have larger receptive fields.
(2) The rate of firing of a complex cell to any given stimulus depends very little on its position within the cell's receptive field.

(3) Most complex cells respond well to moving contours, whereas simple cells respond only to stationary or slowly moving contours.

There is also evidence for the existence of hypercomplex cells. These cells respond most to rather more complex patterns than do simple or complex cells. For example, some respond maximally to corners, whereas others repond to other various specific angles.

Cortical cells provide *ambiguous* information, because they respond in the same way to different stimuli. For example, a cell that responds maximally to a horizontal line moving slowly may respond moderately to a horizontal line moving rapidly and to a nearly horizontal line moving slowly. Thus, as Sekuler and Blake (1994, p. 134) pointed out, "Neurons in the visual cortex cannot really be called 'feature detectors', . . . because individual cells cannot signal the presence of a particular visual feature with certainty."

Hubel and Wiesel (1962) argued that processing in the visual cortex is based on straight lines and edges. An alternative view is based on gratings, which are patterns consisting of alternating lighter and darker bars. Of particular importance are *sinusoidal gratings*, in which there are gradual intensity changes between adjacent bars. According to Sekuler and Blake (1994), gratings possess four properties:

(1) *Spatial frequency*: the spacing of bars as imaged on the retina.
(2) *Contrast*: the difference in intensity of light and dark bars.
(3) *Orientation*: the angle at which the bars of the grating are presented.
(4) *Spatial phase*: the position of the grating with respect to some landmark (e.g., edge of a display).

It is possible to construct any desired visual pattern by manipulating each of these four properties.

Campbell and Robson (1968) assumed that the visual system contains sets of neurons (or channels) that respond to different spatial frequencies of gratings, and this assumption formed the basis of their multi-channel model. They obtained some support for their model by presenting people with a compound grating, which was formed by combining a number of simple sinusoidal gratings. The visual system responded differently to each of the components of these compound gratings, presumably because the channels appropriate to each component were being activated. Subsequent research has indicated that most cells in the primary visual cortex respond more strongly to sinusoidal gratings than to lines and edges (see Pinel, 1997).

Harvey, Roberts, and Gervais (1983) presented individual letters very briefly, and asked their participants to name them. Some letters (e.g., "K" and "N") having several features in common were not confused, which is contrary to the prediction of feature theory. In contrast, letters with similar spatial frequencies tended to be confused, even if they shared few common features. These findings suggest that spatial frequency is more important than features in the representation of letters within the visual system.

Evaluation

Stimulus features play a role in pattern recognition. However, feature theories omit much that is of importance. First, they de-emphasise the effects of context and of expectations on pattern recognition. Weisstein and Harris (1974) used a task involving detection of a line embedded either in a briefly flashed three-dimensional form or in a less coherent form. According to feature theorists, the target line should always activate the same feature detectors, and so the coherence of the form in which it is embedded should not affect detection. In fact, target detection was best when the target line was part of a three-dimensional form. Weisstein and Harris (1974) called this the "object-superiority effect", and it is inconsistent with many feature theories.

Second, pattern recognition does not depend solely on listing the features of a stimulus. For example, the letter "A" consists of two oblique uprights and a dash, but these three features can be presented in such a way that they are not perceived as an A: \/ –. In order to understand pattern recognition, we need to consider the *relationships* among features as well as simply the features themselves.

Third, the limitations of feature theories are clearer with three-dimensional than with two-dimensional stimuli. The fact that observers can generally recognise three-dimensional objects even when some of the major features are hidden from view is hard to account for on a theory that emphasises the role of features in recognition.

Fourth, global processing often precedes feature processing (e.g., Navon, 1977). Additional evidence for this comes from research on face processing (discussed later). Thus, feature processing often plays a more minor role in visual processing than is assumed within feature theories.

Object recognition

It is now time to turn our attention to the recognition of three-dimensional stimuli. Numerous theories have been put forward to account for object recognition, but we will focus mainly on those proposed by Marr (1982) and by Biederman (1987). These theories have been very influential, and provide a way of addressing the key issues.

Marr's computational approach

Marr's (1982) key assumption was that three visual representations of increasing complexity and richness are formed during visual perception. The first representation is the *primal sketch*, which consists largely of information about features such as edges, contours, and blobs. More specifically, there are two versions of the primal sketch. First, there is the raw primal sketch, which contains information about light-intensity changes in the visual scene. Second, there is the full primal sketch, which makes use of the information from the raw primal sketch to identify the number and outline shapes of visual objects.

The primal sketch is used to form a second representation, which is called the *2½-D sketch*. This representation is more detailed than the primal sketch, and includes information about the depth and orientation of visible surfaces. It is a viewer-centred representation, meaning that the visual information in it is essentially retinal in nature and depends on the precise angle from which an object is viewed.

What information is used in changing the primal sketch into the 2½-D sketch? The main kinds of information are those relating to shading, motion, texture, shape, and binocular disparity.

Finally, there is the *3-D model representation*, which is a complete representation free of the limitations of the 2½-D sketch. This representation incorporates a three-dimensional representation that is independent of the viewer's viewpoint (this is known as viewpoint-invariant). In other words, this representation remains the same regardless of the viewing angle.

According to Marr and Nishihara (1978), object recognition involves matching the 3-D model representation against a set of 3-D model representations stored in memory. They argued that concavities (area where the contour points into the object) are identified first. With the human form, for example, there is a concave area in each armpit. These concavities are used to divide the visual image into segments (e.g., arms, legs, torso, head). Finally, the main axis of each segment is found.

Why is there this emphasis on axes? One reason is because it is possible to calculate the lengths and arrangement of axes of most visual objects regardless of the viewing angle. Another reason is that information about the axes of an object can assist in the process of object recognition. As Humphreys and Bruce (1989) pointed out, it is easy to distinguish humans from gorillas on the basis of the relative lengths of the axes of the segments corresponding to arms and legs: our legs are longer than our arms, whereas the opposite is true of gorillas.

Evaluation

Marr (1982) argued correctly that object recognition depends on several very complex processes. This led him to provide a more detailed and systematic account of those processes than any previous theorist. However, his theory has various limitations. First, it is very largely a bottom-up theory, and the role of top-down processes (e.g., expectations) in perception is neglected. Second, the theory is designed to account for unsubtle perceptual discriminations (e.g., that object is a cup), but not for more precise discriminations *within* a class of objects (e.g., that object is my favourite cup). Third, Marr's account of the 3-D model representation is less complete than his description of the primal sketch.

Biederman's recognition-by-components theory

Biederman (1987, 1990) proposed a theory of object recognition, which built on the foundations of Marr's (1982) theoretical approach. The central assumption of his recognition-by-components theory is that objects consist of basic shapes or components known as "geons" (geometric ions). Examples of geons are blocks, cylinders, spheres, arcs, and wedges. According to Biederman (1987), there are about 36 different geons, which can be arranged in almost endless different ways. For example, a cup can be described by an arc connected to the side of a cylinder, and a pail can be described by the same two geons, but with the arc connected to the top of the cylinder.

The stage we have discussed so far is that of the determination of the components or geons of a visual object and their relationships (see Figure 3.3). When this information is available, it is matched with stored object representations or structural models containing infor-

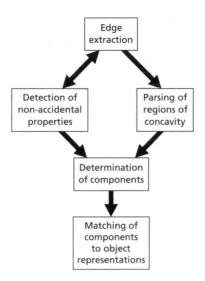

Figure 3.3. An outline of Biederman's recognition-by-components theory. Adapted from Biederman (1987).

mation about the nature of the relevant geons, their orientations, sizes, and so on. The identification of any given visual object is determined by whichever stored object representation fits best with the component- or geon-based information obtained from the visual object.

Only part of Biederman's theory has been presented so far (see Figure 3.3). What has been omitted is any analysis of how an object's components or geons are determined. The first step is edge extraction: "An early edge extraction stage, responsive to differences in surface characteristics namely, luminance, texture, or colour, provides a line drawing description of the object" (Biederman, 1987, p. 117).

The next step is to decide how a visual object should be segmented to establish the number of its parts. Biederman (1987) argued that the concave (curving inwards) parts of an object's contour are of particular value in accomplishing this task.

Which edge information from an object remains invariant across different viewing angles? According to Biederman (1987), there are five invariant properties of edges:

- *Curvature*: points on a curve.
- *Parallel*: sets of points in parallel.
- *Cotermination*: edges terminating at a common point.
- *Symmetry*: versus asymmetry.
- *Co-linearity*: points in a straight line.

The components or geons of a visual object are constructed from these invariant properties. Thus, for example, a cylinder has curved edges and two parallel edges connecting the curved edges, whereas a brick has three parallel edges and no curved edges. Biederman (1987, p. 116) argued that the five properties:

> have the desirable properties that they are invariant over changes in orientation and can be determined from just a few points on each edge. Consequently, they allow a primitive [component or geon] to be extracted with great tolerance for variations of viewpoint, occlusion [obstruction], and noise.

According to Biederman (1987), there are various reasons why we can achieve object recognition when the viewing conditions are poor:

- The invariant properties (e.g., curvature, parallel lines) can be detected even when only parts of edges can be seen.
- Provided that the concavities of a contour are visible, there are mechanisms allowing the missing parts of a contour to be restored.
- There is normally much redundant information available for recognising complex objects (e.g., a giraffe could be identified from its neck alone).

Experimental evidence

Biederman, Ju, and Clapper (1985) tested the notion that complex objects can be detected even when some of the geons are missing. Line drawings of complex objects having six or nine components were presented briefly. Even when only three or four of the components were present, participants identified the objects 90% of the time.

Biederman (1987) discussed a study in which degraded line drawings of objects were presented (see Figure 3.4). Object recognition was much harder to achieve when parts of the contour providing information about concavities were omitted than when other parts of the contour were deleted. Thus, information about concavities is important for object recognition, as is predicted by the theory.

According to Biederman's theory, object recognition depends on edge information rather than on surface information (e.g., colour). However, Joseph and Proffitt (1996) found that colour helped object recognition, especially for objects (e.g., cherries) having a characteristic colour. Their findings seem inconsistent with the theory.

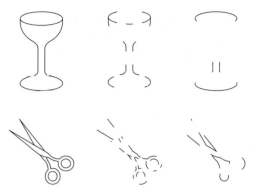

Figure 3.4. Intact figures (left column), with degraded line drawings either preserving (middle column) or not preserving (right column) parts of the contour providing information about concavities. Adapted from Biederman (1987).

Biederman (1987) argued that the input image is initially organised into its constituent parts or geons, with geons forming the building blocks of object recognition. However, as we saw earlier, global processing of an entire object often precedes more specific processing of its parts (see Kimchi, 1992).

In sum, there is experimental support for the kind of theory proposed by Biederman (1987). However, the central theoretical assumptions have not been tested directly. For example, there is no convincing evidence that the 36 components or geons proposed by Biederman do actually form the building blocks of object recognition.

Evaluation

There are various limitations with Biederman's recognition-by-components theory. First, Biederman (1987) argued that edge-based extraction processes provide enough information to permit object recognition. Evidence for this hypothesis was reported by Biederman and Ju (1988), who found that object recognition was as good with line drawings as with colour photographs. Such evidence supports the hypothesis provided that line drawings include all of the edges present in the original stimulus. In fact, line drawings are usually idealised versions of the original edge information (e.g., edges that are irrelevant to the object are often omitted). Edge-extraction processes are more likely to lead to accurate object recognition when objects are presented on their own, because it can be hard to decide which edges belong to which objects when several objects are presented together (Sanocki et al., 1998).

Sanocki et al. (1998) obtained strong support for the view that edge information is often insufficient to allow object recognition. Their

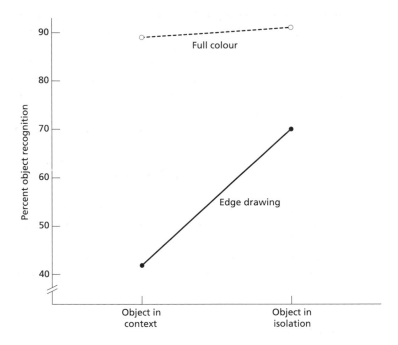

Figure 3.5. Object recognition as a function of stimulus type (edge drawings versus colour photographs) and presence versus absence of context. Data from Sanocki et al. (1998).

participants were presented briefly with objects presented in the form of edge drawings or full-colour photographs, and these objects were presented in isolation or in context. Object recognition was much worse with the edge drawings, especially when objects were presented in context (see Figure 3.5).

Second, Biederman put forward a viewpoint-invariant theory, according to which ease of object recognition is unaffected by the observer's viewpoint. This part of his theory resembles Marr's (1982) viewpoint-invariant 3-D model representation. This approach can be contrasted with viewpoint-dependent theories (e.g., Tarr & Bülthoff, 1998), according to which changes in viewpoint reduce the speed and/or accuracy of object recognition. Several findings support each type of theory. Biederman and Gerhardstein (1993) found that object naming was primed as well by two different views of an object as by two identical views, supporting the viewpoint-invariant position. However, Tarr and Bülthoff (1995) found that the speed and accuracy of object naming depended on the familiarity of the viewpoint, which is in line with viewpoint-dependent theories.

What is going on here? According to Tarr and Bülthoff (1995), viewpoint-invariant mechanisms are more important when the task involves making easy categorical discriminations. As Hayward and Williams (2000, p. 11) pointed out, "Under some circumstances, shape differences may be large enough, distinctive enough, or over-learned enough to support viewpoint-invariant recognition (e.g., distinguishing a square from a line drawing of a car could surely be done in a viewpoint-invariant manner)." In contrast, viewpoint-dependent mechanisms are more important when the task requires hard within-category discriminations (e.g., between different makes of car).

Third, as with Marr's (1982) approach, Biederman's theory only accounts for fairly unsubtle perceptual discriminations. Thus, it allows us to decide whether the animal in front of us is a dog or cat, but not whether it is our dog or cat. Fifth, Biederman's theory de-emphasises the role played by context. For example, as mentioned earlier, Palmer (1975) found that pictures of objects (e.g., a loaf) presented briefly were more likely to be identified when preceded by an appropriate context (e.g., kitchen) than when there was no context.

Visual agnosia

According to Farah (1999, p. 181), *visual agnosia* is "the impairment of visual object recognition in people who possess sufficiently preserved visual fields, acuity and other elementary forms of visual ability to enable object recognition, and in whom the object recognition impairment cannot be attributed to . . . loss of knowledge about objects . . . [Agnosics'] impairment is one of visual recognition rather than naming, and is therefore manifest on naming and non-verbal tasks alike." A distinction has often been made between two forms of visual agnosia:

(1) *Apperceptive agnosia*: object recognition is impaired because of deficits in perceptual processing.
(2) *Associative agnosia*: perceptual processes are essentially intact, but object recognition is impaired because of difficulties in accessing relevant knowledge about objects from memory.

How can we distinguish between patients with apperceptive agnosia and those with associative agnosia? As Humphreys (1999) pointed out, a common practice has been to assess patients' ability to copy objects that cannot be recognised. Patients who can copy objects are said to have associative agnosia, and those who cannot have apperceptive agnosia.

The distinction between apperceptive and associative agnosia is a simple one, and is of some use in classifying visual agnosics. However, the distinction has various limitations. First, while the perceptual abilities of associative agnosics are greatly superior to those of apperceptive agnosics, these abilities are not at normal level. For example, in spite of the fact that associative agnosics produce normal copies of objects, "the process by which [they] produce their good copies is invariably characterised as slow, slavish, and line-by-line" (Farah, 1999, p. 191).

Second, the notion that the underlying mechanisms in apperceptive agnosia and associative agnosia are entirely perceptual and associative, respectively, is a substantial oversimplification. Third, there is increasing evidence that there are actually several agnosias. There is little agreement on the number and nature of the agnosias, but Bauer (1993) proposed a fairly representative categorisation. In addition to apperceptive agnosia and associative agnosia, he argued that there are various other forms of agnosia, including the following:

(1) *Optic aphasia*: Object recognition is impaired on naming tasks only.
(2) *Prosopagnosia*: There are impairments in distinguishing among visually similar members of the same category, especially faces.
(3) *Category-specific agnosia*: There is impaired recognition of objects from a given category (e.g., living things).

In the next few sections, we will consider some of the evidence relating to some of the major forms of agnosia. The emphasis will be on those forms that are of current interest, but leaving a discussion of prosopagnosia until later in the chapter.

Apperceptive agnosia

Warrington and Taylor (1978) argued that the key problem in apperceptive agnosia is an inability to achieve object constancy, which involves being able to identify objects regardless of viewing conditions. They tested this hypothesis using pairs of photographs, one of which was a conventional or usual view and the other of which was an unusual view. For example, the usual view of a flat-iron was photographed from above, whereas the unusual view showed only the base of the iron and part of the handle. The patients were reasonably good at identifying the objects when they were shown one at a time in the usual or conventional view, but were very poor at identifying the same objects shown from an unusual angle.

Humpreys and Riddoch (1984, 1985) argued that the view of an object can be unusual in at least two ways:

(1) The object is foreshortened, thus making it hard to determine its principal axis of elongation.
(2) A distinctive feature of the object is hidden from view.

They used photographs in which some of the unusual views were based on obscuring a distinctive feature, whereas others were based on foreshortening. In four patients having right posterior cerebral lesions, Humphreys and Riddoch (1984, 1985) found that they had poor object recognition with the foreshortened photographs but not with those lacking a distinctive feature.

Warrington and James (1988) studied three patients with right-hemisphere damage and apperceptive agnosia. Their findings confirmed previous ones, in that all three patients had severe problems on *perceptual categorisation* tasks (e.g., tasks on which they had to categorise different versions of the same object as equivalent). In spite of the patients' problems with perceptual categorisation, they performed surprisingly well on various tasks involving *semantic categorisation*. For example, they knew which object out of a display of objects is found in the kitchen, and they could match pairs of drawings having the same function and names (e.g., two types of boat).

The key findings of Warrington and James (1988) were that their patients showed good semantic categorisation, and had no significant problems in everyday life, in spite of having seriously deficient perceptual categorisation ability. What do these findings mean? In general terms, they suggest that perceptual categorisation is of less importance in visual perception than might have been supposed. Rudge and Warrington (1991) proposed that there is a perceptual categorisation system in the right hemisphere and a semantic categorisation system in the left hemisphere. There is a route from basic visual analysis to semantic categorisation that bypasses the perceptual categorisation system. In other words, as Davidoff and Warrington (1999, p. 74) argued, "the right hemisphere perceptual categorisation system is an optional resource rather than an obligatory stage of visual analysis."

In sum, "the apperceptive impairment can be considered as one in which the patient has lost an ability to categorise different versions of the same object as equivalent" (Davidoff & Warrington, 1999, p. 75). This impairment has relatively little impact on access to semantic knowledge in some patients. However, it is very likely that severely impaired perceptual categorisation ability is associated with more widespread impairments in many patients.

Category-specific impairments

Some patients show the phenomenon of category specificity, meaning that they have special problems in recognising certain categories of objects. For example, Warrington and Shallice (1984) studied a patient, J.B.R., who suffered from severe associative agnosia. He had much greater problems in identifying pictures of living than of non-living things, having success rates of 6% and 90%, respectively. The pattern shown by J.B.R. is much more common than the opposite pattern, i.e., worse recognition of non-living than of living things. However, Warrington and McCarthy (1994) did report on one patient (D.R.S.) who showed consistently worse performance with drawings of objects than with drawings of animals. The task involved deciding which of five drawings was most closely associated with the target drawing.

How can we account for the generally worse recognition performance on living than non-living things? Perhaps the finding reflects the fact that we have more familiarity with non-living than with living things (e.g., foreign animals). Funnell and De Mornay Davies (1996) examined the effects of familiarity with J.B.R., who had previously been studied by Warrington and Shallice (1984). There was no difference in object recognition for living and non-living things with highly familiar items. However, with less familiar objects, performance was much better (44% versus 11%) for non-living than for living things. Thus, familiarity had an effect, but there was still evidence for a category-specific impairment.

Forde et al. (1997) studied a patient, S.R.B. He was worse at naming living than non-livings things in terms of both accuracy and speed. This difference was not due to familiarity or name frequency. However, it did depend in part on structural similarity, which was defined as the amount of contour overlap between the members of a category. When S.R.B was presented with colour photographs of structurally similar items (cats and dogs), he performed relatively poorly with both living and non-living things. However, his performance was significantly worse with dogs than with cats (17% versus 57%), suggesting that there was a genuine category-specific impairment.

In sum, it has proved difficult to demonstrate convincingly that there are patients with category-specific impairments unconfounded by other factors such as familiarity or structural similarity. In addition, it remains unclear whether any category-specific impairments reflect damage to the semantic memory system or to some more perceptual system. As Forde (1999, p. 124) concluded in his review of studies on patients with category-specific impairments, "There is considerable debate over the locus (loci) of the impairment in information-processing terms."

Integrative agnosia

Humphreys (1999) discussed what he termed *integrative agnosia*, a condition in which the patient has great difficulties in combining or integrating visual information about the parts of objects in order to identify them. Humphreys and Riddoch (1987) studied H.J.A., who produced accurate drawings of objects he could not recognise, and who could draw objects from memory. However, he found it very hard to integrate visual information. In H.J.A.'s own words: "I have come to cope with recognising many common objects, if they are standing alone . . . When objects are placed together, though, I have more difficulties. To recognise one sausage on its own is far from picking one out from a dish of cold foods in a salad" (Humphreys & Riddoch, 1987).

Evidence that H.J.A. had a serious problem in grouping or organising visual information was obtained by Humphreys et al. (1992). The task of searching for an inverted T target among a homogeneous set of distractors (upright T's) is easy for most people. However, H.J.A.'s performance was very slow and error prone, presumably because he found it very hard to group the distractors together.

H.J.A. is not the only agnosic patient to have problems with integrating visual information. For example, Behrmann, Moscovitch, and Winocur (1994) studied C.K., a man who had suffered head injury in a car crash. C.K. was reasonably good at copying a figure consisting of three touching geometric shapes (two diamonds and a circle). Nearly all normal individuals would copy this figure object by object. What C.K. did was to follow the outer boundary of the whole figure, which meant that he often moved on to the next shape before completing his drawing of the last one.

Humphreys (1999, p. 555) concluded his discussion of patients with integrative agnosia as follows: "The deficit appears to affect a stage of visual processing intermediate between basic shape coding and visual access to memory representations, concerned with parallel perceptual grouping and the integration of perceptual parts into wholes . . . [the] distinction between apperceptive and associative agnosia needs to be fractionated further, to reflect the sub-processes involved at the different processing stages."

Summary

The distinction between apperceptive agnosia and associative agnosia is oversimplified, and fails to encompass the wide range of visual agnosias that have been observed. According to Humphreys and Riddoch (1993), visual object recognition involves a series of stages: feature coding, feature integration, accessing stored structural object descriptions, and accessing semantic knowledge about objects. Problems with visual object recognition can occur because of impairments at any of these stages, and the study of agnosic patients can help to identify the major processes involved in normal object recognition. This is a more complex (but realistic) position than the simple distinction between apperceptive and associative agnosia.

Humphreys et al.'s (1995) model

Humphreys, Lamote, and Lloyd-Jones (1995) produced an interactive activation and competition model of object recognition and naming from the cognitive science perspective. This model has also been applied to visual agnosia. The model contains pools of units of four kinds (see Figure 3.6):

(1) Stored structural descriptions of objects.
(2) Semantic representations.
(3) Name representations.
(4) Superordinate units or category labels.

Activation from the structural units proceeds initially to semantic units before proceeding to name representations. There are bidirectional excitatory connections between related units at adjacent levels of the model. In addition, there are mutually inhibitory connections between units *within* each level. According to the model, the structural descriptions of objects visually similar to the object actually

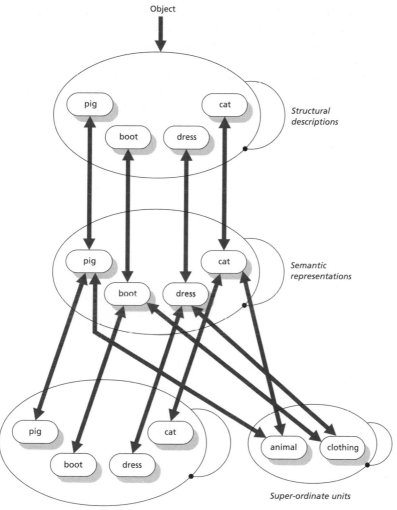

Object

Structural
descriptions

Semantic
representations

Super-ordinate units

Name representations

Figure 3.6. The interactive activation and competition model of object recognition proposed by Humphreys et al. (1995).

presented are activated to some extent. Of particular importance, it is assumed that living things are typically more visually similar to other members of the same category than is the case with non-living things.

Evidence

According to the model, living things should generally be named slower than non-living things, but should be categorised more rapidly. Why is this so? Living things are more visually similar to each other than are non-living things. This causes more activation of irrelevant structural representations and name representations, which inhibits naming living things and slows performance. In contrast, the additional activation of irrelevant representations from the same category as the presented object for living objects increases activation of the appropriate category label and so speeds up categorisation. Both predictions were confirmed in simulations of the model, and are in line with findings on people (Humphreys et al., 1995).

Humphreys, Riddoch, and Quinlan (1988) found that objects with common names were named faster than objects with rare names, and that this frequency effect was greater for non-living things than for living things. Humphreys et al. (1995) found that their model produced the same pattern of findings. According to the model, the activation from semantic representations to name representations is greater for objects with more common names, and this produces the overall frequency effect. The greater activation of irrelevant structural and name representations when living objects are presented reduces this advantage.

Associative agnosics typically show worse identification of living things than of non-living things, but are reasonably good at categorising objects (e.g., Sheridan & Humphreys, 1993). When the model was "lesioned" in various places, this reduced its ability to name objects and especially living objects. The greater effect on living objects occurred because the presentation of a living object tends to activate the structural representations of various visually similar objects, and this makes naming more difficult.

Patients with category-specific anomia have selective impairment in the ability to name certain categories of objects (typically living objects), in spite of being able to access much semantic information about objects (e.g., Farah & Wallace, 1992). Humphreys et al. (1995) tried to mimic the effects of category-specific anomia by "lesioning" connections between the semantic and name representations in their model. The model showed worse naming performance for living things than for non-living things, in line with the evidence from patients. The model is an interactive one, with the consequence that the greater activation of irrelevant structural representations when living objects are seen has knock-on effects that influence naming.

Evaluation
The interactive activation and competition model of Humphreys et al. (1995) provides accounts of object recognition in both normal individuals and in those with various visual disorders. It also provides a

detailed process model which can be applied to object recognition, object naming, and object categorisation. One of its greatest achievements is that it shows how evidence from agnosic patients can play an important role in the development of a model of object recognition in normals.

The model does not provide a convincing explanation of patients with poorer naming and access to semantic information with non-living than with living things (e.g., Warrington & McCarthy, 1994). However, Ellis and Humphreys (1999, p. 554) argued that "the effects can be accounted for if the lesion is not global but more selective, affecting the stored units and connections for the representations of non-living relative to living things."

Face recognition

Why should we study face recognition? Face recognition is the most common way of identifying people, and so the ability to recognise faces is of great significance in our everyday lives. In addition, face recognition differs from other forms of object recognition. For example, consider a condition known as *prosopagnosia*. Prosopagnosic patients cannot recognise familiar faces, and this can even extend to their own faces in a mirror. However, they generally have few problems in recognising other familiar objects.

Models of face recognition

Influential models of face recognition were put forward by Bruce and Young (1986) and Burton and Bruce (1993), the latter model being based on the theoretical views of Valentine et al. (1991). There are eight components in the Bruce and Young (1986) model (see Figure 3.7):

- *Structural encoding*: This produces various representations or descriptions of faces.
- *Expression analysis*: People's emotional states can be inferred from their facial features.
- *Facial speech analysis*: Speech perception can be aided by observation of a speaker's lip movements.
- *Directed visual processing*: Specific facial information may be processed selectively.
- *Face recognition units*: They contain structural information about known faces.

Figure 3.7. The
model of face
recognition put forward
by Bruce and Young
(1986).

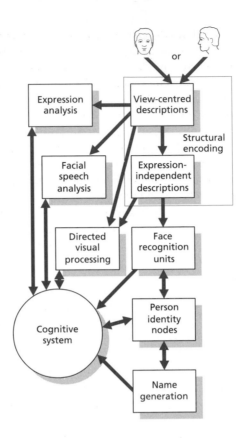

- *Person identity nodes*: They provide information about individuals (e.g., their occupation, interests).
- *Name generation*: A person's name is stored separately.
- *Cognitive system*: This contains additional information (e.g., that actors and actresses tend to have attractive faces); this system also influences attentional processes.

The recognition of familiar faces depends mainly on structural encoding, face recognition units, person identity nodes, and name generation. In contrast, the processing of unfamiliar faces involves structural encoding, expression analysis, facial speech analysis, and directed visual processing.

Experimental evidence
Bruce and Young (1986) assumed that familiar and unfamiliar faces are processed differently. If it were possible to find patients who

showed good recognition of familiar faces but poor recognition of unfamiliar faces, and other patients who showed the opposite pattern, this *double dissociation* would suggest that the recognition processes are different for familiar and unfamiliar faces. Malone et al. (1982) tested one patient who showed reasonable ability to recognise photographs of famous statesmen (14 out of 17 correct), but who was very impaired at matching unfamiliar faces. A second patient performed normally at matching unfamiliar faces, but had great difficulties in recognising photographs of famous people (5 out of 22 correct). However, as we will see shortly, this double dissociation has not been obtained in other research.

According to the model, the name generation component can be accessed only via the appropriate person identity node. Thus, we should be unable to put a name to a face in the absence of other information about that person (e.g., his or her occupation). Young, Hay, and Ellis (1985) asked participants to keep a diary record of problems in face recognition. There were 1008 incidents altogether, but participants never reported putting a name to a face while knowing nothing else about that person. In contrast, there were 190 occasions on which a participant could remember a fair amount of information about a person, but not their name.

According to the model, another kind of problem should be fairly common. If the appropriate face recognition unit is activated, but the person identity node is not, there should be a feeling of familiarity coupled with an inability to think of any relevant information about the person. This was reported on 233 occasions.

Reference back to Figure 3.7 suggests further predictions. When we look at a familiar face, familiarity information from the face recognition unit should be accessed first, followed by information about that person (e.g., occupation) from the person identity node, followed by that person's name from the name generation component. As predicted, familiarity decisions about a face were made faster than decisions based on person identity nodes (Young et al., 1986a). The prediction that decisions based on person identity nodes should be made faster than those based on the name generation component has also been supported (Young et al., 1986b).

Evaluation

The model of Bruce and Young (1986) provides a coherent account of the various kinds of information we possess about faces, and the ways in which these kinds of information are related to each other.

Another significant strength is that differences in the processing of familiar and unfamiliar faces are spelled out.

There are various limitations with the model. First, the cognitive system is vaguely specified. Second, some evidence is inconsistent with the assumption that names can be accessed only via relevant autobiographical information stored at the person identity node. An amnesic patient, M.E., could match the faces and names of 88% of famous people for whom she was unable to recall any autobiographical information (de Haan, Young, & Newcombe, 1991).

Third, the theory predicts that some patients should have better recognition for familiar faces than unfamiliar faces, with others showing the opposite pattern. This double dissociation was obtained by Malone et al. (1982), but has proved difficult to replicate. Young et al. (1993) studied 34 brain-damaged men, and assessed their familiar face identification, unfamiliar face matching, and expression analysis. There was only very weak evidence of selective impairment of familiar or unfamiliar face recognition.

Interactive activation and competition model

Burton and Bruce (1993) developed the Bruce and Young (1986) model and the theory of Valentine et al. (1991). Their interactive activation and competition model adopted a connectionist approach (see Figure 3.8). The face recognition units (FRUs) and the name recognition units (NRUs) contain stored information about specific faces and names, respectively. Person identity nodes (PINs) are gateways into semantic information, and can be activated by verbal input about people's names as well as by facial input. Thus, they provide information about the familiarity of individuals based on either verbal or facial information. Finally, the semantic information units (SIUs) contain name and other information about individuals (e.g., occupation).

Experimental evidence

The model has been applied to associative priming effects. For example, the time taken to decide whether a face is familiar is reduced when the face of a related person is shown immediately beforehand (e.g., Bruce & Valentine, 1986). According to the model, the first face activates SIUs, which feed back activation to the PIN of that face and related faces. This then speeds up the familiarity decision for the second face. Since PINs can be activated by both names and faces, it follows that associative priming for familiarity decisions on faces

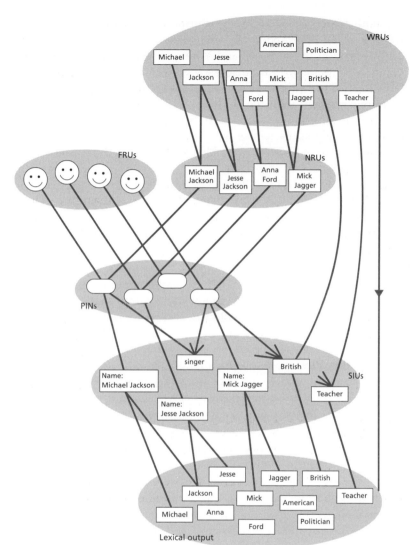

Figure 3.8. The interactive activation and competition model put forward by Burton and Bruce (1993). WRUs, word recognition units; FRUs, face recognition units; NRUs, name recognition units; PINs, person identity nodes; SIUs, semantic units.

should be found when the name of a person (e.g., Prince Philip) is followed by the face of a related person (e.g., Queen Elizabeth). Precisely this has been found (e.g., Bruce & Valentine, 1986).

One difference between the interactive activation and competition model and Bruce and Young's (1986) model concerns the storage of name and autobiographical information. These kinds of information are both stored in SIUs in the Burton and Bruce (1993) model, whereas name information can only be accessed *after* autobiographical information in the Bruce and Young (1986) model. The fact that the amnesic patient, M.E. (discussed above), could match names to faces in spite of being unable to access autobiographical information is more consistent with the Burton and Bruce (1993) model. Cohen (1990) found that faces produced better recall of names than of occupations when the names were meaningful and the occupations were meaningless. This poses problems only for the Bruce and Young (1986) model.

The interactive activation and competition model can also be applied to the findings from patients with prosopagnosia. These findings will be discussed shortly.

Configurational information

When we recognise a face shown in a photograph, there are two major kinds of information we might use: (1) information about the *individual features* (e.g., eye colour); or (2) information about the *configuration* or overall arrangement of the features. Many approaches to face recognition are based on a feature approach. For example, police forces often make use of Identikit to aid face recognition in eyewitnesses. Identikit involves constructing a face resembling that of the criminal on a feature-by-feature basis.

Searcy and Bartlett (1996) studied configurational and feature processing. Facial distortions in photographs were produced in two different ways:

(1) Configurational distortions (e.g., moving the eyes up and the mouth down).
(2) Component distortions (e.g., blurring the pupils of the eyes to produce cataracts, blackening teeth, and discolouring remaining teeth).

The photographs were then presented upright or inverted, and given grotesqueness ratings on a 7-point scale. The participants readily detected component distortions in both upright and inverted faces, but configurational distortions were often not detected in inverted faces (see Figure 3.9). Thus, configurational and component processing can both be used with upright faces, but the processing of inverted faces is largely limited to component processing.

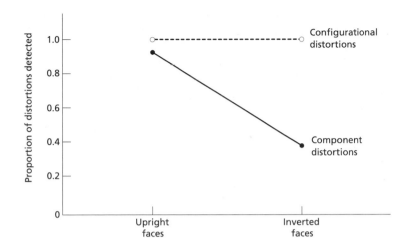

Figure 3.9. Detection of component and configurational distortions in upright and inverted faces. Based on data in Searcy and Bartlett (1996).

Most research on face recognition has used photographs or other two-dimensional stimuli. There are two potential limitations of such research. First, viewing an actual three-dimensional face provides more information for the observer than does viewing a two-dimensional representation. Second, people's faces are normally mobile, registering emotional states, agreement or disagreement with what is being said, and so on. None of these dynamic changes over time is available in a photograph. The importance of such changes was shown by Bruce and Valentine (1988). Small illuminated lights were spread over a face, which was then filmed in the dark so that only the lights could be seen. Participants showed some ability to determine the sex and the identity of each face on the basis of the movements of the lights.

Prosopagnosia

Patients with prosopagnosia cannot recognise familiar faces but can recognise other familiar objects. This might occur simply because more precise discriminations are required to distinguish between faces than to distinguish between other kinds of objects (e.g., a chair and a table). Alternatively, there may be specific processing mechanisms used only for face recognition.

Farah (1994) obtained evidence that prosopagnosic patients can be good at making precise discriminations for stimuli other than faces. She studied L.H., who developed prosopagnosia as a result of a car

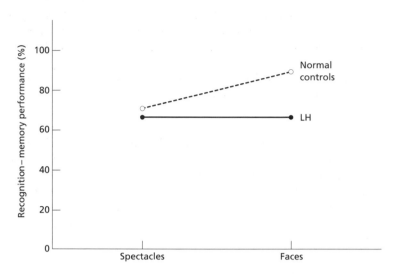

Figure 3.10.
Recognition memory
for faces and pairs of
spectacles in a
prosopagnosic patient
(L.H.) and normal
controls. Data from
Farah (1994).

crash. L.H. and controls were presented with various faces and pairs of spectacles, and were then given a recognition-memory test. L.H. performed at about the same level as the normal controls in recognising pairs of spectacles, but was at a great disadvantage on face recognition (see Figure 3.10).

The notion that face processing involves specific mechanisms would be strengthened if it were possible to show a *double dissociation*, with some patients having normal face recognition but poor recognition or visual agnosia for objects. Such patients have been identified (e.g., Moscovitch, Winocur, & Behrmann, 1997). If face processing involves specific mechanisms, we might also expect to find somewhat separate brain regions associated with face and object recognition. Kanwisher, McDermott, and Chun (1997) used fMRI to compare brain activity to faces, scrambled faces, houses, and hands. There was face-specific activation in parts of the right fulsiform gyrus.

Implict knowledge and connectionist models

Most prosopagnosics possess some implicit knowledge (knowledge not available to consciousness) about the familiarity of faces, face identity, and semantic information that is accessed through faces (e.g., occupation). For example, Bauer and Verfaellie (1988) asked a prosopagnosic patient to select the names corresponding to presented famous faces. The patient had no explicit knowledge about the faces, and so his performance was at chance level. However, there were greater electrodermal responses when the names matched the faces than when they did not, indicating the existence of relevant implicit knowledge.

Burton and Bruce's (1993) interactive activation and competition model (discussed earlier) provides a connectionist account of prosopagnosia and the use of implicit knowledge. Burton et al. (1991) simulated prosopagnosia by reducing the weights on the connections from the FRUs to the PINs. This reduced the activation of PINs to faces, and meant that faces were often not identified or recognised as familiar. Burton et al. (1991) found that their "lesioned" model used implicit knowledge in a similar way to prosopagnosic patients. Presentation of a face produced some activation of its PIN and the relevant SIUs, and this facilitated performance on tasks requiring the use of implicit knowledge.

Evaluation

The connectionist model of Burton and Bruce (1993) accounts for many of the basic phenomena of prosopagnosia. However, it has problems with findings reported by Young and de Haan (1988). Their prosopagnosic patient showed evidence of using implicit knowledge about faces by learning face–name pairings faster when they were accurate than when they were inaccurate, but did not learn accurate face–occupation pairings faster than inaccurate ones. According to the model, faces partially activate relevant semantic knowledge, and so both types of accurate pairings should have been learned more readily than incorrect pairings.

Farah's two-process model

Farah (1990, 1994) proposed a two-process model of object recognition of relevance to understanding face recognition. The model distinguishes between two processes or forms of analysis:

(1) Holistic analysis, in which the configuration or overall structure of an object is processed.
(2) Analysis by parts, in which processing focuses on the constituent parts of an object.

Farah (1990) argued that both forms of analysis are involved in the recognition of most objects. However, face recognition depends

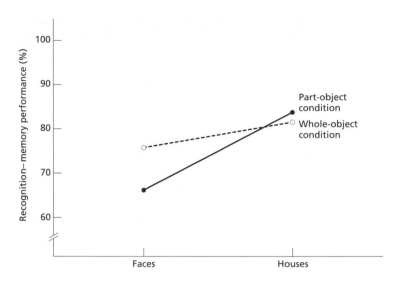

Figure 3.11.
Recognition memory
for features of houses
and faces when
presented with whole
houses or faces or with
only features. Data
from Farah (1994).

mainly on holistic analysis, and reading words or text mostly involves analytic processing. Evidence that face recognition depends more than object recognition on holistic analysis was reported by Farah (1994). The participants were presented with drawings of faces or houses, and associated a name with each face and each house. Then the participants were presented with whole faces and houses or with only a single feature (e.g., mouth, front door), and decided whether a given feature belonged to the individual whose name they had been given previously.

Recognition performance for facial features was much better when the whole face was presented (see Figure 3.11). In contrast, recognition for house features was very similar in whole and single-feature conditions. These findings suggest that holistic analysis is much more important for face recognition than for object recognition.

Farah (1994) obtained additional support for her model by studying the *face inversion effect*. In this effect, the ability to recognise faces is significantly poorer when they are presented in an inverted (upside-down) way than when presented upright. Normal individuals showed the face inversion effect. However, the prosopagnosic patient, L.H., showed the opposite effect, having better face recognition for inverted faces. How can we explain these findings? According to Farah (1994), the face inversion effect occurs because the holistic or configural processing that normal individuals apply to upright faces cannot easily be used with inverted faces. However, prosopagnosic patients have very limited ability to use holistic or configural processing, and so do not show the face inversion effect.

Brain damage

Farah (1990) discussed evidence based on patients suffering from one or more of the following: *prosopagnosia, visual agnosia,* and *alexia* (problems with reading in spite of good ability to comprehend spoken language and good object recognition). According to the theory, prosopagnosia involves impaired holistic or configurational processing, alexia involves impaired analytic processing, and visual agnosia involves impaired holistic and analytic processing. It should be noted that Farah (1990) did not distinguish between apperceptive and associative agnosia.

Farah (1990) considered the co-occurrence of the above three conditions in 87 patients. What would we expect from her theory? First, patients with visual agnosia (having impaired holistic and analytic processing) should also suffer from prosopagnosia or alexia, or both. This prediction was confirmed. There were 21 patients with all three conditions, 15 patients with visual agnosia and alexia, 14 patients with visual agnosia and prosopagnosia, but only 1 patient who may have had visual agnosia on its own.

Second, and most importantly, there was a *double dissociation* between prosopagnosia and alexia. There were 35 patients suffering from prosopagnosia without alexia, and there are numerous patients having alexia without prosopagnosia. Thus, the processes and brain systems underlying face recognition seem to differ from those under-lying word recognition.

The above conclusion receives support from attempts to identify the brain areas damaged in prosopagnosia and alexia using MRI and other neuroimaging techniques (see Chapter 1). Most prosopagnosic patients have damage to the occipital and/or temporal lobes of the cortex. In contrast, alexia "is typically associated with lesions of the left hemisphere, particularly lesions encompassing the angular gyrus in the posterior region of the parietal lobe" (Gazzaniga et al., 1998, pp. 202–203).

Third, it is assumed within the theory that reading and object recognition both involve analytic processing. Thus, patients with alexia (who have problems with analytic processing) should be impaired in their object recognition. This contrasts with the conven-tional view that patients with "pure" alexia have impairments only to reading abilities. Behrmann, Nelson, and Sekuler (1998) studied six patients who seemed to have "pure" alexia. Five of them were

significantly slower than normal participants to name visually complex pictures, which is as predicted from Farah's theory.

Evaluation

The processes typically involved in face recognition differ somewhat
from those involved in object recognition and reading. The two-
process model describes some of the major similarities and differences in processing across these three types of stimuli.

On the negative side, Farah's approach is at a very general and
oversimplified level. Farah argued that faces are processed holis-
tically, but there is evidence of a left-hemisphere system involved in
processing faces more analytically in terms of their features (Parkin &
Williamson, 1986). More importantly, Rumiati et al. (1994) studied a
patient, Mr W., who suffered from visual agnosia for real objects and
for pictures, but showed no signs of either prosopagnosia or alexia.
According to Farah's theory, the existence of visual agnosia means
that Mr W. must have deficit holistic and/or analytic processing.
However, that would mean that he would suffer from prosopagnosia
or alexia. Thus, the pattern shown by Mr W. is not possible within
Farah's theory.

Finally, Farah's failure to distinguish between apperceptive and
associative agnosia seems ill advised. For example, H.O. had essentially perfect performance on the unusual views test (see above), and
performed well on the object decision test (Stewart, Parkin, & Hunkin,
1992). However, he could name only 50% of objects on a naming task,
and he did not know the functions of most objects. H.O.'s problems
are clearly related to associative agnosia rather than to apperceptive
agnosia, and cannot readily be accounted for by Farah's theory.

Perceptual development

How much can the newborn baby (or neonate) see and hear? It used
to be assumed that the answer was "very little". William James,
towards the end of the nineteenth century, described the world of the
newborn baby as a "buzzing, blooming confusion, where the infant is
seized by eyes, ears, nose and entrails all at once." This suggests that
the infant is bombarded by information in all sense modalities, and
cannot attach meaning to this information. That view underestimates
the capabilities of infants. Many basic perceptual mechanisms are

working at a very early age, and infants are not merely helpless observers of their world.

Research methods

It is hard to assess perception in infants, because they cannot tell us what they can see. However, several methods have been developed to assess their visual abilities:

- *Behavioural method*: Various behavioural measures can be taken to discover what infants can perceive. For example, Butterworth and Cicchetti (1978) tested infants in a room in which the walls and the ceiling moved towards and away from them. The infants lost balance, and this loss of balance was always in the expected direction.
- *Preference method*: Two or more stimuli are presented together, and the experimenter simply observes which stimulus attracts the most attention. If infants systematically prefer one stimulus to another, this indicates that they can discriminate between them.
- *Habituation method*: A stimulus is presented repeatedly until the infant no longer attends to it; this is known as *habituation*. When the infant shows habituation to one stimulus, he or she is shown a different stimulus. If the infant responds to the new stimulus, he or she must have discriminated between the two stimuli.
- *Eye-movement method*: The eye movements of infants can provide information about their visual perception. For example, if infants are presented with a moving stimulus, the tracking response or optokinetic nystagmus can be recorded. This indicates whether or not they can distinguish between the moving stimulus and the background against which it is presented.
- *Physiological method*: Various physiological measures can be used. One way of telling whether infants can discriminate between two stimuli is to measure their event-related potentials (brain-wave activity) to each stimulus. Alternatively, if infants show different patterns of heart rate and/or breathing rate to two stimuli, this suggests that the infants perceive the two stimuli to be different.
- *Visual reinforcement method*: The basic idea is that the infant is given control over the stimulus or stimuli presented to it. For

example, Siqueland and DeLucia (1969) gave infants a dummy wired up so that their sucking rate could be assessed. A stimulus may be presented only for as long as it continues to produce a high sucking rate, being replaced when it does not. Stimuli of interest to infants are associated with a high sucking rate.

Basic aspects of vision

Newborns are at a great disadvantage to adults with respect to several basic aspects of vision. For example, they have very poor visual acuity. We can assess visual acuity by presenting a display of alternating black and white lines, and then making the lines progressively narrower until they can no longer be separated in vision. In order for newborns to detect the separation of the lines, they need to be about 30 times wider than is the case for adults (Atkinson & Braddick, 1981).

Colour vision is either non-existent or nearly so during the first weeks of life. Teller (1997, p. 2197) considered the evidence and concluded that newborns probably have no colour vision, and that "By two months, rudimentary colour vision has arrived. Most infants can probably discriminate red, blue, and green from each other, but not yet yellows and yellow-greens."

Another basic aspect of visual perception is binocular disparity (see Chapter 2). There is a disparity or difference in the images projected on to the retinas of the two eyes, and this disparity is useful for depth perception. Teller (1997, p. 2193) discussed three studies that had assessed the development of binocular disparity in different ways: "Remarkably, investigators in all three studies agree that the response to binocular disparity is absent in almost all infants less than 3 months old, and has its onset between 3 and 6 postnatal [afterbirth] months."

How do these basic aspects of vision develop during the early months of life? So far as visual acuity is concerned, it seems likely that maturational changes are of primary importance. For example, the eye is shorter in the newborn than in older infants, and the pupil is smaller. As a consequence, the image of a visual stimulus falls on a smaller area of the retina of newborns than of older infants. The development of colour vision also probably depends on maturational changes (Teller, 1997).

The position with respect to binocular disparity may be more complicated. Banks, Aslin, and Letson (1975) studied adults who had problems with binocular vision because of having a squint in childhood that was subsequently corrected. Their degree of binocular disparity was assessed as follows: The participants first stared at tilted gratings with one eye, and then stared at vertical gratings with the other eye. Individuals with normal binocular disparity show a tilt after-effect, in which the vertical gratings appear tilted in the opposite direction to the original gratings.

The findings obtained by Banks et al. (1975) depended on the age at which squint was detected, and the age at which corrective surgery was carried out:

(1) *Squint at birth or shortly thereafter, and surgery by 30 months of age*: There was a nearly normal tilt after-effect, indicating reasonable binocular disparity.

(2) *Squint diagnosed between 2 and 7 years of age, and surgery 2 or 3 years after diagnosis*: There were reasonable levels of tilt after-effect, and thus binocular disparity.

(3) *Squint at birth or shortly thereafter, and surgery between the ages of 4 and 20*: There was little evidence of tilt after-effect, and thus little or no binocular disparity.

What do these findings mean? They suggest there is a critical or sensitive period for the development of binocularity during the early years of life. If children are unable to develop binocularity during the first few years of life because of having an uncorrected squint, then it may be virtually impossible to develop it thereafter.

Preference method: Faces

Fantz (1961) used the preference method. He showed infants (aged between 4 days and 5 months) pairs of face-shaped discs and measured the amount of time spent fixating each one. There were realistic faces, scrambled faces, and blank faces. Infants of all ages looked most at the realistic face and least at the blank face. These findings led Fantz (1961, p. 70) to conclude as follows: "The degree of preference for the 'real' face . . . was consistent among individual infants. The experiment suggested that there is an unlearned primitive meaning in the form perception of infants."

It is hard to know whether infants look at the real face because it is a face or because it is a complex, symmetrical visual stimulus. However, Dannemiller and Stephens (1988) made use of computer-generated faces constructed to control for these factors. Thus, for example, they produced human faces and patterns having the same level of complexity and symmetry. Three-month-old infants preferred human faces, thus confirming Fantz's findings under well-controlled conditions.

Another potential problem with Fantz's (1961) research was that the infants were all at least several days old. Thus, it is possible that learning influenced their performance on the preference task. Evidence from newborns in the first hour after birth was obtained by Johnson et al. (1991). The newborns showed more visual tracking of realistic faces than of scrambled but symmetrical faces, suggesting that some aspects of face perception do not depend on learning.

Walton, Bower, and Bower (1992) presented infants between 1 and 4 days of age with videotapes of their mother's face and the face of a similar-looking woman. Eleven out of 12 infants preferred their mother's face, indicating that infants can discriminate among faces at a very early age.

In sum, it appears that there is something special about faces. Faces are preferred to scrambled faces within an hour of birth, and the mother's face is preferred to a similar face at 1 or 2 days of age. It is not known how best to interpret these findings. However, Johnson et al. (1991) suggested that newborns are pre-wired to orient towards the faces of other members of the human species.

Depth perception

Gibson and Walk (1960) also argued that infants possess well-developed perceptual skills. They designed a "visual cliff", which was actually a glass-top table (see Figure 3.12). A check pattern was positioned close to the glass under one half of the table (the "shallow" side) and far below the glass under the other half (the "deep" side). Infants between the ages of 6½ and 12 months were placed on the shallow side of the table, and encouraged to crawl over the edge of the visual cliff on to the deep side by being offered toys or having their mothers call them. Most failed to respond to these incentives, suggesting that they possessed at least some of the elements of depth perception.

Research on the visual cliff does not necessarily indicate that depth perception is innate. Infants who are several months old might have learned about depth perception from experience. There is some intriguing evidence pointing to the importance of learning in the visual cliff situation. Nine-month-old infants had faster heart rates than normal when placed on the deep side, presumably because they

Figure 3.12. A drawing of Gibson and Walk's "visual cliff".

were frightened (Campos et al., 1978). However, infants between 2 and 5 months actually had *slower* heart rates than usual when placed on the deep side. This slowing of heart rate probably reflected interest, and certainly indicates that the infants detected some difference between the deep and shallow sides of the visual cliff situation.

Bower, Broughton, and Moore (1970) obtained more convincing evidence that infants have some aspects of depth perception. They showed two objects to infants under 2 weeks of age. One was large and approached to within 20 cm of the infant, whereas the other was small and approached to 8 cm. The two objects had the same retinal size (i.e., size at the retina) at their closest point to the infant. However, the infants were more disturbed by the object that came closer to them, rotating their heads upwards and pulling away from it.

Evaluation

There is evidence that some aspects of depth perception are present very early. However, several factors are involved in depth perception (see Chapter 2). Movement cues to depth (e.g., approaching objects) are used at a very early age, whereas binocular disparity is only used at about 4 or 5 months of age. Other depth cues (e.g. texture, shading) only begin to be used at about 6 months of age (Yonas & Granrud, 1985).

Size and shape constancy

Nearly all adults display *size constancy* and *shape constancy*. Size constancy means that a given object is perceived as having the same size regardless of its distance from us, and shape constancy means that an object is seen to have the same shape regardless of its orientation. Thus, we see things "as they really are," and are not taken in by variations in the information presented to the retina. It is of interest to discover whether infants show size and shape constancy.

There is evidence from studies using the habituation method that size constancy is an innate visual capacity. For example, Slater, Matock, and Brown (1990) familiarised newborns with either a small or large cube over a number of trials. After that, the two cubes were presented successively. The larger cube was presented at a greater distance from the newborns than was the smaller cube, so that the size of the retinal image was the same in both cases. All of the newborns looked longer at the new cube, because they had habituated to the old one. The fact that they could distinguish between two cubes having the same-sized retinal image suggests that the newborns possessed at least some of the elements of size constancy.

Slater and Morison (1985) used the habituation method to study shape constancy in newborns (average age 1 day, 23 hours). The newborns were shown a given shape until they had habituated to it. Then, they were shown the same shape from a novel angle. The newborns paid little attention to it, presumably because they did not perceive the same shape at a different angle as a new shape; in other words, they showed evidence of shape constancy.

Cross-cultural studies

Nearly all the research we have considered so far has been carried out in Western societies. If the development of visual perception depends on certain kinds of learning experiences, then it might be expected that there would be some important cross-cultural differences in perception. We will briefly consider some cross-cultural studies.

Segall, Campbell and Herskovits (1963) argued that the Müller–Lyer illusion (see Chapter 2) would only be perceived by those with experience of a "carpentered environment" containing numerous rectangles, straight lines, and regular corners. People living in Western societies live in a carpentered environment, whereas Zulus living in tribal communities do not. Segall et al. (1963) found that rural Zulus did not show the Müller–Lyer illusion. However, they did show the horizontal–vertical illusion, which involves over-estimating vertical extents relative to horizontal ones in a two-dimensional drawing.

Gregor and McPherson (1965) compared two groups of Australian Aborigines, only one of which lived in a carpentered environment. The two groups did not differ on either the Müller–Lyer or horizontal–vertical illusions. They concluded that cross-cultural differences in visual illusions may depend more on training and education than on whether or not a given group lives in a carpentered environment.

Additional evidence of cross-cultural differences in perception was reported by Turnbull (1961). He studied a pygmy who lived in dense forests, and so had limited experience of looking at distant objects. This pygmy was taken to an open plain, and shown a herd of buffalo a long way away. He argued that the buffalo were insects, and refused to believe that they really were buffalo. When he was driven towards the buffalo, he thought that witchcraft was responsible for the insects "growing" into buffalo. Presumably he had never learned to use depth cues effectively. However, this study is limited because only one person was studied.

Annis and Frost (1973) studied Canadian Cree Indians, some of whom lived in tepees in the countryside, and others of whom lived in cities. They argued that those in cities would be exposed mainly to vertical and horizontal lines, whereas those living in tepees would come across lines in all orientations. Both groups were given the task of deciding whether two lines were parallel. Cree Indians living in tepees were good at this task regardless of the angle at which the lines were presented, whereas those living in cities did much better when the lines were horizontal or vertical. These findings suggest the importance of relevant experience to visual perception.

Allport and Pettigrew (1957) used an illusion based on a nearly rectangular or trapezoidal "window" fitted with horizontal and vertical bars. When this "window" revolves in a circle, it looks like a rectangular window moving backwards and forwards. People living in cultures without rectangular windows tended not to experience the illusion. Zulus living in rural areas were less likely than Europeans or Zulus living in urban areas to see a rectangle moving backwards and forwards.

Evaluation

The findings from cross-cultural studies suggest that visual perception depends in part on the learning experiences that are available in a given culture. However, there are at least two major limitations of this research. First, much of it has focused on two-dimensional visual illusions. Cross-cultural differences in perception may be greater for such illusions than for more typical visual stimuli. Second, it is easy to underestimate the visual abilities of those from other cultures. Deregowski, Muldrow, and Muldrow (1972) found that members of the Me'en tribe in Ethiopia did not respond to drawings of animals on paper, which was an unfamiliar material for them. This might suggest that they could not make sense of two-dimensional representations. However, when the tribespeople were shown animals drawn on cloth (a familiar material to them), they generally recognised the animals.

Nature–nurture debate

There has been much controversy as to whether visual perception depends mainly on innate factors (nature) or on learning and environmental factors (nurture). No easy resolution of the controversy is possible, and it is important to avoid oversimplifying complex issues and de-emphasising interactions between heredity and environment. We will briefly consider some of the findings in the light of the controversy.

Some aspects of visual perception (e.g., size constancy, shape constancy, basic face processing) seem to be present at birth, or at least within a very short time thereafter. It is possible that these aspects reflect innate visual capacities. Other aspects of visual perception (e.g., visual acuity, colour vision) develop several weeks after birth, and may well depend on maturational factors. There are still other aspects of perception for which there may be a critical or sensitive period for their development (e.g., binocular disparity). Finally, there are other aspects of perception (e.g., perception of texture and shading) that develop only after several months of life, and may require certain kinds of learning.

The notion that specific forms of learning are important has been confirmed in animal research. For example, Blakemore and Cooper (1970) reared kittens in an environment consisting only of horizontal or vertical contours. Thereafter, the kittens were better at detecting contours that were in the familiar orientation.

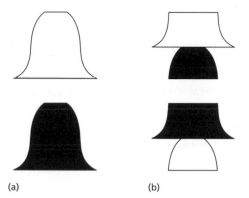

(a)   (b)

Figure 3.13.
Schematic depiction of
two types of displays:
(a) homogeneous
displays and (b)
heterogeneous
displays. From Spelke
et al. (1993) with
permission from
Elsevier.

Theoretical account

How can we explain the order in which the various visual capacities appear developmentally? Kellman (1996, pp. 40–41) proposed the following answer: "The order of appearance of perceptual capacities closely parallels their ecological validity; that is, information that most closely specifies the environment is usable first . . . For infants, perceiving comprehensively is not nearly so crucial as perceiving *accurately*. If the infant is built as risk aversive in this sense, we would expect perceptual abilities to appear in order of ecological validity."

Evidence consistent with the predictions of this approach was reported by Spelke et al. (1993). They presented infants aged 3, 5, and 9 months and adults with simple but unfamiliar displays (see Figure 3.13). Each display could be perceived as a single object or as two joined objects. In these displays, three Gestalt principles (colour and texture similarity, good continuation, and good form; see Chapter 2) indicated that there were one or two objects in the display. Adults used the three principles as expected by Gestalt theory. In contrast, nearly all the infants saw most of the displays as single objects. They made use of the law of proximity (visual elements that are close to each other belong together), and largely ignored the Gestalt principles of similarity, good continuation, and good form. This makes sense if we assume that proximity is a more accurate predictor than the other three principles of which visual elements belong to the same object.

Finally, much of the perceptual learning of infants involves the attachment of meaning and significance to visual stimuli. These developments relate to the distinction between seeing and seeing as (Fodor & Pylyshyn, 1981; see Chapter 2). Seeing involves basic visual perception, whereas seeing as involves realising the significance of what is seen. Infants rapidly develop seeing abilities, but it takes a prolonged period of learning before they are able to appreciate the significance of visual stimuli.

Piaget's approach

According to Piaget, children up to the age of 2 years are in the sensorimotor stage of development. Infants acquire their knowledge of the world mainly by acting on it through mouthing, grasping, and manipulating objects. During this stage, thought and action are almost identical to each other. The main implication of this approach is that the development of perception depends to a large extent on the infant's growing mobility and ability to act on the environment. For example, depth perception should be acquired when the infant starts crawling and interacting directly with its surroundings.

Piaget exaggerated the importance of action in the development of perception. Arterberry, Yonas, and Bensen (1989) showed infants between the ages of 5 and 7 months two identical objects placed on a grid that created the illusion of depth. The two objects were actually the same distance away, but 7-month-old infants reached for the object that looked closer, whereas the 5-month-olds did not. The key finding was that those infants who had had the most experience of crawling showed no more depth perception than the others.

Meadows (1986) discussed other findings that do not seem to fit well with Piaget's theoretical approach. For example, 5-month-olds do not generally reach for objects that are out of reach. This suggests that they have well-developed perceptual abilities, even though they have only limited experience of moving around their environment.

Theoretical overview

There have been various attempts to provide a theoretical overview of findings on early visual perception. We will consider two of these attempts here.

Teller (1997, p. 2196) focused on the situation in which newborn infants find themselves: "Their acuity and contrast sensitivity are very poor but are measurable. Their . . . eye movements reveal the capacity to analyse the direction of motion of large, high-contrast objects . . . However, they should reveal no appreciation of stereo depth, no capacity to respond to low contrasts or to fine spatial details, and probably no colour vision. Their visual worlds are probably marked less by blooming and buzzing than by the haziness of low-contrast-sensitivity, the blurriness of spatial filtering, and the blandness of monochrome [black-and-white]."

Slater (1990, p. 262) summarised the perceptual skills of infants in the following way: "No modality [none of the senses] operates at adult-like levels at birth, but such levels are achieved surprisingly early in infancy, leading to recent conceptualisations of the 'competent infant' . . . early perceptual competence is matched by cognitive incompetence, and much of the reorganisation of perceptual representation is dependent upon the development and construction of cognitive structures that give access to a world of objects, people, language, and events."

In sum, both theorists accept that newborns immediately possess some of the main aspects of visual perception, and that there are rapid and substantial improvements in visual perceptual abilities during the early months of life. Many of these improvements depend on maturational changes in basic aspects of vision (Teller, 1997). Other developments in visual perception probably depend more on the development of the cognitive system, and on the child's growing store of knowledge (Slater, 1990).

Evaluation

Most research provides only limited information about the perceptual abilities of infants. The habituation and physiological methods tell us which stimuli can be discriminated by infants, and the preference and visual reinforcement methods also tell us which stimuli are preferred by infants. However, these methods generally do *not* tell us in detail how the stimuli are perceived and interpreted. The eye-movement and behaviour methods sometimes provide more information about the significance of stimuli for infants, but leave many questions unanswered. For example, infants of 8 months will not crawl over the deep side of the visual cliff, and their heart rate goes up when they are placed on the deep side. These findings indicate clearly that infants find *something* disturbing about the visual cliff, but do not show that they perceive depth like adults. More generally, as Daw (1995, p. 30) pointed out, "All measurements give a lower limit for the capability of the infant, and the actual capability may be higher."

Summary: Object recognition

- *Pattern recognition*: Template theories assume there is a template or miniature copy in long-term memory of each visual pattern, and pattern recognition depends on a matching process. Multiple-template theories that make use of information from all templates are more powerful than those that do not. Most template theories ignore context effects. Feature theories are based on the assumption that visual processing proceeds from a detailed analysis of a pattern or object to a global or general analysis. However, global analysis sometimes precedes feature analysis. Neurons in the visual cortex respond to visual features, but do not indicate for certain whether a given visual feature is present in the stimulus. Basic visual processing may be based on sinusoidal gratings. Most feature theories neglect context effects and the relationships among features.

- *Object recognition*: Marr (1982) argued that three successive representations are formed during visual perception: a primal sketch; a 2½-D sketch, and a 3-D model representation. This theory is more detailed than previous accounts. However, Marr's theory does not account for perceptual discriminations within classes of objects, and the role of top-down processes was de-emphasised. According to Biederman's (1987) recognition-by-components theory, information about the components or geons of a visual object is matched with stored object representations. Biederman attached too much weight to edge-based extraction processes in object recognition, but insufficient weight to the role of surface information. Biederman put forward a viewpoint-invariant theory, but the evidence suggests that viewpoint-dependent mechanisms are important when observers must make difficult within-category discriminations.

- *Visual agnosia*: Some patients with visual agnosia find it hard to recognise objects when they are foreshortened, perhaps because this makes it hard to attain a 3-D model representation. Some patients with associative agnosia have much greater problems in recognising living than non-living things, probably because pictures of living things are more visually similar to each other. Many patients with visual agnosia cannot readily integrate visual features into a coherent whole. The interactive activation and competition model of Humphreys et al. (1995) accounts for object recognition in normals, associative agnosics, and some patients with category-specific anomia. However, it does not provide a convincing explanation of patients with worse object recognition for non-living than for living things.

- *Face recognition*: Bruce and Young (1986) proposed an eight-component model, according to which familiar and unfamiliar faces are processed differently, and the name of a face cannot be retrieved in the absence of other information about that person. There is some support for these predictions. Burton and Bruce (1993) proposed an interactive activation and competition model that accounts for some of the findings that are problematical for the Bruce and Young model. Farah (1990) argued that object recognition involves holistic and analytic processing, face recognition depends mainly on holistic processing, and reading mostly involves analytic processing. The theory is oversimplified, and cannot explain cases of visual agnosia without alexia or prosopagnosia.

- *Perceptual development*: Infants cannot tell us what they can see. However, various methods of assessing their visual abilities have been developed, including those based on behaviour, preference, habituation, eye movements, physiology, and visual reinforcement. Newborns are deficient in some of the basic aspects of vision, having poor visual acuity, an inability to see colour, and a lack of binocular disparity. Infants show a preference for faces over non-faces almost from birth, and newborns can discriminate between their mother's face and the faces of other women. Most of the visual constancies are present at an early age, and their development does not seem to depend on the infant's growing mobility. Some of the developments in visual perception (e.g., visual acuity) seem to depend on maturational changes, whereas others (e.g., attachment of meaning to stimuli) depend on learning.

Essay questions

(1) Compare and contrast theories of pattern recognition.
(2) Describe the main processes involved in object recognition.
(3) What is visual agnosia? How has it been explained?

(4) How special are the processes involved in face recognition?
(5) What are the factors underlying the rapid development of visual perception in infants?

Further reading

Eysenck, M.W., & Keane, M.T. (2000). *Cognitive psychology: A student's handbook* (4th ed.). Hove, UK: Psychology Press. Chapter 4 in this book contains more detailed accounts of most of the topics discussed here.

Gazzaniga, M.S., Ivry, R.B., & Mangun, G.R. (1998). *Cognitive neuroscience: The biology of the mind*. New York: W.W. Norton. Chapter 5 of this book deals at length with neuroimaging and neuropsychological evidence on object recognition.

Slater, A. (1996). The organisation of visual perception in early infancy. In F. Vital-Durand, J. Atkinson, & O. Braddick (Eds.), *Infant vision*. Oxford: Oxford University Press. This chapter provides a well-informed view of the early development of visual perception.

Attention and pattern recognition 4

Introduction

The concept of attention has been used in several senses. It sometimes means concentration, but at other times it refers to our ability to select some aspect of incoming stimulation for further analysis. It has been argued that there are close links between attention and arousal, with aroused individuals being more attentive than drowsy individuals to the environment. However, attention is most often used to refer to selectivity of processing.

There is an important distinction between focused attention and divided attention. *Focused attention* is studied by presenting people with two or more stimulus inputs at the same time, and instructing them to respond to only one. Work on focused attention tells us how well people can *select* certain inputs rather than others. It also allows us to study the nature of the selection process and the fate of unattended stimuli. Focused attention is involved when students taking examinations have to try to avoid being distracted by other students, noises outside the room, and so on.

What is the purpose of attention? According to Behrmann and Tipper (1999, p. 83), "Attention appears to be a mechanism that selects a salient item from the essentially parallel visual perceptual system in the service of the serial motor system. Through the operation of such a mechanism, action may be directed toward one of the many objects that potentially evoke a response." Thus, our actions are most likely to be effective if attentional processes lead us to focus on the most important part of the visual environment.

Divided attention is studied by presenting two stimulus inputs at the same time, with the instructions indicating that both inputs should be attended to and responded to. Studies of divided attention (*dual-task studies*) provide useful information about an individual's processing limitations. They may also tell us something about attentional mechanisms and their capacity. An everyday example of divided attention is when students do their homework while listening to music. Is it really possible to do both things at once?

We can also learn much about the workings of attention by studying *action slips*, which are actions that are not carried out as intended. The most important reason for action slips is a failure to attend sufficiently to what we are doing. An example of an action slip is feeding baked beans to the cat, because the tin looks very similar to the tin of cat food.

Focused auditory attention

Colin Cherry became interested in the "cocktail party" problem during the early 1950s. The problem is to explain our ability to follow just one conversation when several people are talking at once. Cherry (1953) found that we make use of physical differences between the various auditory messages to select the one of interest. These physical differences include differences in the sex of the speaker, in voice intensity, and in the location of the speaker. When Cherry presented two messages in the same voice to both ears at once (thereby removing these physical differences), the participants found it very hard to separate out the two messages purely on the basis of meaning.

Cherry (1953) also carried out studies using a *shadowing task*, in which one auditory message had to be shadowed (repeated back out aloud) while a second auditory message was presented to the other ear. Very little information seemed to be obtained from the second or non-attended message. Listeners rarely noticed when that message was spoken in a foreign language or in reversed speech. In contrast, physical changes (e.g., the insertion of a pure tone) were usually detected, and listeners noticed the sex of the speaker and the intensity of sound of unattended messages. The conclusion that unattended auditory information receives minimal processing is supported by other evidence. For example, there is very little memory for words on the unattended message even when they are presented 35 times each (Moray, 1959).

Broadbent (1958) discussed findings from what is known as the *dichotic listening task*. What usually happens is that three digits are presented one after the other to one ear, while at the same time three different digits are presented to the other ear. After the three pairs of digits have been presented, the participants recall them in whatever

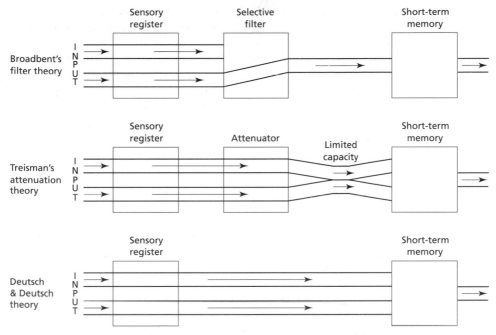

Figure 4.1. A diagrammatic representation contrasting Broadbent's theory (top); Treisman's theory (middle); and Deutsch & Deutsch's theory (bottom).

order they prefer. Recall is typically ear by ear rather than pair by pair. Thus, for example, if 496 were presented to one ear and 852 to the other ear, recall would be 496852 rather than 489562. It should be mentioned that all kinds of verbal stimuli can be used with the dichotic listening task.

Broadbent's filter theory

Broadbent (1958) put forward the first detailed theory of attention. It was also one of the first information-processing theories (see Chapter 1). Broadbent's (1958) filter theory used findings from the shadowing and dichotic listening tasks to propose a filter theory of attention. The key assumptions in this theory were as follows (see Figure 4.1):

- Two stimuli or messages presented at the same time gain access in parallel (at the same time) to a *sensory buffer*, which contains information briefly before it is attended to or disappears from the processing system.

- One of the inputs is then allowed through a filter on the basis of its physical characteristics, with the other input remaining in the buffer for later processing.
- This filter prevents overloading of the limited-capacity mechanism beyond the filter; this mechanism processes the input thoroughly.

This theory handles Cherry's basic findings, with unattended messages being rejected by the filter and thus receiving very little processing. It also accounts for performance on Broadbent's original dichotic listening task, since it is assumed that the filter selects one input on the basis of the most obvious physical characteristic distinguishing the two inputs (i.e., the ear of arrival). However, it does not explain other findings. For example, it is assumed within filter theory that the unattended message is *always* rejected at an early stage of processing, but this assumption is wrong. The original shadowing studies involved participants with no previous experience of shadowing messages, who had to devote nearly all of their processing resources to the shadowing task. Underwood (1974) asked participants to detect digits presented on either the shadowed or the non-shadowed message. Participants who had not done the task before detected only 8% of the digits on the non-shadowed message. In contrast, an experienced researcher in the area detected 67% of the non-shadowed digits.

The two messages were very similar (i.e., both auditorily presented verbal messages) in early studies on the shadowing task. Allport, Antonis, and Reynolds (1972) found that the degree of similarity between the two messages had a major impact on memory for the non-shadowed message. When shadowing of auditorily presented passages was combined with auditory presentation of words, memory for the words was very poor. However, when shadowing was combined with picture presentation, memory for the pictures was very good (90% correct). If two inputs differ clearly from each other, then they can both be processed more thoroughly than was allowed for on Broadbent's filter theory.

The findings of Allport et al. (1972) shed some light on how it was that Broadbent (1958) came to the mistaken conclusion that there is very little processing of unattended auditory messages. The experimental evidence prior to 1958 nearly all involved two very similar auditory inputs, and it is precisely in those conditions that there is minimal processing of the unattended input.

Broadbent (1958) assumed that there was no processing of the meaning of unattended messages, because the participants had no conscious awareness of their meaning. However, meaning might be processed without awareness. Von Wright, Anderson, and Stenman (1975) gave their participants two auditorily presented lists of words. They told them to shadow one list and ignore the other. When a word previously associated with electric shock was presented on the non-attended list, there was sometimes a physiological response. There was the same effect when a word very similar in sound or meaning to the shocked word was presented. Thus, information on the unattended message was processed in terms of both sound and meaning. These physiological reactions occurred even though the participants were not consciously aware that the previously shocked word or its associates had been presented. Since physiological responses were observed on only relatively few trials, it seems that thorough processing of unattended information occurred only some of the time.

Evaluation

Broadbent's filter theory of attention is of great historical importance. The notion of an information-processing system, with a number of processes linked to each other, first saw the light of day in filter theory. That notion has been very influential, with information-processing systems being proposed for memory, language processing, and so on, as well as attention. Indeed, cognitive psychology as it is today owes more to Broadbent's filter theory than to any other single contribution (Eysenck, 2000).

On the negative side, Broadbent's theory is too *inflexible*. The theory predicts that an unattended input will receive minimal processing. In fact, however, there is great variability in the amount of processing devoted to such input. A similar inflexibility of filter theory is shown in its assumption that the filter selects information on the basis of physical features of the input. This assumption is supported by the tendency of participants on the dichotic listening task to recall digits ear by ear. However, a small change in the task produces very different results. Gray and Wedderburn (1960) used a version of the dichotic listening task in which "who 6 there" might be presented to one ear while "4 goes 1" was presented to the other ear. The preferred order of report was *not* the usual ear by ear; instead, it was determined by meaning (e.g., "who goes there" followed by "4 6 1"). Thus, selection can occur either *before* or *after* the processing of information from both inputs. The fact that selection can be based on the meaning of presented information is inconsistent with filter theory.

Alternative theories

Treisman (1964) proposed an attenuation theory of attention, in which the processing of unattended information is attenuated or reduced. In Broadbent's filter theory, it was proposed that there is a bottleneck early in processing. In Treisman's theory, the location of the bottleneck is more flexible (see Figure 4.1). It is as if people possess a "leaky" filter making selective attention less efficient than assumed by Broadbent (1958).

According to Treisman (1964), stimulus processing proceeds systematically, starting with analyses based on physical cues, and then moving on to analyses based on meaning. If there is insufficient processing capacity to allow full stimulus analysis, then some of the later analyses are omitted with "unattended" stimuli. This theory neatly predicts Cherry's (1953) finding that it is usually the physical characteristics of unattended inputs (e.g., sex of the speaker) which are noticed rather than their meaning.

The extensive processing of unattended sources of information that was embarrassing for filter theory can be accounted for by Treisman's attenuation theory. However, the same findings were also explained by Deutsch and Deutsch (1963). They claimed that all stimuli are analysed fully, with the most important or relevant stimulus determining the response. This theory differs from filter theory and attenuation theory in placing the bottleneck closer to the response end of the processing system (see Figure 4.1).

It has proved very hard to decide conclusively between the theory of Treisman and that of Deutsch and Deutsch. Treisman's theory seems more plausible. The assumption made by Deutsch and Deutsch that all stimuli are analysed completely, but that most of the analysed information is lost almost at once, seems rather wasteful. In fact, studies by Treisman and Geffen (1967) and by Treisman and Riley (1969) provided support for attenuation theory rather than the theory of Deutsch and Deutsch (1963).

Treisman and Geffen (1967) told participants to shadow one of two auditory messages, having been told to tap whenever they detected a target word in either message. According to attenuation theory, there should be reduced analysis of the non-shadowed message, and so fewer targets should be detected on that message than on the shadowed one. According to Deutsch and Deutsch, there is complete processing of all stimuli, and so it might be predicted that there would be no difference in detection rates between the two messages. In fact, the detection rate on the shadowed or attended message was much higher.

Deutsch and Deutsch (1967) pointed out that their theory assumes that only *important* inputs lead to responses. As the task used by Treisman and Geffen (1967) required their participants to make two responses (i.e., shadow and tap) to shadowed target words, but only one response (i.e., tap) to non-shadowed targets, the shadowed targets were more important than the non-shadowed ones. Thus, their theory could account for the findings.

Treisman and Riley (1969) retaliated by carrying out a study in which exactly the same response was made to targets in either message. Their participants were told to stop shadowing and to tap whenever they detected a target in either message. Many more target words were detected on the shadowed message than on the non-shadowed one, a finding that is hard to explain on the theory of Deutsch and Deutsch.

Neurophysiological studies provide support for early-selection theories (see Luck, 1998, for a review). Woldorff et al. (1993) used the task of detecting auditory targets presented to the attended ear, with fast trains of non-targets being presented to each ear. *Event-related potentials* (regularities in the brain-wave responses to repeated stimuli) were recorded from attended and unattended stimuli. There were greater event-related potentials to attended than unattended stimuli 20–50 ms after stimulus onset, suggesting that attended stimuli were processed more thoroughly.

Section summary

The analysis of unattended auditory inputs can be greater than was originally thought. However, the full analysis theory of Deutsch and Deutsch (1963) seems dubious. The most reasonable account of focused auditory attention may be along the lines suggested by Treisman (1964), with reduced or attenuated processing of sources of information outside focal attention. The extent of such processing is probably flexible. Styles (1997, p. 28) made a telling point: "Discovering precisely where selection occurs is only one small part of the issues surrounding attention, and finding *where* selection takes place may not help us to understand *why* or *how* this happens."

Focused visual attention

Over the past 25 years, far more researchers have studied visual than auditory attention. Why is this? One reason is because it is easier to control the presentation times of visual stimuli than of auditory stimuli. Another reason is that most early research on focused attention had been concerned with auditory attention, and so there was much to be discovered about focused visual attention. Some of the most important research on focused visual attention has involved the study of attentional disorders, and that is where we will begin our coverage.

Disorders of visual attention

Cognitive neuropsychologists have studied three visual attentional disorders in detail: unilateral neglect, extinction, and Balint's syndrome (see Driver, 1998, for a review). *Unilateral neglect* is typically found after brain damage to the right parietal lobe, with patients failing to notice objects presented to the left visual field. For example, when patients with unilateral neglect copy a drawing, they typically leave out everything on the left side of it. In addition, neglect patients show a similar phenomenon on tasks involving visual imagery (Bisiach & Luzzatti, 1978).

Patients with unilateral neglect fail to report stimuli presented to the left visual field, but there is often some perceptual processing of these stimuli. For example, Marshall and Halligan (1988) presented a neglect patient with two drawings of a house that were identical, except that the house presented to the left visual field had flames coming out of one of its windows. The patient could not report any differences between the two drawings, but said that she would prefer to live in the house on the right.

How can we explain neglect? According to Parkin (1996, p. 108), "The most convincing class of theories concerning neglect are those that propose some form of attentional deficit. Essentially these theories suggest that there is an imbalance in the amount of attention allocated to left and right . . . However, the idea that a single theory of neglect will emerge is highly unlikely because of the diversity of defects being discovered."

Extinction is a phenomenon often found in neglect patients. A single stimulus on either side of the visual field can be judged normally. However, when two stimuli are presented, the one further toward the side of the visual field that is neglected tends to go undetected.

Why does extinction occur? The fact that single stimuli on the impaired side of the visual field are perceived normally suggests that extinction patients have essentially intact sensory processing, and so problems with sensory processing do not account for extinction. An alternative explanation was favoured by Driver (1998, p. 301): "Many authors . . . regard extinction as primarily a deficit in covert spatial attention." Convincing evidence that *covert attention* (a shift in attention occurring in the absence of eye movements) is involved was reported by Di Pellegrino and De Renzi (1995). They found that a stimulus on the impaired side could be identified even when a second stimulus was presented to the unimpaired side at the same time, provided that the extinction patients were instructed to ignore any stimulus on the unimpaired side. Covert rather than overt attention was involved, because the use of brief displays prevented eye movements from having any real impact on performance.

Balint's syndrome is associated with lesions in both hemispheres involving the posterior parietal lobe or parieto-occipital junction. Patients with this syndrome have various attentional problems, including fixed gazing, gross misreaching for objects, and *simultagnosia*, in which only one object at a time can be seen. Evidence that Balint's patients can attend to only one object at a time was reported by Humphreys and Riddoch (1993). When Balint patients were presented with several red and green circles, they were generally unable to report seeing both colours at the same time. However, when the red and green circles were joined by lines (so that each object contained red and green), they could see red and green at the same time.

The explanation of Balint's syndrome is not altogether clear, although the symptom of simultagnosia presumably represents an attentional deficit. There may be no single explanation of the syndrome. Some Balint patients fail to show all three major symptoms (simultagnosia, fixed gaze, misreaching), suggesting that different processes underlie each one. However, Driver (1998) argued that the central problem is that Balint patients find it hard to "disengage" covert attention from an object.

Components of visual attention

Posner and Petersen (1990) used findings from attentionally disordered patients to propose a theory in which visual attention involves three separate processes or components:

- *Disengagement* of attention from a given visual stimulus: Patients with unilateral neglect (Posner et al., 1984) and Balint patients with simultagnosia have problems of disengagement.
- *Shifting* of attention from one target stimulus to another: Patients with progressive supranuclear palsy (Posner et al.,

1985) and with Balint's syndrome (Humphreys & Riddoch, 1993) have problems with shifting of attention.

- *Engaging* or locking of attention on a new visual stimulus: Patients with damage to the pulvinar nucleus of the thalamus (Rafal & Posner, 1987) have problems with engaging attention.

These three processes are functions of the posterior attention system. In addition, there is an anterior attention system. This co-ordinates the different aspects of visual attention, and resembles the central executive component of the working memory system (see Chapter 5).

In sum, the evidence from attentionally disordered patients is that the attentional system is complex. In the words of Allport (1989, p. 644), "spatial attention is a distributed function in which many functionally differentiated structures participate, rather than a function controlled uniquely by a single centre."

Spotlight or zoom lens?

Focused visual attention seems to resemble a spotlight. Everything within a fairly small region of the visual field can be seen clearly, but it is much harder to see anything not falling within the beam of the attentional spotlight. Attention can be shifted by moving the spotlight, and the simplest assumption is that the attentional spotlight moves at a constant rate (see Yantis, 1998). A more complex view of focused visual attention was put forward by Eriksen and St. James (1986). According to their zoom-lens model, attention is directed to a given region of the visual field. The area of focal attention can be increased or decreased in line with task demands.

Posner (1980) favoured the spotlight notion. He argued that there can be covert attention, with the attentional spotlight shifting to a different spatial location in the absence of an eye movement. In his studies, the participants responded as rapidly as possible when they detected the onset of a light. Shortly before the onset of the light, they were presented with a central cue (arrow pointing to the left or right) or a peripheral cue (brief illumination of a box outline). These cues were mostly valid (i.e., they indicated where the target light would appear), but sometimes they were invalid (i.e., they provided misleading information about the location of the target light).

Posner's (1980) key findings were that valid cues produced faster responding to light onset than did neutral cues (a central cross), whereas invalid cues produced slower responding than neutral cues.

The findings were comparable for central and peripheral cues, and were obtained in the absence of eye movements. When the cues were valid on only a small fraction of trials, they were ignored when they were central cues but affected performance when they were peripheral cues. These findings led Posner (1980) to distinguish between two systems:

(1) An endogenous system, which is controlled by the participant's intentions and is involved when central cues are presented.
(2) An exogenous system, which automatically shifts attention and is involved when peripheral cues are presented.

Evidence in favour of the zoom-lens model was reported by LaBerge (1983). Five-letter words were presented. A probe requiring rapid response was occasionally presented instead of, or immediately after, the word. The probe could appear in the spatial position of any of the five letters of the word. In one condition, an attempt was made to focus the participants' attention on the middle letter of the five-letter word by asking them to categorise that letter. In another condition, the participants were required to categorise the entire word. It was expected that this would lead the participants to adopt a broader attentional beam.

LaBerge (1983) assumed that the probe would be responded to faster when it fell within the central attentional beam than when it did not. On this assumption, the attentional spotlight can have either a very narrow (letter task) or rather broad beam (word task). LaBerge's (1983) findings were as predicted, with the width of the attentional beam being affected by the task (see Figure 4.2).

Evaluation
Visual attention resembles a zoom lens more than a spotlight, because the size of the visual field within focal attention can vary substantially. However, there is a fundamental objection to both the spotlight and zoom lens models. It is assumed within both models that visual attention is directed towards a given region in the visual field. However, visual attention is often directed to *objects* rather than to a particular *region*. Consider, for example, a study by Neisser and Becklen (1975). They superimposed two moving scenes on top of each other. Their participants could easily attend to one scene while ignoring the other. These findings suggest that objects within the visual environment can be the main focus of attention.

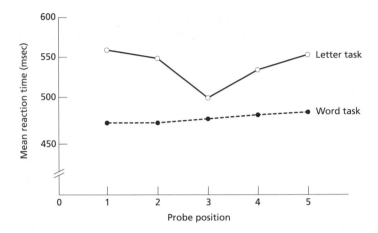

Figure 4.2. Mean reaction time to the probe as a function of probe position. The probe was presented at the time that a letter string would have been presented. Data from LaBerge (1983).

Driver and Baylis (1989) and Baylis and Driver (1992) also obtained evidence against the spotlight and zoom-lens approaches. Driver and Baylis (1989) found that objects having common movement (i.e., moving in the same direction) were attended to at the same time even when they were not close to each other in space. In similar fashion, Baylis and Driver (1992) reported that interference could be produced by distractors which were a long way away from the target, provided that the distractor and target objects had common movement.

The notion that visual attention can be directed to objects has been supported by studies on neglect patients. Unilateral neglect patients with right-hemisphere damage do not notice, or fail to respond to, objects presented to the left side. Marshall and Halligan (1994) presented a patient with neglect in the left visual field with ambiguous displays, each of which could be seen as a black shape against a white background or as a white shape on a black background. There was a jagged edge dividing the two shapes at the centre of each display. The patient copied this jagged edge when asked to draw the shape on the left side of the display, in which case the edge was on its right. However, the patient could not copy the same edge when asked to draw the shape on the right side, in which case the edge was on its left. Thus, the patient attended to objects rather than simply to a region of visual space.

Visual attention is more flexible than has been suggested so far. For example, Behrmann and Tipper (1999, p. 98) carried out a complex attentional study on patients with unilateral neglect, and came to the following conclusion: "Unilateral neglect, assumed to be a pathology [disease] of attention, has been revealed in both location-based and object-centred frames of reference simultaneously." Thus, visual attention can be directed *either* to a specific region of space *or* to a given object.

Unattended visual stimuli

What happens to unattended visual stimuli? Luck (1998) discussed several neurophysiological studies in which the participants fixated a central point while attending to the left or the right visual field. Event-related potentials (ERPs) were larger to attended than to unattended stimuli, suggesting that there was more thorough processing of attended stimuli.

Evidence suggesting that there is very little processing of unattended visual stimuli was reported by Francolini and Egeth (1980). Circular arrays of red and black letters or numerals were presented, and the task was to count the number of red items while ignoring the black items. Performance speed was reduced when the *red* items consisted of numerals conflicting with the answer, but there was no interference effect from the *black* items. These findings suggested there was little or no processing of the to-be-ignored black items.

The findings of Driver and Tipper (1989) contradicted the above conclusion. They used the same task as Francolini and Egeth (1980), but focused on whether conflicting numerical values had been presented on the *previous* trial. There was an interference effect from both red *and* black items. The finding that performance on any given trial was affected by the numerical values of to-be-ignored items from the previous trial means those items must have been processed. This is an example of the phenomenon of *negative priming*. In this phenomenon, the processing of a target stimulus is inhibited if that stimulus or one very similar to it was a to-be-ignored or distracting stimulus on the previous trial.

Further evidence that there is often more processing of unattended visual stimuli than initially seems to be the case has been reported with patients suffering from *unilateral neglect*. McGlinchey-Berroth et al. (1993) asked such patients to decide which of two drawings matched a drawing presented immediately beforehand to the left or the right visual field. Neglect patients performed well when the initial drawing was presented to the right visual field, but at chance level when it was presented to the left visual field (see Figure 4.3a). The latter finding suggests that stimuli in the left visual field were not processed.

A very different conclusion emerged from a second study, in which neglect patients had to decide whether letter strings formed

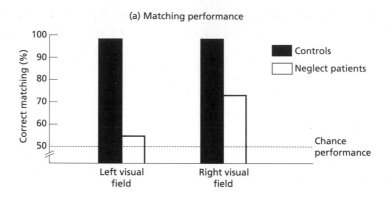

Figure 4.3. Effects of prior presentation of a drawing to the left or right visual field on matching performance and lexical decision in neglect patients. Data from McGlinchey-Berroth et al. (1993).

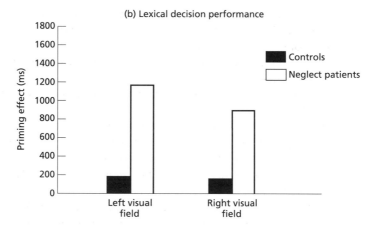

words. Decision times were faster on "yes" trials when the letter string was preceded by a semantically related object rather than an unrelated object. This effect was the same size regardless of whether the object was presented to the left or the right visual field (see Figure 4.3b), indicating some processing of left-field stimuli by neglect patients.

Visual search

One of the main ways we use focused visual attention in our everyday lives is in *visual search* (see Chapter 3), in which a target stimulus presented in the context of other stimuli has to be detected. For example, we look for a friend in a crowded room or for information about a given topic in a book. The processes involved have been studied by using visual search tasks. The participants are presented with a visual display containing a variable number of items (the set or display size). A target (e.g., red G) is presented on half the trials, and the task is to decide as rapidly as possible whether the target is in the display. Some of the factors determining the speed and accuracy of visual search are discussed below.

Feature integration theory

Treisman (e.g., 1988, 1992) distinguished between the features of objects (e.g., colour, size, lines of particular orientation) and the objects themselves Her feature integration theory includes the following assumptions:

- There is a rapid initial parallel process in which the visual features of objects in the environment are processed together; this is not dependent on attention.
- There is then a serial process in which features are combined to form objects.
- The serial process is slower than the initial parallel process, especially when the set size is large.
- Features can be combined by focused attending to the location of the object, in which case focused attention provides the "glue" forming unitary objects from the available features.
- Feature combination can be influenced by stored knowledge (e.g., bananas are usually yellow).
- In the absence of focused attention or relevant stored knowledge, features from different objects will be combined randomly, producing "illusory conjunctions".

Treisman and Gelade (1980) had previously obtained support for this theory. Their participants searched for a target in a visual display having a set or display size of between 1 and 30 items. The target was either an object (a green letter T), or consisted of a single feature (a blue letter or an S). When the target was a green letter T, all the non-targets shared one feature with the target (i e , they were either brown letter Ts or green letter Xs). It was predicted that focused attention would be needed to detect the object target (because it was defined by a combination of features), but would not be needed with the single-feature targets.

Set or display size had a large effect on detection speed when the target was defined by a combination or conjunction of features (i.e., a green letter T), presumably because focused attention was required

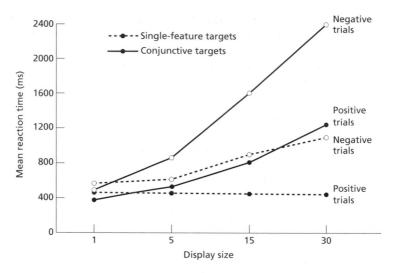

Figure 4.4.
Performance speed on a detection task as a function of target definition (conjunctive versus single feature) and display size. Adapted from Treisman and Gelade (1980).

(see Figure 4.4). However, there was very little effect of display size when the target was defined by a single feature (i.e., a blue letter or an S).

According to feature integration theory, lack of focused attention can produce illusory conjunctions. Treisman and Schmidt (1982) confirmed this prediction. There were numerous illusory conjunctions when attention was widely distributed, but not when the stimuli were presented to focal attention.

Treisman and Sato (1990) developed feature integration theory. They argued that the degree of *similarity* between the target and the distractors influences visual search time. Visual search for an object target defined by more than one feature was typically limited to those distractors having at least one of the target's features. For example, if you were looking for a blue circle in a display containing blue triangles, red circles, and red triangles, you would ignore red triangles. This contrasts with the views of Treisman and Gelade (1980), who argued that none of the stimuli would be ignored.

Guided search theory

Guided search theory was put forward by Wolfe (1998). It represents a substantial refinement of feature integration theory. Wolfe (1998) replaced Treisman and Gelade's (1980) assumption that the initial processing is necessarily parallel and subsequent processing is serial with the notion that processes are more or less efficient. Why did he do this? As Wolfe (1998) pointed out, there should be no effect of set or display size on detection times if parallel processing is used, but a substantial effect of set size if serial processing is used. In fact, most findings fall between these two extremes, suggesting that processing may rarely be purely parallel or purely serial.

According to guided search theory, the initial processing of basic features produces an activation map, in which each of the items in the visual display has its own level of activation. Suppose that someone is searching for red, horizontal targets. Feature processing would activate all red objects and all horizontal objects. Attention is then directed towards items on the basis of their level of activation, starting with those with the highest level of activation. This assumption allows us to understand why search times are longer when some of the non-targets share one or more features with the target stimuli (e.g., Treisman & Sato, 1990).

A great problem with the original version of feature integration theory was that targets in large displays are typically found faster than would be predicted. The activation-map notion provides a plausible way in which visual search can be made more efficient by ignoring stimuli not sharing any features with the target stimulus. This occurs because such stimuli receive little or no activation.

Evaluation

Feature integration theory has influenced theoretical approaches to visual search in various ways. First, it is generally agreed that two successive processes are involved. Second, it is accepted that the first process is fast and efficient, whereas the second process is slower and less efficient. Third, the notion that different visual features are processed independently or separately seems attractive in view of the evidence that different areas of the visual cortex are specialised for processing different features (Zeki, 1993; see Chapter 2).

There were three main weaknesses with early versions of feature integration theory. First, as Wolfe (1998) pointed out, the assumption that visual search is either entirely parallel or serial is too strong and is disproved by the evidence. Second, the search for targets consisting of a conjunction or combination of features is faster than predicted by feature integration theory. Some of the factors involved are incorporated into guided search theory. For example, search for conjunctive targets can be speeded up if non-targets can be grouped together or if non-targets share no features with targets.

Third, it was originally assumed that the effect of set or display size on visual search depends mainly on the nature of the target (single feature or conjunctive feature). In fact, other factors (e.g., similarity of non-targets) also play a role.

Another issue with research on visual search concerns its relevance to the real world. As Wolfe (1998, p. 56) pointed out, "In the real world, distractors are very heterogeneous [diverse]. Stimuli exist in many size scales in a single view. Items are probably defined by conjunctions of many features . . . A truly satisfying model of visual search will need . . . to account for the range of real-world visual behaviour."

Divided attention

What happens when people try to do two things at once? The answer clearly depends on the nature of the two "things". Sometimes the attempt is successful, as when an experienced motorist drives a car while holding a conversation. At other times, as when someone tries to rub their stomach with one hand while patting their head with the other, there can be a complete disruption of performance.

Focused and divided attention are more similar than might have been expected. Factors such as use of different modalities which aid focused or selective attention generally also make divided attention easier. According to Hampson (1989, p. 267), "anything which minimises interference between processes, or keeps them 'further apart' will allow them to be dealt with more readily either selectively or together."

Dual-task studies (studies in which two tasks must be performed at the same time) indicate that there are frequent performance impairments. Some theorists (e.g., Baddeley, 1986; Norman & Shallice, 1986) argue that such impairments often reflect the limited capacity of a single multi-purpose central processor or executive sometimes described as "attention". Other theorists (e.g., Allport, 1989) are more impressed by our apparent ability to perform two fairly complex tasks at the same time without disruption or interference. Such theorists favour the notion of several specific processing resources, arguing that there will be no interference between two tasks provided that they make use of different processing resources.

It is possible to predict fairly accurately whether or not two tasks can be combined successfully, in spite of the fact that the accounts offered by different theorists are very diverse. Accordingly, we will discuss some of the factual evidence before moving on to the more complex issue of how the data are to be explained.

Dual-task performance

Dual-task performance depends on several factors. We will focus on what are perhaps the three most important factors in this section: task similarity, practice, and task difficulty.

Task similarity

When we think of pairs of activities that are performed well together in everyday life, the examples that come to mind usually involve two rather dissimilar activities (e.g., driving and talking; reading and listening to music). As we have seen, when people shadow or repeat back prose passages while learning auditorily presented words (two similar activities), their subsequent recognition–memory performance for the words is at chance level (Allport et al., 1972). However, the same authors found that memory was excellent when the to-be-remembered material consisted of pictures.

There are various kinds of similarity. For example, two tasks can be presented in the same sense modality (e.g., visually or auditorily). Two tasks can also be similar because they require the same type of response. McLeod (1977) asked participants to perform a continuous tracking task with manual responding at the same time as a tone-identification task. Some participants responded vocally to the tones, whereas others responded manually with the hand not involved in the tracking task. Performance on the tracking task was worse with high response similarity (manual responses on both tasks) than with low response similarity (manual responses on one task and vocal ones on the other).

Similarity of stimulus modality was studied by Treisman and Davies (1973). They found two monitoring tasks interfered with each much more when the stimuli on both tasks were in the same sense modality (visual or auditory) than when they were in different modalities.

It is often very hard to measure similarity. How similar are piano playing and poetry writing, or driving a car and watching a football match? Only when there is a better understanding of the processes involved in the performance of such tasks will sensible answers be forthcoming.

Practice

The old saying, "Practice makes perfect", is very applicable to dual-task performance. For example, learner drivers find it almost impossible to drive and hold a conversation, whereas expert drivers find it fairly easy. Evidence for the importance of practice was obtained by Spelke, Hirst, and Neisser (1976) in a study on two students called Diane and John. These students received extensive training on various tasks. Their first task was to read short stories for comprehension while writing down words to dictation. They found this very hard initially, and their reading speed and handwriting both suffered considerably. After 6 weeks of training, however, they could read as rapidly and with as much comprehension when taking dictation as when only reading, and the quality of their handwriting had also improved.

Spelke et al. (1976) were still not satisfied. Diane and John could recall only 35 out of the thousands of words they had written down at dictation. Even when 20 successive dictated words formed a sentence or came from a single semantic category, the two students were unaware of that. With further training, however, they learned to write down the names of the categories to which the dictated words belonged while maintaining normal reading speed and comprehension.

Spelke et al. (1976, p. 229) doubted whether the popular notion that we have limited processing capacity is accurate, basing themselves on the dramatic findings with John and Diane: "People's ability to develop skills in specialised situations is so great that it may never be possible to define general limits on cognitive capacity." However, there are other ways of interpreting their findings. Perhaps the dictation task was performed rather automatically, and so placed few demands on cognitive capacity, or there might have been a rapid alternation of attention between reading and writing.

Hirst et al. (1980) claimed that writing to dictation was *not* done automatically, because the students understood what they were writing. They also claimed that reading and dictation could only be performed together with success by alternation of attention if the reading material were simple and highly redundant. However, they found that most participants could still read and take dictation effectively when less redundant reading matter was used.

Do the studies by Spelke et al. (1976) and by Hirst et al. (1980) show that two complex tasks can be performed together without disruption? One of the participants used by Hirst et al. was tested at dictation *without* reading, and made fewer than half the number of errors that occurred when reading at the same time. Furthermore, the reading task gave the participants much flexibility in terms of when they attended to the reading matter, and so there may well have been some alternation of attention between tasks.

There are other cases of apparently successful performance of two complex tasks, but the requisite skills were always highly practised. For example, expert pianists can play from seen music while repeating back or shadowing heard speech (Allport et al., 1972), and an expert typist can type and shadow at the same time (Shaffer, 1975). These studies are often regarded as providing evidence of completely successful task combination. However, there are some signs of interference (Broadbent, 1982).

Task difficulty

The ability to perform two tasks together depends on their difficulty. For example Sullivan (1976) used the tasks of shadowing an auditory message and detecting target words on a non-shadowed message at the same time. When the shadowing task was made harder by using a less redundant message, fewer targets were detected on the non-shadowed message. However, it is hard to define "task difficulty" with any precision.

The demands for resources of two tasks performed together might be thought to equal the sums of the demands of the two tasks when performed separately. However, the necessity to perform two tasks together often introduces new demands of co-ordination and avoidance of interference. Duncan (1979) asked his participants to respond to closely successive stimuli, one requiring a left-hand response and the other a right-hand response. The relationship between each stimulus and response was either corresponding (e.g., rightmost stimulus calling for response of the rightmost finger) or crossed (e.g., leftmost stimulus calling for response of the rightmost finger). Performance was poor when the relationship was corresponding for one stimulus but crossed for the other. In these circumstances, the participants were sometimes confused, with their errors being largely those expected if the inappropriate stimulus–response relationship had been selected.

Summary

The extent to which two tasks can be performed successfully together depends on various factors. As a rule of thumb, two dissimilar, highly practised, and simple tasks can typically be performed well together, whereas two similar, novel, and complex tasks cannot. In addition, having to perform two tasks together rather than separately often produces entirely new problems of co-ordination. We now consider some of the theoretical accounts that have been offered of these (and other) findings.

Central capacity theories: Kahneman

A simple way of accounting for many dual-task findings is to assume there is some central capacity or resources that can be used flexibly across a wide range of activities. Capacity theories were proposed by Kahneman (1973) and by Norman and Bobrow (1975). Two crucial assumptions are made by such theories:

- There is some central capacity (attention or effort), which has limited resources.
- The ability to perform two tasks together depends on the demands placed on those resources by the two tasks.

It follows that dual-task performance will be poor if the two tasks require more resources than are available. However, the two tasks will be performed successfully if their combined demands for resources are less than the total resources of the central capacity.

Evidence supporting central capacity theories was reported by Bourke, Duncan, and Nimmo-Smith (1996). First of all, they selected four tasks designed to differ as much as possible from each other:

(1) *Random generation*: generating letters in a random order.
(2) *Prototype learning*: working out the features of two patterns or prototypes from seeing various exemplars.
(3) *Manual task*: screwing a nut down to the bottom of a bolt and back up to the top, and then down to the bottom of a second bolt and back up, and so on.
(4) *Tone task*: detecting the occurrence of a target tone.

The participants were given two of these tasks to perform together, with one task being identified as more important than the other. The basic argument was as follows: If there is a central or general capacity, then the task making most demands on this capacity will interfere most with all three of the other tasks. In contrast, the task making fewest demands on this capacity will interfere least with all the other tasks.

What did Bourke et al. (1996) find? First, these very different tasks did interfere with each other. Second, the random generation task interfered the most overall with the performance of the other tasks, and the tone task interfered the least. Third, and of greatest importance, the random generation task consistently interfered most with the prototype, manual, and tone tasks, and it did so whether it was the primary or the secondary task (see Figure 4.5). The tone task consistently interfered least with each of the other three tasks. Thus, the findings accorded with the predictions of a general capacity theory.

The main limitation of the study by Bourke et al. (1996) is that it did not clarify the nature of the central capacity. As they admitted, "The method developed here deals only with the existence of a general factor in dual-task decrements, not its nature" (p. 544).

A well-known capacity theory was put forward by Kahneman (1973). In addition to the assumptions that people have limited capacity, and that the ability to perform two tasks together depends on the total demand on resources, Kahneman (1973) made the following assumptions (see Figure 4.6):

(1) The greater the level of arousal, the greater the pool of resources or capacity available; this relationship may break down at high levels of arousal.
(2) Decisions about how to make use of the available capacity are made by the allocation policy.
(3) The allocation policy is determined by four factors:
    (i) Enduring dispositions (e.g., attend to intense or novel stimuli).
    (ii) Momentary intentions (e.g., attend to your psychology textbook and ignore the television).
    (iii) Evaluation of demands: If there is insufficient capacity to perform two activities at the same time, then one is carried through to completion.
    (iv) The level of arousal produced by external stressors: High arousal produces a narrowing of attention and a reduced ability to discriminate between relevant and irrelevant cues (this is known as Easterbrook's hypothesis).
(4) Individuals evaluate the demands on their available capacity, and this can lead to an increase in effort and in the available capacity.

Figure 4.5.
Performance on
random generation (R),
prototype learning (P),
manual (M), and tone
(T) tasks as a function
of concurrent task.
Adapted from Bourke et
al. (1996).

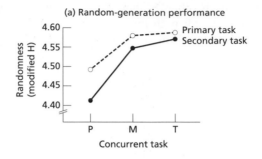

(a) Random-generation performance

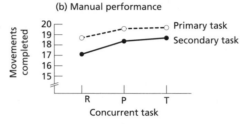

(b) Manual performance

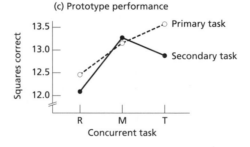

(c) Prototype performance

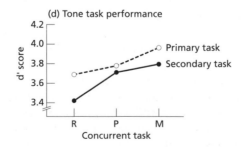

(d) Tone task performance

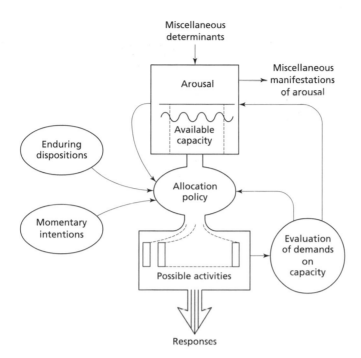

Figure 4.6. A capacity model for attention. From *Attention and Effort* by Kahneman, Daniel, ©1973. Reprinted by permission of Prentice-Hall, Inc., Upper Saddle River, NJ.

Miscellaneous determinants

Arousal

Miscellaneous manifestations of arousal

Available capacity

Enduring dispositions

Allocation policy

Momentary intentions

Possible activities

Evaluation of demands on capacity

Responses

What predictions follow from Kahneman's theory? First, dual-task performance should depend on the demands of each task on the total available capacity. The findings of Bourke et al. (1996) support that prediction. Second, there will be an increase in effort as task demands increase (see Figure 4.7). Supporting evidence was reported by Kahneman et al. (1969) using pupillary dilation as a measure of effort. There was a digit-transformation task, in which the participants were presented with four digits and added one to each digit (e.g., 4826 became 5937). Pupil dilation increased steadily during digit presentation, suggesting that the participants were increasing their level of effort in response to increasing task demands.

Third, the amount of spare processing (the difference between total capacity and capacity supplied to the primary task) decreases as primary task demands increase (see Figure 4.7). This prediction was also tested by Kahneman et al. (1969). Digit transformation was the primary task, and there was a subsidiary task of monitoring a display for a specified letter. As predicted, performance on the subsidiary task became steadily worse throughout digit presentation as the amount of capacity allocated to the primary task increased.

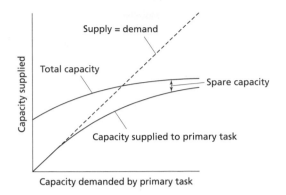

Figure 4.7. Supply of effort as a function of demands of a primary task. From *Attention and Effort* by Kahneman, Daniel, ©1973. Reprinted by permission of Prentice-Hall, Inc., Upper Saddle River, NJ.

Evaluation

The notion that the available processing capacity varies as a function of effort expenditure is plausible, and has received experimental support. However, there are various problems specific to Kahneman's (1973) capacity theory. First, he did not define his key terms very clearly, referring to "a nonspecific input, which may be variously labelled 'effort', 'capacity', or 'attention'." Instead of equating the concepts of "effort" and "attentional capacity", it may be preferable to argue that effort is the cause of increased attention.

Second, Kahneman assumed that effort and attentional capacity are determined in part by task difficulty. However, it is very hard to determine the difficulty of a task with any precision. Third, it is often difficult to make precise predictions. For example, consider a situation in which someone who is highly aroused is exerting much effort on a task. The high arousal may impair performance because of attentional narrowing and reduced ability to discriminate between task-relevant and task-irrelevant stimuli, but the high level of effort will improve performance. Thus, it is impossible to predict whether performance will be improved or impaired.

There are also problems that apply to all central capacity theories. According to such theories, the crucial determinant of dual-task performance is the difficulty level of the two tasks, with difficulty being defined in terms of the demands placed on the resources of the central capacity. However, the effects of task difficulty are often swamped by those of task similarity. For example, Segal and Fusella (1970) combined image construction (visual or auditory) with signal detection (visual or auditory). The auditory image task impaired detection of auditory signals more than the visual task did (see Figure 4.8), suggesting that the auditory image task was more demanding

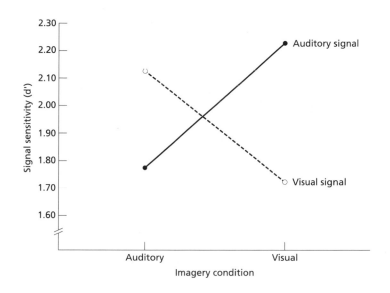

Figure 4.8. Sensitivity (d') to auditory and visual signals as a function of concurrent imagery modality (auditory versus visual). Adapted from Segal and Fusella (1970).

than the visual image task. However, the auditory image task was less disruptive than the visual image task when each task was combined with a task requiring detection of visual signals, suggesting the opposite conclusion. In this study, task similarity was clearly a much more important factor than task difficulty.

Allport (1989, p. 647) argued that such findings "point to a multiplicity of attentional functions, dependent on a multiplicity of specialised subsystems. No one of these subsystems appears uniquely 'central'." It is possible to "explain" dual-task performance by assuming that the resources of some central capacity have been exceeded, and to account for a lack of interference by assuming that the two tasks did not exceed those resources. However, . . . this is simply a re-description of the findings rather than an explanation.

Bottleneck theories

Welford (1952) argued that there is a processing bottleneck making it hard (or impossible) for two decisions about the appropriate responses to two different stimuli to be made at the same time. His views influenced the development of Broadbent's (1958) filter theory, which was discussed earlier in the chapter. Much of the supporting evidence comes from studies of the *psychological refractory period*. There are two stimuli (e.g., two lights) and two responses (e.g., button presses), and the task is to respond rapidly to each stimulus. When the second stimulus is presented very shortly after the first one, there is generally a marked slowing of the response to the second stimulus: This is the psychological refractory period effect (see Welford, 1952).

One objection to the notion that the delay in responding to the second stimulus reflects a bottleneck in processing is that the effect is due to similarity of stimuli and/or similarity of responses. According to the bottleneck theory, the psychological refractory period effect should be present even when the two stimuli and responses differ greatly. In contrast, the effect should disappear if similarity is crucial. Pashler (1990) used a tone requiring a vocal response and a visual letter requiring a button-push response. Some participants were told the order in which the stimuli would be presented, whereas the others were not. In spite of a lack of either stimulus or response similarity, there was a psychological refractory period effect, and it was greater when the order of stimuli was known (see Figure 4.9). Thus, the findings provided strong support for the bottleneck position.

Earlier we discussed studies (e.g., Hirst et al, 1980; Spelke et al., 1976) in which two complex tasks were performed remarkably well together. Such findings may seem inconsistent with the notion that there is a bottleneck in processing. However, studies on the psychological refractory period have the advantage of very precise assessment of the time taken to respond to any given stimulus. The coarse-grained measures obtained in studies such as those of Spelke et al. (1976) and Hirst et al. (1980) may simply be too insensitive to permit detection of a bottleneck.

Evaluation

The evidence from studies of the psychological refractory period indicates that there is a bottleneck in dual-task processing. The implication is that at least some central processing is serial in nature. However, the size of the psychological refractory period effect is typically fairly small. It is thus entirely possible that many of the processes involved in dual-task performance occur in parallel.

Multiple resources

Wickens (1984) argued that people possess multiple resources. He proposed a three-dimensional structure of human processing

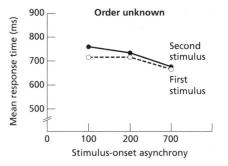
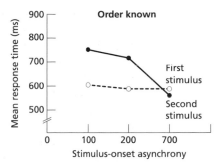

Figure 4.9. Response times to the first and second stimuli as a function of time between the onset of the stimuli (stimulus-onset asynchrony) and whether or not the order of the stimuli was known beforehand. Adapted from Pashler (1990).

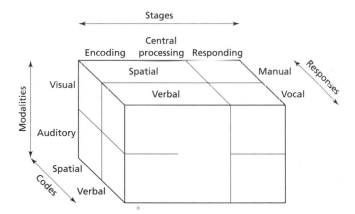

Figure 4.10. A proposed dimensional structure of human processing resources. From "Processing resources in attention" by Wickens, C.D. in *Varieties of Attention*, edited by R. Parasuraman and D.R. Davies ©1984 by Academic Press, reproduced by permission of the publisher.

resources (see Figure 4.10). According to his model, there are three successive stages of processing (encoding, central processing, and responding). Encoding involves the perceptual processing of stimuli, and typically involves the visual or auditory modalities. Encoding and central processing can involve spatial or verbal codes. Finally, responding involves manual or vocal responses. There are two key assumptions in this model:

(1) There are several pools of resources based on the distinctions among stages of processing, modalities, codes, and responses.
(2) If two tasks make use of different pools of resources, then people should be able to perform both tasks without disruption.

There is much support for this multiple-resource model, and its prediction that several kinds of task similarity influence dual-task performance. For example, we have seen that there is more interference when two tasks share the same modality (e.g., Allport et al., 1972; Treisman & Davies, 1973), or when they share the same type of response (e.g., McLeod, 1977).

Evaluation

Most findings from dual-task studies are broadly consistent with the multiple-resource model. However, there are various limitations with it. First, the model focuses only on visual and auditory inputs, but tasks could be presented in other modalities (e.g., touch). Second, there is often some disruption to performance even when two tasks make use of separate pools of resources. For example, Treisman and Davies (1973) found evidence of interference between two tasks presented in different modalities. Third, the model assumes that several tasks could be performed together without interference provided that each task made use of different pools of resources. This assumption seems unlikely to be correct. It minimises the problems associated with the higher-level processes of co-ordinating and organising the demands of tasks being carried out at the same time.

Automatic processing

A key phenomenon in studies of divided attention is the dramatic improvement of performance with practice. The commonest explanation for this phenomenon is that some processing activities become automatic as a result of prolonged practice. There is reasonable agreement on the criteria for automatic processes:

- They are fast.
- They do not reduce the capacity for performing other tasks (i.e., they demand zero attention).
- They are unavailable to consciousness.
- They are unavoidable (i.e., they always occur when an appropriate stimulus is presented).

These criteria are generally hard to satisfy. For example, the requirement that automatic processes should not need attention means that they should have no influence on the concurrent performance of an attention-demanding task. This is rarely the case (see Pashler, 1998). There are also problems with the unavoidability criterion. The *Stroop effect*, in which the naming of the colours in which words are printed is slowed down by using colour words (e.g., the word YELLOW printed in red), has often been regarded as involving unavoidable and automatic processing of the colour words. However, Kahneman and Henik (1979) found that the Stroop effect was much larger when the distracting information (i.e., the colour name) was in the same location as the to-be-named colour rather than in an adjacent location. Thus, the processes producing the Stroop effect are not entirely unavoidable.

Few processes are fully automatic in the sense of conforming to all the criteria, with numerous processes being only partially automatic. Later in this section we consider a theoretical approach (that of Norman & Shallice, 1986) which distinguishes between fully automatic and partially automatic processes.

Shiffrin and Schneider's theory

Shiffrin and Schneider (1977) and Schneider and Shiffrin (1977) distinguished between controlled and automatic processes. According to their theory, controlled processes are of limited capacity, require attention, and can be used flexibly in changing circumstances. Automatic processes suffer no capacity limitations, do not require attention, and are very hard to modify once they have been learned.

Schneider and Shiffrin (1977) tested these ideas in a series of studies. Their basic situation was one in which the participants memorised one, two, three, or four items (consonants or numbers); this was called the memory set. They were then shown a visual display containing one, two, three, or four items (consonants or numbers). Finally, they had to decide rapidly whether any item was present in both the memory set and the visual display.

Of crucial importance is the distinction between *consistent mapping* and *varied mapping*. With consistent mapping, only consonants were used as members of the memory set, and only numbers were used as distractors in the visual display (or vice versa). Consider someone who was given only numbers as members of each memory set. If a number was seen in the visual display, it had to be a member of the current memory set. According to Shiffrin and Schneider (1977), the participants' years of practice at distinguishing between letters and numbers allowed them to perform the consistent-mapping task in an automatic way. With varied mapping, the memory set consisted of a mixture of consonants and numbers, and so did the visual display. In this condition, automatic processes cannot be used.

In order to clarify this key difference between consistent mapping and varied mapping, we will consider a few examples of each:

Consistent mapping

Memory set	Visual display	Response
H B K D	4 3 B 7	Yes
H B K D	9 2 5 3	No
5 2 7 3	J 5 D C	Yes
5 2 7 3	B J G H	No

Varied mapping

Memory set	Visual display	Response
H 4 B 3	5 C G B	Yes
H 4 B 3	2 J 7 C	No
5 8 F 2	G 5 B J	Yes
5 8 F 2	6 D 1 C	No

There was a large difference in performance between the consistent and varied mapping conditions (see Figure 4.11). The number of items in the memory set and the visual display had very little effect on decision time with consistent mapping, but had a large effect with varied mapping. According to Shiffrin and Schneider (1977), performance in the consistent-mapping condition reflects the use of automatic processes operating in parallel. On the other hand, performance in the varied mapping condition reflects the use of attentionally demanding controlled processes operating in a serial fashion. The more items that have to be considered, the slower is the decision time.

The notion that automatic processes develop as the result of prolonged practice was studied by Shiffrin and Schneider (1977). They used consistent mapping, with the memory set items always being drawn from the consonants B to L, and the distractors in the visual display always being drawn from the consonants Q to Z, or vice versa. There were 2100 trials, and the dramatic improvement in performance over these trials presumably reflected the development of automatic processes.

After automatic processes had developed, there were a further 2400 trials with the reverse consistent mapping. Thus, for example, if the memory set items had been drawn from the first half of the

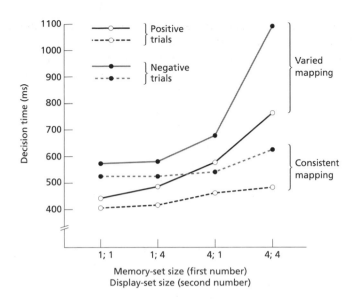

Figure
4.11. Response times on a decision task as a function of memory-set size, display-set size, and consistent versus varied mapping. Data from Shiffrin and Schneider (1977).

alphabet during the initial 2100 trials, they were taken from the second half of the alphabet during the subsequent 2400 trials. Reversing the consistent mapping greatly impaired performance; indeed, it took almost 1000 trials for performance to recover to its level at the very start of the experiment! Thus, it is hard to abandon automatic processes that have outlived their usefulness.

What are the relative advantages and disadvantages of automatic and controlled processes? The greatest advantages of automatic over attentional processes are that they operate much more rapidly, and that many automatic processes can take place at the same time. However, automatic processes are at a disadvantage when there is a change in the environment or in the prevailing conditions, because they lack the adaptability and flexibility of controlled processes. The fact that we possess both automatic and controlled processes allows us to respond rapidly and appropriately to most situations.

Evaluation
The work of Shiffrin and Schneider (1977) and of Schneider and Shiffrin (1977) is important at the theoretical and experimental levels. Theoretically, they drew a clear distinction between automatic and controlled processes, and this distinction has proved very influential. Experimentally, they provided evidence that the speed of performance can be much affected by whether it is based on automatic or controlled processes.

On the negative side, there is a puzzling discrepancy between theory and data with respect to the identification of automaticity. The theoretical assumption that automatic processes operate in parallel and place no demands on capacity means there should be a slope of zero (i.e., a horizontal line) in the line relating decision speed to the number of items in the memory set and/or in the visual display when automatic processes are used. In fact, decision speed was slower when the memory set and the visual display both contained several items even when automatic processes were allegedly being used.

Shiffrin and Schneider's theoretical approach describes rather than explains. The claim that some processes become automatic with practice does not tell us what is actually happening. Practice may simply lead to a speeding up of the processes involved in performing a task, or it may lead to a change in the nature of the processes themselves. Cheng (1985) argued that participants in the consistent mapping conditions did not search through the memory set and visual display looking for a match. If, for example, they knew that any consonant in the visual display had to be an item from the memory set, then they simply scanned the visual display looking for a consonant without any regard to which consonants were actually in the memory set. Cheng (1985) was probably right, but we cannot tell for sure on the basis of the data provided by Shiffrin and Schneider.

Instance theory

Shiffrin and Schneider (1977) did not really explain *how* automatic processes develop through practice. Logan (1988) put forward his instance theory to fill this gap. This theory was based on five main assumptions:

(1) Separate memory traces are stored away each time a stimulus is presented and processed.
(2) Practice with the same stimulus leads to the storage of increased information about the stimulus, and about what to do with it.
(3) This increase in the knowledge base with practice permits rapid retrieval of relevant information when the appropriate stimulus is presented.
(4) "Automaticity is memory retrieval: performance is automatic when it is based on a single-step direct-access retrieval of past solutions from memory" (Logan, 1988, p. 493).

(5) In the absence of practice, responding to a stimulus requires thought and the application of rules; after prolonged practice, the appropriate response is stored in memory and can be accessed very rapidly.

Logan (1988, p. 519) summarised instance theory as follows: "Novice performance is limited by a lack of knowledge rather than by a lack of resources . . . Only the knowledge base changes with practice." Logan is probably right in his basic assumption that an understanding of automatic, expert performance will require detailed consideration of the knowledge acquired with practice, rather than simply processing changes.

Evaluation

Logan's theoretical approach provides a useful account of many aspects of automatic processing. Automatic processes are fast because they require only the retrieval of "past solutions" from long-term memory. Such processes have little or no effect on the processing capacity available to perform other tasks, because the retrieval of heavily over-learned information is fairly effortless. Finally, there is no conscious awareness of automatic processes because few processes intervene between the presentation of a stimulus and the retrieval of the appropriate response.

Norman and Shallice's theory

Norman and Shallice (1986) distinguished between fully automatic and partially automatic processes. They identified three levels of functioning:

- Fully automatic processing controlled by *schemas* (organised plans).
- Partially automatic processing involving contention scheduling without deliberate direction or conscious control; contention scheduling is used to resolve conflicts among schemas.
- Deliberate control by a supervisory attentional system; Baddeley (1986) argued that this system resembled the central executive of the working memory system (see Chapter 6).

According to Norman and Shallice (1986), fully automatic processes occur with very little conscious awareness of the processes involved. However, such automatic processes would often disrupt behaviour if left entirely to their own devices. As a result, there is an automatic conflict resolution process known as contention scheduling. This selects one of the available schemas or organised plans on the basis of environmental information and current priorities when two competing schemas are activated at the same time. There is generally more conscious awareness of the partially automatic processes involving contention scheduling than of fully automatic processes. Finally, the higher-level supervisory system is involved in decision making and troubleshooting, and it permits flexible responding in novel situations. This system may well be located in the frontal lobes (see Chapter 6).

Shallice and Burgess (1996) argued that there are several different processes carried out by the supervisory system. For example, consider how we cope with a novel situation. First of all, we need to *construct* a new schema to control behaviour. After that, it is necessary to *implement* or make use of the new schema. Finally, it is necessary to *monitor* for errors to check that the appropriate schema is being used.

Evidence supporting the distinction between construction and implementation of schemas was reported by Burgess and Shallice (1996). Patients with frontal lesions were given the Brixton spatial anticipation test, on which the participants have to predict which of various circles will be filled on each one of a series of cards. The circle that was filled was determined by various rules, and so successful performance of the task involved constructing a schema corresponding to the rule currently in operation. The errors made by the frontal patients indicated that some of them had problems with schema construction, whereas others had problems mainly with schema implementation. This *double dissociation* suggests that construction and implementation are separate processes.

Evaluation

The theoretical approach of Norman and Shallice (1986) includes the interesting notion that there are two separate control systems: contention scheduling and the supervisory system. This contrasts with the views of many previous theorists that there is a single control system. The approach of Norman and Shallice is preferable, because it provides an explanation for the fact that some processes are fully automatic, but many others are only partially automatic. What remains for the future is to clarify precisely which processes are carried out by the supervisory system, and to determine whether it forms a single unitary system.

Action slips

Action slips involve the performance of actions that were not intended. Attentional failures are usually involved in action slips, and this is recognised in the notion of "absent-mindedness". There are two main ways of investigating action slips: (1) diary studies, and (2) laboratory studies. We will consider these two approaches in turn.

Diary studies

Reason (1979) asked 35 people to keep diaries of their action slips over a 2-week period. Over 400 action slips were reported, most belonging to five major categories. Forty per cent of the slips involved *storage failures*, in which intentions and actions were forgotten or recalled incorrectly. Here is one of Reason's (1979, p. 74) examples of a storage failure: "I started to pour a second kettle of boiling water into a teapot of freshly made tea. I had no recollection of having just made it."

A further 20% of the errors were *test failures*, in which the progress of a planned sequence was not monitored adequately at crucial junctures or choice points. Here is an example from Reason (1979, p. 73): "I meant to get my car out, but as I passed through the back porch on my way to the garage I stopped to put on my Wellington boots and gardening jacket as if to work in the garden." *Subroutine failures* accounted for another 18% of the errors; these involved insertions, omissions, or re-orderings of the various stages in an action sequence. Reason (1979, p. 73) gave this example: "I sat down to do some work and before starting to write I put my hand up to my face to take my glasses off, but my fingers snapped together rather abruptly because I hadn't been wearing them in the first place."

The remaining two categories occurred only rarely in the diary study. *Discrimination failures* (11%) consisted of failures to discriminate between objects (e.g., mistaking shaving cream for toothpaste). *Programme assembly failures* (5%) involved inappropriate combinations of actions. For example, "I unwrapped a sweet, put the paper in my mouth, and threw the sweet into the waste bucket" (Reason, 1979, p. 72).

Evaluation

Diary studies such as that of Reason (1979) provide valuable information about the action slips occurring in everyday life. However, there are various reasons for not attaching much significance to the reported percentage for each category of action slip. First, the figures are based on those action slips that were detected, and we simply do not know how many cases of each kind of slip were never detected. Second, to interpret the percentages, we need to know the number of occasions on which each kind of slip might have occurred but did not. Thus, the small number of discrimination failures may reflect either good discrimination or a relative lack of situations requiring fine discrimination.

Another problem is that two superficially similar action slips may be categorised together, even though the underlying mechanisms are actually different. Grudin (1983) carried out videotape analyses of substitution errors in typing in which the key next to the intended key was struck. Some substitution errors involved the correct finger moving in the wrong direction, but others involved an incorrect key being pressed by the finger that normally strikes it. According to Grudin (1983), the former kind of error is due to faulty execution of an action, whereas the latter is due to faulty assignment of the finger. We would need more information than is usually available in diary studies to identify such subtle differences in underlying processes.

Laboratory studies

In view of the problems with diary studies, it might be argued that laboratory studies are preferable. However, potential disadvantages with the laboratory approach were identified by Sellen and Norman (1992). They pointed out that many naturally occurring action slips occur "when a person is internally preoccupied or distracted, when both the intended actions and the wrong actions are automatic, and when one is doing familiar tasks in familiar surroundings. Laboratory situations offer completely the opposite conditions. Typically, subjects are given an unfamiliar, highly contrived task to accomplish in a strange environment. Most subjects arrive motivated to perform well and . . . are not given to internal preoccupation . . . In short, the typical laboratory environment is possibly the least likely place where we are likely to see truly spontaneous, absent-minded errors" (p. 334).

In spite of the problems, some interesting findings have been obtained from laboratory studies. For example, Hay and Jacoby (1996) argued that action slips are most likely to occur when two conditions are satisfied:

(1) The correct response is *not* the strongest or most habitual one.

(2) Attention is not fully applied to the task of selecting the correct response.

For example, suppose you are looking for your house key. If it is not in its usual place, you are likely to waste time by looking there first of all. If you are late for an important appointment as well, you may find it hard to focus your attention on thinking about other places in which the key might have been put. As a result, you may spend a lot of time looking in several wrong places.

Hay and Jacoby (1996) tested these ideas in a study in which the participants were given a memory test on which they had to complete paired associates (e.g., knee: b_n_) on the basis of a previous learning task. Sometimes the correct response from the learning task was also the strongest response (e.g., bend), and sometimes the correct response was *not* the strongest response (e.g., bone). The participants had either 1 second or 3 seconds to respond. Hay and Jacoby (1996) argued that action slips would be most likely when the correct response was not the strongest one, and when the response had to be made rapidly. As predicted, the error rate in that condition was 45% against a mean of only 30% in the other conditions.

Why is the research by Hay and Jacoby (1996) of importance? As they themselves pointed out, "Very little has been done to examine action . . . slips by directly manipulating the likelihood of their occurrence in experimental situations . . . we not only manipulated action slips, but also teased apart the roles played by automatic and intentional responding in their production" (p. 1332).

Robertson et al. (1997) studied patients with traumatic brain injury causing damage to the frontal lobes and the white matter of the brain. These patients had severe problems with attention and concentration, and so might be expected to produce numerous action slips. Robertson et al. (1997) devised a task (the Sustained Attention to Response Task), in which a long sequence of random digits is presented, and participants respond with a key press to all digits except 3. Failures to withhold responses to the digit 3 are regarded as action slips. As predicted, the patients produced many more action slips than normals (30% vs. 12%, respectively). Within the patient group, there was a correlation of +.58 between pathological severity of their symptoms and the number of action slips produced, suggesting that those patients with most damage to the frontal lobes were most vulnerable to action slips.

Theories of action slips

Several theories of action slips have been proposed, including those of Reason (1992) and Sellen and Norman (1992). In spite of differences between these theories, Reason (1992) and Sellen and Norman (1992) agree that there are two modes of control:

- *An automatic mode*: Motor performance is controlled by schemas or organised plans; the schema that determines performance is the strongest one available.
- *A conscious control mode*: This involves some central processor or attentional system; this mode of control can override the automatic control mode.

The advantages of automatic control are that it is fast and that it permits attentional resources to be devoted to other processing activities. Its disadvantages are that it is inflexible, and that action slips occur when there is too much reliance on this mode of control. Conscious control has the advantages that it is less prone to error than automatic control, and that it responds flexibly to environmental changes. However, it operates fairly slowly, and is an effortful process.

Action slips occur when someone is in the automatic mode of control and the strongest available schema or motor programme is the wrong one. The involvement of the automatic mode of control can be seen in many of Reason's (1979) action slips. One common type of action slip involves repeating an action because the first action has been forgotten (e.g., brushing one's teeth twice in quick succession; trying to start a car engine that has already been started). As we saw earlier in the chapter, unattended information is held very briefly and then forgotten. When brushing one's teeth or starting a car occurs in the automatic mode of control, it would be predicted that later memory for what has been done should be very poor. As a result, the action would often be repeated.

Schema theory

Sellen and Norman (1992) proposed a schema theory, according to which actions are determined by hierarchically arranged schemas or organised plans. Note that the term schemas is being used in a different way from that typically found in theories of memory (see Chapter 13). The highest-level schema represents the overall intention or goal (e.g., buying a present), and the lower-level schemas correspond to the actions involved in achieving that goal (e.g., taking money out of the bank; taking the train to the shopping centre). Any given schema determines action when its level of activation is high enough, and when the appropriate triggering conditions exist (e.g., getting into the train when it stops at the station). The activation level of the schemas is determined by current intentions and by the immediate situation.

Why do action slips occur according to schema theory? There are a number of possible reasons. First, there may be errors in the formation of an intention. Second, there may be faulty activation of a schema, leading to activation of the wrong schema, or to loss of activation in the right schema. Third, the situation may lead to faulty triggering of active schemas, leading to action being determined by the wrong schema.

Many of the action slips recorded by Reason (1979) can be related to schema theory. For example, discrimination failures can lead to errors in the formation of an intention, and storage failures for intentions can produce faulty triggering of active schemas.

Evaluation

It is possible that action slips are special events produced by their own mechanisms. However, it is probably preferable to argue (as is done within schema theory) that action slips are "the normal by-products of the design of the human action system" (Sellen & Norman, 1992, p. 318). In other words, there is a single action system that normally functions well, but occasionally produces errors in the form of action slips.

Recent theories of action slips emphasise the notion of automatic processing. However, automatic processes are hard to define. More needs to be discovered about the factors leading to automatic processes being used at the wrong time. Most theories predict correctly that action slips should occur most often with highly practised activities, because automatic processes are most likely to be used with such activities. However, action slips are much more common with actions of minor importance than those regarded as very important. For example, many circus performers carry out well-practised actions, but the element of danger ensures that they do not make use of the automatic mode of control. Most theories do not provide an adequate account of such phenomena.

Finally, several theorists have argued that insufficient use of the conscious control mode is involved in most action slips. However, we know relatively little about the attentional system associated with the conscious control mode, and it is by no means clear that only a single attentional system is involved.

Summary: Attention and pattern recognition

- *Focused auditory attention*: We can follow one auditory message and ignore another message by making use of physical differences (e.g., sex of speaker) between them. According to Broadbent's filter theory, a filter allows one auditory message at a time through to a limited-capacity mechanism beyond the filter on the basis of its physical characteristics. In fact, there is more processing of unattended messages than predicted by Broadbent. According to Treisman's attenuation theory, the processing of unattended information is attenuated or reduced. According to Deutsch and Deutsch, all stimuli are analysed fully, with the most important or relevant stimulus determining the response. Experimental and neurophysiological evidence suggests that there is fuller processing of attended than of unattended auditory stimuli. This is more consistent with attenuation theory than with Deutsch and Deutsch's late-selection theory.
- *Focused visual attention*: Research on attentionally disordered patients suggests that visual attention involves three separate components: disengagement of attention, shifting of attention, and engaging or locking of attention. In addition, there is an anterior attention system, which co-ordinates the various aspects of visual attention. It has been argued that focused visual attention resembles a spotlight or zoom lens. There is evidence that the attentional spotlight can shift to a different spatial location in the absence of an eye movement. According to the spotlight and zoom-lens models, visual attention is directed towards a given region in the visual field. However, visual attention is often directed to objects rather than to a particular region. There is neurophysiological evidence suggesting that unattended visual stimuli are processed less thoroughly than attended ones. However, normals

and patients with neglect often process the meaning of unattended visual stimuli. Visual search involves two processes. The first process is fast and efficient, whereas the second process is slower and less efficient. Speed of visual search depends on the nature of the target and of the distractors.

- *Divided attention*: Dual-task performance is typically best when the two tasks are dissimilar, highly practised, and easy. Many of the findings from dual-task studies can be accounted for by central capacity theories (e.g., Kahneman, 1973). However, the nature of the central capacity is usually poorly specified, and such theories cannot readily explain the importance of task similarity in determining dual-task performance. Studies on the psychological refractory period indicate the existence of a central bottleneck in which only serial processing is possible.

- *Automatic processing*: In principle, automatic processes are fast, demand zero attention, and are unavoidable. However, all these criteria are rarely satisfied. Shiffrin and Schneider (1977) distinguished between automatic and controlled processes, and showed that automatic processes develop as the result of prolonged practice. They also showed that automatic processes lack the adaptability and flexibility of controlled processes. Shiffrin and Schneider did not explain how automatic processes develop through practice. Logan (1988) put forward his instance theory to fill the gap. According to this theory, increased information is stored in long-term memory as a result of practice, and this permits rapid access to the appropriate responses to stimuli. Norman and Shallice distinguished between fully and partially automatic processes. The notion that many processes are only partially automatic is consistent with the finding that relatively few processes satisfy all the criteria for automaticity.

- *Action slips*. Diary studies indicate that many action slips involve storage failures, test failures, or subroutine failures. A problem with diary studies is that we do not know how many action slips were undetected. Laboratory studies suggest that action slips are most likely to occur when the correct response is not the strongest one, and attention is not fully applied to the task of selecting the correct response. Theoretically, it has been argued that there are two modes of control: (1) an automatic, schema-driven mode; and (2) a conscious control mode. According to schema theory, action slips can occur because of errors in the formation of an intention or faulty activation of a schema. There is limited understanding of the processes involved in automatic and controlled processing, and more needs to be discovered about the factors leading to automatic processes being used at the wrong time.

Essay questions

(1) Describe TWO theories of focused auditory attention, and discuss their strengths and limitations.
(2) To what extent does focused visual attention resemble a spotlight or zoom lens?
(3) What determines how well we can perform two tasks at the same time?
(4) What are action slips, and why do they occur?

Further reading

Gazzaniga, M.S., Ivry, R.B., & Mangun, G.R. (1998). *Cognitive neuroscience: The biology of the mind*. New York: W.W. Norton. Chapter 6 provides detailed coverage of what is currently known about the neurophysiology of attention.

Pashler, H. (1998). *Attention*. Hove, UK: Psychology Press. The chapters in this edited book provide thorough accounts of the main topics in attention.

Styles, E.A. (1997). *The psychology of attention*. Hove, UK: Psychology Press. This book contains a readable introduction to theory and research in attention.

Short-term memory and learning 5

Introduction

This chapter and the next are concerned with human memory. There is much to cover. Human memory ranges from remembering telephone numbers for a few seconds to remembering for a lifetime how to ride a bicycle, and from remembering nonsense syllables to the plot of a long novel.

Theories of memory generally consider both the *structure* of the memory system and the *processes* operating within that structure. Structure refers to the way in which the memory system is organised, and process refers to the activities occurring within the memory system. Structure and process are both important, but some theorists emphasise only one of them in their theoretical formulations.

Learning and memory involve a series of stages. Those stages occurring during the presentation of the learning material are known as "encoding". This is the first stage. As a result of encoding, some information is stored within the memory system. Thus, storage is the second stage. The third, and final, stage is retrieval, which involves recovering or extracting stored information from the memory system.

The distinctions between structure and process, and among encoding, storage, and retrieval, are important. However, there is no structure without process, or retrieval without previous encoding and storage. It is only when processes operate on the essentially passive structures of the memory system that it becomes active and of use. As Tulving and Thomson (1973, p. 359) pointed out, "Only that can be retrieved that has been stored, and . . . how it can be retrieved depends on how it was stored."

Multi-store model

Several memory theorists (e.g., Atkinson & Shiffrin, 1968) have described the basic architecture of the memory system. It is possible

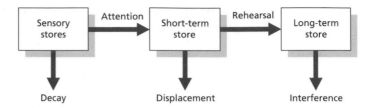

Figure 5.1. The multi-store model of memory.

Sensory stores — Attention → Short-term store — Rehearsal → Long-term store

Decay | Displacement | Interference

to identify a multi-store model on the basis of the common features of their approaches. Three types of memory store were proposed:

- *Sensory stores*, each of which holds information very briefly and is modality specific (limited to one sensory modality).
- *Short-term store* of very limited capacity.
- *Long-term store* of essentially unlimited capacity, which can hold information over extremely long periods of time.

The multi-store proposed by Atkinson and Shiffrin (1968) is shown in Figure 5.1. Environmental information is initially received by the sensory stores. These stores are modality specific (e.g., vision, hearing). Information is held very briefly in the sensory stores, with some being attended to and processed further by the short-term store. Some of the information processed in the short-term store is transferred to the long-term store. Long-term storage of information often depends on rehearsal (according to Atkinson and Shiffrin, 1968), with a direct relationship between the amount of rehearsal in the short-term store and the strength of the stored memory trace.

There is much overlap between the areas of attention and memory. Broadbent's (1958) theory of attention (see Chapter 4) was an important influence on the multi-store approach to memory. For example, there is a clear resemblance between the notion of a sensory store and his "buffer" store, and both theories emphasise the severe limitations on processing capacity.

Within the multi-store approach, the memory stores form the basic structure, and processes such as attention and rehearsal control the flow of information between them. However, the main emphasis within this approach was on structure.

Sensory stores

Our senses are constantly bombarded with information, most of which does not receive any attention. If you are sitting in a chair as you read this, then tactile information from that part of your body in contact with the chair is probably available. However, you have probably been unaware of that tactile information until now. Information in every sense modality persists briefly after the end of stimulation. This is useful, because it aids the task of extracting its key aspects for further analysis.

Classic work on the visual or *iconic store* was carried out by Sperling (1960). When he presented his participants with a visual array containing three rows of four letters each for 50 ms, and asked them to recall as many letters as possible, he discovered that they could usually report only four or five of them. However, most participants claimed that they had actually seen many more letters than they had been able to report.

Sperling (1960) wondered whether the above puzzling discrepancy between performance and self-report was due to the fact that visual information was available after the offset of the stimulus, but so briefly that the information had faded before most of it could be reported. He explored this hypothesis by asking the participants to report only one-third of the presented information, using a cueing tone to signal which row was to be reported. The tone was presented either 0.1 s before the onset of the visual display (which lasted 50 ms) or at intervals of up to 1 s after stimulus offset. Since the three rows were tested at random, Sperling could estimate the total amount of information available to each participant by multiplying the number of items recalled by three. When the tone was presented immediately before or after the onset of the display, about 9 letters seemed to be available, but this dropped to 6 letters when the tone was heard 0.3 s after the presentation of the display, and it fell to only 4.5 letters with an interval of 1 s. Thus, there is a form of visual storage that fades rapidly (within about 0.5 s according to most estimates).

It has often been assumed that information in iconic storage is held in a relatively raw and uninterpreted form. This is supported by the finding that participants can efficiently select items for report on the basis of size or colour, but not category membership (e.g., letters vs. numbers). However, Butler (1974) found that participants do better when the letters in non-cued rows resemble English words than when they do not, suggesting that iconic information is not necessarily in an unanalysed form.

How useful is iconic storage? Haber (1983) claimed it is irrelevant to normal perception, except when trying to read in a lightning storm! His argument was that the icon formed from one visual fixation would be rapidly masked by the next fixation. Haber was mistaken. He assumed that the icon is created at the *offset* of a visual stimulus, but it is actually created at its *onset* (Coltheart, 1983). Thus, even with a continuously changing visual world, iconic information can still be used. The mechanisms responsible for visual perception always operate on the icon rather than directly on the visual environment.

The sensory store in the auditory modality is known as the *echoic store*. The echoic store is a transient store holding relatively unprocessed input. For example, suppose someone reading a newspaper is asked a question. The person addressed will sometimes ask, "What did you say?", but then realise that he or she does know what has been said. This "playback" facility depends on the echoic store.

Treisman (1964) asked people to shadow (repeat back aloud) the message presented to one ear while ignoring a second identical message presented to the other ear. When the second or non-shadowed message preceded the shadowed message, the two messages were only recognised as the same when within 2 s of each other. This suggests the temporal duration of unattended auditory information in echoic storage is about 2 s. However, Darwin, Turvey, and Crowder (1972) argued that the duration was rather longer. They presented different sets of auditory items at the same time to three spatial locations. As Sperling (1960) had done in the visual modality, Darwin et al. (1972) used partial report, in which a visual cue indicated which set of items was to be reported. The key finding was that partial report produced better recall than whole report even with an interval of 4 s between presentation and cue. Thus, some information remains within the echoic store for at least 4 s.

Short- and long-term stores

Trying to remember a telephone number for a few seconds is an everyday example of the use of the *short-term store*. It shows two key characteristics usually attributed to this store:

- Very limited capacity (only about seven digits can be remembered).
- Fragility of storage, as any distraction usually causes forgetting.

The capacity of short-term memory has been assessed by span measures and by the recency effect in free recall. Digit span is a span

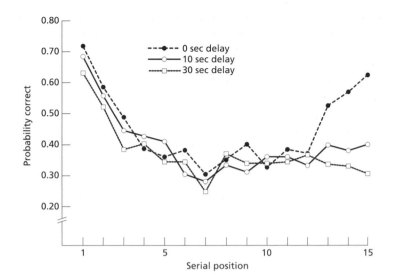

Figure 5.2. Free recall as a function of serial position and duration of the interpolated task. Adapted from Glanzer and Cunitz (1966).

measure, in which participants repeat back a series of random digits in the correct order when they have heard them all. The span of immediate memory is usually "seven plus or minus two" whether the units are numbers, letters, or words (Miller, 1956). Miller claimed that about seven chunks (integrated pieces or units of information) could be held in short-term memory. For example, "IBM" is one chunk for those familiar with the company name International Business Machines, but three chunks for everyone else. However, the span in chunks is less with larger chunks (e.g., eight-word phrases) than with smaller chunks (e.g., one-syllable words; Simon, 1974).

The *recency effect* in *free recall* (recalling the items in any order) refers to the finding that the last few items in a list are usually much better remembered in immediate recall than are the items from the middle of the list. Counting backwards for only 10 s between the end of list presentation and the start of recall mainly affects the recency effect (Glanzer & Cunitz, 1966; see Figure 5.2). The two or three words in the recency effect may be in the short-term store at the end of list presentation, and thus especially vulnerable. However, Bjork and Whitten (1974) found there was still a recency effect in free recall when the participants counted backwards for 12 s after each item in the list was presented. According to Atkinson and Shiffrin (1968), this should have eliminated the recency effect. The findings can be explained by analogy to looking along a row of telephone poles. The closer poles are more distinct than the ones further away, just as the more recent list words are more discriminable than the others (Glenberg, 1987).

You may have noticed in Figure 5.2 that recall was better for the first few items than for those in the middle of the list. This is known as the *primacy effect*. According to Atkinson and Shiffrin (1968), rehearsal plays a key role in determining long-term memory, and so the primacy effect could be explained by assuming that the first few list items receive more rehearsal than do later ones. Evidence for this was obtained by Rundus and Atkinson (1970). Their overt rehearsal technique allowed the participants to rehearse any of the list items, but required them to rehearse aloud. They obtained the usual primacy effect in free recall, and also found that the first few items did receive a disproportionately large amount of rehearsal. This suggests that the primacy effect is due to extra rehearsal. However, other factors are also involved. When steps were taken to equate the amount of rehearsal given to each list item, the primacy effect was reduced but not eliminated (Fischler, Rundus, & Atkinson, 1970).

Forgetting

How is information forgotten or lost from short-term memory? One possibility is that forgetting is due to *displacement*. If we think of the short-term store as resembling a box of limited capacity, then it could be argued that new items can only be entered into the box by displacing or removing one or more of the items currently in it. The problem with this approach is that it assumes that we have very limited short-term memory capacity because of structural limitations. However, it is much more likely that short-term memory capacity is limited because of processing limitations, especially attentional ones.

Some of the research has focused on whether forgetting from short-term memory involves interference or decay. Waugh and Norman (1965) compared these explanations in a study in which the participants heard a series of digits followed by a probe digit, with the task being to recall the digit that had previously followed the probe digit. The number of intervening digits was varied, and the digits were presented either rapidly or slowly. Recall decreased as the number of intervening digits increased, but was unaffected by the rate of presentation. These findings suggested that interference in the form of the intervening digits caused forgetting, but that time-based decay was not a factor.

Many of the key findings come from the Brown–Peterson paradigm. In this paradigm, three consonants (e.g., F B M) are presented, followed immediately by a three-digit number. The participant's task is to count backwards by threes from the number until the signal is given to recall the consonants. Consonant recall is generally almost 100% with no retention interval, but falls to only 10–20% with a retention interval of 18 s.

Forgetting in the Brown–Peterson paradigm may involve interference. Digits are clearly different from consonants, but nevertheless they may be sufficiently *similar* to produce some interference. Evidence supporting that point of view was reported by Reitman (1971). The participants carried out either a syllable detection task or a tone detection task during the retention interval. Those who performed the syllable detection task had much lower recall than those who performed the tone detection task, presumably because syllables interfered much more than tones.

Another possibility is that forgetting occurs in the Brown–Peterson paradigm because attention is diverted away from the to-be-remembered information. This explanation is rather similar to decay theory, because it assumes that forgetting can occur simply because of the passage of time. Watkins et al. (1973) obtained evidence favouring the diversion-of-attention theory. Some of their participants had to listen to musical notes, then hum them, and finally identify them, whereas others simply had to listen to the notes. Those who had to hum and identify the notes showed much forgetting, whereas those who merely listened showed no forgetting. Watkins et al. (1973) argued that forgetting occurred because the requirements to hum and identify the notes diverted attention away from the to-be-remembered information.

Baddeley (1990) obtained evidence that decay may also be involved in forgetting in the Brown–Peterson paradigm. The participants were only presented with a single set of letters in order to minimise any interference effects. The set of letters was longer than in most other studies in order to ensure that forgetting occurred. There was some forgetting, but it was fairly modest and levelled off within 5 s. Baddeley (1990, p. 48) concluded as follows: "Something like trace decay occurs in the Brown–Peterson task, but is complete within five seconds, and is certainly not sufficiently large as to readily explain the substantial forgetting that occurs in the standard paradigm."

In sum, several factors seem to be involved in forgetting from short-term memory. There is considerable evidence for interference, but diversion of attention and decay are also probably involved.

Long-term memory

It has already been mentioned that rehearsal was regarded during the 1960s as the main way in which information enters long-term memory. In contrast to the short-term memory store, the capacity of the long-term memory store is essentially infinite. Most information that is stored in the long-term memory store remains there. However, it may become inaccessible over time because of interference from other information that has been learned.

Separate stores

Probably the most important theoretical assumption of the multi-store model is the notion that there are separate short-term and long-term memory stores. Convincing evidence comes from studies of brain-damaged patients. The logic is as follows. Suppose that there are separate short-term and long-term memory stores in somewhat different areas of the brain. We might then expect to find some brain-damaged patients with damage to the area of the brain involved in short-term memory but not long-term memory, and vice versa. Thus, there might be some patients with good short-term memory but poor long-term memory, and others with good long-term memory but poor short-term memory. This pattern is known as a *double dissociation*, and it has been found. Amnesic patients have fairly intact short-term memory but impaired long-term memory (see Chapter 6). The reverse problem is rare, but some cases have been reported. For example, K.F. had no problem with long-term learning and recall, but his digit span was greatly impaired, and he had a recency effect of only one item under some circumstances (Shallice & Warrington, 1970). However, K.F. did not perform badly on all short-term memory tasks (see next section).

Evaluation

The multi-store model provided a systematic account of the structures and processes involved in memory. The conceptual distinction between three kinds of memory stores (sensory stores, short-term store, and long-term store) makes sense. In order to justify the existence of three qualitatively different types of memory store, we must show major differences among them. Precisely this has been done. The memory stores differ from each other in the following ways:

- Temporal duration.
- Storage capacity.
- Forgetting mechanism(s).
- Effects of brain damage.

There are several limitations with the multi-store model. First, the account given of the short-term store is very oversimplified. It was assumed that it is unitary, and so always operates in a single, uniform way. Evidence that the short-term store is not unitary was reported by Warrington and Shallice (1972). K.F.'s short-term forgetting of auditory letters was much greater than his forgetting of visual stimuli. Shallice and Warrington (1974) then found that K.F.'s short-term memory deficit was limited to verbal materials such as letters, words, and digits, and did not extend to meaningful sounds (e.g., telephones ringing). Thus, it was only part of short-term memory (which Shallice and Warrington, 1974, referred to as the "auditory–verbal short-term store") that was impaired.

Second, the multi-store model provided an oversimplified view of long-term memory. There is an amazing wealth of information stored in long-term memory, and it is simply not the case that all this knowledge is stored within a single long-term memory store (see Chapter 6).

Third, Logie (1999) pointed out that the model assumes that the short-term store acts as a gateway between the sensory stores and long-term memory (see Figure 5.1). However, the information processed in the short-term store has already made contact with information stored in long-term memory. For example, our ability to engage in verbal rehearsal of visually presented words depends on prior contact with stored information about pronunciation. Thus, access to long-term memory occurs *before* information is processed in short-term memory.

Fourth, most multi-store theorists assumed that the main way in which information is transferred to long-term memory is via rehearsal in the short term store. In fact, the role of rehearsal was exaggerated by multi-store theorists: We possess enormous amounts of information in long-term memory, even though most of us rarely rehearse the information presented to us. In addition, rehearsal often has surprisingly small effects on long-term memory (e.g., Glenberg, Smith, & Green, 1977; see later in the chapter). More generally, multi-store theorists focused too much on structural aspects of memory rather than on memory processes

Working memory

One of the reasons why the multi-store model fell into disfavour was because its account of short-term memory was oversimplified. Baddeley and Hitch (1974) argued that the concept of the short-term store should be replaced with that of working memory. According to them, the working memory system consists of three components:

- *Central executive*: This is a modality-free component of limited capacity; it is like attention.
- *Articulatory or phonological loop*: This holds information briefly in a phonological (i.e., speech-based) form.
- *Visuospatial scratch (or sketch) pad*: This is specialised for spatial and/or visual coding.

The most important component is the central executive. It has limited capacity, and is used when dealing with most cognitive tasks. The phonological loop and the visuospatial sketchpad are slave systems used by the central executive for specific purposes. The phonological loop preserves the order in which words are presented, and the visuospatial sketchpad is used for the storage and manipulation of spatial and visual information.

The working memory model can be used to predict whether or not two tasks can be performed successfully at the same time. Every component of the working memory system has limited capacity, and is relatively independent of the other components. Two predictions follow:

(1) If two tasks make use of the same component, they cannot be performed successfully together.
(2) If two tasks make use of different components, it should be possible to perform them as well together as separately.

Numerous dual-task studies have been carried out on the basis of these assumptions. For example, Robbins et al. (1996) considered the involvement of the three components of working memory in the selection of chess moves by weaker and stronger players. The main task was to select continuation moves from various chess positions while performing one of the following concurrent tasks:

- Repetitive tapping: This was the control condition.
- Random number generation: This involved the central executive.

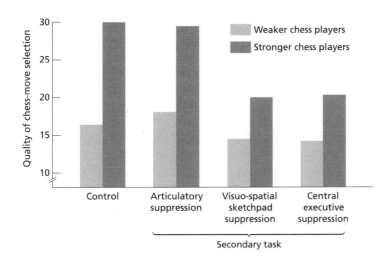

Figure 5.3. Effects of secondary tasks on quality of chess-move selection in stronger and weaker players. Adapted from Robbins et al. (1996).

- Pressing keys on a keypad in a clockwise fashion: This used the visuospatial sketchpad.
- Rapid repetition of the word see-saw: This used the phonological loop.

The findings are shown in Figure 5.3. Random number generation and pressing keys in a clockwise fashion both reduced the quality of the chess moves selected. Thus, selecting chess moves involves the central executive and the visuospatial sketchpad. However, rapid word repetition did not affect the quality of chess moves, and so the phonological loop is not involved in selecting chess moves. The effects of the various concurrent tasks were similar on stronger and weaker players, suggesting that both groups use the working memory system in the same way.

Phonological loop

Most is known about the phonological loop, which was studied by Baddeley et al. (1975). They asked their participants to recall immediately sets of five words in the correct order. Their ability to do this was better with short words than with long ones. Further investigation of this *word-length effect* showed that the participants could recall as many words as they could read out loud in 2 s. This suggested that the capacity of the articulatory loop is determined by time duration in the same way as a tape loop.

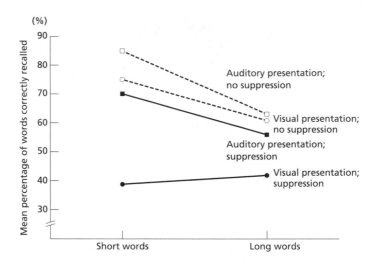

Figure 5.4. Immediate word recall as a function of modality of presentation (visual vs. auditory), presence versus absence of articulatory suppression, and word length. Adapted from Baddeley et al. (1975).

(%)

Mean percentage of words correctly recalled

90
80
70
60
50
40
30

Auditory presentation; no suppression

Visual presentation; no suppression

Auditory presentation; suppression

Visual presentation; suppression

Short words   Long words

The phonological loop is more complex than was assumed by Baddeley and Hitch (1974). For example, although Baddeley et al. (1975) found that articulatory suppression eliminated the word-length effect with visual presentation, it did *not* do so with auditory presentation (see Figure 5.4). Vallar and Baddeley (1984) studied a patient, P.V., who did not seem to use the articulatory loop when tested on memory span. However, her memory span for spoken letters was worse when the letters were phonologically similar (i.e., they sounded alike). Thus, PV seemed to be processing phonologically (in a speech-based manner), but *without* making use of articulation.

Baddeley (1986, 1990) drew a distinction between a phonological or speech-based store and an articulatory control process (see Figure 5.5). According to Baddeley, the phonological loop consists of:

- A passive phonological store directly concerned with speech perception.
- An articulatory process linked to speech production that gives access to the phonological store.

According to this revised account, words that are presented auditorily are processed differently from those presented visually. Auditory presentation of words produces *direct* access to the phonological store regardless of whether the articulatory control process is used. However, this direct access would not produce the word-length effect unless the auditorily presented words were rehearsed. In

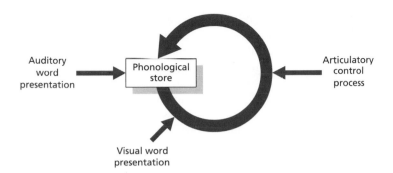

Figure 5.5.
Phonological loop system as envisaged by Baddeley (1990).

Auditory word presentation → Phonological store

Articulatory control process

Visual word presentation

contrast, visual presentation of words only permits *indirect* access to the phonological store through subvocal articulation.

This revised account makes sense of many findings. Suppose the word-length effect observed by Baddeley et al. (1975) depends on the rate of articulatory rehearsal. Articulatory suppression eliminates the word-length effect with visual presentation because access to the phonological store is prevented. It does *not* affect the word-length effect with auditory presentation, because information about the words enters the phonological store directly.

Why was P.V.'s letter span with auditory presentation affected by phonological similarity even though she did not use subvocal articulation? The effects of phonological similarity occurred because the auditorily presented letters entered *directly* into the phonological store even in the absence of subvocal articulation. It is likely that P.V. has a deficient phonological store, and she does not use the articulatory control process because there is little information in the store to rehearse (G. Quinn, pers. comm.).

Smith and Jonides (1997) used two tasks designed to differ in their demands on the phonological store and the articulatory process. PET scans indicated that there was heightened activity in the parietal lobe when the phonological store was being used, and increased activity in Broca's (language) area when the articulatory process was being used. Thus, the two subsystems of the phonological loop depend on different parts of the brain.

Evaluation

The theory accounts well for the word-length effect, the effects of articulatory suppression, and the performance of various brain-damaged patients. In addition, the theory accounts for two other effects.

(1) *The irrelevant speech effect*: The finding that irrelevant or unattended speech impairs immediate recall is explained by assuming that all spoken material necessarily enters the phonological store.

(2) *The phonological similarity effect*: The finding that immediate recall is impaired when the memorised items are phonologically similar is explained by assuming that this reduces the discriminability of items in the phonological store.

According to the model, irrelevant speech and phonological similarity both affect *only* the phonological store. This leads to two predictions:

(1) Irrelevant speech and phonological similarity should both affect the same brain area.

(2) The effects of irrelevant speech and phonological similarity should be *interactive* rather than *independent*.

Martin-Loeches, Schweinberger, and Sommer (1997) tested the above predictions. They recorded event-related potentials (ERPs), and found that different areas were most active in response to irrelevant speech and to phonological similarity. They also failed to support the second prediction (as had some previous researchers).

Is the phonological loop of much use in everyday life? According to Baddeley, Gathercole, and Papagno (1998, p. 158), "the phonological loop does have a very important function to fulfil, but it is one that is not readily uncovered by experimental studies of adult participants. We suggest that the function of the phonological loop is not to remember familiar words but to learn new words."

Evidence supporting the above viewpoint was reported by Papagno, Valentine, and Baddeley (1991). Native Italian speakers learned pairs of Italian words and pairs of Italian–Russian words. Articulatory suppression (which reduces use of the phonological loop) greatly slowed the learning of foreign vocabulary, but had little effect on the learning of pairs of Italian words.

Visuospatial sketchpad

The characteristics of the visuospatial sketchpad are less clear than those of the articulatory loop. However, it is used in the temporary storage and manipulation of spatial and visual information. Baddeley and Lieberman (1980) studied the visuospatial sketchpad. Partici-

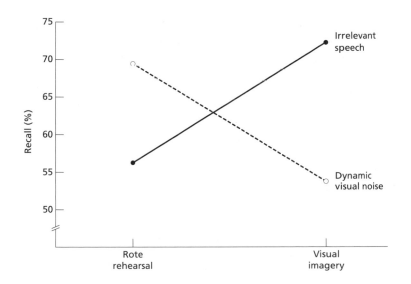

**Figure
5.6.** Percentage recall
as a function of learning
instructions (visual
imagery versus rote
rehearsal) and of
interference (dynamic
visual noise or
irrelevant speech).
Data from Quinn and
McConnell (1996).

pants heard the locations of digits within a matrix described by an
auditory message that was either easily visualised or was rather hard
to visualise. They then reproduced the matrix. In one condition, a
spatial task with no visual input was performed during message
presentation. This involved participants trying to point at a moving
pendulum while blindfolded, with auditory feedback being provided. This spatial tracking task greatly reduced recall of visualisable
messages, but had little effect on non-visualisable messages. These
findings suggest that processing of visualisable messages within the
visuospatial sketchpad involves spatial coding.

Visual coding can also be of importance within the visuospatial
sketchpad. Quinn and McConnell (1996) told their participants to
learn a list of words using either visual imagery or rote rehearsal.
This learning task was performed either on its own or in the presence
of dynamic visual noise (a meaningless display of dots that changed
randomly) or irrelevant speech in a foreign language. It was assumed
that dynamic visual noise would gain access to the visuospatial
sketchpad, whereas irrelevant speech would gain access to the
phonological loop.

The findings were clear (see Figure 5.6): "Words processed under
mnemonic (imagery) instructions are not affected by the presence of
a concurrent verbal task but are affected by the presence of a
concurrent visual task. With rote instructions, the interference pattern
is reversed" (Quinn & McConnell, 1996, p. 213). Thus, imaginal

processing used the visuospatial sketchpad, whereas rote rehearsal used the phonological loop.

Logie (1995) argued that visuospatial working memory can be subdivided into two components:

- The *visual cache*, which stores information about visual form and colour.
- The *inner scribe*, which deals with spatial and movement information. It rehearses information in the visual cache and transfers information from the visual cache to the central executive.

Beschin et al. (1997) studied a man, N.L., who had suffered a stroke. He performed very poorly on tasks thought to require use of the visuospatial sketchpad, unless stimulus support in the form of a drawing or other physical stimulus was present. According to Beschin et al. (1997), N.L. had sustained damage to his visual cache, which meant that he could only create impoverished mental representations of objects and scenes. Stimulus support counteracted the negative effects of his damaged visual cache.

Evaluation

How useful is the visuospatial sketchpad in everyday life? According to Baddeley (1997, p. 82), "The spatial system is important for geographical orientation, and for planning spatial tasks. Indeed, tasks involving visuospatial manipulation . . . have tended to be used as selection tools for professions . . . such as engineering and architecture."

Is there a *single* visuospatial sketchpad or *separate* visual and spatial systems? Evidence suggesting that there may be separate systems was reported by Smith and Jonides (1997). They carried out an ingenious study in which two visual stimuli were presented together, followed by a probe stimulus. The participants had to decide either whether the probe was in the same location as one of the initial stimuli (spatial task) or had the same form (visual task). The stimuli were identical in the two tasks, but there were clear differences in brain activity as revealed by PET. Regions in the right hemisphere (prefrontal cortex; premotor cortex; occipital cortex; and parietal cortex) became active during the spatial task. In contrast, the visual task produced activation in the left hemisphere, especially the parietal cortex and the inferotemporal cortex. In spite of such evidence, it remains likely that the visual and spatial systems are closely linked to each other.

Central executive

The central executive, which resembles an attentional system, is the most important and versatile component of the working memory system. Baddeley (1996) argued that damage to the frontal lobes of the cortex can cause impairments to the central executive. Rylander (1939, p. 20) described the classical frontal syndrome as involving "disturbed attention, increased distractibility, a difficulty in grasping the whole of a complicated state of affairs . . . well able to work along old routine lines . . . cannot learn to master new types of task, in new situations." Thus, patients with the frontal system damaged behave as if they lacked a control system allowing them to direct, and to re-direct, their processing resources appropriately. Such patients are said to suffer from *dysexecutive syndrome* (Baddeley, 1996).

Evidence

Baddeley (1996) identified and assessed some of the major functions of the central executive, such as the following:

(1) Switching of retrieval plans.
(2) Timesharing in dual-task studies.
(3) Selective attention to certain stimuli while ignoring others.
(4) Temporary activation of long-term memory.

One task Baddeley has used to study the workings of the central executive is random generation of digits or letters. The basic idea is that close attention is needed on this task to avoid producing stereotyped (and non-random) sequences. Baddeley (1996) reported a study in which the participants held between one and eight digits in short-term memory while trying to generate a random sequence of digits. It was assumed that the demands on the central executive would be greater as the number of digits to be remembered increased. As predicted, the randomness of the sequence produced on the generation task decreased as the digit memory load increased (see Figure 5.7).

Baddeley (1996) argued that performance on the random generation task might depend on the ability to switch retrieval plans rapidly and so avoid stereotyped responses. This hypothesis was tested as follows. The random digit generation task involved pressing

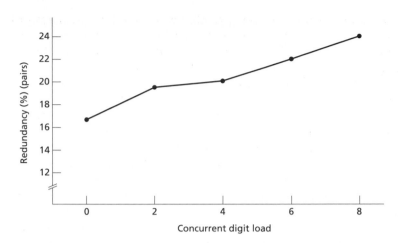

Figure 5.7.
Randomness of digit generation (greater redundancy means reduced randomness) as a function of concurrent digit memory load. Data from Baddeley (1996).

numbered keys. This task was done on its own, or in combination with reciting the alphabet, counting from 1, or alternating numbers and letters (A 1 B 2 C 3 D 4 . . .). Randomness on the random generation task was reduced by the alternation task, presumably because it required constant switching of retrieval plans. This suggests that rapid switching of retrieval plans is one of the functions of the central executive.

The notion that the central executive may play an important part in timesharing or distributing attention across two tasks was considered in a number of studies discussed by Baddeley (1996). One study involved patients with *Alzheimer's disease*, a disease involving progressive loss of mental powers and reduced central executive functioning. First of all, each participant's digit span was established. Then they were given several digit-span trials with that number of digits. Finally, they were given more digit-span trials combined with the task of placing a cross in each of a series of boxes arranged in an irregular pattern (dual-task condition). All of the Alzheimer's patients showed a marked reduction in digit-span performance in the dual-task condition, but none of the normal controls did. These findings are consistent with the view that Alzheimer's patients have particular problems with the central executive function of distributing attention between two tasks.

Evaluation

There is growing evidence that the central executive is not unitary in the sense of forming a unified whole. For example, Eslinger and Damasio (1985) studied a former accountant, E.V.R., who had had a large cerebral tumour removed. He had a high IQ, and performed well on tests requiring reasoning, flexible hypothesis testing, and resistance to distraction and memory interference, suggesting that his central executive was essentially intact. However, he had very poor decision making and judgements (e.g., he would often take hours to decide where to eat). As a result, he was dismissed from various jobs. Presumably E.V.R.'s central executive was partially intact and partially damaged. This implies that the central executive consists of two or more component systems. Such evidence is consistent with the growing body of evidence that the attentional system is not unitary (see Chapter 4).

Shah and Miyake (1996) studied the complexity of the central executive by presenting students with tests of verbal and spatial working memory. The verbal task was the reading span task (Daneman & Carpenter, 1980). In this task, the participants read a series of sentences for comprehension, and then recall the final word of each sentence. The reading span is the maximum number of sentences for which they can do this. There was also a spatial span task. The participants had to decide whether each of a set of letters was in normal or mirror-image orientation. After that, they had to indicate the direction in which the top of each letter had been pointing. The spatial span was the maximum number of letters for which they were able to do this.

The correlation between reading span and spatial span was a non-significant +.23, suggesting that verbal and spatial working memory are rather separate. Their other findings supported this conclusion. Reading span correlated +.45 with verbal IQ, but only +.12 with spatial IQ. In contrast, spatial span correlated +.66 with spatial IQ, and only +.07 with verbal IQ. As Mackintosh (1998, p. 293) concluded, "Within the constraints of this study, and particularly the subject population studied [university students], . . . verbal and spatial working-memory systems seem relatively independent." Shah and Miyake (1996) favoured a multiple-resource model, and this was developed by Shah and Miyake (1999).

Evaluation

The working memory model represents an advance over the account of short-term memory provided by the multi-store model in various ways. First, the working memory system is concerned with both active processing and the brief storage of information. Thus, it is relevant to activities such as mental arithmetic, verbal reasoning, and comprehension, as well as to traditional short-term memory tasks. Second, the working memory model accounts for many findings that are hard to explain within the multi-store approach, especially our ability to perform some tasks together without disruption. Third, the working memory model views verbal rehearsal as an *optional* process occurring within the articulatory or phonological loop. This is more realistic than the central importance of verbal rehearsal in the multi-store model.

On the negative side, little is known about the central executive. It has limited capacity, but this capacity has not been measured accurately. It is argued that the central executive is "modality free" and used in many different processing operations, but the precise details of its functioning are not known. Most importantly, it remains unclear whether the central executive forms a unitary system.

Levels of processing

The notion that long-term memory for words or events depends on the processes occurring at the time of learning sounds fairly obvious. However, Craik and Lockhart (1972) were among the first memory theorists to construct a theoretical approach based on this notion. In their levels-of-processing theory, they assumed that attentional and perceptual processes at the time of learning determine what information is stored in long-term memory. There are various levels of processing, ranging from shallow or perceptual analysis of a stimulus (e.g., detecting specific letters in words) to deep or semantic analysis. Craik (1973, p. 48) defined depth as "the meaningfulness extracted from the stimulus rather than . . . the number of analyses performed upon it."

The key theoretical assumptions made by Craik and Lockhart (1972) were as follows:

- The level or depth of processing of a stimulus has a large effect on its memorability.
- Deeper levels of analysis produce more elaborate, longer-lasting, and stronger memory traces than do shallow levels of analysis.

Craik and Lockhart (1972) distinguished between maintenance and elaborative rehearsal. *Maintenance rehearsal* involves repeating analyses that have previously been carried out, whereas *elaborative rehearsal* involves deeper or more semantic analysis of the learning material. According to levels-of-processing theory, only elaborative rehearsal improves long-term memory. This contrasts with the view of Atkinson and Shiffrin (1968) that rehearsal *always* enhances long-term memory.

Evidence

The most direct way of testing levels-of-processing theory is to present the same list of words to different groups of participants, with each group being asked to process the words in a different way. The effects of these various processing or orienting tasks on long-term memory are then assessed. For example, Hyde and Jenkins (1973) used the following orienting tasks: rating the words for pleasantness; estimating the frequency with which each word is used in the English language; detecting the occurrence of the letters "e" and "g" in the lists words; deciding on the part of speech of each word; and deciding whether the words fitted sentence frames. It was assumed that only the tasks of rating pleasantness and rating frequency of usage involved processing of meaning.

Free recall for lists containing words either associatively related or unrelated in meaning in the Hyde and Jenkins (1973) study is shown in Figure 5.8. Recall was 51% higher after the semantic tasks than the non-semantic tasks with associatively unrelated words, and it was 83% higher with associatively related words. Similar findings have been reported in numerous other studies.

Studies on rehearsal have generally found that elaborative rehearsal leads to better long-term memory than maintenance rehearsal, which is as predicted by Craik and Lockhart, 1972. However, maintenance rehearsal usually has some beneficial effect on memory, which is contrary to prediction. For example, Glenberg, Smith, and Green (1977) found that a ninefold increase in the time devoted to maintenance rehearsal only increased recall by 1.5%, but increased recognition memory by 9%. Maintenance rehearsal may have prevented the formation of associations among the items in the list, and such associations benefit recall more than recognition.

In the years after 1972, it became clear that long-term memory does not depend only on the depth or level of processing. For example, elaboration of processing (i.e., the amount of processing of a particular kind) and the distinctiveness or uniqueness of processing

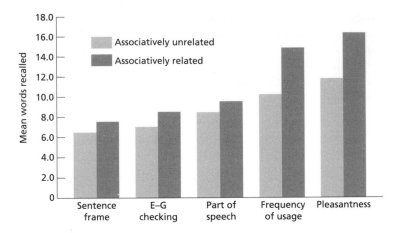

Figure 5.8. Mean words recalled as a function of list type (associatively related or unrelated) and orienting task. Data from Hyde and Jenkins (1973).

are also important. Craik and Tulving (1975) showed the value of elaboration of processing in a study in which the participants had to decide whether list words fitted the blanks in sentences. Some of the sentences were high in elaboration (e.g., "The great bird swooped down and carried off the struggling ____"), whereas others were low in elaboration (e.g., "She cooked the ____"). Subsequent cued recall for the list words was twice as great when they accompanied high-elaboration sentences.

Bransford et al. (1979) showed that distinctiveness or uniqueness of processing can be more effective than elaboration of processing. They presented participants with distinctive but not elaborate similes (e.g., "A mosquito is like a doctor because they both draw blood") and with non-distinctive but elaborate similes (e.g., "A mosquito is like a raccoon because they both have heads, legs, jaws"). Recall was much better for the distinctive similes than for the non-distinctive ones.

Evaluation

The levels-of-processing approach has had a major impact on memory research. It is generally accepted that the processes occurring at the time of learning are important in determining long-term memory. However, there are at least four major problems with the approach. First, Craik and Lockhart (1972) tended to ignore the role of the particular memory test used in influencing the magnitude to the levels-of-processing effect. Morris, Bransford, and Franks (1977) argued that information is remembered only if it is of *relevance* to

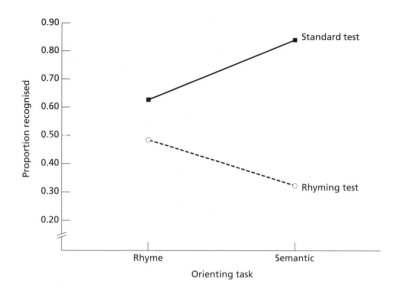

Figure 5.9. Mean proportion of words recognised as a function of orienting task (semantic or rhyme) and of the type of recognition task (standard or rhyming). Data are from Morris et al. (1977), and are from positive trials only.

the memory test. Their participants answered semantic or shallow (rhyme) questions for lists of words. After that, two kinds of memory test were used: (1) a standard recognition test (list and non-list words presented); and (2) a rhyming recognition test, on which the list words themselves were not presented, and the task was to select words that rhymed with list words. For example, if the word FABLE appeared on the test and TABLE was a list word, then the participants should have selected it.

The findings of Morris et al. (1977) are shown in Figure 5.9. There was the typical superiority of deep over shallow processing with the standard recognition test, but the *opposite* finding was obtained with the rhyme test. This latter finding represents an experimental disproof of the notion that deep processing always enhances long-term memory. Morris et al. (1977) proposed a transfer-appropriate processing theory to explain their findings. According to this theory, whether the information stored as a result of the processing at acquisition leads to subsequent retention depends on the *relevance* of that information to the memory test. For example, stored semantic information is essentially irrelevant when the memory test requires the selection of words rhyming with list words. What is required for this kind of test is shallow rhyme information.

Second, the levels-of-processing approach was designed to account for performance on tests of *explicit memory* such as recall and recognition, on which there is a conscious and deliberate retrieval of past events. The theory works less well with tests of *implicit memory*, which does not depend on conscious recollection (see Chapter 6). An example of such a test is word-fragment completion, in which participants write down the first word they think of that completes a word fragment (e.g., –en–i– is a fragment for "tennis"). There is typically only a small (and often non-significant) levels-of-processing effect on such tests (Challis & Brodbeck, 1992).

Third, it is hard to be sure of the level of processing used by learners, because there is generally no independent measure of processing depth. For example, it is not really clear whether the part-of-speech task used by Hyde and Jenkins (1973) involves deep or semantic processing. However, Gabrieli et al. (1996) argued that functional magnetic resonance imaging (fMRI) could be used to identify the brain regions used in different kinds of processing. They used fMRI with semantic and perceptual (shallow) processing tasks, and concluded: "The fMRI found greater activation of left inferior prefrontal cortex for semantic than for perceptual encoding" (Gabrieli et al., 1996, p. 282).

Fourth, the levels-of-processing approach is descriptive rather than explanatory. In other words, Craik and Lockhart (1972) failed to explain in detail *why* deep or semantic processing is so effective.

Update

Lockhart and Craik (1990) accepted that their levels-of-processing approach was greatly oversimplified. They also accepted the notion of transfer-appropriate processing proposed by Morris et al. (1977). However, they argued that the two approaches are compatible. According to Lockhart and Craik (1990), transfer-appropriate theory predicts that there will be interactions between the type of processing at learning and the type of processing at retrieval (see Figure 5.9), and levels-of-processing theory predicts a main effect of processing depth when transfer appropriateness is held constant. There is supporting evidence in the findings of Morris et al. (1977). Transfer appropriateness was high with semantic processing followed by a standard recognition test and with rhyme processing followed by a rhyming test. However, as predicted by levels-of-processing theory, memory performance was much higher in the former condition.

Lockhart and Craik (1990) accepted that their original theory implied that processing proceeds in an ordered sequence from shallow sensory levels to deeper semantic levels. They proposed a more realistic (but vaguer) view: "It is likely that an adequate model will comprise complex interactions between top-down and bottom-up processes, and that processing at different levels will be temporally parallel or partially overlapping" (Lockhart & Craik, 1990, p. 95).

Implicit learning

The levels-of-processing approach was concerned with the processes involved in the conscious acquisition and retrieval of information. However, it has been increasingly recognised that some learning is not of that type; the term "implicit learning" has been used to refer to such learning. According to Seger (1994, p. 63), *implicit learning* is "learning complex information without complete verbalisable knowledge of what is learned." There are clear similarities between implicit learning and *implicit memory*, which is memory that does not depend on conscious recollection (see Chapter 6). According to Seger (1994, p. 165), "there is probably no firm dividing line between implicit memory and implicit learning."

The reader may wonder why implicit learning and implicit memory are not discussed together. After all, there can be no memory without prior learning, and learning necessitates the involvement of a memory system. There are two reasons. First, studies of implicit learning have typically used relatively complex, novel stimulus materials, whereas most studies of implicit memory have used simple, familiar stimulus materials. Thus, the tasks used are very different. Second, as Reber (1993, p. 109) pointed out, "The two research programs have, unfortunately, travelled parallel courses with precious little interaction."

What are the characteristics of the systems involved in implicit learning and memory that distinguish them from the systems involved in explicit learning and memory? Reber (1993) proposed five such characteristics:

(1) *Robustness*: Implicit systems should be relatively unaffected by disorders (e.g., amnesia) that affect explicit systems.
(2) *Age independence*: Implicit learning is little influenced by age or developmental level.
(3) *Low variability*: There are smaller individual differences in implicit learning and memory than in explicit learning and memory.

(4) *IQ independence*: Performance on implicit tasks is relatively unaffected by IQ.

(5) *Commonality of process*: Implicit systems are common to most species.

Evidence

Much of the research on implicit learning has made use of a complex task on which the participants learn to decide whether strings of letters conform to the rules of an artificial grammar. Most participants learn to discriminate reasonably well between grammatical and ungrammatical strings, even though they cannot verbalise the rules of the grammar (see Reber, 1993). A particularly interesting study on artificial-grammar learning was reported by Knowlton, Ramus, and Squire (1992). They studied amnesic patients, who have been found to be severely impaired in explicit learning and memory (see Chapter 6). The amnesic patients performed as well as normal individuals in learning to distinguish between grammatical and ungrammatical strings of letters. Thus, amnesic patients showed intact implicit learning.

Knowlton et al. (1992) found that the findings were different when the participants were instructed to try to recall the specific strings used during learning, and to use these strings to aid task performance. The amnesics performed much worse than the normal participants in this condition, presumably because performance depended more on explicit learning. These findings can be regarded as confirming Reber's (1993) view that implicit systems are more robust than explicit systems.

Berry and Broadbent (1984) studied implicit learning by using a complex task in which a sugar-production factory had to be managed to maintain a specified level of sugar output. The participants learned to perform this task effectively, but most of them could not report the principles underlying their performance. Those participants whose reports revealed good knowledge of these principles tended to perform the task *worse* than those with poor knowledge. Thus, the task information available to consciousness seemed to be of no value to the learners.

Squire and Frambach (1990) used the same complex task as Berry and Broadbent (1984). Amnesic patients performed as well as normal controls when they carried it out for the first time. However, a questionnaire that was given after the task revealed that the amnesics possessed less explicit knowledge than the normal controls concerning simple facts about the experiment. This deficient explicit learning may explain why the amnesic patients performed the task less well than the normal controls when they carried it out for a second time 27 days after the first occasion.

A possible problem with the task used by Berry and Broadbent (1984) and by Squire and Frambach (1990) is that the participants may have had conscious access to task-relevant knowledge, but found it hard to express this knowledge in words. Evidence of implicit learning avoiding that problem was reported by Howard and Howard (1992). They used a task in which an asterisk appeared in one of four positions on a screen, under each of which there was a key. The task was to press the key corresponding to the position of the asterisk as rapidly as possible. The position of the asterisk over trials conformed to a complex pattern. The participants showed clear evidence of learning the pattern by responding faster and faster to the asterisk. However, when asked to predict where the asterisk would appear next, their performance was at chance level. Thus, the participants showed implicit learning of the pattern, but no explicit learning.

The notion that implicit learning is separate from explicit learning would receive support if different brain regions were found to underlie the two types of learning. Grafton, Hazeltine, and Ivry (1995) obtained PET scans from participants engaged in learning motor sequences under implicit learning conditions or under conditions making it easier for them to become consciously aware of the sequence. The motor cortex and the supplementary motor area were activated during implicit learning. In contrast, "Explicit learning and awareness of the sequences required more activations in the right premotor cortex, the dorsolateral cingulate, areas in the parietal cortex associated with working memory, the anterior cingulate, areas in the parietal cortex concerned with voluntary attention, and the lateral temporal cortical areas that store explicit memories" (Gazzaniga et al., 1998, p. 279). Thus, there seem to be clear differences between the systems involved in explicit and implicit learning.

Theoretical considerations

A key theoretical issue is whether learning is possible with little or no conscious awareness of what has been learned. Shanks and St. John (1994) proposed two criteria for learning to be regarded as unconscious:

(1) *Information criterion*: The information that the participants are asked to provide on the awareness test must be the information that is responsible for their improved level of performance.

(2) *Sensitivity criterion*: "We must be able to show that our test of awareness is sensitive to all of the relevant knowledge" (Shanks & St. John, 1994, p. 11). People may be consciously aware of more task-relevant knowledge than appears on an insensitive awareness test, and this may lead us to underestimate their consciously accessible knowledge.

The two criteria proposed by Shanks and St. John (1994) may seem reasonable, but they are hard to use in practice. However, Shanks and St. John argued that the sensitivity criterion could be replaced provided that the performance and awareness tests resemble each other as closely as possible. This was precisely what was done in the study by Howard and Howard (1992), and so their findings provide strong support for implicit learning. The evidence from neuro-imaging also points to the same conclusion.

Another important theoretical issue concerns the relationship between explicit and implicit learning. One view was expressed by Anderson (e.g., 1983, 1996) in various versions of his Adaptive Control of Thought (ACT) model (see Chapter 9). According to ACT, what happens during the development of automatic skills is that conscious representations are gradually transformed into unconscious ones. In other words, there is an initial process of explicit learning, which is then followed by implicit learning. A different view was expressed by Willingham and Goedert-Eschmann (1999), who argued that explicit and implicit learning develop together in parallel rather than one preceding the other. According to this theoretical position, performance is initially supported by explicit processes. After sufficient practice, implicit processes that are acquired at the same time as the explicit processes become strong enough to support performance on their own.

Willingham and Goedert-Eschmann (1999) obtained evidence supporting the hypothesis that explicit and implicit learning develop together. The task involved responding rapidly with the appropriate responses to four different stimuli over a long series of trials. It was a motor sequencing task because the stimuli were arranged in a given sequence. Participants in the explicit learning condition were told there was a repeating sequence, and they were encouraged to memorise it. In contrast, participants in the implicit learning condition were not informed about the sequencing.

The participants were then given a further series of transfer trials designed to assess implicit knowledge. The stimuli on these trials were mostly presented in a random order, and the participants who had engaged in explicit learning were told that the purpose of these trials was to see how rapidly they could respond when the stimuli were in a random order. However, the previously learned sequence or a novel sequence was introduced during the course of the trials without the awareness of the participants. What happened on this test of implicit knowledge? According to Willingham and Goedert-Eschmann (1999), "Participants with explicit training showed sequence knowledge equivalent to those with implicit training, implying that implicit knowledge had been acquired in parallel with explicit knowledge."

Much more evidence is needed to clarify the relationship between explicit and implicit learning. It may be, for example, that the two forms of learning develop together on simple motor tasks such as the one used by Willingham and Goedert-Eschmann (1999), but that explicit learning precedes implicit learning on more complex or non-motor tasks.

Summary: Short-term memory and learning

- *Multi-store model*: There are three types of memory store within the multi-store model: sensory stores, short-term store, and long-term store. The sensory stores are modality specific, and hold information very briefly. The short-term store has very limited capacity. Information is lost from this store because of interference, diversion of attention, and decay. Evidence from brain-damaged patients supports the distinction between short-term and long-term memory stores. The memory stores differ with respect to temporal duration, storage capacity, and forgetting mechanisms. The multi-store model is very oversimplified in its account of unitary short-term and long-term stores, and the notion that access to long-term memory occurs only after information is processed in the short-term store. In addition, the role of rehearsal is exaggerated.

- *Working memory*: The working memory system consists of a central executive, a phonological loop, and a visuospatial sketchpad. Two tasks can be performed successfully together only when they use different components of the working memory system. The phonological loop consists of a passive phonological store and an articulatory process. Its primary function is to assist in the learning of new words. The visuospatial sketchpad consists of a visual cache and an inner scribe. It is possible that there are separate visual and spatial systems rather than a single sketchpad. The central executive is involved in various functions such as switching of retrieval plans, time-sharing, selective attention, and temporary activation of long-term memory. There may be relatively separate verbal and spatial working memory systems. The working memory approach has the advantage over the multi-store model that it can be applied to most cognitive activities rather than only being of relevance to memory tasks.
- *Levels of processing*: According to levels-of-processing theory, long-term memory is better for information that is processed deeply or semantically at the time of learning. In addition, elaborative rehearsal improves long-term memory but maintenance rehearsal does not. Some evidence supports these theoretical assumptions. However, long-term memory depends on elaboration and distinctiveness of processing as well as on depth of processing. Long-term memory depends on the relevance of the stored information to the requirements of the memory test (transfer-appropriate processing). The theory is more applicable to tests of explicit memory than to those of implicit memory. Finally, the theory provides a description rather than an explanation of certain memory phenomena. In an updated account of levels-of-processing theory, it was argued that depth of processing and transfer-appropriate processing jointly determine long-term memory performance.
- *Implicit learning*: There have been numerous apparent demonstrations of implicit learning. However, the participants in some studies may have found it hard to express task-relevant knowledge to which they had conscious access. There is some evidence that different cortical areas are activated during explicit and implicit

learning. Shanks and St. John (1994) proposed the information and sensitivity criteria for learning to be regarded as unconscious. These criteria are hard to use in practice, but some studies (e.g., Howard & Howard, 1992) seem to satisfy them. Some evidence suggests that explicit and implicit learning develop in parallel, rather than explicit learning preceding implicit learning.

Essay questions

(1) Describe the multi-store model of memory. What are its strengths and limitations?
(2) What has the working memory model contributed to our understanding of human memory and cognition?
(3) Evaluate the levels-of-processing approach to long-term memory.
(4) Evaluate the evidence for implicit learning.

Further reading

Baddeley, A. (1997). *Human memory: Theory and practice* (rev. ed.). Hove, UK: Psychology Press. This is a well-written book by an outstanding cognitive psychologist.

Eysenck, M.W., & Keane, M.T. (2000). *Cognitive psychology: A student's handbook* (4th ed.). Hove, UK: Psychology Press. Chapters 6 and 7 in this book provide more detailed coverage of the topics dealt with in this chapter.

Haberlandt, K. (1999). *Human memory: Exploration and application*. Boston, MA: Allyn & Bacon. There is accessible coverage of topics on short-term memory in this book.

Long-term memory 6

Introduction

In the previous chapter, we considered some of the main issues related to short-term memory and learning. In this chapter, the main focus is on long-term memory. We start with theoretical attempts to explain how information in long-term memory is forgotten, followed by an evaluation of major theories of long-term memory. After that, the ways in which the study of amnesia has furthered our understanding of long-term memory are considered.

Influential theories of long-term memory have been based on the assumption that much of the information in long-term memory is stored in the form of schemas or integrated packages of knowledge. The value of such theories is considered. Finally, there has been a marked increase in studies of everyday memory. Some of the key topics in everyday memory are discussed at the end of the chapter.

Theories of forgetting

We all know that our memory for information tends to become worse as the time since learning increases. The first systematic attempt to establish the forgetting function over time was made by Hermann Ebbinghaus (1885/1913). He carried out numerous studies using himself as the only participant. Forgetting of lists of nonsense syllables was very rapid over the first hour or so after learning, with the rate of forgetting slowing considerably thereafter (see Figure 6.1).

Ebbinghaus's findings suggested that the forgetting function is approximately logarithmic. This was confirmed by Rubin and Wenzel (1996). They analysed the forgetting functions from 210 data sets

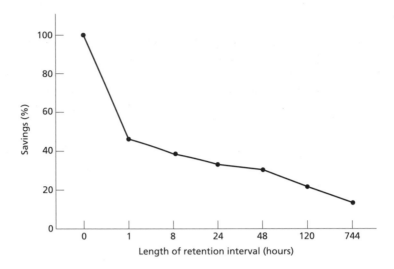

Figure 6.1. Forgetting over time as indexed by reduced savings. Data from Ebbinghaus (1885/1913).

involving many different kinds of learning and several types of memory test, and concluded as follows: "We have established a law: the logarithmic-loss law" (Rubin & Wenzel, 1996, p. 758). This law described most of the data very well, except for those involving autobiographical memory where the rate of forgetting was relatively slow. It is not known why the forgetting function is different for autobiographical memory. However, it is probably relevant that participants in studies on autobiographical memory are typically free to produce any memory they want from their lives, and the retention interval can be decades rather than minutes or hours.

Most studies of forgetting have focused on explicit memory, in which there is conscious recollection of information. However, a few studies have considered implicit memory, in which memory performance does not involve conscious recollection. McBride and Dosher (1999) considered both kinds of memory over retention intervals of between 1 and 60 min. Their findings were as follows: "Either conscious and automatic [implicit] memory reflect different systems with very similar forgetting characteristics, or they reflect different types of information in a common memory store" (McBride & Dosher, 1999, p. 583).

Some of the major theories of forgetting are discussed below. However, the reader should be forewarned that it has proved very difficult to clarify the processes underlying forgetting. It is possible that the various theories are all partially correct, in that each one may explain forgetting in some circumstances.

Repression

Sigmund Freud (1915, 1943) emphasised the importance of emotional factors in forgetting. He argued that very threatening or anxiety-provoking material is often unable to gain access to conscious awareness, and he used the term *repression* to refer to this phenomenon. According to Freud (1915, p. 86), "The essence of repression lies simply in the function of rejecting and keeping something out of consciousness." However, Freud sometimes used the concept to refer merely to the inhibition of the capacity for emotional experience (Madison, 1956). Thus, threatening material could be said to be repressed even when it is available to consciousness, provided that it did not produce an emotional reaction.

Evidence

Freud's ideas on repression emerged from his clinical experiences with patients who found great difficulty in remembering traumatic events that had happened to them. The central problem in testing Freud's theory is that there are obvious ethical reasons why repression cannot be produced under laboratory conditions. However, relevant evidence has been obtained from normal individuals known as *repressors*, who have low scores on trait anxiety (a personality factor relating to anxiety susceptibility) and high scores on defensiveness. Repressors describe themselves as controlled and relatively unemotional. According to Weinberger, Schwartz, and Davidson (1979), those who score low on trait anxiety and on defensiveness are the truly low-anxious, those high on trait anxiety and low on defensiveness are the high-anxious, and those high on both trait anxiety and defensiveness are the defensive high-anxious.

Myers and Brewin (1994) assessed the time taken to recall negative childhood memories by members of all four personality groups. Repressors were much slower than any of the other groups (see Figure 6.2), suggesting a repression-like phenomenon. This slowness to recall did not happen because repressors had experienced happier childhoods than members of the other groups. Detailed questioning by means of semi-structured interviews indicated that they had experienced the most indifference and hostility from their fathers.

At a non-experimental level, large numbers of adults have apparently recovered repressed memories of childhood physical and/or sexual abuse. There has been a fierce controversy about the genuineness of these recovered memories. The issues involved are complex, and we will consider only briefly some of the relevant findings. Some

Figure 6.2. Speed of recall of negative childhood memories by high-anxious, defensive high-anxious, low-anxious, and repressor groups. Data from Myers and Brewin (1994).

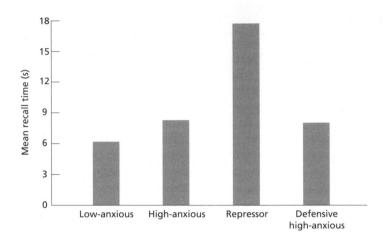

of the most convincing evidence that recovered memories can be genuine was reported by Williams (1994). She interviewed 129 women who had suffered acts of rape and sexual abuse more than 17 years previously. All of these women had been 12 or younger when the abuse happened, and 38% of them had no recollection of it. In addition, Williams (1994) found that 16% of those women who recalled being abused said that there had been periods of time in the past when they had been unable to remember the abuse.

Andrews et al. (1999) obtained detailed information from 108 therapists about recovered memories from a total of 236 patients. Their evidence suggested that most recovered memories may well be genuine. For example, 41% of the patients reported that there was corroborative or supporting evidence. The most common form of such evidence was that someone else had also reported being abused by the alleged perpetrator. Those who believe that most recovered memories are false typically assume that such false memories are generally produced as a result of direct pressure from the therapist. However, only 28% of the patients studied by Andrews et al. (1999) claimed that the trigger for the first recovered memory occurred during the course of a therapeutic session. In 22% of cases, the trigger occurred before therapy had even started, and so could not have been influenced by the therapist.

Those who claim that most recovered memories are false emphasise two points. First, some patients have admitted to reported false memories of childhood abuse. For example, Lief and Fetkewicz (1995) studied 40 patients who had retracted their "memories" of childhood abuse. In about 80% of these cases, the therapist had made direct suggestions that the patient was the victim of sexual abuse. In 68% of cases, hypnosis (which is known to produce mistaken memories) had been used to recover memories, and in 40% of cases the patient had read numerous books about sexual abuse.

Second, most people can be misled into believing in the existence of events that never actually happened. For example, Ceci (1995) asked preschool children to think about various real events and fictitious but plausible events over a 10-week period. Fifty-eight per cent of the children provided detailed stories about fictitious events which they falsely believed had happened. Psychologists experienced in interviewing children watched videotapes of the stories, and were unable to tell which events were real and which were false. However, it is probably much easier to produce false memories of fairly trivial events than of traumatic events such as childhood abuse.

Evaluation

Studies on repressors have provided evidence of a phenomenon resembling repression. However, the negative childhood memories that are retrieved are rarely traumatic, and these negative memories are retrieved slowly rather than not at all. These facts suggest that what is being observed in such studies is only a weak form of repression.

So far as recovered memories are concerned, it is likely that most are genuine even though some clearly are not. Brewin, Andrews, and Gotlib (1993, p. 94) considered the evidence in detail, and concluded as follows: "Provided that individuals are questioned about the occurrence of specific events or facts that they were sufficiently old and well placed to know about, the central features of their accounts are likely to be reasonably accurate."

Interference theory

According to interference theory, our ability to remember what we are currently learning can be disrupted or interfered with by what we have previously learned or by what we learn in the future. When previous learning interferes with our memory of later learning, we have *proactive interference*. When later learning disrupts memory for earlier learning, there is *retroactive interference*. Methods of testing for proactive and retroactive interference are shown in Figure 6.3. In general terms, both proactive and retroactive interference are

Figure 6.3. Methods of testing for proactive and retroactive interference.

Proactive interference

Group	Learn	Learn	Test
Experimental	A–B (e.g. Cat–Tree)	A–C (e.g. Cat–Dirt)	A–C (e.g. Cat–Dirt)
Control	–	A–C (e.g. Cat–Dirt)	A–C (e.g. Cat–Dirt)

Retroactive interference

Group	Learn	Learn	Test
Experimental	A–B (e.g. Cat–Tree)	A–C (e.g. Cat–Dirt)	A–B (e.g. Cat–Tree)
Control	A–B (e.g. Cat–Tree)	–	A–B (e.g. Cat–Tree)

Note: for both proactive and retroactive interference, the experimental group exhibits interference. On the test, only the first word is supplied, and the subjects must provide the second word.

maximal when two different responses have been associated with the same stimulus; intermediate when two similar responses have been associated with the same stimulus; and minimal when two different stimuli are involved (Underwood & Postman, 1960).

Strong evidence for retroactive interference has been obtained in studies of eyewitness testimony, in which memory of an event is interfered with by post-event questioning (see later in the chapter). However, most of the evidence for retroactive interference has come from studies using lists of paired associates (see Figure 6.3). It is generally assumed that retroactive interference occurs simply because two different responses become associated to the same stimulus (e.g., participants cannot recall that 79 was paired with Picasso if they have subsequently learned to associate Picasso with 18). In fact, matters are more complicated. *All* of the response terms in both lists generally belong to the same category, and Bower, Thompson-Schill, and Tulving (1994) found that this is crucially important to producing retroactive interference. There was practically no evidence of retroactive interference when several different categories were used in the list even though the B and C terms in each A–B, A–C set were from the same category (see Figure 6.4). Thus, retroactive interference does *not* depend solely on similarities within the A–B, A–C pairings.

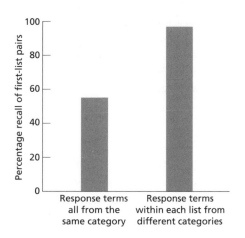

Figure 6.4.
Percentage recall of first-list (A–B) pairs originally learned completely as a function of whether the response terms came from the same category or from different categories. Based on data in Bower et al. (1994).

An example of proactive interference you may have encountered is when a woman marries and changes her surname. It is easy to fall into the error of continuing to use her maiden name, because the stimulus (the woman) has remained the same, but the response (surname) has changed.

The importance of proactive interference was shown by Underwood (1957), who reviewed studies on forgetting over a 24-hour retention interval. About 80% of what had been learned was forgotten in one day if the participants had previously learned 15 or more lists in the same experiment, against only 20% or so if no earlier lists had been learned. These findings suggested that proactive interference can produce a massive amount of forgetting. However, there is a problem with these studies. The learning of each list was equated in that all lists were learned to the same criterion (e.g., all items recalled correctly on an immediate test). However, the participants reached the criterion more rapidly with the later lists. Thus, they had less exposure to the later lists, and perhaps learned them less thoroughly. When the amount of exposure to all lists was equated (Warr, 1964), the amount of proactive interference was much less than reported by Underwood (1957). Proactive interference undoubtedly occurs, but may well account for less forgetting than was assumed by Underwood (1957).

Evaluation
There are literally hundreds of studies showing the existence of proactive and retroactive interference. Why, then, is interference theory less popular than it used to be? There are three main reasons.

First, interference theory tells us very little about the internal processes involved in forgetting. Second, it requires special conditions for substantial interference effects to occur (i.e., the same stimulus paired with two different responses), and these conditions may be infrequent in everyday life. Third, associations learned *outside* the laboratory seem less susceptible to interference than those learned *inside* the laboratory (Slamecka, 1966).

Cue-dependent forgetting or retrieval failure

According to Tulving (1974), there are two main reasons for forgetting. First, there is *trace-dependent forgetting*, in which the information is no longer stored in memory. Second, there is *cue-dependent forgetting*, in which the information is in memory, but cannot be accessed. Such information is said to be available (i.e., it is still stored) but not accessible (i.e., it cannot be retrieved). In other words, forgetting is based on *retrieval failure*. It is often argued that most forgetting is cue dependent or dependent on retrieval failure. Evidence of cue-dependent forgetting will be discussed in this section and the following one on context effects.

Tulving and Psotka (1971) compared the cue-dependent approach with interference theory. There were between one and six word lists, with four words in six different categories in each list. After each list had been presented, the participants recalled as many words as possible. That was the original learning. After all the lists had been presented, the participants tried to recall the words from *all* the lists that had been presented. That was total free recall. Finally, all the category names were presented, and the participants tried again to recall all the words from all the lists. That was total free cued recall.

Retroactive interference appeared in total free recall, with word recall from any list decreasing as the number of other lists intervening between learning and recall increased (see Figure 6.5). This finding would be interpreted within interference theory by assuming there had been unlearning of the earlier lists. However, this interpretation does not fit with the findings from total cued recall. There was essentially *no* retroactive interference or forgetting when the category names were available to the participants. Thus, the forgetting observed in total free recall was basically cue dependent and involved retrieval failure.

We can obtain some theoretical understanding of what is involved in cue-dependent forgetting by considering the *encoding specificity principle*, which was defined as follows by Tulving (1979, p. 408): "The

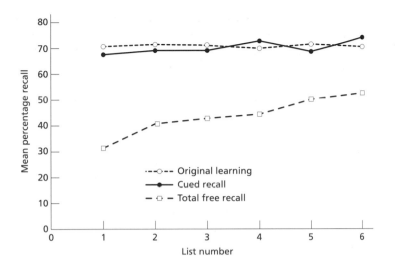

Figure 6.5. Original learning, total free recall, and total free cued recall as a function of the number of interpolated lists. Data from Tulving and Psotka (1971).

probability of successful retrieval of the target item is a monotonically increasing function of informational overlap between the information present at retrieval and the information stored in memory." A monotonically increasing function is one which is generally rising and which does not decrease at any point. Of crucial importance, Tulving assumed that the information stored in memory would typically include contextual information. This contextual information can include information about the external learning environment, current mood state, and so on.

The major prediction from the encoding specificity principle is as follows: Memory performance will be worse (and so forgetting will be greater) when the contextual information present at retrieval *differs* from the contextual information stored in memory. Kenealy (1997) tested this prediction. In one study, the participants looked at a map and learned a set of instructions concerning a particular route until their learning performance exceeded 80%. The following day they were given tests of free recall and cued recall (the visual outline of the map). Context was manipulated by using music to create happy or sad mood states at learning and at retrieval. The findings are shown in Figure 6.6. As predicted, free recall was better when the context (mood state) was the same at learning and retrieval than when it differed (this is known as mood-state-dependent retrieval). However, there was no context effect with cued recall. Thus, context in the form of mood state can affect memory, but does so only when no other powerful retrieval cues are available.

Figure 6.6. Free and cued recall as a function of mood state (happy or sad) at learning and at recall. Based on data in Kenealy (1997).

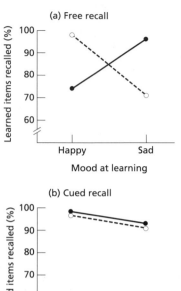

(a) Free recall

(b) Cued recall

●———● Sad at recall
○- - - -○ Happy at recall

There is a further, more unexpected, prediction that follows from the encoding specificity principle. As you would expect, recognition memory is generally much better than recall. According to Tulving, however, recall in the presence of much relevant context could be better than recognition in the absence of contextual information. Relevant evidence was reported by Muter (1978). Participants were presented with names of people (e.g., DOYLE, FERGUSON, THOMAS) and asked to circle those they "recognised as a person who was famous before 1950." They were then given recall cues in the form of brief descriptions plus first names of the famous people whose surnames had appeared on the recognition test (e.g., author of the Sherlock Holmes stories: Sir Arthur Conan ____; Welsh poet: Dylan ____). Participants recognised only 29% of the names but recalled 42%.

Evaluation
In spite of its many successes, there are various limitations with Tulving's approach. First, he assumed that context affects recall and

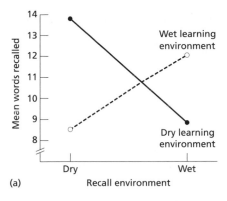
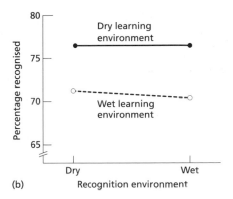

Figure 6.7. (a) Recall in the same versus different contexts. Data from Godden and Baddeley (1975). (b) Recognition in the same versus different contexts. Data from Godden and Baddeley (1980).

recognition in the same way. However, that is not the case according to Baddeley (1982). He proposed a distinction between intrinsic context and extrinsic context. *Intrinsic context* has a direct impact on the meaning of significance of a to-be-remembered item (e.g., strawberry vs. traffic as intrinsic context for the word "jam"), whereas *extrinsic context* (e.g., the room in which learning takes place) does not. According to Baddeley (1982), recall is affected by both intrinsic and extrinsic context, but recognition memory is affected only by intrinsic context.

Relevant evidence was obtained by Godden and Baddeley (1975, 1980). Godden and Baddeley (1975) asked participants to learn a list of words either on land or 20 feet underwater, and they were then given a test of free recall on land or underwater. Those who had learned on land recalled more on land, and those who learned underwater did better when tested underwater. Retention was about 50% higher when learning and recall took place in the same extrinsic context (see Figure 6.7). Godden and Baddeley (1980) carried out a very similar study, but using recognition instead of recall. Recognition memory was not affected by extrinsic context (see Figure 6.7).

Second, there is a danger of circularity in applying the encoding specificity principle. Memory is said to depend on "informational overlap", but there is seldom any direct measure of that overlap. If we infer the amount of informational overlap from the level of memory performance, this produces completely circular reasoning.

Third, Tulving assumed that the information available at the time of retrieval is compared in a simple and direct fashion with the information stored in memory to ascertain the amount of informational overlap. This is implausible if one considers what happens if memory is tested by asking the question, "What did you do six days ago?" Most people answer such a question by engaging in a complex problem-solving strategy to reconstruct the relevant events. Tulving's approach has little to say about how retrieval operates under such circumstances.

Conclusions

Studies designed to test cue-dependent forgetting and the encoding specificity principle have shown that changes in contextual information between storage and test can produce substantial reductions in memory performance. It is tempting to assume that forgetting over time can be explained in the same way. According to Bouton, Nelson, and Rosas (1999, p. 171), "The passage of time can create a mismatch because internal and external contextual cues that were present during learning may change or fluctuate over time . . . Thus, the passage of time may change the background context and make it less likely that target material will be retrieved . . . We call this approach the *context-change account of forgetting*." This theoretical approach is plausible, but there is little direct evidence to support it.

Theories of long-term memory

Our long-term memories contain an amazing variety of different kinds of information. As a result, it is tempting to assume there are various long-term memory systems, each specialised for certain types of information. There have been several attempts to identify these memory systems. In this section, we focus on two of the most important theoretical approaches in this area. In the following section of the chapter, these approaches are considered in terms of their ability to explain the findings from brain-damaged patients suffering from amnesia, which involves a substantial impairment of long-term memory.

Episodic versus semantic memory

Tulving (1972) argued for a distinction between *episodic memory* and *semantic memory*. According to Tulving (1972) episodic memory refers to the storage (and retrieval) of specific events or episodes occurring in a particular place at a particular time. Thus, memory for what you had for breakfast this morning is an example of episodic memory. In contrast, semantic memory contains information about our stock of knowledge about the world. Tulving (1972, p. 386) defined semantic memory as follows:

> It is a mental thesaurus, organized knowledge a person possesses about words and other verbal symbols, their meanings and referents, about relations among them, and about rules, formulas, and algorithms for the manipulation of these symbols, concepts, and relations.

Wheeler, Stuss, and Tulving (1997, p. 333) defined episodic memory rather differently, arguing that its main distinguishing characteristic is "its dependence on a special kind of awareness that all healthy human adults can identify. It is the type of awareness experienced when one thinks back to a specific moment in one's personal past and consciously recollects some prior episode or state as it was previously experienced." In contrast, retrieval of semantic memories does not possess this sense of conscious recollection of the past. It involves instead thinking objectively about something one knows.

How do the definitions of episodic and semantic memory offered by Wheeler et al. (1997) differ from those of Tulving (1972)? According to Wheeler et al. (1997, pp. 348–349), "The major distinction between episodic and semantic memory is no longer best described in terms of the type of information they work with. The distinction is now made in terms of the nature of subjective experience that accompanies the operations of the systems at encoding and retrieval."

In spite of the major differences between episodic and semantic memory, there are also important similarities: "The manner in which information is registered in the episodic and semantic systems is highly similar—there is no known method of readily encoding information into an adult's semantic memory without putting corresponding information in episodic memory or vice versa . . . both episodic and semantic memory obey the principles of encoding specificity and transfer appropriate processing" (Wheeler et al., 1997, p. 333).

Evidence

The key theoretical assumption made by Wheeler et al. (1997) is that episodic memory depends on various cortical and subcortical networks in which the prefrontal cortex plays a central role. Evidence from brain damaged patients and from PET scans has been obtained to test this assumption. For example, Janowsky, Shimamura, and Squire (1989) studied memory in frontal lobe patients. They focused especially on *source amnesia*, which involves being unable to remember where or how some piece of factual information was learned. This study is relevant, because it can be argued that source amnesia typically reflects a failure of episodic memory. Frontal lobe patients showed considerable source amnesia, which is consistent with the view that the frontal cortex is involved in episodic memory.

Additional evidence comes from PET studies. In 25 out of 26 studies reviewed by Wheeler et al. (1997), the right prefrontal cortex was more active during episodic memory *retrieval* than during semantic memory retrieval. The same approach was used in 20 studies to identify those brain regions involved in episodic encoding but not in semantic encoding. In 18 out of the 20 studies, the left prefrontal cortex was more active during episodic *encoding*.

In sum, Wheeler et al. (1997) argued there are two major differences between episodic and semantic memory. First, episodic memory involves the subjective experience of consciously recollecting personal events from the past whereas semantic memory does not. Second, the prefrontal cortex is much more involved in episodic memory than in semantic memory. Many higher-level cognitive processes take place in the prefrontal cortex, and it is assumed that the "sophisticated form of self-awareness" (Wheeler et al., 1997, p. 349) associated with episodic memory involves a higher-level cognitive process.

Evaluation

The theoretical views of Wheeler et al. (1997) represent an advance in our understanding of long-term memory. In particular, the notion that there is a major distinction between episodic and semantic memory seems plausible. However, there are doubts about the empirical support for the distinction. The finding that patients with damage to the frontal lobes show impaired episodic memory is open to various interpretations. One possibility is that the actual processes involved in episodic memory are *specifically* affected by the brain damage. Another possibility is that the effects of frontal lobe damage are more *general* (e.g., loss of some higher-level cognitive processes). As a result, such brain damage disrupts the performance of numerous kinds of cognitive tasks, including those involving episodic memory.

The findings from PET studies are consistent with the notion that the distinction between episodic and semantic memory is of major importance. However, there are some doubts about the value of this distinction, especially when applied to amnesic patients (see later in the chapter).

What remains for the future is to consider more closely the relationship between episodic and semantic memory. Research so far has focused on the differences between episodic and semantic memory, in spite of the fact that there are several similarities and inter-connections between them.

Implicit versus explicit memory

Traditional measures of memory (e.g., free recall, cued recall, and recognition) involve the use of direct instructions to retrieve specific information. Thus, they can all be regarded as measures of explicit memory (Graf & Schacter, 1985, p. 501): "*Explicit memory* is revealed when performance on a task requires conscious recollection of previous experiences." In contrast, "*Implicit memory* is revealed when performance on a task is facilitated in the absence of conscious recollection."

In order to understand what is involved in implicit memory, we will consider a study by Tulving, Schacter, and Stark (1982). Their participants learned a list of multi-syllabled and relatively rare words (e.g., "toboggan"). One hour or one week later, they were simply asked to fill in the blanks in word fragments to make a word (e.g., _ O _ O _ G A _). The solutions to half of the fragments were words from the list that had been learned, but the participants were not told this. As conscious recollection was not required on the word-fragment completion test, it can be regarded as a test of implicit memory.

There was evidence for implicit memory, with the participants completing more of the fragments correctly when the solutions matched list words. This is known as *repetition priming*, and is found when the processing of a stimulus is faster and/or easier when it is presented on more than one occasion. You might imagine that repetition priming occurred because the participants deliberately searched through the previously learned list, so that the test actually involved explicit memory. However, Tulving et al. (1982) reported an additional finding that goes against that possibility. Repetition priming was no greater for target words that were recognised than for those that were not. Thus, the repetition priming effect was *unrelated* to explicit memory performance as assessed by recognition memory. This finding suggests that repetition priming and recognition memory involve different forms of memory.

If explicit and implicit memory really are separate forms of memory, then they probably involve different brain regions. This issue was explored by Schacter et al. (1996) in a study using PET scans. When the participants performed an explicit memory task (recall of semantically processed words), there was much activation of the hippocampus. In contrast, when they performed an implicit memory task (word-stem completion), there was reduced blood flow in the bilateral occipital cortex, but the task did not affect hippocampal activation.

Does implicit memory form a *single* memory system? The fact that there are numerous kinds of implicit memory tasks ranging from motor skills to word completion suggests that various memory systems and brain areas are involved. Tulving and Schacter (1990) distinguished between perceptual and conceptual implicit memory. On most perceptual implicit tests, the stimulus presented at study is presented at test in a degraded form (e.g., word-fragment completion; word-stem completion; perceptual identification). On conceptual implicit tests, on the other hand, the test provides information *conceptually* related to the studied information, but there is no *perceptual* similarity between the study and test stimuli (e.g., general knowledge questions such as "What is the largest animal on earth?").

Neuroimaging studies suggest that different brain areas are involved in perceptual and conceptual implicit memory. As we have seen, Schacter et al. (1996) found in a PET study that perceptual priming reduced activity in bilateral occipito-temporal areas. In contrast, Wagner et al. (1997) found that conceptual priming reduced activity in the left frontal neocortex. Why was brain activity reduced rather than increased in these studies? Processing is more efficient when a stimulus is re-presented than on its original presentation.

Evaluation
There appears to be a distinction of major importance between explicit and implicit memory. However, it can be argued that the distinction only *describes* different forms of memory, and fails to *explain* what is happening. The crucial difference between explicit and implicit memory is in terms of the involvement of conscious recollection, and it is not easy to decide whether someone's memory performance depends on conscious recollection. Finally, implicit memory is defined by the absence of conscious recollection. There is increasing evidence that there are several forms of memory not involving conscious recollection, but the number and nature of such forms of implicit memory remain unclear.

Amnesia

Memory researchers have carried out numerous studies on brain-damaged patients suffering from a range of memory problems. Of particular interest have been patients with *amnesia*, a condition in which there are severe problems with long-term memory. Why have amnesic patients been the focus of research? One reason is that the study of such patients provides a good *test-bed* for existing theories of normal memory. Another important reason is that research on amnesia has suggested theoretical distinctions that have proved relevant to our understanding of memory in normal individuals. Some examples are discussed later in the chapter.

Patients become amnesic for various reasons. Closed head injury is the most common cause of amnesia, and other causes include bilateral stroke and chronic alcoholism. Most research has involved sufferers from *Korsakoff's syndrome*, which occurs through chronic alcohol abuse. There has been less research on patients with closed head injury. Such patients often have a range of cognitive impairments, and this makes it hard to interpret their memory deficit.

Two major symptoms are exhibited by most amnesic patients. First, there is *anterograde amnesia*, in which there is a marked impairment in the ability to remember new information learned after the onset of the amnesia. Second, there is *retrograde amnesia*, in which there is great difficulty in remembering events from before the onset of amnesia, especially those that occurred shortly beforehand.

Amnesia can be produced by damage to various brain structures. These structures are in two areas of the brain: a subcortical region called the diencephalon, and a cortical region known as the medial temporal lobe (see Figure 6.8). Patients with Korsakoff's syndrome have brain damage in the diencephalon, especially the medial thalamus and the mamillary nuclei, but typically the frontal cortex is also damaged. Other patients have damage in the medial–temporal region. This can happen as a result of herpes simplex encephalitis, anoxia (due to lack of oxygen), infarction, or sclerosis (involving a hardening of tissue or organs).

Our understanding of the brain systems involved in amnesia has been hampered by the difficulty of locating the precise location of damage in any given patient. Attempts to do so used to rely mainly on post-mortem examination. However, the development of neuro-imaging techniques has allowed accurate assessment of the damaged areas while the patient is alive. Aggleton and Brown (1999, p. 426)

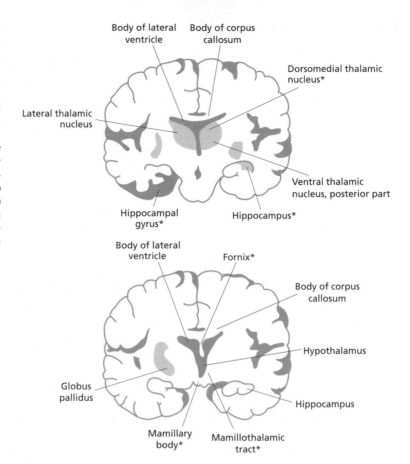

Figure 6.8. Some of the brain structures involved in amnesia (indicated by asterisks). Figure from "Clinical symptoms, neuropathology and etiology" by Nelson Butters and Laird S. Cermak in *Alcoholic Korsakoff's syndrome: An information-processing approach to amnesia.* Copyright © 1980 by Academic Press, reproduced by permission of the publisher.

made use of evidence obtained from neuroimaging to propose a new theory: "The traditional distinction between temporal lobe and diencephalic amnesics is misleading: both groups have damage to the same functional system . . . The proposed hippocampal–diencephalic system is required for the encoding of episodic information, permitting the information to be set in its spatial and temporal context."

Are different parts of the brain involved in anterograde and retrograde amnesia? Evidence that this may be the case was reported by Reed and Squire (1998) in a study of four amnesic patients. Magnetic resonance imaging (MRI) examinations revealed that all four had hippocampal damage, but only two also had temporal lobe damage. The two patients with temporal lobe damage had much more severe retrograde amnesia than the other two, suggesting that retrograde amnesia involves the temporal lobe.

Residual learning ability

We know that amnesics are generally poor at remembering information learned after the onset of amnesia. However, it is important to discover those aspects of learning and memory that remain fairly intact in amnesic patients. A comparison of the lists of those memory abilities impaired and not impaired in amnesia might facilitate the task of identifying the processes and/or memory structures affected in amnesic patients. Some of the main memory abilities that remain in amnesic patients are as follows:

(1) *Short-term memory*: Amnesic patients perform almost as well as normals on digit span (immediate ordered recall of random digits; Butters & Cermak, 1980).
(2) *Skill learning*: Amnesic patients have normal rates of learning for serial reaction time, mirror tracing, and the pursuit rotor (Gabrieli, 1998). Mirror tracing involves tracing with a stylus a figure seen reflected in a mirror. The pursuit rotor involves manual tracking of a moving target.
(3) *Repetition priming*: Amnesics show normal or nearly normal repetition priming effects across a range of tasks (see earlier in the chapter). For example, Cermak et al. (1985) used a perceptual identification task, which involved presenting words at the minimal exposure time needed to identify them correctly. Some of these words were primed, in the sense that they had previously been presented in a list of words to be learned. Amnesic patients showed a similar priming effect to controls, i.e., primed words were detected at shorter presentation times than non-primed words.
(4) *Conditioning*: Many amnesic patients show normal eyeblink conditioning (see Gabrieli, 1998). This is a form of classical conditioning in which individuals learn to blink to a tone that has previously been paired with a puff of air delivered to the eyes.

It is hard to detect much similarity among these different memory abilities. However, a common theme running through most of them is that they do not necessarily require conscious recollection of previous stimuli or events. More specifically, the assessment of skill learning, repetition learning, and conditioning is based on behavioural measures of performance rather than on the ability to bring previously acquired knowledge into consciousness. As we will see, some theories of amnesia have been constructed on this basis.

Theories of amnesia

Episodic vs. semantic memory

As we saw earlier, Tulving (1972) distinguished between *episodic memory*, which is concerned with events or episodes happening at a given time in a given place, and *semantic memory*, which is concerned with general knowledge about the world. Amnesic patients clearly have problems with episodic memory, because they often cannot remember recent events in which they have been involved. In contrast, much of semantic memory seems to be intact. They generally possess good language skills, including vocabulary and grammar, and their performance is essentially normal on intelligence tests. However, those aspects of semantic memory that are intact are mainly those that were acquired *before* the onset of amnesia, and most amnesics find it hard to acquire new semantic memories *after* the onset of amnesia. For example, Gabrieli, Cohen, and Corkin (1988) found an amnesic patient with an almost complete inability to acquire new vocabulary.

The fact that most amnesics have great difficulties in acquiring new episodic and semantic memories has led many theorists to argue that the distinction is of limited value to an understanding of amnesia. However, Vargha-Khadem et al. (1997) produced evidence supporting the distinction. They studied two patients (Beth and Jon) who had suffered bilateral hippocampal damage at an early age before they had had the opportunity to develop semantic memories. Both patients had very poor episodic memory for the day's activities, television programmes, and so on. In spite of this, they both attended ordinary schools, and their levels of speech and language development, literacy, and factual knowledge (e.g., vocabulary) were within the normal range.

Vargha-Khadem et al. (1997, p. 376) explained their findings by arguing that episodic and semantic memory depend on somewhat different brain regions: "Episodic memory depends primarily on the hippocampal component of the larger system [i.e., hippocampus and underlying entorhinal, perihinal, and parahippocampal cortices], whereas semantic memory depends primarily on the underlying cortices." Why, then, do so many amnesics have great problems with both episodic and semantic memory? According to Vargha-Khadem et al. (1997), most amnesics have damage to the hippocampus *and* to the nearby underlying cortices.

Explicit vs. implicit memory

Schacter (1987) argued that amnesic patients are at a severe disadvantage when tests of explicit memory (requiring conscious recollection) are used, but that they perform at normal levels on tests of implicit memory (not requiring conscious recollection). As predicted by this theory, most amnesic patients display impaired performance on tests of recently acquired episodic and semantic memories. Most studies on motor skills and on various repetition-priming effects are also consistent with Schacter's theoretical perspective, in that they are basically implicit memory tasks on which amnesic patients perform normally or nearly so.

Striking findings were reported by Graf, Squire, and Mandler (1984). Word lists were presented, with each list being followed by one of four memory tests. Three of the tests were conventional explicit memory tests (free recall; recognition memory; cued recall), but the fourth test (word completion) involved implicit memory. On this last test, participants were given three-letter word stems (e.g., STR___) and simply wrote down the first word they thought of starting with those letters (e.g., STRAP; STRIP). Implicit memory was assessed by the extent to which the word completions corresponded to words from the previous list. The amnesic patients did much worse than normals on all three explicit memory tests, but performed as well as normals on the implicit memory test (see Figure 6.9).

Schacter and Church (1995) reported further evidence of intact implicit memory in amnesic patients. The participants initially heard a series of words spoken in the same voice. After that, they tried to

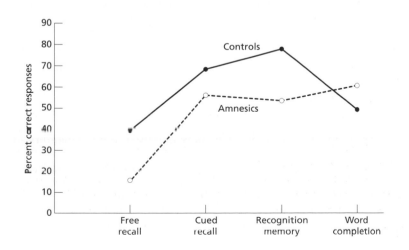

Figure 6.9. Free recall, cued recall, recognition memory, and word completion in amnesic patients and controls. Data from different experiments reported by Graf et al. (1984).

Figure 6.10. Auditory word identification for previously presented words in amnesics and controls. All words originally presented in the same voice. Data from Schacter and Church (1995).

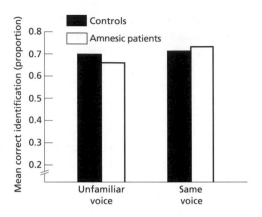

identify the same words passed through an auditory filter; the words were either spoken in the same voice or in an unfamiliar voice. Amnesic patients and normal controls both showed implicit memory or perceptual priming, in that word-identification performance was better when the words were spoken in the same voice (see Figure 6.10).

Evaluation

The distinction between explicit and implicit memory is of great value in categorising tests of long-term memory on which amnesic patients do and do not perform poorly. However, there are some limitations with this approach to amnesia. First, the notion that amnesic patients have deficient explicit memory does not in and of itself provide an *explanation* of their memory impairments. As Schacter (1987, p. 501) pointed out, implicit and explicit memory "are descriptive concepts that are primarily concerned with a person's psychological experience at the time of retrieval." Second, the finding that amnesics have nearly intact short-term memory does not fit, because tests of short-term memory typically involve explicit rather than implicit memory. Third, there are an increasing number of studies of long-term memory that show impaired implicit memory in amnesic patients (see below).

Declarative versus procedural memory

Cohen and Squire (1980) drew a distinction between declarative memory and procedural memory. Their distinction was closely related to that made by Ryle (1949) between knowing that and knowing how. *Declarative memory* corresponds to knowing that (e.g., knowing that Paris is the capital of France), and covers both episodic and semantic memory. *Procedural memory* corresponds to knowing how, and refers to the ability to perform skilled actions (e.g., knowing how to ride a bicycle) without the involvement of conscious recollection. Thus, declarative memory corresponds fairly closely to explicit memory and procedural memory to implicit memory.

Cohen, Poldrack, and Eichenbaum (1997) redefined somewhat the distinction between declarative memory and procedural memory. Declarative memory was defined as "a fundamentally relational representation supporting memory for the relationships among perceptually distinct objects that constitute the outcomes of processing of events" (Cohen et al., 1997, p. 138). In contrast, procedural memory "accomplishes experience-based tuning and modification of individual processors, and involves fundamentally inflexible, individual (i.e., nonrelational) representations" (Cohen et al., 1997, p. 138). It remains the case that declarative memory resembles explicit memory, in that it involves the integration or linkage of information. In contrast, procedural memory still resembles implicit memory, in that it involves specific forms of processing. According to Cohen et al. (1997, p. 138), "*The fundamental deficit in amnesia is the selective disruption of declarative memory.*"

The theoretical approach of Cohen et al. (1997) is similar to that of Schacter (1987). However, there is at least one crucial difference. Suppose that we consider implicit memory for information that needs to be integrated. According to Schacter (1987), amnesics should perform normally on this task. According to Cohen et al. (1997), they should not. We turn to an experimental test of these predictions.

Whitlow, Althoff, and Cohen (1995) presented amnesic patients and normal controls with real-world scenes, and asked them to respond as rapidly as possible to questions (e.g., "Is there a chair behind the oranges?"). After that, the participants answered questions when presented with three kinds of scenes:

(1) Repeated old scenes.
(2) New scenes.
(3) Manipulated old scenes, in which the positions of some of the objects had been rearranged.

The participants' eye movements were recorded as they viewed the scenes.

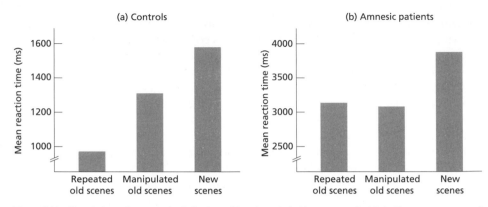

Figure 6.11. Speed of question answering in three conditions (repeated old scenes; manipulated old scenes; new scenes). Data from Whitlow et al. (1995).

What did Whitlow et al. (1995) find? Both groups answered questions faster to old scenes (whether repeated or rearranged) than to new scenes. This could be explained on the basis that the task relies on implicit memory, which is intact in amnesic patients. However, the crucial findings were that normal controls responded faster to *repeated* old scenes than to *rearranged* old scenes, whereas the amnesic patients did not (see Figure 6.11). The lack of advantage for repeated old scenes in amnesic patients suggests that their implicit memory is *not* always intact. The findings suggest that amnesic patients failed to store integrated information about the relative positions of the objects in the scenes. This conclusion was supported by the eye movement data. The normal controls had numerous eye movements directed to the parts of rearranged old scenes that had changed, whereas the amnesics showed no tendency to fixate on these altered aspects.

Kroll et al. (1996) also found that amnesics have difficulty in storing integrated information. They studied conjunction errors, which occur when new objects formed out of conjunctions or combinations of objects seen previously are mistakenly recognised as old. Amnesic patients made numerous conjunction errors, presumably because they remembered having seen the elements of the new objects but did not realise that the combination of elements was novel.

Cohen et al. (1994) used fMRI to identify the brain regions involved in the integration of information. Seven normal participants were presented with three kinds of information at the same time (faces, names, and occupations). On some trials, they were told to learn the associations among these kinds of information, a task involving integrative processes. On other trials, the participants simply made gender decisions about each face, a task not requiring the integration of information. All the participants had more activation in the hippocampus on the task requiring the integration of information. Thus, the hippocampus seems to play a central role in processes of association or integration.

Evaluation

The notion that amnesic patients have particular problems with storing integrated or linked information has become extremely popular. For example, it has influenced theorists who favour the distinction between explicit and implicit memory: "Implicit memory reflects primarily the bottom-up, nonconscious effects of prior experience on single brain subsystems . . . Explicit memory reflects the top-down, simultaneous retrieval of information from multiple information-processing brain mechanisms. This massive integration of information (e.g., perceptual, semantic, temporal, spatial, etc.) may be necessary to support conscious recollection of previous experiences" (Curran & Schacter, 1997, p. 45).

In spite of the impressive theoretical progress that has been made in recent years, there are some unresolved issues. As you have probably noticed, there have been clear changes over the years in the definitions of key concepts such as declarative memory, procedural memory, explicit memory, implicit memory, episodic memory, and semantic memory. Most of these changes have brought these concepts closer together. As a result, it is increasingly difficult to decide on the extent to which different theories actually make significantly different predictions.

Schema theories

Most of the research we have considered so far has been concerned with words, pictures, or sentences. However, it is also important to consider our long-term memory for stories, events, and so on. Theories in this area have focused on *schemas*, which are well-integrated packages of information about the world, events, people, and actions. Scripts and frames are relatively specific kinds of schemas. Scripts deal with knowledge about events and consequences of events, and frames deal with knowledge about the properties of objects and locations.

Schemas or scripts allow us to form *expectations*. In a restaurant, for example, we expect to be shown to a table, to be given a menu by the waiter or waitress, to order the food and drink, and so on. If any of these expectations is violated, then we usually take appropriate action. For example, if no menu is forthcoming, we try to catch the eye of the waiter or waitress. As our expectations are generally confirmed, schemas help to make the world a reasonably predictable place.

We will consider two schema or script theories here. First, and of great historical importance, there is Bartlett's (1932) schema theory. Second, there is the script-pointer-plus-tag hypothesis of Schank and Abelson (1977).

Bartlett's schema theory

According to Bartlett (1932), what we remember from stories is determined not only by the story itself, but also by our store of relevant prior knowledge in the form of schemas. He tested this notion by presenting his participants (mostly Cambridge University students) with stories producing a *conflict* between what was presented to them and their prior knowledge. The prediction was that people reading a story from a different culture (e.g., North American Indian culture) would have a distorted memory of the story, making it more conventional and acceptable from the standpoint of their own cultural background.

Bartlett's (1932) findings supported the above prediction. In particular, a substantial proportion of the recall errors were in the direction of making the story read more like a typical English story. He used the term *rationalisation* to refer to this type of error. Bartlett (1932) reported findings supporting this prediction. He also found other kinds of errors, including flattening (failure to recall unfamiliar details) and sharpening (elaboration of certain details).

Bartlett's studies are open to criticism. He did not give very specific instructions to his participants (Bartlett, 1932, p. 78: "I thought it best, for the purposes of these experiments, to try to influence the subjects' procedure as little as possible." As a result, some of the distortions observed by Bartlett were due to conscious guessing rather than deficient memory. Gauld and Stephenson (1967) found that instructions stressing the need for accurate recall eliminated almost half the errors usually obtained.

Bartlett (1932) assumed that memory for the precise material presented is forgotten over time, whereas memory for the underlying schemas is not. Thus, rationalisation errors (which depend on

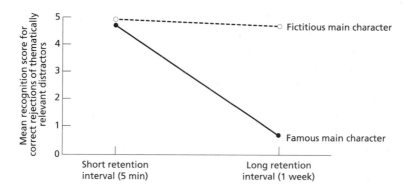

Figure 6.12. Correct rejection of thematic distractor as a function of main actor (Gerald Martin or Adolf Hitler) and retention interval. Data from Sulin and Dooling (1974).

schematic knowledge) should increase in number at longer retention intervals. Supporting evidence was reported by Sulin and Dooling (1974). They presented some of their participants with a story about Gerald Martin: "Gerald Martin strove to undermine the existing government to satisfy his political ambitions . . . He became a ruthless, uncontrollable dictator. The ultimate effect of his rule was the downfall of his country" (Sulin & Dooling, 1974, p. 256). Other participants were given the same story, but the name of the main actor was given as Adolf Hitler. Those participants told the story was about Adolf Hitler were much more likely than the other participants to believe incorrectly that they had read the sentence, "He hated the Jews particularly and so persecuted them." Their schematic knowledge about Hitler distorted their recollections of what they had read. As Bartlett (1932) predicted, this type of distortion was more frequent at a long than a short retention interval (see Figure 6.12).

Bartlett (1932) assumed that memorial distortions occur mainly because of schema-driven reconstructive processes operating at the time of retrieval. However, schemas can influence story comprehension rather than just retrieval. For example, Bransford and Johnson (1972, p. 722) presented a passage in which it was hard to work out which schemas were relevant. Part of it was as follows:

> The procedure is quite simple. First, you arrange items into different groups. Of course one pile may be sufficient depending on how much there is to do. If you have to go somewhere else due to lack of facilities that is the next step; otherwise, you are pretty well set.

The participants who heard the passage in the absence of a title rated it as incomprehensible, and recalled an average of only 2.8 idea

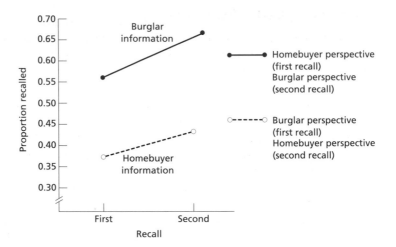

Figure 6.13. Recall as a function of perspective at the time of retrieval. Based on data from Anderson and Pichert (1978).

units. In contrast, those who were supplied beforehand with the title "Washing clothes" found it easy to understand and recalled 5.8 idea units on average. This effect of relevant schema knowledge occurred because it helped comprehension of the passage. Bransford and Johnson (1972) favoured a constructive theory, according to which schematic knowledge affects the way in which stories and other material are interpreted and comprehended.

Evidence more supportive of Bartlett (1932) was reported by Anderson and Pichert (1978). Participants read a story from the perspective of either a burglar or of someone interested in buying a home. After they had recalled as much as they could of the story from the perspective they had been given, they shifted to the alternative perspective, and recalled the story again. On the second recall, participants recalled more information that was important only to the second perspective or schema than they had done on the first recall (see Figure 6.13).

There are doubts as to whether Bartlett's main findings can be replicated under more naturalistic conditions. Wynn and Logie (1998) tested students' recall of "real-life" events experienced during their first week at university at various intervals of time ranging from 2 weeks to 6 months. What they found was as follows: "The initial accuracy sustained throughout the time period, together with the relative lack of change over time, suggests very limited use of reconstructive processes" (Wynn & Logie, 1998, p. 1). This failure may have occurred in part because the students were only able to make limited use of schema-based processes.

Script-pointer-plus-tag hypothesis

The script-pointer-plus-tag hypothesis was put forward by Schank and Abelson (1977). It consists of various assumptions about memory for script- or schema-based stories:

- Information from the story is combined with information from the underlying script or schema in memory.
- Actions in a story are either typical (consistent with the underlying script or schema) or atypical (inconsistent with the underlying script).
- Information about atypical actions is tagged individually to the underlying script.
- Recognition memory will be worse for typical than for atypical actions, because typical actions *present* in the story are hard to discriminate from typical actions *absent* from the story.
- Initial recall for atypical actions should be better than for typical actions, because they are tagged individually in memory.
- Recall for atypical actions at long retention intervals should be worse than for typical actions, because recall increasingly relies on the underlying script or schema.

Evidence

Most studies support the prediction that recognition memory for atypical actions is better than for typical ones at all retention intervals (Davidson, 1994). However, the findings with respect to recall are more inconsistent. Davidson (1994) shed light on these inconsistencies. She used routine atypical actions that were irrelevant to the story and atypical actions that interrupted the story. For example, in a story about going to the cinema, "Sarah mentions to Sam that the screen is big" belongs to the former category and "Another couple, both of whom are very tall, sits in front of them and blocks their view" belongs to the latter category. Both kinds of atypical actions were better recalled than typical ones at a relatively short retention interval (1 hour), which is in line with prediction. After 1 week, the routine atypical actions were worse recalled than typical or script actions, but the interruptive atypical actions were better recalled than typical actions.

What is going on here? Presumably, interruptive atypical actions are well recalled at the longer retention interval because they remain clearly differentiated from the underlying script or schema. As Davidson (1994, p. 772) concluded, "Part of the problem with existing schema theories is that they do not specify how different types of atypical actions will be recalled."

Evaluation

Our organised knowledge of the world is used to help text comprehension and recall. However, it has proved hard to identify the characteristics of schemas. More importantly, most versions of schema theory are rather lacking in testability. If we are trying to explain text comprehension and memory in terms of the activation of certain schemas, then we really require independent evidence of the characteristics (and appropriate activation) of those schemas. Such evidence is generally not available, but was provided in a study by Bower, Black, and Turner (1979). They asked students to list 20 actions or events associated with various events (e.g., eating at a restaurant, attending a lecture). There was a considerable amount of agreement across participants, suggesting that different people have similar schemas. When Bower et al. (1979) presented stories eliciting specific underlying schemas or scripts, they found that unstated schema-relevant actions were often recalled or falsely recognised.

According to schema theory, top-down processes lead to the generation of numerous inferences during story comprehension. Most early research provided support for this assumption. For example, Bransford, Barclay, and Franks (1972) presented sentences such as "Three turtles rested on a floating log, and a fish swam beneath them." They argued that the inference would be drawn that the fish swam under the log. To test this, some participants on a subsequent recognition-memory test were given the sentence, "Three turtles rested on a floating log, and a fish swam beneath it." Most participants were confident that this inference was the original sentence. Indeed, their level of confidence was as high as it was when the original sentence was re-presented on the memory test!

Graesser, Singer, and Trabasso (1994) argued that most schema theories fail to specify *which* inferences are drawn when people read a story. They remedied this omission in their search-after-meaning theory, which was based on the following assumptions:

- *The reader goal assumption*: Readers construct a meaning for the text that addresses their goals.
- *The coherence assumption*: Readers try to construct a coherent meaning for the text.
- *The explanation assumption*: Readers try to explain the actions, events, and states referred to in the text.

Readers will draw few inferences if their goals do not require them to understand the meaning of the text (e.g., in proofreading), if the text appears to lack coherence, or if they lack the necessary background knowledge to make sense of the text. Even if readers do search after meaning, there are several kinds of inference that are not normally drawn: ones about future developments (causal consequence); the precise way in which actions are accomplished (subordinate goal-actions); and the author's intent (see Graesser et al., 1994). Schema theories do not make it clear why such inferences are not drawn. Issues relating to inference drawing in discourse comprehension are discussed more fully in Chapter 7.

Everyday memory

Most research on human memory has been carried out in the laboratory, and may appear to have little relevance to real life. This state of affairs has led many researchers to study everyday memory. As Koriat and Goldsmith (1996) pointed out, many everyday memory reseachers differ from other memory researchers in their answers to three questions:

(1) *What* memory phenomena should be studied? According to everyday memory researchers, the kinds of phenomena people experience every day should be the main focus.

(2) *How* should memory be studied? Everyday memory researchers emphasise the importance of the ecological validity of memory research. *Ecological validity* consists of two aspects: (1) *representativeness*, and (2) *generalisability* (Kvavilashvili & Ellis, in press). Representativeness refers to the naturalness of the experimental situation, stimuli, and task, whereas generalisability refers to the extent to which the findings of a study are applicable to the real world. Generalisability is more important than representativeness.

(3) *Where* should memory phenomena be studied? Some everyday memory researchers argue in favour of naturalistic settings.

In fact, matters are not as neat and tidy as suggested so far. As Koriat and Goldsmith (1996) pointed out, "Although the three dimensions—the what, how, and where dimensions are conceptual in the reality of memory research, they are not logically inter-dependent. For instance, many everyday memory topics can be studied in the laboratory, and memory research in naturalistic settings may be amenable to strict experimental control" (p. 168).

Neisser (1996) identified a crucial difference between memory as studied traditionally and memory in everyday life. The participants in traditional memory studies are generally motivated to be as *accurate* as possible in their memory performance. In contrast, everyday memory research should be based on the notion that "remembering is a form of purposeful action" (Neisser, 1996, p. 204). This approach involves three assumptions about everyday memory:

(1) It is purposeful.
(2) It has a personal quality about it, meaning that it is influenced by the individual's personality and other characteristics.
(3) It is influenced by situational demands (e.g., the wish to impress one's audience) rather than by the need to be accurate.

Numerous topics have been studied within everyday memory. We will focus on two of the most important ones: eyewitness testimony and flashbulb memories. Research on eyewitness testimony has possibly been of more practical benefit than any other research in memory. Research on flashbulb memories has addressed the fascinating issue of our vivid memories for dramatic world events (e.g., the sudden death of Princess Diana).

Eyewitness testimony

Thousands of people have been put in prison purely on the basis of eyewitness testimony. Even if the rate of mistaken identification is low, it would still follow that many innocent individuals languish in prison because of the fallibility of eyewitness testimony. As we will see, eyewitness testimony is often inaccurate. Why is that so? One obvious reason is because eyewitnesses often do not realise initially that a crime or other event is happening, and so do not attend fully to it. In addition, there is strong evidence that the memory that an eyewitness has of an event is fragile, in the sense that it can easily be distorted by questioning or information occurring after the event (post-event information). We will start by considering evidence for this fragility.

Post-event information

Loftus and Palmer (1974) showed their participants projected slides of a multiple car accident. After that, the participants described what had happened, and answered specific questions. Some were asked, "About how fast were the cars going when they smashed into each other?", whereas for other participants the verb "hit" was substituted for "smashed into". Control participants were not asked a question about car speed. The estimated speed was affected by the verb used in the question, averaging 41 mph when the verb "smashed" was used vs. 34 mph when "hit" was used. Thus, the information implicit in the question affected the way in which the accident was remembered.

One week later, all the participants were asked, "Did you see any broken glass?" There was actually no broken glass in the accident, but 32% of the participants who had been asked previously about speed using the verb "smashed" said they had seen broken glass. Only 14% of the participants asked using the verb "hit" said they had seen broken glass, and the figure was 12% for the control participants. Thus, our memory for events is fragile and susceptible to distortion.

Why does post-event information distort what eyewitnesses report? At the most general level, what we have here is simply retroactive interference (see earlier in the chapter). Some understanding of what is involved can be obtained with reference to the source monitoring framework (Johnson, Hashtroudi, & Lindsay, 1993). A memory probe (e.g., question) activates memory traces having informational overlap with it; this memory probe may activate memory from various sources. The individual decides on the source of any activated memory on the basis of the information it contains. If the memories from one source resemble those from another source, this increases the chances of source misattribution. If eyewitnesses falsely attribute the source of misinformation to the original event, then the misinformation will form part of their recall of the event.

A key prediction from the source monitoring framework is as follows: Any manipulation that increases the extent to which memories from one source resemble those from another source increases the likelihood of source misattribution. Allen and Lindsay (1998) presented two narrative slide shows 48 hours apart describing two different events with different people in different settings. Thus, the participants knew that the post-event information contained in the second slide show was not relevant to the event described in the first slide show. However, some of the details in the two events were rather similar (e.g., a can of Pepsi versus a can of Coca-Cola). This caused source misattribution, and led the participants to substitute details from the post-event information for details of the event itself.

Loftus (1979) argued that information from the misleading questions permanently alters the memory representation of the incident: The previously formed memory is "overwritten" and destroyed. In one study, she offered her participants $25 if their recall of an incident was accurate. Their recollections were still distorted by the misleading information they had heard, suggesting that the information might have been destroyed. However, the views of Loftus (1979) are *not* generally accepted, because there is evidence that the original information remains in long-term memory. For example, Dodson and Reisberg (1991) used an implicit memory test to show that misinformation had *not* destroyed the original memories of an event. They concluded that misinformation simply makes these memories inaccessible.

Loftus (1992) emphasised the notion of *misinformation acceptance*: The participants "accept" misleading information presented to them after an event, and subsequently regard it as forming part of their memory of that event. There is a greater tendency to accept post-event information in this way as the time since the event increases. This resembles a schema theory: Eyewitnesses form a coherent memory structure or schema of the event they have witnessed, and post-event information is simply added to the event schema.

Verbal overshadowing of visual memories

The notion that eyewitness memory is fragile and easily distorted was confirmed strikingly by Schooler and Engstler-Schooler (1990). Participants viewed a film of a crime. After that, some participants provided a detailed verbal report of the criminal's appearance, whereas others did an unrelated task. Finally, all the participants tried to select the criminal's face on a recognition test. Those who had provided the detailed verbal report performed *worse* than the other participants on this test. This phenomenon (verbal overshadowing of visual memories) presumably occurred because the verbal reports interfered with recollection of the purely visual information about the criminal's face.

Face recognition

Eyewitnesses are often asked to describe the facial features of the criminal, and may be asked to pick out the criminal from among other people at an identity parade. In order to do this successfully, the eyewitness needs to be good at face recognition. The evidence suggests that there is generally accurate memory for faces in laboratory experiments, but face recognition is often poor in everyday life. Bruce (1982) pointed out that face recognition in the laboratory typically involves presenting the participants with identical pictures at study and at test, which does not correspond to what happens on identification parades. She found in a laboratory study that recognition memory was 90% correct when identical pictures of faces were used at study and test, but it dropped to 60% when the viewpoint and expression changed. Patterson and Baddeley (1977) also found that changes in the appearance of a face between study and test produced a substantial reduction in face recognition. Among the changes they used were false beards and wigs.

Beales and Parkin (1984) studied the effects of the context in which someone is seen. Face recognition from photographs was better when the face was in the same context at study and at test than when a different context was used. An important limitation on these studies was identified by Groeger (1997, p. 182): "Even though recognition judgements can be unreliable when the individual is portrayed in a different location, or where their physical appearance is different, these difficulties probably only apply to people who are not known to the witness."

Another factor influencing the likelihood of mistakes being made on identification parades is the *functional size* of the line-up. This is the number of people in the line-up matching the eyewitness's description of the culprit. When the actual culprit is absent, low functional size of line-up is associated with a greater probability of mistaken identification (Lindsay & Wells, 1980).

The probability of mistaken identification is also influenced by whether or not the eyewitness is warned that the culprit may not be in the line-up (Wells, 1993). This is especially important with real-life line-ups, since eyewitnesses may feel the police would not have set up an identification parade unless they were fairly certain the actual culprit was present.

Wells (1993, p. 560) argued that eyewitnesses use *relative judgements*: "The eyewitness chooses the line-up member who most resembles the culprit relative to the other members of the line-up." How can we reduce eyewitnesses' reliance on the relative judgement strategy? One approach is sequential line-ups, in which members of the line-up or identification parade are presented one at a time. Sequential line-ups reduce the effects of functional size and failure to warn of possible culprit absence on mistaken identification (Lindsay et al., 1991).

Confidence

Most people assume that an eyewitness's confidence is a good predictor of his or her identification accuracy. This assumption is actually false. For example, Perfect and Hollins (1996) gave their participants recognition memory tests for the information contained in a film about a girl who was kidnapped, and for general knowledge questions. Accuracy of memory was *not* associated with confidence for questions about the film, but it was with general knowledge questions.

Perfect and Hollins (1996, p. 379) explained the above difference as follows: "Individuals have insight into their strengths and weaknesses in general knowledge, and tend to modify their use of the confidence scale accordingly . . . So, for example, individuals will know whether they tend to be better or worse than others at sports questions. However, eyewitnessed events are not amenable to such insight: subjects are unlikely to know whether they are better or worse . . . than others at remembering the hair colour of a participant in an event, for example."

Perfect and Hollins (1996) found that eyewitnesses typically had more confidence in their accurate answers than in their inaccurate ones. Thus, they could decide on the quality of their own memories to some extent, even though they did not know whether they were better or worse than others at remembering details of an event.

Confirmation bias

One way in which eyewitness testimony can be distorted is via *confirmation bias*. This occurs when what is remembered of an event is influenced by the observer's expectations. For example, students from two universities in the United States (Princeton and Dartmouth) were shown a film of a football game involving both universities. The students showed a strong tendency to report that their opponents had committed many more fouls than their own team.

Weapon focus

One of the factors that may be involved in eyewitness testimony is *weapon focus*. This was described in the following way by Loftus (1979, p. 75): "The weapon appears to capture a good deal of the victim's attention, resulting in, among other things, a reduced ability to recall other details from the environment, to recall details about the assailant, and to recognise the assailant at a later time."

Loftus, Loftus, and Messo (1987) asked their participants to watch one of two sequences: a person pointing a gun at a cashier and receiving some cash; a person handing a cheque to the cashier and receiving some cash. Loftus et al. (1987) recorded the participants' eye movements, and found that they looked more at the gun than at the cheque. In addition, memory for details unrelated to the gun/cheque was poorer in the weapon condition.

Evaluation

Research into eyewitness testimony has convincingly shown that the memories of eyewitnesses are fragile, and are susceptible to retro-active interference. The evidence that post-event information can easily distort an eyewitness's recollections of an incident indicates the necessity of being very careful when questioning eyewitnesses. However, an important limitation of most research on post-event information is its focus on memory for *peripheral* details of events (e.g., presence or absence of broken glass). As Fruzzetti et al. (1992) pointed out, it is harder to use post-event information to distort witnesses' memory for key details (e.g., the murder weapon) than for minor details.

Flashbulb memories

Brown and Kulik (1977) were impressed by the very vivid and detailed memories that people have of certain dramatic world events (e.g., the assassination of President Kennedy). They argued that a special neural mechanism may be activated by such events, provided that they are seen by the individual as surprising and having real consequences for that person's life. This mechanism "prints" the details of such events permanently in the memory system. According to Brown and Kulik (1977), such *flashbulb memories* are not only accurate and very long-lasting, but also often include the following categories of information:

- Informant (person who supplied the information).
- Place where the news was heard.
- Ongoing event.
- Individual's own emotional state.
- Emotional state of others.
- Consequences of the event for the individual.

Brown and Kulik's (1977) central point was that flashbulb memories are very different from other memories in their longevity, accuracy, and reliance on a special neural mechanism. As we will see, this view is controversial.

Evidence and theory

Bohannon (1988) tested people's memory for the explosion of the space shuttle *Challenger* 2 weeks or 8 months afterwards. Recall fell from 77% at the short retention interval to 58% at the long retention interval, suggesting that flashbulb memories are forgotten in the same way as ordinary memories. However, long-term memory was best when the news had caused a strong emotional reaction, and the event had been rehearsed several times (see Figure 6.14).

Conway et al. (1994) refused to accept that flashbulb memories are simply stronger versions of ordinary memories. According to them, the participants in the study by Bohannon (1988) may not have regarded the explosion of *Challenger* as having consequences for their lives. If they did not, one of the main criteria for flashbulb memories proposed by Brown and Kulik (1977) was not fulfilled.

Conway et al. (1994) studied flashbulb memories for the resignation of Mrs Thatcher in 1990. This event was regarded as surprising and consequential by many British people, and so should theoretically have produced flashbulb memories. Memory for this event by students was tested within a few days, after 11 months, and after 26 months. Flashbulb memories were found in 86% of British participants after 11 months, compared to 29% in other countries.

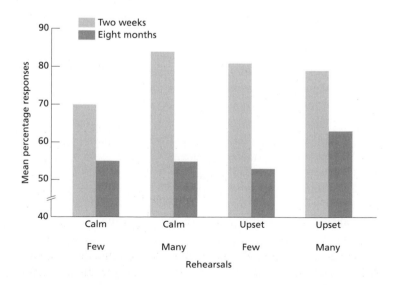

Figure 6.14. Memory for the *Challenger* explosion as a function of whether the event upset the participants, the extent of rehearsal, and the retention interval. Based on data in Bohannon (1988).

Conway et al. (1994, pp. 337–338) concluded: "The striking finding of the present study was the high incidence of very detailed memory reports provided by the U.K. subjects, which remained consistent over an 11-month retention interval and, for a smaller group, over a 26-month retention interval."

Conway et al. (1994) argued that flashbulb memories depend on three main processes plus one optional process:

(1) *Prior knowledge*: This aids in relating the event to existing memory structures.
(2) *Personal importance*: The event should be perceived as having great personal relevance.
(3) *Surprise and emotional feeling state*: The event should produce an emotional reaction.
(4) *Overt rehearsal*: This is an optional process (some people with flashbulb memories for Mrs Thatcher's resignation had not rehearsed the event). However, rehearsal was generally strongly linked to the existence of flashbulb memories.

Evaluation

Flashbulb memories can be very vivid and unusually memorable. However, they are not found very often or for large numbers of people. Wright and Gaskell (1995, p. 70) pointed out that "The only study that has found a high percentage of subjects reporting what can realistically be considered memories that differ from ordinary memories investigated memories for Margaret Thatcher's resignation" (Conway et al., 1994). Wright, Gaskell, and Muircheartaigh (1998) carried out a large population survey in England about 18 months after Mrs Thatcher's resignation, and found that only 12% of those sampled remembered the event vividly. The fact that Conway et al. (1994) used a student sample may help to explain the high percentage of flashbulb memories they reported.

The crucial issue is whether flashbulb memories are radically different from other memories, as was suggested by Brown and Kulik (1977). Most of the evidence suggests they are not. Finkenauer et al. (1998, p. 526) argued that flashbulb memories depend on several key variables: "(1) the reaction of surprise upon learning about the original event, (2) the appraisal of importance or consequentiality of the original event, (3) an intense emotional feeling state, and (4) rehearsal." However, *all* of these factors can be involved in the formation of any memory. This led them to the following conclusion: "FBMs [flashbulb memories] are the result of ordinary memory mechanisms. However, the great number of details constituting FBMs, their clarity, and their durability suggest that a particularly efficient encoding took place" (Finkenauer et al., 1998, p. 530).

An important limitation of some studies on flashbulb memories is that it is difficult to check on the accuracy of those memories. The experimenter was not present when the flashbulb memories were formed, and so has no direct evidence of what happened.

Summary: Long-term memory

- *Theories of forgetting*: The forgetting function is generally logarithmic with a few exceptions (e.g., autobiographical memory). There is evidence of a repression-like phenomenon in normal repressors, and controversial evidence concerning recovered memories of childhood abuse. There is convincing evidence of the existence of proactive and retroactive interference. However, special conditions are required for substantial interference effects to occur, and interference theory is relatively uninformative about the processes involved in forgetting. Most forgetting seems to be cue dependent, and is greater when the contextual information present at retrieval differs from the contextual information stored in memory.
- *Theories of long-term memory*: Tulving argued that there is an important distinction between episodic and semantic memory. There is evidence from PET studies that the prefrontal cortex is much more involved in episodic memory than in semantic memory. It remains unclear whether there is a fundamental distinction between episodic and semantic memory, in part because there are several similarities and interconnections between them. There is a major distinction between explicit and implicit memory. PET studies have revealed that rather different areas of the brain are activated in explicit and implicit memory tasks. There is increasing evidence (e.g., from PET studies) that there are different types of implicit memory (e.g., perceptual and conceptual).
- *Amnesia*: Most amnesic patients suffer from anterograde and retrograde amnesia, but somewhat different parts of the brain may underlie them. Amnesics have fairly intact short-term memory, skill learning, repetition priming, and

conditioning. It has been argued that most amnesics have impaired episodic memory but intact semantic memory. However, they typically have great difficulties in acquiring new episodic and semantic memories. This may be because the brain areas underlying these two types of memory are very close to each other. Amnesic patients generally have relatively intact implicit memory but severely impaired explicit memory. However, amnesic patients have impaired implicit memory for information that needs to be integrated. The poor ability to integrate different kinds of information may be the central memory problem of amnesic patients.

- *Schema theories*: Schemas are well-integrated packages of information that allow us to form expectations and to draw inferences. Bartlett found that systematic schema-based distortions (e.g., rationalisations) in the recall of stories from a different culture increased over time. Schemas can influence both comprehension and retrieval processes. According to the script-pointer-plus-tag hypothesis, recognition memory should always be better for atypical actions than for typical ones, whereas recall for atypical actions should be worse than for typical ones at long retention intervals. However, interruptive atypical actions are better recalled than typical ones at all retention intervals. Most schema theories are low in testability, because it is hard to obtain independent evidence of the information contained in schemas. The range of inferences drawn during story comprehension is less than predicted by most schema theories.

- *Everyday memory*: Eyewitness memory for an event is easily distorted by post-event information. This is an example of retroactive interference, and can be partially understood within the source monitoring framework. Face recognition is reduced when there are changes in the appearance of a face between study and test or the context changes. Eyewitness confidence is a poor predictor of his or her identification accuracy. Other problems with eyewitness testimony stem from confirmation bias and weapon focus. Flashbulb memories are claimed to differ from other memories in their longevity, accuracy, and reliance on a special neural mechanism. In fact, flashbulb memories probably resemble other memories, and owe their long-lastingness to the importance of the event concerned, its distinctiveness, and frequent rehearsal.

Essay questions

(1) Consider some of the main theories of forgetting.
(2) How useful is the distinction between explicit and implicit memory?
(3) What has the study of amnesic patients contributed to our understanding of normal memory?
(4) What are the strengths and weaknesses of schema theories of memory?
(5) Discusss research on eyewitness testimony.

Further reading

Davies, G.M., & Logie, R.H. (1998). *Memory in everyday life*. Amsterdam: Elsevier. There is up-to-date coverage of numerous topics in everyday memory in this book.

Eysenck, M.W., & Keane, M.T. (2000). *Cognitive psychology: A student's handbook* (4th ed.). Hove, UK: Psychology Press. The topics discussed in this chapter are dealt with in more detail in Chapters 6, 7, and 8 of this book.

Haberlandt, K. (1999). *Human memory: Exploration and applications*. Boston: Allyn and Bacon. Several chapters in this book (e.g., 4, 5, and 10) provide readable accounts of major topics within long-term memory.

Basic language processes 7

Introduction

Language is an impressive human achievement, and one that gives us clear advantages over other species. However, in spite of its importance, progress in understanding the psychology of language has been slow. As Bishop (1997, p. 1) remarked, "Despite years of research, we still understand remarkably little about how language works." Why is that so? There are several reasons, but the most obvious one is that language is a very complex phenomenon.

This chapter is concerned with some of the basic processes involved in language. We start by considering young children's acquisition of language. This is followed by a discussion of the processes involved in speech perception and in reading. Other aspects of language (e.g., comprehension of text or spoken language) are discussed in Chapter 8.

Language acquisition

Young children acquire language with breathtaking speed. By the age of 2 years, most children use language to communicate hundreds of messages. By the age of 5 years, children have mastered most of the grammatical rules of their native language. However, very few parents are consciously aware of the rules of grammar. Thus, young children simply "pick up" the complex rules of grammar without the benefit of much formal teaching.

Stages of language development

Language development can be divided into *receptive language* (language comprehension) and *productive language* (language expression or speaking). One-year-old children (and adults) have better receptive than productive language. We underestimate the language skills of children if we assume that their speech reflects all their knowledge of language.

Children need to learn four kinds of knowledge about language (Shaffer, 1993):

- *Phonology*: The sound system of a language.
- *Semantics*: The meaning conveyed by words and sentences.
- *Syntax*: The set of grammatical rules indicating how words may be combined to make sentences.
- *Pragmatics*: The principles determining how language should be modified to fit the context (e.g., we speak in a simpler way to a child than an adult).

Children typically acquire these kinds of knowledge in the order listed. They first of all learn to make sounds, followed by developing an understanding of what those sounds mean. After that, they learn grammatical rules, and how to change what they say to fit the situation.

Early vocalisations

Infants between the ages of about 3 and 5 weeks start to coo, producing vowel-like sounds (e.g., "ooooh") over and over again. Between 4 and 6 months of age, infants start to babble. Babbling consists of combinations of vowels and consonants that seem to lack meaning for the infants.

The babbling of infants up to about 6 months of age is similar in all parts of the world and in deaf infants as well as hearing ones. However, by about 8 months of age, infants start to show in their babbling signs of the language they have heard. Indeed, adults can sometimes guess accurately from their babbling whether infants have been exposed to French, Chinese, Arabic, or English (De Boysson-Bardies, Sagart, & Durand, 1984).

One-word stage

Up until the age of about 18 months, young children are limited to single-word utterances. Nelson (1973) studied the first 50 words used by infants, and put those words into categories. The largest category was classes of objects (e.g., cat, car), followed by specific objects (e.g., Mummy, Daddy). The other four categories used by young children were (in descending order of frequency): action words such as "go" and "come"; modifiers (e.g., "mine", "small"); social words (e.g., "please", "no"); and function words (e.g., "for", "where").

Almost two-thirds of the words used by young children refer to objects or to people. Why is this so? Children naturally refer to things of interest to them, which consist mainly of the people and objects that surround them.

Young children often make mistakes with word meanings. Some words are initially used to cover more objects than they should (over-extension). It can be embarrassing, as when a child refers to every man as "Daddy". The opposite mistake is known as under-extension. For example, a child may think that the word "cereal" refers only to the brand of cereal he or she eats for breakfast.

McNeill (1970) referred to the one-word stage as the *holophrastic period*. In this period, young children try to convey much more meaning than their utterances would suggest. For example, an infant who says "ball" while pointing to a ball may mean that he or she would like to play with the ball. Infants produce one-word utterances because of a limited attention span and a small vocabulary (McNeill, 1970).

It is hard to test McNeill's notion of a holophrastic period. In its favour is the fact that young children often suggest by their actions or by their tone of voice that they are trying to communicate more than just one word. On the other hand, young children have very limited cognitive development. This must restrict their ability to have complex ideas.

Telegraphic period

The second stage of language development is the *telegraphic period*. It begins at, or shortly after, 18 months of age. Its name arises because the speech of children in this stage is like a telegram. Telegrams cost so much per word, and so senders of telegrams make them short. Content words such as nouns and verbs are included, but function words such as "a", "the", "and", pronouns, and prepositions are left out. The same is true of the speech of young children. However, they leave out even more than is left out of a telegram (e.g., plurals and tenses).

Even though young children are largely limited to two-word utterances, they can still communicate numerous meanings. A given two-word utterance can mean different things in different situations. "Daddy chair" may mean "I want to sit in Daddy's chair", "Daddy is sitting in his chair", or "Daddy, sit in your chair!"

Braine (1963) found that early speech consists of two main classes of words: *pivot words* and *open words*. Pivot words always occur in the same place within an utterance, they are few in number, and they are used very often. In contrast, open words appear in different places in different utterances, they are numerous, and each open word is used rarely. Most telegraphic utterances consist of a pivot word plus an open word, and this seems to be a rule that children use. Braine (1963) recorded these examples of a pivot word followed by an open word from one child: all clean; all done; all dressed; all messy.

Another way in which telegraphic speech is based on rules was identified by Roger Brown (1973). He argued that young children possess a basic order rule: A sentence consists of agent + action + object + location (e.g., "Daddy eats lunch at home"). Their two-word utterances follow the basic order rule. For example, an utterance containing an agent and an action will be in the order agent–action (e.g., "Daddy walk") rather than the reverse ("walk Daddy"). Similarly, action and object will be spoken in the order action–object (e.g., "drink Coke"). Children everywhere construct two-word utterances obeying the basic order rule.

Subsequent developments

Children's language develops considerably between 2½ years and 5 years of age. The most obvious change is in the mean length of utterance measured in terms of the number of morphemes (meaningful units) produced. Another important change is based on the learning of what are known as *grammatical morphemes*. These include prepositions, prefixes, and suffixes (e.g., "in", "on", plural -s; "a"; "the"), and they serve to alter the meaning of words or phrases. All children learn the various grammatical morphemes in the same order (de Villiers & de Villiers, 1973). They start with simple ones (e.g., including "in" and "on" in sentences) followed by more complex ones (e.g., reducing "they are" to "they're").

Do children simply imitate the speech of adults rather than learning rules? Evidence that they do not comes from children's grammatical errors. For example, a child will say, "The dog runned away", which parents and other adults are unlikely to produce. Presumably the child makes that mistake because he or she is applying the rule that the past tense of a verb is usually formed by adding -ed to the present tense. Using a grammatical rule in situations in which it does not apply is known as *over-regularisation*.

It could be argued that over-regularisation occurs because children imitate what other children say. However, this cannot explain the findings of Berko (1958). Children were shown two pictures of an imaginary animal or bird. They were told, "This is a wug. This is another wug. Now there are two . . ." Even young children produced the regular plural form "wugs", despite the fact they had never heard the word before.

Finally, children at this stage develop a good grasp of pragmatics, in which what they say fits the situation. Shatz and Gelman (1973) analysed the speech of 4-year-old children when talking about a new toy to a 2-year-old or to an adult. They used longer and more complex sentences when talking to the adult.

Nativist theories of child language

How do young children learn the complexities of language so rapidly and easily? Nativist theorists argue that infants are born with knowledge of the structure of human languages. For example, Chomsky (1965) argued that humans possess a *language acquisition device*, which consists of innate knowledge of grammatical structure.

In developing this notion, Chomsky (1965) distinguished between the surface structure and the deep structure of a sentence. The surface structure is based on the actual phrases used in a sentence, whereas the deep structure reflects its meaning. For example, the sentence, "Visiting relatives can be boring", has only one surface structure. However, it can mean either that it is sometimes tedious to visit relatives, or that relatives who come on a visit can be boring. The two meanings of this, and other sentences are distinguished in the deep structure. Chomsky (1965) introduced the notion of a *transformational grammar*. This allows us to transform the meaning, or deep structure, of a sentence into the actual words in the sentence (the surface structure). It also allows us to transform basic sentences into negative statements, questions, and so on. According to Chomsky, this transformational grammar is innate, and forms a key part of the language acquisition device.

Chomsky (1986) later replaced the notion of a language acquisition device with the idea of a universal grammar, which forms part of our innate knowledge of language. According to Chomsky (1986), there are *linguistic universals*, which are features found in nearly every language. There are substantive universals and formal universals. Substantive universals concern categories that are common to all languages (e.g., noun and verb categories). Formal universals are concerned with the general form of syntactic or grammatical rules.

Evidence

Chomsky assumed that there are numerous linguistic universals, of which word order is a good example. Consider the preferred word order for expressing the subject, verb, and object within sentences. There are six possible orderings, two of which (object–verb–subject; object–subject–verb) are not found among the world's languages (Greenberg, 1963). The most popular word order is subject–object–verb (44% of languages), followed by the subject–verb–object word order found in English (35% of languages). The subject precedes the object in 98% of languages, presumably because it makes sense to consider the subject of a sentence before the object.

Chomsky (1986) assumed that linguistic universals are innate, but there are other possibilities. Consider the linguistic universals of nouns and verbs, with nouns referring to objects and verbs to actions. Perhaps objects and actions are distinguished in all languages simply because the distinction is such an obvious feature of the environment.

Another line of research supporting the notion of an innate grammar was developed by Bickerton (1984). He proposed the language bioprogramme hypothesis, according to which children will create a grammar even if not exposed to a proper language during their early years. Evidence for this hypothesis was obtained by considering labourers from China, Japan, Korea, Puerto Rico, Portugal, and the Philippines who were taken to the sugar plantations of Hawaii about 100 years ago. In order to communicate with each other, these labourers developed a pidgin language, which was very simple and lacked most grammatical structures. Here is an example of this pidgin language: "Me cape buy, me check make", which was intended to mean, "He bought my coffee; he made me out a cheque" (Pinker, 1984). The key finding was that the offspring of these labourers developed a language known as Hawaiian Creole. This is a proper language and is fully grammatical. Here is an example of this language: "Da firs japani came ran away from japan come." This means, "The first Japanese who arrived ran away from Japan to here."

Research in genetic linguistics has been claimed to support the view that language is partly innate. Gopnik (1990, 1994) considered three generations of a family known as the K's. About half the members of this family displayed specific language impairment (very poor acquisition of language but near-normal non-verbal IQ). The pattern of affected and unaffected individuals within this family suggested that a single dominant gene was involved. Gopnik (1990) suggested that the affected individuals lacked some of the genetic endowment required for language acquisition. More specifically,

Gopnik (1990) proposed the feature-blindness hypothesis, according to which the genetic make-up of the affected individuals made it very hard to mark grammatical features such as number, gender, and tense. However, other researchers have described the deficit more simply in terms of over-regularisation errors (Vargha-Khadem et al., 1995).

Evaluation

Chomsky's theory seems to explain how it is that nearly all children master their native language very rapidly. It is supported by the way in which pidgin languages develop into creole languages. It is also supported (but more controversially) by studies of genetic linguistics, in which specific language impairment runs in families. Finally, the theory makes sense of the fact that language appears to be rule-based even though few speakers of a language can express these rules explicitly.

Several criticisms have been made of the theory. First, it is very difficult to test. Chomsky (1980, p. 80) argued that "An innatist hypothesis is a refutable hypothesis", but there are formidable obstacles to doing so. For example, Chomsky assumed that very young children have access to a considerable amount of grammatical knowledge. However, when their language performance fails to match up to this alleged knowledge or competence, there are several ways of salvaging the theory. As Bishop (1997, p. 130) pointed out, "The problem is . . . that limitations of memory and attention, biases to prefer particular options, or motivational factors interfere with their ability to demonstrate this knowledge."

Second, Chomsky argued that children must possess innate knowledge of grammatical structure, because the language they hear is too full of errors and lacks adequate information to allow them to work out grammatical rules from scratch. This argument is not persuasive. As is discussed later, mothers and other adults typically talk to young children using child-directed speech or motherese. Such speech involves using simple, short sentences, which facilitates children's language acquisition.

Third, Chomsky (and many other theorists) have assumed that all children learn complex grammatical rules as they master language. However, this assumption has been challenged. For example, Plunkett and Marchman (1991) argued that connectionist networks can "learn" to produce what look like rule-governed responses using only very simple processes and no rules. However, this connectionist approach remains controversial.

Fourth, the whole idea of an innate grammar seems implausible. According to Bishop (1997, p. 123), "What makes an innate grammar a particularly peculiar idea is the fact that innate knowledge must be general enough to account for acquisition of Italian, Japanese, Turkish, Malay, as well as sign language acquisition by congenitally deaf children."

Critical period hypothesis

Did you find it easier to learn your native language as a young child than other languages that you learned later? It probably seems that it was much easier to learn your own language. Lenneberg (1967) and other nativists argued that this common experience supports the *critical period hypothesis*. According to this hypothesis, language learning depends on biological maturation, and is easier before puberty.

Lenneberg (1967) claimed that the two hemispheres of the brain have the same potential at birth. However, their functions become more specialised and rigid over the years, with language functions typically being located mainly in the left hemisphere. It follows that damage to the left hemisphere at an early age can be overcome by language functions moving to the right hemisphere. This would be harder if the brain damage occurred during adolescence, by which time language is well established in the left hemisphere.

Deprived children

In principle, the best way to test the critical period hypothesis is to consider children who have little chance to learn language during their early years. There have been various reports on wild or feral children abandoned at birth. For example, the "Wild Boy of Aveyron" was found in an isolated place in the south of France. A French educationalist, Dr Itard, tried to teach him language, but he only managed to learn two words.

Genie spent most of her time up to the age of 13 years in an isolated room (Curtiss, 1977). She had practically no contact with other people, and was punished if she made any sounds. After Genie was rescued, she learned some aspects of language (especially vocabulary), but showed very poor learning of grammatical rules. However, there are problems in interpreting the evidence from Genie. She was exposed to great social as well as linguistic deprivation, and her father's justification for keeping her in isolation was that he thought she was very retarded. Thus, there are various possible reasons for Genie's limited ability to learn language.

Evaluation

There may well be a critical period (or at least a sensitive period) for the learning of syntax, as well as for phonology. However, there is less evidence of a critical period for the learning of vocabulary, and many language skills can be acquired after the critical period. It is reasonable to argue for a weakened version of the critical period hypothesis, according to which some aspects of language are harder to acquire outside the critical period Harley, 1995).

Environmental theories

Skinner (1957) claimed that language is acquired via *operant conditioning*, in which learning is controlled by reward or reinforcement. According to this approach, only those utterances of the child that are rewarded become stronger. Language develops through a process of *shaping*, in which responses need to become progressively closer to the correct response to be rewarded.

Imitation is often involved, with the child trying to repeat what his or her parent has just said. This is known as an echoic response. Children imitate particular words spoken by their parents and by others, and also imitate grammatical structures that they hear. Skinner (1957) also focused on tacts and mands. A tact is involved when the child is rewarded for producing a sound that resembles the correct pronunciation of a word. A mand is involved when the child learns a word whose meaning has significance for him or her.

Evaluation

Children sometimes learn words by imitation or because they are rewarded for saying them. However, detailed analysis of the language behaviour of young children provides evidence against Skinner's theory. Brown, Caxden, and Bellugi (1969) observed the interactions between middle-class American parents and their young children. Parents rewarded or reinforced the speech of their children on the basis of its accuracy or truth rather than the grammar used. According to Skinner, this should produce adults whose speech is very truthful but ungrammatical. In fact, of course, the speech of most adults is grammatical but not always very truthful.

Most children master language very rapidly. Many experts (e.g., Chomsky, 1959) doubt whether such rapid language acquisition would be possible on the basis of imitation and reinforcement. It can take some time to learn a single word via reinforcement, and yet children learn thousands of words and a good understanding of grammar.

According to Skinner's approach, children should imitate or copy what they have heard other people say. In fact, the telegraphic speech of children under the age of 2 years does not usually closely resemble the utterances of other people. As children's language develops, they often produce novel sentences.

Finally, and most importantly, Skinner focused mainly on the learning of specific responses (e.g., pressing a lever, saying a word) by reinforcement. However, much of the knowledge of language possessed by children is not in the form of specific responses at all. They know a lot about grammatical rules, but a grammatical rule is not a specific response that can be rewarded.

Motherese

The most important environmental factor in language acquisition is the nature of the social interaction between the mother and her child. Most mothers adopt a style of speaking to their children known as *motherese*. This involves using very short, simple sentences, which gradually become longer and more complex as the child's own use of language develops (Shatz & Gelman, 1973). In order to help their children, mothers typically use sentences slightly longer and more complicated than the sentences produced by their child (Bohannon & Warren-Leubecker, 1989).

Mothers, fathers, and other adults also help children's language development by means of expansions. These consist of fuller and more grammatical versions of what the child has just said. For example, a child might say, "Cat out," with his or her mother responding, "The cat wants to go out."

Evidence that the way in which the mother talks to her child affects its language development was reported by Harris et al. (1986; see Figure 7.1). They found that 78% of what mothers said to their 16-month-old children related to the objects to which the children were attending. However, the situation was different in a group of children whose language development at the age of 2 years was poor. Among these children, only 49% of what mothers said to their children at the age of 16 months related to the object of the child's attention.

The language development of children is helped by conversations with adults involving motherese, expansions, and so on. However, it is not certain that this kind of help is essential for normal language

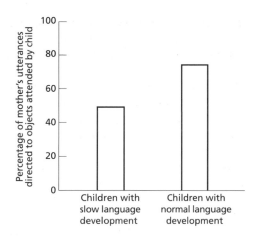

Figure 7.1. The percentages of mother's utterances related to an object currently attended by her child in children with slow or normal language development. Data from Harris et al. (1986).

development. As Shaffer (1993) pointed out, there are several cultures (e.g., the Kaluli of New Guinea) in which adults talk to children as if they were adults. In spite of this, children in these cultures develop language at about the normal rate. Perhaps the most reasonable conclusion is that children require a modest amount of environmental support in the form of motherese (or other effective language input from adults) for normal language development.

Specific language impairment

The term *specific language impairment* has been used to describe children with severe language problems having no obvious explanation. More specifically, children are often said to have specific language impairment when there is a substantial discrepancy between their language ability and non-verbal intelligence.

What causes specific language impairment? There is no simple answer, in part because the precise language problems experienced by children with specific language impairment vary from child to child. However, most children with specific language impairment have difficulties with auditory processing. For example, Tallal (1976) presented two tones at varying intervals, and the task was to identify each tone in the correct sequence. Children with specific language impairment performed better than younger control children when the interval between the tones was long, but performed much worse when the interval was short. Such findings led Tallal (e.g., 1990) to propose the *temporal processing hypothesis*, according to which children with specific language impairment have difficulty in discriminating between brief or rapid stimuli in any sensory stimuli. This difficulty has serious consequences for language acquisition, which involves recognising briefly presented auditory stimuli.

The problem with most research in this area is that the evidence is essentially correlational. Problems in discriminating briefly presented auditory stimuli are associated with specific language impairment, but this does not prove that these problems are *causally related* to the language impairment. The best way to support the causal account would be to show that improved auditory functioning in children with specific language impairment hastens language development. Precisely this was claimed by Merzenich et al. (1996) and by Tallal et al. (1996) in an intervention study. Children with specific language impairment were given extensive training on auditory tasks such as the sequence task used by Tallal (1976). The children were also presented with speech in which the duration of the speech signal was increased. These interventions improved the children's language development, but the findings are only preliminary (see Bishop, 1997).

Vocabulary learning is very deficient in children with specific language impairment. Gathercole and Baddeley (1989) looked at the growth of receptive vocabulary in normally developing children over a 2-year period. The best predictor of vocabulary growth was a test of non-word repetition, in which non-words (e.g., pennel, woolgalamic) had to be repeated back immediately after being heard. Children with specific language impairment perform especially poorly on non-word repetition (Bishop, North, and Donlan, 1996; see Figure 7.2).

What do the above findings mean? According to Gathercole and Baddeley (1990), poor performance on the non-word repetition test (and hence on vocabulary learning) occurs because of deficiencies within the phonological loop (see Chapter 5). However, there are other possible explanations. As Bishop (1997, p. 97) argued, "Poor nonword repetition in SLI [specific language impairment] might simply reflect the fact that initial perception and encoding of phonological information was inadequate."

Evaluation

There are probably several reasons why children suffer from specific language impairment. However, some progress has been made by focusing on their deficiencies in basic cognitive processes. For example, children with specific language impairment may have problems in discriminating between rapidly presented stimuli, and their phonological loop seems to be impaired. It is likely that these children have problems with such basic processes rather than high-level cognitive processes, because their non-verbal intelligence is normal.

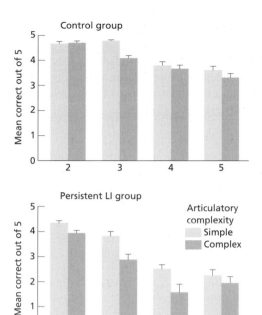

Figure 7.2. Data on the Children's Nonword Repetition test for language-impaired versus control children, in relation to articulatory complexity (i.e., whether the non-word contains consonant clusters or not) and length in syllables. Error bars show standard errors. The language-impaired children obtain lower scores at all lengths except the two-syllable items, where both groups are at ceiling. Data from Bishop et al. (1996).

Speech perception

Accurate perception of speech is a more complex achievement than might be imagined. Language is spoken at a rate of up to 12 *phonemes* (basic speech sounds) per second. Amazingly, we can understand speech artificially speeded up to 50–60 sounds per second (Werker & Tees, 1992). In normal speech, phonemes overlap, and there is *co-articulation*, in which producing one speech segment affects the production of the following segment. The "linearity problem" refers to the difficulties for speech perception produced by co-articulation.

Another related problem is the "non-invariance problem". This arises because the sound pattern for any given speech component such as a phoneme is affected by the sound or sounds preceding and following it. Speech typically consists of a continuously changing pattern of sound with few periods of silence. This contrasts with our perception of speech as consisting of separate sounds. The continuous nature of the speech signal produces the "segmentation problem", that is, deciding how the continuous stream of sound should be divided up into words.

Word recognition

A key issue is to identify the processes involved in spoken word recognition. There are numerous studies on this topic (see Moss & Gaskell, 1999, for a review). We will first consider some of the major processes involved, and will then turn to a discussion of influential theories of spoken word recognition.

Bottom-up and top-down processes

Spoken word recognition is generally achieved by a mixture of bottom-up or data-driven processes triggered by the acoustic signal, and top-down or conceptually driven processes generated from the linguistic context. However, there have been disagreements about precisely how these processes combine to produce word recognition.

Spoken language consists of a series of sounds or phonemes incorporating various features. Among the features for phonemes are the following:

- *Manner of production* (oral versus nasal versus fricative, involving a partial blockage of the airstream).
- *Place of articulation*.
- *Voicing*: The larynx vibrates for a voiced but not for a voiceless phoneme.

The notion that bottom-up processes in word recognition make use of feature information was supported by Miller and Nicely (1955). They gave their participants the task of recognising consonants presented auditorily against a background of noise. The most frequently confused consonants were those differing on the basis of only one feature.

Evidence that top-down processing based on context is involved in speech perception was obtained by Warren and Warren (1970). They studied the *phonemic restoration effect*. Participants heard one of the following sentences in which a small portion had been removed and replaced with a meaningless sound (the asterisk indicates a deleted portion of the sentence):

- It was found that the *eel was on the axle.
- It was found that the *eel was on the shoe.
- It was found that the *eel was on the table.
- It was found that the *eel was on the orange.

The perception of the crucial element in the sentence (i.e., *eel) was influenced by sentence context. Participants listening to the first sentence heard "wheel", those listening to the second sentence heard "heel", and those exposed to the third and fourth sentences heard "meal" and "peel", respectively. The auditory stimulus was identical in all cases, so all that differed was the contextual information.

Samuel (1981) identified two possible explanations for the phonemic restoration effect. First, context may interact directly with bottom-up processes; this would be a sensitivity effect. Second, the context may simply provide an additional source of information; this would be a response bias effect. Participants listened to sentences, and meaningless noise was presented briefly during each sentence. On some trials, this noise was superimposed on one of the phonemes of a word; on other trials, that phoneme was deleted. The task was to decide whether or not the crucial phoneme had been presented. Finally, the word containing this phoneme was predictable or unpredictable from the sentence context.

Performance in Samuel's (1981) study was better when the word was predictable, indicating the importance of context. If context improves sensitivity, then the ability to discriminate between phoneme plus noise and noise alone should be greater with predictable context. If context affects response bias, then participants should simply be more likely to decide that the phoneme was presented when the word was presented in a predictable context. Context affected response bias but not sensitivity, suggesting that contextual information did *not* influence bottom-up processing.

Samuel (1990) carried out further studies. He concluded that contextual information influences the listener's expectations in a top-down fashion, but these expectations then need to be confirmed with reference to the sound that is actually presented.

Prosodic patterns

Spoken speech contains *prosodic cues* (e.g., stress, intonation). These cues can be used by the listener to work out syntactic or grammatical structure. For example, in the ambiguous sentence, "The old men and women sat on the bench", the women may or may not be old. If the women are not old, then the spoken duration of the word "men" will be relatively long, and the stressed syllable in "women" will have a steep rise in pitch contour. Neither of these prosodic features will be present if the sentence means that the women are old.

Lip-reading

Many people (especially the hard of hearing) are aware of using lip-reading to understand speech. However, this happens far more than is generally believed among those whose hearing is normal. McGurk and MacDonald (1976) provided a striking demonstration of the importance of lip-reading. They prepared a videotape of someone repeating "ba" over and over again. The sound channel then changed so there was a voice saying "ga" repeatedly in synchronisation with the lip movements still indicating "ba". Participants reported that they heard "da", representing a blending of the visual and the auditory information.

The so-called McGurk effect is surprisingly robust. Green et al. (1991) found the effect even when there was a female face and a male voice. They suggested that information about pitch becomes irrelevant early in speech processing, and this is why the McGurk effect is found even with a gender mismatch between vision and hearing.

Why do listeners resort to lip-reading? Visual information from lip movements is used to make sense of speech sounds because the information conveyed by the speech sounds is often inadequate.

Theories of word recognition

There are several theories of spoken word recognition. However, two theories (cohort theory and the TRACE model) have been very influential, and our discussion will focus on them.

Cohort theory

Marslen-Wilson and Tyler (1980) put forward the original version of their cohort theory based on the following assumptions:

- Early in the auditory presentation of a word, those words known to the listener conforming to the sound sequence that has been heard so far become active; this collection of words is the "word-initial cohort".
- Words in this cohort are then eliminated because they cease to match further information from the presented word, or because they are inconsistent with the semantic or other context.
- Processing of the presented word continues only until contextual information and information from the word itself are sufficient to eliminate all but one of the words in the word-initial cohort; this is the "recognition point" of a word.

According to cohort theory, various knowledge sources (e.g., lexical, syntactic, semantic) *interact* and combine with each other in complex ways to produce an efficient analysis of spoken language.

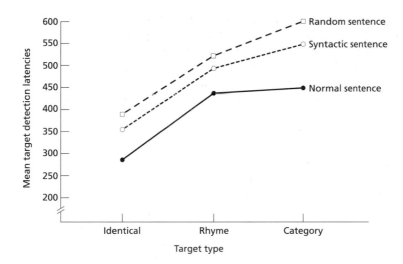

Figure 7.3. Detection times for word targets presented in sentences. Adapted from Marslen-Wilson and Tyler (1980).

Marslen-Wilson and Tyler (1980) tested their theoretical notions in a word-monitoring task, in which participants had to identify pre-specified target words presented within spoken sentences as rapidly as possible. There were normal sentences, syntactic sentences (grammatically correct but meaningless), and random sentences (unrelated words), and the target was a member of a given category, a word that rhymed with a given word, or a word that was identical to a given word.

According to cohort theory, sensory information from the target word and contextual information from the rest of the sentence are both used at the same time. As expected, complete sensory analysis of the longer words was not needed when there was adequate contextual information (see Figure 7.3). It was only necessary to listen to the entire word when the sentence context contained no useful syntactic or semantic information (i.e., random condition).

Undue significance was given to the initial part of the word in the original cohort theory. It was assumed that a spoken word will generally not be recognised if its initial phoneme is unclear or ambiguous. However, Connine, Blasko, and Titone (1993) referred to a study in which a spoken word ending in "ent" had an ambiguous initial phoneme between "d" and "t". There was evidence that the words "dent" and "tent" could both be activated at a short delay when the target word was presented. This finding was inconsistent with the original theory.

Marslen-Wilson (1990) and Marslen-Wilson and Warren (1994) revised cohort theory. In the original version, words were either in or out of the word cohort. In the revised version, candidate words vary in activation level, and so membership of the word cohort is a matter of degree. Marslen-Wilson (1990) assumed that the word-initial cohort may contain words having similar initial phonemes, rather than being limited only to words having the initial phoneme of the presented word. This revised version accounts for the findings of Connine et al. (1993).

There is a second major difference between the original and revised versions of cohort theory. In the original version, context influenced word recognition very early in processing. In the revised version, the effects of context occur only at a fairly late stage of processing. The evidence supports the revised theory. For example, Zwitserlood (1989) found that context did not influence the initial activation of words, but did so *after* the point at which a spoken word could be uniquely identified.

Evaluation

Cohort theory is an influential approach to spoken word recognition. The revised version of the theory is preferable to the original version for two reasons:

(1) Its assumption that membership of the word cohort is flexible is more in line with the evidence.
(2) Contextual effects on spoken word recognition typically occur late rather than early in processing, as proposed within the revised theory.

The major disadvantage with the revised theory is that it is less precise than the original theory. As Massaro (1994, p. 244) pointed out, "These modifications are necessary to bring the model in line with empirical results, but they . . . make it more difficult to test against alternative models."

TRACE model

McClelland and Elman (1986) and McClelland (1991) produced a network model of speech perception based on connectionist principles (see Chapter 1). Their TRACE model of speech perception resembles the original version of cohort theory. It is argued within both theories that several sources of information combine interactively in word recognition.

The TRACE model is based on the following theoretical assumptions:

- There are individual processing units or nodes at three different levels: features (e.g., voicing, manner of production), phonemes, and words.
- Feature nodes are connected to phoneme nodes, and phoneme nodes are connected to word nodes.
- Connections *between* levels operate in both directions, and are only facilitatory.
- There are connections among units or nodes *within* the same level; these connections are inhibitory.
- Nodes influence each other in proportion to their activation levels and the strengths of their interconnections.
- As excitation and inhibition spread among nodes, a pattern of activation develops.
- The word that is recognised is determined by the activation level of the possible candidate words.

The TRACE model assumes that bottom-up and top-down processing interact during speech perception. Bottom-up activation proceeds upwards from the feature level to the phoneme level and on to the word level. In contrast, top-down activation proceeds in the opposite direction from the word level to the phoneme level and on to the feature level. Evidence that top-down processes are involved in spoken word recognition was discussed earlier in the chapter (e.g., Marslen-Wilson & Tyler, 1980; Warren & Warren, 1970).

Cutler et al. (1987) studied a phenomenon lending itself to explanation by the TRACE model. They used a phoneme monitoring task, in which participants had to respond immediately to the presence of a target phoneme. They observed a word superiority effect, in that phonemes were detected faster when they were presented in words than in non-words. According to the TRACE model, this phenomenon occurs because of top-down activation from the word level to the phoneme level.

Marslen-Wilson, Moss, and van Halen (1996) presented their participants with "words" such as p/blank, in which the initial phoneme was halfway between a /p/ and a /b/. They wanted to see whether this "word" would facilitate lexical decision for words related to plank (e.g., wood) or to blank (e.g., page). The TRACE model predicts a significant facilitation or priming effect because of spreading activation. In contrast, the original cohort theory assumed that only words matching the initial phoneme of the presented word are activated. Thus, there should be no priming effect. The findings supported the cohort theory and were inconsistent with the TRACE model.

Evaluation

The TRACE model provides reasonable accounts of phenomena such as the word superiority effect in phoneme monitoring. A significant general strength of the TRACE model is its assumption that bottom-up and top-down processes both contribute to spoken word recognition, combined with explicit assumptions about the processes involved. However, the theory predicts that speech perception depends *interactively* on top-down and bottom-up processes, and this was not confirmed by Massaro (1989) on a phoneme-discrimination task. He found that bottom-up effects stemming from stimulus discriminability and top-down effects stemming from phonological context both influenced performance, but they did so in an *independent* rather than *interactive* way.

There are other problems with the TRACE model. First, it is assumed that words phonologically similar to a presented word will be activated immediately, even though they do not match the presented word in the initial phoneme. In fact, this is typically not the case (e.g., Marslen-Wilson et al., 1996).

Second, the theory exaggerates the importance of top-down effects. For example, Frauenfelder, Segui, and Dijkstra (1990) gave their participants the task of detecting a given phoneme. The key condition was one in which a non-word closely resembling an actual word was presented (e.g., "vocabutaire" instead of "vocabulaire"). According to the model, top-down effects from the word node corresponding to "vocabulaire" should have inhibited the task of identifying the "t" in "vocabutaire", but they did not.

Third, as Protopapas (1999, p. 420) pointed out, TRACE "does not learn anything. It is prewired to achieve all its remarkable results."

Section summary

Theories of spoken word recognition are becoming increasingly similar. Most theorists agree that activation of several candidate words occurs early in the process of word recognition. It is also agreed that the speed of word recognition indicates that most of the processes involved proceed in parallel (at the same time) rather than serially. There is also general agreement that the activation levels of candidate words vary in degree rather than being either very high or very low. Finally, nearly all theorists agree that bottom-up and top-down processes combine to produce word recognition, although they disagree on how this happens. The revised version of cohort theory and the TRACE model both incorporate all these assumptions.

An issue in need of further research is that of precisely *when* contextual and other forms of top-down information are used in spoken word recognition. As Harley (1995, p. 56) concluded, "It is difficult to draw any definite conclusions about the role of context in spoken word recognition . . . it is difficult to be sure that these experiments [on context] are tapping processes before the selection of a unique candidate rather than reflecting post-access effects."

Cognitive neuropsychology of speech perception

Repeating a spoken word immediately after hearing it is apparently simple. However, many brain-damaged patients experience difficulties with this task, even though audiometric testing reveals they are not deaf. Detailed analysis of these patients suggests various processes can be used to permit repetition of a spoken word.

Information from such patients was used by Ellis and Young (1988) to propose a model of the processing of spoken words (see Figure 7.4 for a modified version):

- The *auditory analysis system* extracts phonemes or other sounds from the speech wave.
- The *auditory input lexicon* contains information about spoken words known to the listener, but not about their meaning. The lexicon permits recognition of familiar words via the activation of the appropriate word units.
- The meanings of words are stored within the *semantic system* (cf. *semantic memory*, which is discussed in Chapter 6).
- The *speech output lexicon* provides the spoken forms of words.
- The *phoneme response buffer* provides distinctive speech sounds.
- These components can be used in various combinations, producing three different routes between hearing a spoken word and saying it

The most striking assumption is that saying a spoken word can be achieved in three different ways. It is this assumption to which we will devote the most attention. Before doing so, however, we consider the role of the auditory analysis system in speech perception.

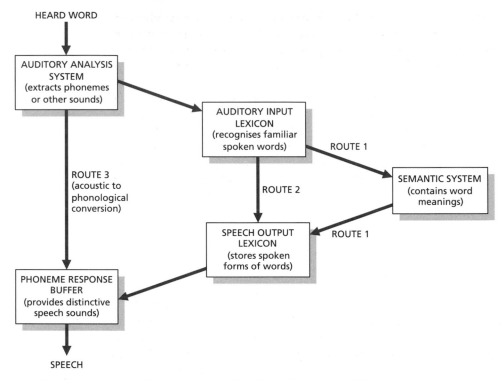

HEARD WORD

AUDITORY ANALYSIS
SYSTEM
(extracts phonemes
or other sounds)

AUDITORY INPUT
LEXICON
(recognises familiar
spoken words)

ROUTE 1

SEMANTIC SYSTEM
(contains word
meanings)

ROUTE 3
(acoustic to
phonological
conversion)

ROUTE 2

SPEECH OUTPUT
LEXICON
(stores spoken
forms of words)

ROUTE 1

PHONEME RESPONSE
BUFFER
(provides distinctive
speech sounds)

SPEECH

Figure 7.4. Processing and repetition of spoken words. Adapted from Ellis and Young (1988).

Auditory analysis system

Suppose a patient had damage only to the auditory analysis system, thereby producing a deficit in phonemic processing. Such a patient would have impaired speech perception for words and non-words, especially for words containing phonemes that are hard to discriminate. However, such a patient would have generally intact speech production, reading, and writing, would have normal perception of non-verbal environmental sounds (e.g., coughs, whistles), and unimpaired hearing. Several patients conforming to this pattern have been identified (see Parkin, 1996), and the term *pure word deafness* has been used to describe their condition.

If patients with pure word deafness have a severe deficit in phonemic processing, then their speech perception should improve when they have access to other kinds of information. Okada et al. (1963) studied a patient with pure word deafness who could use contextual information. The patient understood spoken questions much better when they all referred to the same topic than when they did not. Auerbach et al. (1982) found that patients with pure word deafness had better speech perception when lip-reading was possible.

A crucial aspect of pure word deafness is that auditory perception problems are highly *selective*, and do not apply to non-speech sounds. Evidence that separate systems deal with speech and non-speech sounds was reported by Fujii et al. (1990). They studied a patient with brain damage in the right hemisphere. He found it very hard to name familiar environmental sounds, but his language abilities were only modestly affected. This is in some ways the opposite pattern to that found in pure word deafness.

Route 1

This route uses the auditory input lexicon, the semantic system, and the speech output lexicon. It represents the normal way in which familiar words are identified and comprehended by those with no brain damage. If a brain-damaged patient could use only this route (plus perhaps Route 2), then familiar words would be said correctly. However, there would be severe problems with saying unfamiliar words and non-words, because they do not have entries in the auditory input lexicon, and so use of Route 3 would be required.

McCarthy and Warrington (1984) described a patient, O.R.F., who seems to fit the bill fairly well. O.R.F. repeated words much more accurately than non-words (85% vs. 39%, respectively), indicating that Route 3 was severely impaired. However, he made several errors in repeating words, suggesting impairment to other parts of the system.

Route 2

If patients could use Route 2, but Routes 1 and 3 were severely impaired, they would be able to repeat familiar words but would often not understand their meaning. In addition, they would have problems with non-words, because non-words cannot be handled through Route 2. Finally, since such patients would make use of the input lexicon, they would distinguish between words and non words.

Patients suffering from *word meaning deafness* fit the above description. One of the clearest cases, Dr O., was studied by Franklin et al.

(1996). Dr O. showed "no evidence of any impairment in written word comprehension, but auditory comprehension was impaired, particularly for abstract or low-imageability words" (Franklin et al., 1996, p. 1144). His ability to repeat words was dramatically better than his ability to repeat non-words, 80% vs. 7%, respectively. Finally, Dr O. was 94% correct at distinguishing between words and non-words.

Dr O. has reasonable access to the input lexicon as shown by his greater ability to repeat words than non-words, and by his almost perfect ability to distinguish between words and non-words. He clearly has some problem relating to the semantic system. However, the semantic system itself does not seem to be damaged, because his ability to understand written words is intact.

Route 3

A patient with damage to Route 3 only would show good ability to perceive and to understand spoken familiar words, but would be impaired at perceiving and repeating unfamiliar words and non-words. This is the case in patients with *auditory phonological agnosia*. Such a patient was studied by Beauvois, Dérousné, and Bastard (1980). Their patient, J.L., had almost perfect repetition and writing to dictation of spoken familiar words, but his repetition and writing of non-words was very poor. However, he was very good at *reading* non-words. J.L. had an intact ability to distinguish between words and non-words, indicating that there were no problems with access to the input lexicon.

Deep dysphasia

Some brain-damaged patients have extensive problems with speech perception, suggesting that several parts of the speech perception system are damaged. For example, patients with *deep dysphasia* make semantic errors when asked to repeat spoken words (i.e., they say words related in meaning to those spoken). They also find it harder to repeat abstract words than concrete ones, and have very poor ability to repeat non-words. It could be argued that none of the three routes between heard words and speech is intact (see Figure 7.4). The presence of semantic errors suggests there is some impairment in (or near) the semantic system.

Valdois et al. (1995) studied E.A., a 72-year-old man who had suffered a stroke. He exhibited all the symptoms of deep dysphasia, including numerous semantic errors when trying to repeat spoken words having a synonym. In addition, E.A. had very poor short-term memory for auditory and visual verbal material. These latter findings led Valdois et al. (1995, p. 711) to conclude as follows: "The impairment responsible for both E.A.'s language performance and his short-term memory deficit is rooted in the inability to maintain a sufficiently activated phonological representation [in the response buffer]."

Valdois et al. (1995) discussed six deep dysphasics who had a very severe short-memory memory deficit (memory span of one or two items). These patients conformed to the theoretical expectation of Valdois et al. (1995), in that there was evidence of damage to the response buffer. However, three other patients had only slightly impaired short-term memory, suggesting that their theory does not apply to all deep dysphasics. Perhaps these patients had damage to all three routes between heard words and speech.

Section summary

There has been relatively little research on auditory word recognition and comprehension in brain damaged patients. However, there are clearly different patterns of impairment in the ability to repeat and to understand spoken words. This suggests strongly that there is more than one route between hearing a word and then saying it. Figure 7.4 represents a possible set of components and their interactions, but its validity will become clear only after much further research.

Basic reading processes

Why is it important to study reading? Skilled reading has much value in contemporary society, and adults without effective reading skills are at a great disadvantage. Thus, it is important to discover enough about reading processes to be able to sort out the problems of poor readers.

Some reading processes are concerned with identifying and extracting meaning from individual words, whereas others deal with the overall organisation of an entire story or book. However, research has focused mainly on a few of these processes: "Scanning the literature on skilled reading, one could be forgiven for thinking that the goal of reading is to turn print into speech. Of course, it is not: the goal of reading is to understand (perhaps even to enjoy) a piece of text" (Ellis, 1993, p. 35).

Research methods

Several methods are available for studying reading. The method of recording eye movements during reading has two particular strengths: (1) it provides a detailed moment-by-moment record; and (2) it is unobtrusive. The only major restriction on readers whose eye movements are being recorded is that they should keep their heads fairly still. However, it is hard to know *what* processing occurs during each fixation.

Another method for studying reading involves using various techniques to assess the time taken for word identification. There is the *lexical decision task* (deciding whether a string of letters forms a word) and the *naming task* (saying a word as rapidly as possible). These techniques ensure that certain processing has occurred within a given time, whereas identification may *not* occur during word fixation. However, there are some disadvantages. Normal reading processes are disrupted by the additional task, and it is not clear precisely what processes are involved in lexical decision or naming.

Balota, Paul, and Spieler (1999) argued that reading involves several kinds of processing: *orthography* (the spelling of words); *phonology* (the sound of words); word meaning; syntax; and higher-level discourse integration. The naming task emphasises the links between orthography and phonology, whereas lexical decision emphasises the links between orthography and meaning. Thus, performance on naming and lexical decision tasks may not accurately reflect normal reading processes.

Eye movements in reading

We feel that our eyes move smoothly across the page while reading. In fact, they actually move in rapid jerks (*saccades*). Saccades are ballistic (once initiated their direction cannot be changed). There are regressions, in which the eyes move backwards in the text, accounting for about 10% of all saccades. Saccades take 10–20 ms to complete, and are separated by fixations lasting about 200–250 ms. The length of each saccade is about eight letters or spaces. Information is extracted from the text only during each fixation, and not during the intervening saccades.

The perceptual span is defined as the amount of text from which useful information is obtained on each fixation. It is affected by the difficulty of the text, the size of the print, and so on. However, it usually extends to no more than about three or four letters to the left of fixation and 15 letters to the right.

E-Z Reader model

Reichle et al. (1998) explained the pattern of eye movements during reading in their E-Z Reader model (note that Z is pronounced "zee" in American English!). About 80% of content words (nouns, verbs, and adjectives) are fixated, so it is important to identify the factors determining the length of fixation on such words. Only about 20% of function words (articles, conjunctions, prepositions, and pronouns) are fixated, and we need to identify the factors leading some words to be "skipped" or not fixated.

The model was designed to explain the following findings (see Reichle et al., 1998):

- Rare words are fixated for longer than common words.
- Words that are more predictable in the sentence context are fixated for less time.
- Words that are not fixated tend to be common, short, or predictable.
- The fixation time on a word is longer when it is preceded by a rare word: the "spillover" effect.

What would be the most obvious kind of model? Perhaps readers fixate on a word until they have processed it sufficiently, after which they move their eyes immediately to the next word. However, there are two major problems with this approach:

(1) It takes about 150–200 ms to execute an eye-movement programme. If readers behaved according to this simple model, they would waste time waiting for their eyes to move.
(2) Readers could not safely skip words, because they would know nothing about the next word until they fixated it.

How can we get round these problems? Reichle et al. (1998) argued that the next eye movement is programmed after only *part* of the processing of the currently fixated word has occurred. This greatly reduces the time between completion of processing on the current word and movement of the eyes to the next word. Any spare time is used to start processing the next word. If the processing of the next word is completed rapidly enough, it is skipped.

Reichle et al. (1998) emphasised several general assumptions in their E-Z Reader model:

(1) Readers check the frequency of the word they are currently fixating.

(2) Completion of frequency checking of a word initiates an eye-movement program.

(3) Readers also engage in *lexical access,* in which stored information (e.g., semantic) about the word is retrieved. This takes longer to complete than does frequency checking.

(4) Completion of lexical access is the signal to shift covert (internal) attention to the next word.

(5) Frequency checking and lexical access are completed faster for common words than for rare ones, especially lexical access.

(6) Frequency checking and lexical access are completed faster for predictable than for unpredictable words.

Assumptions (2) and (5) together predict that the time spent fixating common words will be less than the time fixating rare words, which is consistent with the evidence. According to the model, readers spend the time between completion of lexical access to a word and the next eye movement in processing the next word outside the central or foveal part of the retina. The amount of time spent in such parafoveal processing is less when the fixated word is rare than when it is common (see Figure 7.5). Thus, the word following a rare word generally needs to be fixated for longer than the word following a common word (the spillover effect described earlier).

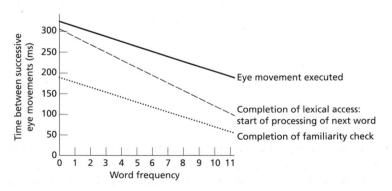

Figure 7.5. Effects of word frequency on eye movements according to the E-Z Reader model. Adapted from Reichle et al. (1998).

Why are words that are common, predictable, or short more likely than other words to be skipped or not fixated? According to the model, a word is skipped when its lexical access is completed while the previous word is still fixated. This is most likely to happen for common, predictable, or short words, because lexical access is faster for these words than for others (assumptions 5 and 6).

Evaluation

The model specifies the major factors determining eye movements in reading. It shows that reading occurs on a word-by-word basis, and that parafoveal processing increases the efficiency of the reading process. The predictions of the model are generally in good agreement with eye-movement data, suggesting that its central assumptions are correct.

The E-Z Reader model de-emphasises the impact of higher-level cognitive processes. For example, readers fixate for a long time on the word "seems" when presented with the sentence, "Since Jay always jogs a mile seems like a short distance" (Frazier & Rayner, 1982). They cannot fit "seems" into the syntactic structure they have formed, and so there is disruption. This disruption affects eye fixations, but is not adequately explained by the model.

Reichle et al. (1998) identified another problem. According to the model, the motor programming system translates the signal to move to the next word into a saccade. However, it is not clear how this system produces saccades of the appropriate length.

Word identification

College students typically read at about 300 words per minute, thus averaging only 200 ms to identify each word. It has proved hard to decide exactly how long word identification normally takes, in part because of imprecision about the meaning of "word identification". The term can refer to accessing either the name of a word or its meaning. However, reading rate is slowed by only about 15% when a mask appears 50 ms after the start of each eye fixation (Rayner et al., 1981). This suggests that word identification in both senses takes only a little more than 50 ms.

Automatic processing

Rayner and Sereno (1994) argued that word identification is generally fairly automatic. This makes intuitive sense if you consider that most college students have already read between 20 and 70 million words.

It has been argued that automatic processes are unavoidable and unavailable to consciousness (see Chapter 5). Evidence that word identification may be unavoidable comes from the *Stroop effect* (Stroop, 1935). The colours in which words are printed are named as rapidly as possible, and naming speed is slowed when the words are conflicting colour names (e.g., the word RED printed in green). The Stroop effect suggests that word meaning is extracted even when people try not to process it.

Cheesman and Merikle (1984) replicated the Stroop effect. They also found that the effect could be obtained even when the colour name was presented below the level of conscious awareness, suggesting that word identification does not depend on conscious awareness.

Context effects

Is word identification influenced by context? This issue was addressed by Meyer and Schvaneveldt (1971) in a study in which the participants had to decide whether letter strings were words. On this lexical decision task, the decision time for a word (e.g., DOCTOR) was shorter when the preceding context or prime was a semantically related word (e.g., NURSE) than when it was an unrelated word (e.g., LIBRARY) or when there was no prime. This is known as the *semantic priming effect*.

Why does the semantic priming effect occur? Perhaps the context or priming word *automatically* activates the stored representations of all the words related to it due to massive previous learning. Alternatively, *controlled processes* may be involved, with a prime (e.g., NURSE) leading participants to expect that a semantically related word will follow.

Neely (1977) tested the above explanations of the semantic priming effect. The priming word was the name of a semantic category (e.g., "Bird"), and it was followed by a letter string at one of three intervals: 250, 400, or 700 ms. In the key manipulation, participants expected that a particular category name would usually be followed by a member of a different, pre-specified category (e.g., "Bird" followed by the name of part of a building). There were two kinds of trials:

(1) The category name was followed by a member of a different, but expected, category (e.g., Bird–Window).
(2) The category name was followed by a member of the same, but unexpected, category (e.g., Bird–Magpie).

There were two priming or context effects (see Figure 7.6). First, there was a rapid, automatic effect based on semantic relatedness.

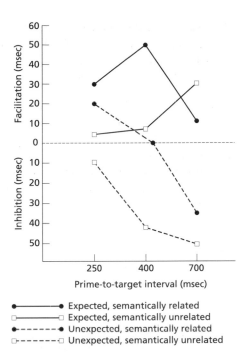

Figure 7.6. Time course of inhibitory and facilitatory effects of priming as a function of whether or not the target word was related semantically to the prime, and of whether or not the target word belonged to the expected category. Data from Neely (1977).

●————● Expected, semantically related
□————□ Expected, semantically unrelated
●------● Unexpected, semantically related
□------□ Unexpected, semantically unrelated

Second, there was a slower-acting attentional effect based on expectation. Subsequent research has generally confirmed Neely's (1977) findings, except that automatic processes can cause inhibitory effects at short intervals (see Rayner & Pollatsek, 1989).

It is hard to know whether Neely's (1977) findings apply to normal reading, because the situations are so different. However, context does influence reading. For example, Ehrlich and Rayner (1981) found that words fitting the sentential context were fixated for 40 ms less than other words.

Word identification is affected by context, but it is more controversial whether context effects occur *before* or *after* the individual has gained *lexical access* to the stored information contained in the internal *lexicon*. Neely (1977) found that semantic or associative priming had a very rapid effect on word identification, suggesting that this effect of context occurs pre-lexically. He also found that the effects of participants' expectancies were slow to develop, suggesting that these expectancies (and probably sentence context as well) affect post-lexical processing.

Lucas (1999) carried out a *meta-analysis* (statistical analysis based on combining data across studies) focusing on context effects in lexical access. In most of the studies, each context sentence contained an ambiguous word (e.g., "The man spent the entire day fishing on the *bank*"). The ambiguous word was immediately followed by a target on which a naming or lexical decision task was performed. The target word was either appropriate (e.g., "river") or inappropriate (e.g., "money") to the meaning of the ambiguous word in the sentence context. Overall, the 17 studies in the meta-analysis "showed a small effect of context on lexical access of about two-tenths of a standard deviation: the appropriate interpretation of a word consistently showed greater priming than the inappropriate interpretation" (Lucas, 1999, p. 394).

Letter versus word identification

Common sense indicates that the recognition of a word on the printed page involves two successive stages:

(1) Identification of the individual letters in the word.
(2) Word identification.

However, the notion that letter identification must be complete before word identification can begin is wrong. Consider the *word superiority effect* (Reicher, 1969). A letter string is presented very briefly followed by a pattern mask. The task is to decide which of two letters was presented in a particular position (e.g., the third letter). The word superiority effect is defined by the fact that performance is better when the letter string forms a word than when it does not.

The word superiority effect suggests that information about the word presented can facilitate identification of the letters of that word. However, there is also a pseudo-word superiority effect: Letters are better recognised when presented in pronounceable non-words (e.g., "MAVE") than in unpronounceable non-words (e.g., Cole et al., 1980).

Interactive activation model

McClelland and Rumelhart (1981) put forward an influential inter-active activation model of visual word recognition. The key assumptions of this model are as follows: "Visual word recognition involves a process of mutual constraint satisfaction between the bottom-up information gained about the features in the words and the top-down knowledge about word and letter identities" (Ellis & Humphreys, 1999, p. 315). The more detailed theoretical assumptions made by McClelland and Rumelhart (1981) are as follows (see Figure 7.7):

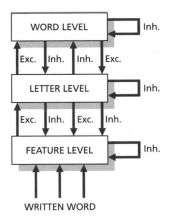

Figure 7.7.
McClelland and
Rumelhart's (1981)
interactive activation
model of visual word
recognition. Adapted
from Ellis (1984).

Inh. = Inhibitory process
Exc. = Excitatory process

- There are recognition units at three levels: the feature level, the letter level, and the word level.
- When a feature in a letter is detected (e.g., vertical line at the right-hand side of a letter), activation goes to all letter units containing that feature (e.g., H, M, N), and inhibition to all other letter units.
- Letters are identified at the letter level. When a letter in a particular position within a word is identified, activation is sent to the word level for all four-letter word units containing that letter in that position, and inhibition is sent to all other word units.
- Words are recognised at the word level. Activated word units increase the level of activation in the letter-level units for the letters forming that word (e.g., activation of the word SEAT would increase activation for the four letters S, E, A, and T at the letter level) and inhibit activity of all other letter units.
- At each level in the system, activation of one particular unit leads to suppression or inhibition of competing units.

Bottom-up processes stemming directly from the written word proceed from the feature level through the letter level to the word level by means of activation and inhibition. Top-down processing is involved in the activation and inhibition processes going from the word level to the letter level. The word superiority effect occurs because of the top-down influences of the word level on the letter level. Suppose the word SEAT is presented, and the participants are asked whether the third letter is an A or an N. If the word unit for SEAT is activated at the word level, then this will increase the activation of the letter A at the letter level, and inhibit the activation of the letter N.

How can the pseudo-word superiority effect be explained? When letters are embedded in pronounceable non-words, there will generally be some overlap of spelling patterns between the pseudo-word and genuine words. This overlap produces additional activation of the letters presented in the pseudo-word and thus generates the pseudo-word superiority effect.

Evaluation

The interactive activation model has been very influential. It shows how a connectionist processing system (see Chapter 1) can be applied to visual word recognition. It accounts for various phenomena, including the word superiority effect and the pseudo-word superiority effect.

According to the model, letters are coded in terms of their precise locations in the visual field. In fact, however, the coding seems to be based on the *relative* positions of letters rather than their precise positions. Experimental evidence that the relative positions of words are important in reading was reported by McClelland and Mozer (1986). They found that pairs of words such as LINK and MINE were sometimes misread as LINE and MINK.

The model put forward by McClelland and Rumelhart (1981) is limited. For example, it was only designed to account for performance on four-letter words written in capital letters. High-frequency or common words are more readily recognised than low-frequency or rare words. This can be explained by assuming either that stronger connections are formed between the letter and word units of high-frequency words, or that high-frequency words have a higher resting level of activation. It follows that there should be a larger word superiority effect for high-frequency words than for low-frequency words due to more top-down activation from the word level to the letter level. However, the word superiority effect is the same with high- and low-frequency words (Gunther, Gfoerer, & Weiss, 1984).

The model proposed by McClelland and Rumelhart (1981) assumes that lexical access is determined by visual information. However, there has been much controversy on this issue. Frost (1998) claimed that phonological coding is nearly always used prior to lexical access.

Development of the model

The original interactive activation model was deterministic, meaning that any given input would *always* produce the same output. This contrasts with human performance, which is somewhat variable. Accordingly, McClelland (1993) developed the model by including variable or stochastic processes within it. This permitted the model to simulate the response distributions of human participants given various word-recognition tasks.

Routes from print to sound

Suppose you were asked to read out the following list of words and non-words:

> CAT FOG COMB PINT MANTINESS FASS

You would probably find it a simple task, but it actually involves some hidden complexities. For example, how do you know that the "b" in "comb" is silent, and that "pint" does not rhyme with "hint"? Presumably you have specific information stored in long-term memory about how to pronounce these words. However, this does not seem to explain how you are able to pronounce non-words such as "mantiness" and "fass", because you lack specific stored information about their pronunciation. Perhaps non-words are pronounced by analogy with real words (e.g., "fass" is pronounced to rhyme with "mass"). Another possibility is that people make use of rules governing the translation of letter strings into sounds.

The study of brain-damaged patients with impaired reading skills has proved useful in understanding the processes and structures involved in reading. It suggests that there are several reading disorders, depending on which parts of the cognitive system involved in reading are damaged. Some of the major findings from the cognitive neuropsychological approach are discussed in the next section.

Cognitive neuropsychology

Processes and structures that may be involved in reading are shown in Figure 7.8. Ellis and Young (1988) identified these components on the basis of the study of acquired dyslexias (i.e., impairments of reading produced by brain damage in adults who were previously skilled readers). Only selected aspects of the cognitive neuropsychological account of reading will be presented here.

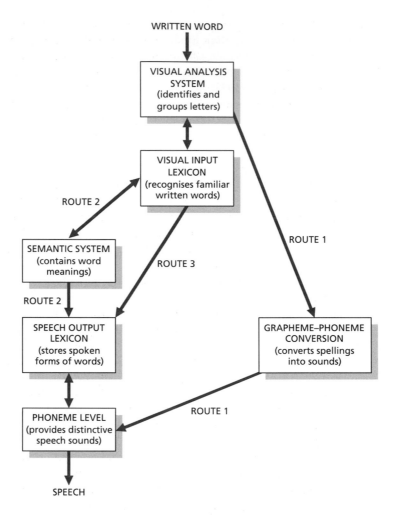

Figure 7.8. Some of the processes involved in reading. Adapted from Ellis and Young (1988).

WRITTEN WORD

VISUAL ANALYSIS
SYSTEM
(identifies and
groups letters)

VISUAL INPUT
LEXICON
(recognises familiar
written words)

ROUTE 2

SEMANTIC SYSTEM
(contains word
meanings)

ROUTE 3

ROUTE 1

ROUTE 2

SPEECH OUTPUT
LEXICON
(stores spoken
forms of words)

GRAPHEME–PHONEME
CONVERSION
(converts spellings
into sounds)

PHONEME LEVEL
(provides distinctive
speech sounds)

ROUTE 1

SPEECH

The most important message of Figure 7.8 is that there are three routes between the printed word and speech. All three routes start with the visual analysis system, which has the functions of identifying and grouping letters in printed words. We will consider each of the three routes in turn.

Route 1 (grapheme–phoneme conversion)

Route 1 differs from the other routes in making use of the process of grapheme–phoneme conversion. This process may well involve working out pronunciations for unfamiliar words and non-words by translating letters or letter groups into phonemes by the application of rules. However, Kay and Marcel (1981) argued that unfamiliar words and non-words are actually pronounced by analogy with familiar words. They found that the pronunciations of non-words by normal readers were sometimes altered to rhyme with real words that had just been presented. For example, a non-word such as "raste" is generally pronounced to rhyme with "taste", but is more likely to be pronounced to rhyme with "mast" if preceded by the word "caste".

If a brain-damaged patient could use only Route 1 when pronouncing words and non-words, what would one expect to find? The use of grapheme–phoneme conversion rules should permit accurate pronunciation of words having regular spelling–sound correspondences, but not of irregular words. If an irregular word such as "pint" has grapheme–phoneme conversion rules applied to it, it should be pronounced to rhyme with "hint"; this is known as regularisation. Finally, the grapheme–phoneme conversion rules can be used to provide pronunciations of non-words.

Patients who adhere most closely to exclusive use of Route 1 are surface dyslexics (Marshall and Newcombe, 1973). *Surface dyslexia* is a condition in which patients have particular problems in reading irregular words. For example, the surface dyslexic patient, M.P., read non-words well, and had a reading accuracy of over 90% with common and rare regular words. In contrast, although common irregular words were read with an accuracy of about 80%, only 40% of rare irregular words were read accurately (Bub, Cancelliere, & Kertesz, 1985).

The evidence from surface dyslexics suggests they have a strong (but not exclusive) reliance on Route 1. If all words were read by means of grapheme–phoneme conversion, then all irregular words would be mispronounced, and this simply does not happen. Presumably surface dyslexics make some use of routes other than Route 1, even though these other routes are severely damaged.

Route 2 (lexicon plus semantic system)
Route 2 is the route generally used by adult readers. The basic idea is that representations of thousands of familiar words are stored in a visual input lexicon. Visual presentation of a word leads to activation in the visual input lexicon. This is followed by obtaining its meaning from the semantic system after which the word is spoken (see Figure 7.8).

How could we identify patients who use Route 2 but not Route 1? Their intact visual input lexicon means that they should experience little difficulty in pronouncing *familiar* words (regular and irregular). However, their inability to use grapheme–phoneme conversion should mean they find it very hard to pronounce relatively *unfamiliar* words and non-words.

Phonological dyslexics fit this predicted pattern fairly well. *Phonological dyslexia* is a condition in which there are particular problems with reading unfamiliar words and non-words. The first case of phonological dyslexia reported systematically was R.G. (Beauvois & Dérouesné, 1979). R.G. successfully read 100% of 40 real words but only 10% of 40 non-words.

Deep dyslexia is a condition in which there are particular problems in reading unfamiliar words, and in which there are semantic reading errors (e.g., "ship" read as "boat"). Deep dyslexics resemble phonological dyslexics in finding it very hard to read unfamiliar words and non-words, suggesting they cannot use grapheme–phoneme conversion effectively. Deep dyslexics also make semantic errors, in which a word related in meaning to the printed word is read instead of the printed word. Deep dyslexics may mainly use Route 2, but damage within the semantic system itself or in the connections between the visual input lexicon and the semantic system makes this route error prone.

Route 3 (lexicon only)

Route 3 resembles Route 2 in that the visual input lexicon and the speech output lexicon are involved in reading. However, the semantic system is bypassed in Route 3, so that printed words that are pronounced are not understood. Otherwise, the expectations about reading performance for users of Route 3 are the same as those for users of Route 2: Familiar regular and irregular words should be pronounced correctly, whereas most unfamiliar words and non-words should not (see Figure 7.8).

Schwartz, Saffran, and Marin (1980) reported the case of W.L.P., a 62-year-old woman suffering from senile dementia. She could read most familiar words whether they were regular or irregular, but she often indicated that these words meant nothing to her. She was totally unable to relate the written names of animals to pictures of them, although she was fairly good at reading animal names aloud. These findings are consistent with the view that W.L.P. was bypassing the semantic system when reading words.

Evaluation of the dual-route (or triple-route) model

The above approach to reading can be regarded as the triple-route model. However, as the fundamental distinction is between reading based on a lexical or dictionary look-up procedure and reading based on a non-lexical letter-to-sound procedure, it is often referred to as the dual-route model.

Coltheart et al. (1993) put forward a dual-route computational model of reading based loosely on the processes and structures shown in Figure 7.8. Their focus was on non-lexical reading via Route 1, with the computational system learning the grapheme–phoneme rules embodied in an initial set of words. These rules were later applied to previously unseen letter strings.

Coltheart et al. (1993) trained their computational model on 2897 words. They then tested its performance when reading various non-words on which it had not been trained. It scored 90% correct, which is very close to the figure of 91.5% obtained by human participants.

According to the dual-route model, normal readers use both routes with familiar words, but the direct route will generally be much faster. It was also assumed originally that the main two routes to reading are *independent* of each other. Some evidence is inconsistent with this assumption. For example, non-words are supposed to be read by means of grapheme–phoneme correspondence rules without reference to the lexicon. Glushko (1979) compared naming times to two kinds of non-words: (1) those having irregular word neighbours (e.g., "have" is an irregular word neighbour of "mave", whereas "gave" and "save" are regular word neightbours); and (2) non-words having only regular word neighbours. Non-words of the former type were named more slowly, suggesting that the lexical route can affect the non-lexical route.

The basic dual-route model predicts that the naming of familiar words should not be influenced by the regularity of their spelling-to-sound correspondences. In fact, however, irregular words are generally named slower than regular ones (see Harley, 1995). Seidenberg et al. (1984) found this regularity effect with low-frequency words but not with high-frequency ones. Perhaps the direct route operates relatively slowly with low-frequency words, and so allows the indirect route to influence naming performance. As a result, phonological processing (which is crucial to the indirect route) plays an important role in the naming of low-frequency words and in the regularity effect.

Connectionist approaches

Within the dual-route approach, it is assumed that separate mechanisms are required to pronounce irregular words and non-words. This contrasts with the connectionist approach of Plaut et al. (1996), according to which, "All of the system's knowledge of spelling–sound correspondences is brought to bear in pronouncing all types of letter strings [words *and* non-words]. Conflicts among possible alternative pronunciations of a letter string are resolved . . . by cooperative and competitive interactions based on how the letter string relates to all known words and their pronunciations." Thus, Plaut et al. (1996) assumed that pronunciation of words and non-words is based on a highly *interactive* system.

The two approaches can be contrasted by considering the distinction between regularity and consistency. Dual-route theorists divide words into two categories: *regular*, meaning their pronunciation can be generated by applying rules; and *irregular*, meaning their pronunciation is not rule based. Regular words can generally be pronounced more rapidly. In contrast, Plaut et al. (1996) argued that words vary in *consistency* (the extent to which their pronunciation agrees with those of similarly spelled words). Highly consistent words are pronounced faster and more accurately than inconsistent words, because more of the available knowledge supports the correct pronunciation of such words. Word naming is generally predicted better by consistency than by regularity (e.g., Glushko, 1979), as is predicted by the connectionist model.

Plaut et al. (1996) tried various simulations based on two crucial notions:

(1) The pronunciation of a word or non-word is influenced strongly by consistency based on the pronunciations of all those words similar to it.
(2) Pronunciation of a word is more influenced by high-frequency or common words than by low-frequency or rare words: high-frequency words are encountered more often, and so contribute more to changes in the network.

The network learns to pronounce words accurately as connections develop between the visual forms of letters and combinations of letters (grapheme units) and their corresponding phonemes (phoneme units). The network based on this architecture learns by the use of *back-propagation*, in which the actual outputs or responses of the system are compared against the correct ones. The network received prolonged training with a set of 2998 words, after which the performance of the network closely resembled that of adult readers:

(1) Inconsistent words took longer to name than consistent ones.
(2) Rare words took longer to name than common ones.
(3) There was an interaction between word frequency and consistency, with the effects of consistency being much greater for rare words than for common ones.
(4) The network pronounced over 90% of non-words "correctly", which resembles the performance of adult readers; this finding is especially impressive, because the network received no direct training on non-words.

The above simulation did not take semantic information into account. However, Plaut et al. (1996) expanded their network model to include semantic information, assuming that such information has more impact on high-frequency words. A network based on this assumption learned to read regular and exception words much faster than a network lacking semantic information.

Surface dyslexia and phonological dyslexia

Plaut et al. (1996, p. 95) advanced the following theory of surface dyslexia: "Partial semantic support for word pronunciations alleviates the need for the phonological pathway to master all words such that, when the support is eliminated by brain damage, the surface dyslexic reading pattern emerges." Plaut et al. (1996) tested this theory by making "lesions" to the network to reduce or eliminate the contribution from semantics. The network's reading performance was very good on regular high- and low-frequency words and on non-words, worse on irregular high-frequency words, and worst on irregular low-frequency words. This is the same pattern of reading performance found in surface dyslexics.

What about phonological dyslexia? Plaut et al. (1996, p. 99) only considered this disorder in general terms: "In the limit of a complete lesion between orthography and phonology, nonword reading would be impossible. Thus, a lesion to the network that severely impaired the phonological pathway while leaving the contribution of semantics to phonology (relatively) intact would replicate the basic characteristics of phonological dyslexia."

Evaluation

The connectionist approach has various advantages over the traditional dual-route approach. First, the apparent non-independence between the two routes of the dual-route approach poses no problems for the connectionist approach, which assumes that the processing system is interactive. Second, the connectionist approach (unlike the dual-route approach) does not draw a sharp distinction between regular and irregular words. This is an advantage, because the evidence does not support the notion of a rigid distinction, and there is no agreement on the rules determining which words belong to each category. Third, speed and accuracy of word and non-word pronunciation seem to depend more on consistency than on regularity. Fourth, Plaut et al. (1996) predicted correctly that damage to the semantic system can affect reading performance in surface dyslexics. In contrast, "dual-route theories that include a lexical, nonsemantic pathway (e.g., . . . Coltheart et al., 1993) predict that selective semantic damage should never affect [word] naming accuracy" (Plaut et al., 1996, p. 102).

The connectionist model has various limitations. First, as Plaut et al. (1996, p. 108) admitted, "the nature of processing within the semantic pathway has been characterised in only the coarsest way." Second, the approach has only been tested with one-syllabled words. Third, the approach provides only a sketchy account of some key issues, such as the nature of the impairment in phonological dyslexia. Fourth, as Ellis and Humphreys (1999, p. 537) argued, "Plaut et al. proposed that their second route was semantic in nature; however, they did not attempt to represent semantic knowledge in any plausible manner."

Phonological theory of reading

According to the dual-route model, the reading performance of normal individuals is generally little affected by phonological coding. This is because reading via the indirect route (grapheme–phoneme conversion) tends to be much slower than reading via the direct route. Frost (1998, 76) argued that phonological coding is much more important in reading than is implied by the dual-route model: "A phonological representation is a necessary product of processing printed words, even though the explicit pronunciation of their phonological structure is not required. Thus, the strong phonological model would predict that phonological processing will be mandatory [obligatory], perhaps automatic."

One prediction of the phonological model (but inconsistent with the dual-route model) is as follows: Phonological coding will occur even when it impairs performance. This prediction was supported by Tzelgov et al. (1996). It was based on the *Stroop effect*, in which naming the colours in which words are printed is slowed when the words themselves are different colour names (e.g., the word RED printed in green). The participants in the study were English–Hebrew bilinguals, and in the key condition they had to name the colours of non-words in one of the two languages. Each non-word had an unfamiliar printed form, but its phonological translation was a colour name in the other language. There was a strong Stroop effect with these non-words, because the participants engaged in phonological coding of the non-words even though it was disadvantageous to do so.

Evaluation

There is reasonable support for the central assumption of the phonological model that phonological coding typically occurs during the processing of printed words, even when it disrupts performance. Phonological coding occurs more often and more rapidly than assumed by the dual-route model.

On the negative side, the phonological model does not provide a detailed account of reading processes. In addition, it seems more applicable to reading in normals than in dyslexics. For example, phonological dyslexics have great difficulties with phonological coding, but are reasonably good at reading familiar words. This is puzzling if one assumes that phonological coding is of major importance in reading. As Frost (1998, p. 93) admitted, "Evidence that is . . . damaging to the strong phonological model comes from phonological dyslexia."

Section summary

There is still controversy about the processes involved in reading individual words, in large part because of the inconclusiveness of much of the evidence. One reason for this inconclusiveness is that naming and other methods provide evidence about the overall accuracy and speed of word reading, but are relatively uninformative about the underlying processes. As Frost (1998, p. 95) suggested, "Instead of setting one's experimental camera at the finish line of the cognitive events, one should aim at filming their on-line, step-by-step development."

Summary: Basic language processes

- *Language acquisition*: Children acquire language very rapidly, generally in the order of phonology first, followed by semantics, syntax, and pragmatics. After the one-word or holophrastic period comes the telegraphic period. According to Chomsky's nativist theory, part of our innate knowledge is in the form of a universal grammar. This theory receives some support from the way in which pidgin languages develop into creole languages, and by studies in genetic linguistics. However, the theory is hard to test, and grammatical rules are probably not acquired in the all-or-none way predicted. There is some evidence for a critical (or sensitive) period for the learning of syntax and phonology, but not for vocabulary. Skinner argued that language is acquired by operant conditioning based on shaping. However, children acquire the rules of grammar even though they are not generally rewarded for using grammar correctly. Skinner's approach does not account for the creativity in children's language. The most important environmental influence on language acquisition is probably the social interaction between mother and child, and her use of motherese. Specific language impairment depends in part on difficulties in distinguishing between brief auditory stimuli and on deficiencies in the phonological loop.
- *Speech perception*: Listeners to speech have to confront the linearity, non-invariance, and segmentation problems. Studies on the phonemic restoration effect suggest that contextual information can influence speech perception in a top-down way. Prosodic cues are often used by listeners. The role played by lip-reading is shown by the McGurk effect. According to the original version of cohort theory, the initial sound of a word is used to construct a word-initial cohort that is reduced to only one word by using additional information from the presented word and from contextual information. Cohort theory has been revised to make it more flexible. According to the TRACE model, bottom-up and top-down processes interact during speech perception. This assumption is probably incorrect, and the importance of top-down processes is exaggerated in the TRACE model.

- *Cognitive neuropsychology of speech perception*: Evidence from brain-damaged patients suggests that saying a spoken word can be achieved using three different routes. Patients with pure word deafness have problems with speech perception because of impaired phonemic processing in the auditory analysis system. Patients with word meaning deafness can repeat familiar words without understanding their meaning, but have problems with non-words. Patients with auditory phonological agnosia have damage within Route 3. Deep dysphasia may reflect damage to all three routes used to repeat spoken words, or it may involve damage to the response buffer.

- *Basic reading processes*: According to the E-Z Reader model, the next eye movement in reading is programmed after only part of the processing of the currently fixated word has occurred. Completion of lexical access to the currently fixated word produces a shift of covert attention to the next word. The model de-emphasises the impact of higher-level cognitive processes on fixation times. Word identification is affected by context, and there is a small effect of context on lexical access. According to the interactive activation model, word recognition depends on top-down as well as bottom-up processes. The word superiority effect occurs because of top-down influences of the word level on the letter level of processing. The model incorrectly assumes that letters are coded in terms of their precise locations, and neglects the possible influence of phonological coding on word access and identification.

- *Routes from print to sound*: According to the dual-route theory, there are two main routes between the printed word and speech, one used mainly for familiar words, and the other used for unfamiliar words and non-words. This theory is supported by evidence from surface dyslexics and phonological dyslexics. However, the two main routes are probably not independent of each other, and phonological coding is more important than is implied by the model. Plaut et al. (1996) put forward a connectionist model, according to which the pronunciation of words and non-words is based on a highly interactive system. They "lesioned" their connectionist network to simulate the reading performance of surface dyslexics. Plaut et al. provided a sketchy account of phonological dyslexia, and had little to say about the role of semantic processing in reading.

Essay questions

(1) Discuss the role of environmental factors in language acquisition.
(2) What processes are involved in spoken word recognition?
(3) What has the cognitive neuropsychological approach contributed to our understanding of speech perception?
(4) Discuss the basic processes involved in reading text.
(5) Evaluate the evidence for the notion that there are two or three routes between the printed word and speech.

Further reading

Garrod, S., & Pickering, M.J. (1999). *Language processing*. Hove, UK: Psychology Press. Chapters 2–4 provide thorough accounts of the basic processes involved in speech perception and reading.

Harley, T.A. (1995). *The psychology of language: From data to theory*. Hove, UK: Psychology Press. There is detailed but accessible coverage of the topics discussed here in several chapters (e.g., 2, 3, 4, 10, and 11) of this well-written book.

Parkin, A.J. (1996). *Explorations in cognitive neuropsychology*. Oxford: Blackwell. This book contains good coverage of the ways in which the study of brain-damaged patients has increased our understanding of speech perception and reading.

Language comprehension and production 8

Introduction

In the previous chapter, we focused on the processing of individual words and sentences. In real life, however, we are generally presented with connected *discourse* (written text or speech), the first topic discussed in this chapter. According to Graesser, Millis, and Zwaan (1997, p. 164), there are important differences between the processing of sentences and discourse: "A sentence out of context is nearly always ambiguous, whereas a sentence in a discourse context is rarely ambiguous . . . Both stories and everyday experiences include people performing actions in pursuit of goals, events that present obstacles to these goals, conflicts between people, and emotional reactions."

The second major topic dealt with in this chapter is speech production. This is concerned with the complex processes involved in speaking fluently. Studying brain-damaged patients with speech problems has clarified what is involved, as has research within cognitive neuroscience.

The third major topic of this chapter is the relationship between language and thought. Our focus will be mainly on whether language influences or determines thought.

Discourse processing

Most research on discourse comprehension has been based on written texts. Some researchers have used published texts written by professional writers, whereas others have used specially constructed texts. The former approach has the advantage of *ecological validity* (applicability to real life), but provides poor control over many variables affecting comprehension. The latter approach has the advantage that textual variables can be manipulated systematically, but the resulting texts tend to be artificial and uninteresting.

Inference drawing

In order to comprehend discourse, we need to gain access to relevant stored knowledge. This is especially obvious when we use such knowledge to draw inferences so that we can fill in the frequent gaps in what we listen to or read. Some idea of how readily we make inferences can be formed by reading the following story (Rumelhart and Ortony, 1977):

(1) Mary heard the ice-cream van coming.
(2) She remembered the pocket money.
(3) She rushed into the house.

You probably made various inferences while reading the story. Possible inferences include the following: Mary wanted to buy some ice-cream; buying ice-cream costs money; and Mary had only a limited amount of time to get hold of some money before the ice-cream van arrived. None of these assumptions is explicitly stated.

A distinction can be drawn between *bridging inferences* and *elaborative inferences*. Bridging inferences need to be made to establish coherence between the current part of the text and the preceding text, whereas elaborative inferences simply add details to the text. Readers generally draw bridging inferences, which are essential for under-standing. It is less clear which non-essential or elaborative inferences are drawn.

Anaphora

Perhaps the simplest form of bridging inference is involved in *anaphora*, in which a pronoun or noun has to be identified with a previously mentioned noun or noun phrase (e.g., "Fred sold John his lawn mower, and then he sold him his garden hose"). It requires a bridging inference to realise that "he" refers to Fred.

The ease of establishing the appropriate anaphoric inference often depends on the distance between the pronoun and the noun to which it refers: this is the distance effect. However, Clifton and Ferreira (1987) showed that distance is not always important. The reading time for a critical phrase containing a pronoun was faster if the relevant noun was still the topic of discourse, but distance as such had no effect.

When are inferences drawn?

Consider the following passage (O'Brien et al., 1988):

> All the mugger wanted was to steal the woman's money. But when she screamed, he stabbed her with his weapon in an attempt to quiet her. He looked to see if anyone had seen him. He threw the knife into the bushes, took her money, and ran away.

O'Brien et al. (1988) were interested in seeing when readers drew the inference that the "weapon" in the second sentence was a knife. They compared the reading time on the last sentence in the passage quoted here, and in an almost identical passage with the word "weapon" replaced by "knife". There was no difference, suggesting that the inference that the weapon was a knife was drawn immediately.

O'Brien et al. (1988) also considered the reading time for the last sentence when the second sentence was altered so that the inference that the weapon was a knife was less clear ("But when she screamed, he assaulted her with his weapon in an attempt to quiet her"). The last sentence now took longer to read, presumably because the inference that the weapon was a knife was drawn only while the last sentence was being read.

Which inferences are drawn?

Various inferences are made while people are reading text or listening to speech. *Why* are inferences made, and *which* inferences are likely to be made in any given situation? McKoon and Ratcliff (1992, p. 440) proposed the *minimalist hypothesis*: "In the absence of specific, goal-directed strategic processes, inferences of only two kinds are constructed: those that establish locally coherent representations of the parts of a text that are processed concurrently and those that rely on information that is quickly and easily available." They made the following assumptions:

- Inferences are either automatic or strategic (goal directed).
- Some automatic inferences establish local coherence (two or three sentences making sense on their own or in combination with easily available general knowledge).
- Other automatic inferences rely on information that is readily available because it forms part of general knowledge or is explicitly stated in the text.
- Strategic inferences are formed in pursuit of the reader's goals.

Those who favour the minimalist hypothesis claim that there are very definite constraints on the number of inferences that are generated automatically. In contrast, those who support the constructionist viewpoint (e.g., Bransford, 1979) argue that numerous automatic inferences are drawn in reading. According to constructionist theorists, these automatic inferences facilitate full comprehension of what is being listened to or read.

McKoon and Ratcliff (1986) compared these two theories. They argued that a sentence such as "The actress fell from the fourteenth storey" would automatically lead to the inference that she died from the constructionist (but not the minimalist) viewpoint. Participants read several short texts containing such sentences, followed by a recognition memory test. There were critical test words that represented inferences from a presented sentence (e.g., "dead" for the sentence about the actress). The correct response to these critical test words was "No". However, if participants had formed the inference, they might make errors.

There were generally very few errors. However, when they were preceded by a word from the relevant sentence (e.g., "actress"), there were several errors. Thus, the inferences were not generated fully, in line with the minimalist hypothesis. However, they were formed to a limited extent, which provides some support for the constructionists.

Evidence opposing the constructionist position was obtained by Dosher and Corbett (1982). They used instrumental inferences (e.g., a sentence such as "Mary stirred her coffee" has "spoon" as its instrumental inference). In order to decide whether participants generated these instrumental inferences during reading, Dosher and Corbett used an unusual procedure. It is known from research on the Stroop effect that the time taken to name the colour in which a word is printed is affected if the word has recently been activated. Thus, if presentation of the sentence "Mary stirred her coffee" activates the word "spoon", then this should slow the time taken to name the colour in which the word "spoon" is printed on the Stroop task. In a control (out-of-context) condition, the words presented on the Stroop task bore no relationship to the preceding sentences. With normal reading instructions, there was no evidence that the instrumental inferences had been formed with normal reading instructions (see Figure 8.1). However, when the participants were instructed to guess the instrument in each sentence, then there were effects on the Stroop task.

The above findings indicate clearly that whether an inference is drawn can depend on the reader's intentions or goals, as assumed by

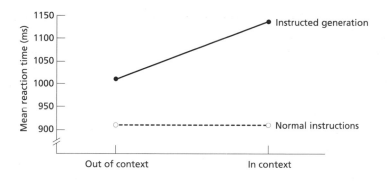

Figure 8.1. Colour-naming time in the Stroop task as a function of whether or not participants had been asked to guess the instrument in preceding sentences, and as a function of whether the words on the Stroop test were in or out of context with the preceding sentences. Based on data in Dosher and Corbett (1982).

McKoon and Ratcliff (1992). These findings are at variance with the constructionist position. It is necessary to infer the instrument used in stirring coffee to attain full understanding, but such instrumental inferences are not normally drawn.

McKoon and Ratcliff (1992) assumed that automatic inferences are drawn to establish local coherence for information contained in working memory, but global inferences (inferences connecting widely separated pieces of textual information) are not drawn automatically. They tested these assumptions with short texts containing a global goal (e.g., assassinating a president) and one or two local or subordinate goals (e.g., using a rifle). Active use of global and local inferences was tested by presenting a test word after each text, and instructing the participants to decide rapidly whether the word had appeared in the text.

Local inferences were drawn automatically, but global ones were not. These findings are more consistent with the minimalist hypothesis than with the constructionist position, in which no distinction is drawn between local and global inferences.

Evaluation

The minimalist hypothesis clarifies which inferences are drawn automatically. In contrast, constructionist theorists often argue that those inferences needed to understand fully the situation described in a text are drawn automatically. This is rather vague, as it is often unclear what information needs to be encoded for full understanding. Another strength of the minimalist hypothesis is that it emphasises the distinction between automatic and strategic inferences. The notion that many inferences will be drawn only if they are consistent with the reader's goals in reading is an important one.

On the negative side, we cannot always predict accurately from the hypothesis which inferences will be drawn. For example, automatic inferences are drawn if the necessary information is "readily available", but it can be hard to establish the precise degree of availability of some piece of information.

Search-after-meaning theory

Graesser, Singer, and Trabasso (1994) put forward a search-after-meaning theory, according to which readers engage in a search after meaning based on the following:

- *The reader goal assumption*: The reader constructs a meaning for the text addressing his or her goals.
- *The coherence assumption*: The reader tries to construct a meaning for the text that is coherent locally and globally.
- *The explanation assumption*: The reader tries to explain the actions and events described in the text.

According to the theory, the reader will not search after meaning if his or her goals do not require the construction of a meaning representation of the text (e.g., in proofreading), if the text seems to lack coherence, or if the reader does not possess the necessary background knowledge to make sense of the text.

Evaluation

Search-after-meaning theory provides a reasonably clear account of the types of inferences that are generally drawn. The theory predicts that more inferences will be drawn than does the minimalist hypothesis, but fewer than does the constructionist approach. The evidence is more in line with the predictions of the search-after-meaning theory than those of the other two theories.

Section summary

Graesser et al. (1997, p. 183) discussed the evidence relating to theories of inference, and concluded as follows: "Each of the . . . models is correct in certain conditions. The minimalist hypothesis is probably correct when the reader is very quickly reading the text, when the text lacks global coherence, and when the reader has very little background knowledge. The constructionist [or search-after-meaning] theory is on the mark when the reader is attempting to comprehend the text for enjoyment or mastery at a more leisurely pace."

Some theorists (e.g., Kintsch, 1988, 1994) have argued that readers often construct a mental model or representation of the situation described by the text. The information contained in mental models can go well beyond the information contained in a text, and such information is based on inferences. The notion of situational representations plays an important part in the theory of story processing proposed by Kintsch (1988, 1994), and so further discussion will be deferred until that theory is considered later.

Story processing

If someone asks us to tell them about a story or book we have read recently, we discuss its major events and themes, and leave out the minor details. In other words, our description of the story is highly *selective*, and is determined by its meaning.

Gomulicki (1956) showed the selective way in which stories are comprehended and remembered. One group of participants wrote a précis (summary) of a story that was visible in front of them, and a second group recalled the story from memory. A third group of participants who were given each précis and recall found it very hard to tell them apart. Thus, story memory resembles a précis with people focusing mainly on important information.

Story grammars

Most (or all) stories possess some kind of structure. Some psychologists have argued that all stories share common elements at a very general level. This led to the notion of a *story grammar* or set of rules from which the structure of any given story can be generated. Thorndyke (1977) considered a hierarchical story grammar, with the major categories of setting, theme, plot, and resolution at the top of the hierarchy. Thorndyke (1977) tested this story grammar by presenting a story in which the theme was in its usual place at the start of the story, or it was placed at the end of the story, or it was omitted altogether. Memory for the story was best when the theme was presented at the start of the story, and it was better when it had been presented at the end rather than not at all.

Other research has supported the view that stories are hierarchically organised. For example, Meyer and McConkie (1973) found that an event low down in the story hierarchy was much more likely to be recalled if the event immediately above it in the hierarchy had been recalled.

Evaluation

The notion that stories have an underlying structure is reasonable, but the story grammar approach has not proved of lasting value. Why is this? According to Harley (1995, p. 233): "There is no agreement on story structure: virtually every story grammatician has proposed a different grammar." Another limitation is that story grammars are not very informative about the processes involved in story comprehension.

Kintsch's construction–integration model

Kintsch (1988, 1994) put forward a construction–integration model (see Figure 8.2). According to the model, the following stages occur during comprehension:

- Sentences in the text are turned into propositions representing the meaning of the text.
- These propositions are entered into a short-term buffer and form a *propositional* net.

Figure 8.2. The construction–integration model. Adapted from Kintsch (1992).

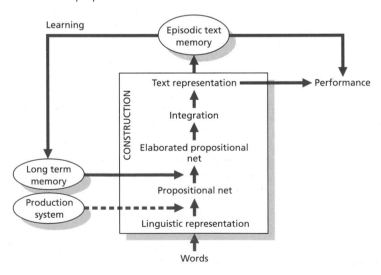

- Each proposition constructed from the text retrieves associatively related propositions (including inferences) from long-term memory.
- The propositions constructed from the text plus those retrieved from *long-term memory* jointly form the *elaborated propositional net*; this net contains many irrelevant propositions.
- A spreading activation process is then used to select propositions for the text representation; clusters of highly interconnected propositions attract most of the activation and are most likely to be included in the text representation: "things that belong together contextually become stronger, and things that do not, die off" (Kintsch, 1994, p. 732): this is the *integration process*.
- The *text representation* is an organised structure stored in *episodic text memory*; information about the relationship between any two propositions is included if the two propositions were processed together in the short-term buffer.
- Three levels of representation are constructed: surface representation (the text itself); propositional representation or textbase (propositions formed from the text); and situational representation (a mental model describing the situation referred to in the text). Schemas can help the construction of situational representations or models.

A distinctive feature of this model is the assumption that the processes involved in the construction of the elaborated propositional net are relatively inefficient, with many irrelevant propositions being included. This is basically a bottom-up approach, in that the elaborated propositional net is constructed ignoring the context provided by the overall theme of the text. In contrast, "most other models of comprehension attempt to specify strong, 'smart' rules which, guided by schemata, arrive at just the right interpretations, activate just the right knowledge, and generate just the right inferences" (Kintsch et al., 1990, p. 136). Such strong rules are very complex and lack flexibility. The weak rules incorporated into the construction–integration model are much more robust, and can be used in virtually all situations.

Evidence
Kintsch et al. (1990) tested the theoretical assumption that text processing produces three levels of representation (surface, propositional,

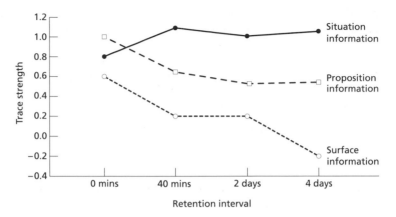

Figure 8.3. Forgetting functions for situation, proposition, and surface information over a 4-day period. Adapted from Kintsch et al. (1990).

and situational). Participants were presented with brief descriptions of very stereotyped situations (e.g., going to see a film), and then their recognition memory was tested immediately or at times ranging up to four days.

The forgetting functions for the surface, propositional, and situational representations were distinctively different (see Figure 8.3). There was rapid and complete forgetting of the surface representation, whereas information from the situational representation showed no forgetting over 4 days. Propositional information differed from situational information in that there was forgetting over time, and differed from surface information in that there was only partial forgetting. As Kintsch et al. (1990) had predicted, the most complete representation of the meaning of the text (i.e., the situational representation) was best remembered, and the least complete representation (i.e., the surface representation) was worst remembered.

Zwaan (1994) tested the psychological reality of some of the levels of representation identified in the construction–integration model. He argued that the reader's goals influence the extent to which different representational levels are constructed. For example, someone reading an excerpt from a novel might focus on the text itself (e.g., the wording, stylistic devices), and so form a strong surface representation. In contrast, someone reading a newspaper article may focus on updating his or her representation of a real-world situation, and so form a strong situation representation. Zwaan (1994) devised texts that were described as either literary extracts or news stories. As predicted, memory for surface representations was better for stories described as literary, whereas

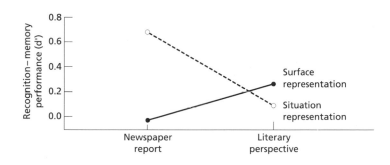

Figure 8.4. Memory for surface and situation representations for stories described as literary or as newspaper reports. Data from Zwaan (1994).

memory for situation representations was better for stories described as newspaper reports (see Figure 8.4).

Glenberg, Meyer, and Linden (1987) reported a study comparing the mental or situational model approach against the propositional approach, according to which the meaning of a passage is stored in the form of a string of propositions. They presented short passages such as the following:

> John was preparing for a marathon in August. After doing a few warm-up exercises, he (took off/put on) his sweatshirt and went jogging. He jogged halfway round the lake without too much difficulty. Further along the route, however, his muscles began to ache.

The participants were then probed with the word "sweatshirt", and decided whether it had occurred in the passage. They responded significantly faster with the version of the story in which John put on his sweatshirt than when he took it off. This finding is rather mystifying from the perspective of a propositional theory, because the probe word is represented in only one proposition in both versions of the passage. However, the finding is readily explicable from the mental or situational model approach: If participants construct mental models depicting the events described in the passage, then the sweatshirt has much greater prominence when John puts it on than when he takes it off.

Evaluation

The construction–integration model possesses various strengths. First, the ways in which text information combines with the reader's knowledge are spelled out in detail. Second, there is good support for the notion that three levels of representation of the text are constructed. Third, the emphasis on spreading activation points to important similarities between story processing and the processing of individual words.

On the negative side, situational representations are not always constructed. Zwaan and van Oostendop (1993) asked some of their participants to read the description of a murder scene, including the locations of the body and various clues. Most participants did not construct a situational representation. However, when the initial instructions emphasised the importance of constructing a spatial representation, then a situational representation was constructed at the cost of a marked increase in reading time. Thus, limited processing capacity may often restrict the formation of situational representations.

Another limitation with the model relates to the assumption that numerous inferences are considered initially, with most of them being discarded before the reader becomes aware of them. This key theoretical assumption has not been tested properly. Finally, there may be more levels of representation than the three levels identified by Kintsch (1988, 1994). For example, Graesser et al. (1997) identified the genre level, which is concerned with the nature of the text (e.g., narration, description, persuasion).

Event-indexing model

The construction–integration model is not specific about the processes involved in the construction of situation models. However, Zwaan, Langston, and Graesser (1995) put forward an event-indexing model to remedy this omission. According to this model, readers monitor five aspects or indexes of the evolving situation model when they read stories:

(1) *The protagonist*: The central character or actor in the present event compared to the previous event.
(2) *Temporality*: The relationship between the times at which the present and previous events occurred.
(3) *Causality*: The causal relationship of the current event to the previous event.
(4) *Spatiality*: The relationship between the spatial setting of the current event and that of the previous event.
(5) *Intentionality*: The relationship between the character's goals and the present event.

Key predictions of the event-indexing model are that *discontinuities* in any of these aspects (e.g., a change in the spatial setting, a flashback in time) create difficulties in situation-model construction, and increase reading times for events. Zwaan and Radvansky (1998) discussed a study in which they assessed the overlap (or lack of discontinuity) between the target sentence and the previous sentence with respect to the five situational aspects. The greater was the level of discontinuity, the lower were the participant ratings of how well the target sentence fitted in with the previous sentence.

Additional support for the event-indexing model was reported by Zwaan et al. (1995). The reading times for events in a story increased as a function of the number out of the five situational dimensions on which there was discontinuity with the previous event. In addition, each of the five dimensions was found to influence reading time.

Evaluation

The event-indexing model identifies key processes involved in creating and updating situation models. The emphasis of the model on the construction of situation models is probably well placed. As Zwaan and Radvansky (1998, p. 177) argued, "Language can be regarded as a set of processing instructions on how to construct a mental representation of the described situation."

On the negative side, the event-indexing model, "treats the individual dimensions as independent entities" (Zwaan & Ravansky, 1998, p. 180). In fact, the various situational dimensions seem to interact. Consider the following sentence provided by Zwaan and Radvansky (1998): "Someone was making noise in the backyard; Mike had left hours ago." This sentence provides information about temporality. However, it also has relevance to the causality issue, because it permits the causal inference that Mike was not the person making the noise.

Speech production

Speech nearly always occurs as conversation in a social context. Grice (1967) argued that the key to successful communication is the Co-operative Principle, according to which speakers and listeners should try to be co-operative.

In addition to the Co-operative Principle, Grice proposed four maxims the speaker should heed:

- *Maxim of quantity*: The speaker should be as informative as necessary, but not more so.
- *Maxim of quality*: The speaker should be truthful.
- *Maxim of relation*: The speaker should say things relevant to the situation.
- *Maxim of manner*: The speaker should make his or her contribution easy to understand.

What needs to be said (maxim of quantity) depends on what the speaker wishes to describe (often called the referent). It is also necessary to know the objects from which the referent must be differentiated. It is sufficient to say "The boy is good at football" if the other players are all men, but not if some of them are also boys. In the latter case, it is necessary to be more specific (e.g., "The boy with red hair is good at football").

According to Clark and Carlson (1981), the speaker must take account of what they called the "common ground". The common ground between two people consists of their mutual beliefs, expectations, and knowledge. If you overhear a conversation between two friends, it can be very hard to follow, because you lack the common ground that they share.

Horton and Keysar (1996) distinguished between two theoretical positions:

(1) *The initial design model*: The speaker's initial plan for an utterance takes full account of the common ground with the listener.

(2) *The monitoring and adjustment model*: Speakers plan their utterances initially on the basis of information available to them *without* considering the listener's perspective. Then they monitor and correct their plans to take account of the common ground.

Horton and Keysar (1996) tested these models. Their participants' descriptions were in line with the initial design model when they had enough time to plan their utterances in detail. However, their descriptions were more in accord with the monitoring and adjustment model when they had little time available. Presumably the common ground was not used properly in this speeded condition because there was insufficient time for the monitoring process to operate.

Would it not be better if we constantly operated on the basis of the initial design model? One obvious advantage is that we would communicate more effectively with other people. However, the processing demands involved in always taking account of the listener's knowledge when planning utterances could be excessive. In fact, the information available to the speaker often happens to be shared with the listener. As a result, many utterances will be appropriate for the listener even though the speaker has not devoted processing resources to common ground knowledge.

Processes in speech production

Speech production is a complex activity involving various skills. These include deciding what one wants to say, selecting the appropriate words to express it, organising those words grammatically, and turning the sentences one wants to say into actual speech.

Speakers use *prosodic cues* in their speech (e.g., rhythm, stress, and intonation), which make it easier for listeners to understand what they are saying. However, Allbritton, McKoon, and Ratcliff (1996) found that very few of their participants (even trained actors and broadcasters) consistently produced prosodic cues when asked to read short passages containing ambiguous sentences that were disambiguated by the passage context. In contrast, Lea (1973) analysed hundreds of naturally occurring spoken sentences, and found that syntactic boundaries (e.g., ends of sentences) were generally signalled by prosodic cues.

A consideration of hesitations and pauses in speech production suggests that speech is planned in phrases or clauses. Pauses in spontaneous speech occur more often at grammatical junctures (e.g., the ends of phrases) than anywhere else. Boomer (1965) found that such pauses last longer on average than those at other locations (1.03 s vs. 0.75 s, respectively). Pauses coinciding with phrase boundaries tend to be filled with sounds such as "um", "er", or "ah", whereas those occurring within a phrase tend to be silent (Maclay & Osgood, 1959). These longish pauses at the end of phrases or clauses probably permit forward planning of the next utterance.

Speech errors

It is hard to identify the processes involved in speech production, partly because they normally occur so rapidly (we produce two or three words per second on average). One approach is to focus on the errors in spoken language. As Dell (1986, p. 284) pointed out, "The inner workings of a highly complex system are often revealed by the way in which the system breaks down."

There are various collections of speech errors (e.g., Garrett, 1975; Stemberger, 1982), consisting of those personally heard by the researchers concerned. This procedure poses some problems, because some kinds of error are more readily detectable than others. Thus, we should be sceptical about percentage figures for the different kinds of speech errors. However, there are no major problems with the main categories of speech errors. The existence of some types of speech errors has been confirmed by experimentation in which errors have been created under laboratory conditions (see Dell, 1986).

We will consider some of the main types of speech errors here, and then discuss their theoretical significance in the next section. Several forms of speech error involve problems with selecting the correct word (lexical selection). A simple kind of lexical selection error is *semantic substitution* (the correct word is replaced by a word of similar meaning, e.g., "Where is my tennis bat?" instead of "Where is my tennis racquet?"). In 99% of cases, the substituted word is of the same form class as the correct word (e.g., nouns substitute for nouns).

Blending is another kind of lexical selection error (e.g., "The sky is shining" instead of "The sky is blue" or "The sun is shining"). A further kind of lexical selection error is the *word-exchange error*, in which two words switch places (e.g., "I must let the house out of the cat" instead of "I must let the cat out of the house"). The two words involved in a word-exchange error are typically further apart in the sentence than the two words involved in *sound-exchange errors* (two sounds switching places) (Garrett, 1980).

Morpheme-exchange errors involve inflections or suffixes remaining in place but attached to the wrong words (e.g., "He has already trunked two packs"). These errors suggest that the positioning of inflections or suffixes is dealt with by a rather separate process from the one responsible for positioning word stems (e.g., "trunk", "pack"). The word stems seem to be worked out *before* the inflections are added. Smyth et al. (1987) pointed out that inflections are generally altered to fit in with the new word stems to which they are linked. For example, the "s" sound in the phrase "the forks of a prong" is pronounced in a way that is appropriate within the word "forks", but this is different from the "s" sound in the original word "prongs".

One of the best-known speech errors is the spoonerism, in which the initial letter or letters of two or more words are switched. The Rev. William Archibald Spooner is credited with several memorable examples, including "You have hissed all my mystery lectures" and "The Lord is a shoving leopard to his flock." Alas, most of the Rev.

Spooner's gems were the result of much painstaking effort. Consonants always exchange with consonants and vowels with vowels in spoonerisms, and the exchanging phonemes are generally similar in sound (see Fromkin, 1993). Garrett (1976) reported that 93% of the spoonerisms in his collection involved a switching of letters between two words within the same clause, suggesting that the clause is an important unit in speech production.

Theories of speech production

Several researchers (e.g., Dell, 1986; Dell & O'Seaghdha, 1991; Garrett, 1976) have used evidence from speech errors to construct theories of speech production. These theories have much in common. First, it is assumed that there is much pre-production planning of speech. Second, most theorists agree that there is a series of processing stages in speech production, and there is even agreement that there are four processing stages. Third, the processes move from the general (the intended meaning) to the specific (the units of sound to be uttered).

We will consider mainly the spreading-activation theory of Dell (1986), Dell and O'Seaghdha (1991), and Dell, Burger, and Svec (1997). In addition, there will be a brief consideration of the theoretical approach of Levelt (e.g., Levelt, 1989; Levelt, Roelofs, & Meyer, 1999).

Spreading-activation theory

Spreading-activation theory is based on connectionist principles (see Chapter 1), and consists of four levels. The main assumptions of the theory (including descriptions of the four levels) are as follows:

- *Semantic level*: the meaning of what is to be said; this level is not considered in detail within the theory.
- *Syntactic level*: the grammatical structure of the words in the planned utterance.
- *Morphological level*: the morphemes (basic units of meaning or word forms) in the planned sentence.
- *Phonological level*: the phonemes or basic units of sound within the sentence.
- A representation is formed at each level.
- Processing during speech planning occurs at the same time at all four levels, and is both parallel and interactive; however, it typically proceeds more rapidly at higher levels (e.g., semantic and syntactic).

According to spreading-activation theory, there are *categorical rules* at each level. These rules are constraints on the acceptable categories of items and the combinations of categories. The rules at each level define categories appropriate to that level. In addition to the categorical rules, there is a *lexicon* (dictionary) in the form of a constructionist network. It contains nodes for concepts, words, morphemes, and phonemes. When a node is activated, it sends activation to all the nodes connected to it (see Chapter 1).

The most important assumption of the theory relates to the *insertion rules*. These rules select the items for inclusion in the representation at each level according to the following criterion: *The most highly activated node belonging to the appropriate category is chosen.* For example, if the categorical rules at the syntactic level dictate that a verb is required at a particular point within the syntactic representation, then that verb whose node is most activated will be selected. After an item has been selected, its activation level immediately reduces to zero; this prevents it from being selected repeatedly.

Speech errors occur when an incorrect item has a higher level of activation than the correct item. The existence of spreading activation means that numerous nodes are all activated at the same time, and this increases the likelihood of speech errors.

Evidence

What kinds of errors are predicted by the theory? First, errors should belong to the appropriate category (e.g., an incorrect noun replacing the correct noun), because of the operation of the categorical rules. As expected, most errors do belong to the appropriate category (Dell, 1986).

Second, many errors should be anticipation errors, in which a word is spoken earlier in the sentence than is appropriate (e.g., "The sky is in the sky"). This happens because all of the words in the sentence tend to become activated during the planning for speech. As predicted, speakers make several anticipation errors.

Third, anticipation errors should often turn into exchange errors, in which two words within a sentence are swapped (e.g., "I must write a wife to my letter"). Remember that the activation level of a selected item immediately reduces to zero. Therefore, if "wife" has been selected too early, it is unlikely to compete successfully to be selected in its correct place in the sentence. This allows a previously unselected and highly activated item such as "letter" to appear in the wrong place. Many speech errors are of the exchange variety.

Fourth, anticipation and exchange errors generally involve words moving only a relatively short distance within the sentence. Those words relevant to the part of the sentence that is under current consideration will tend to be more activated than those words relevant to more distant parts of the sentence.

Fifth, speech errors should tend to consist of actual words or morphemes (the lexical bias effect). This effect was demonstrated by Baars, Motley, and MacKay (1975). Word pairs were presented briefly, and participants had to say both words as rapidly as possible. The error rate was twice as great when the word pair could be reformed to create two new words (e.g., "lewd rip" can be turned into "rude lip") than when it could not (e.g. "Luke risk" turns into "ruke lisk").

Sixth, the notion that the various levels of processing interact flexibly with each other means that speech errors can be multiply determined. Dell (1986) quoted the example of someone saying "Let's stop" instead of "Let's start". The error is certainly semantic. However, it is also phonological, because the substitute word shares a common sound with the appropriate word. Detailed investigation of such word-substitution errors reveals that the spoken word and the intended word are more similar in sound than would be expected by chance alone (Dell & O'Seaghdha, 1991; Harley, 1984).

According to the theory, most errors are caused by spreading activation. Would it not be preferable if activation did not spread so widely through the lexicon? Dell (1986) argued that widespread activation facilitates the production of novel sentences, and so prevents our utterances from becoming too stereotyped.

Evaluation
One of the strengths of spreading-activation theory is that it makes precise predictions about the kinds of errors that should occur most often in speech production. Another strength is that the emphasis on spreading activation provides links between speech production and other cognitive activities (e.g., word recognition: McClelland & Rumelhart, 1981).

On the negative side, the focus of spreading-activation theory is mainly on individual words or concepts, with broader issues relating to the construction of a message being de-emphasised. The theory predicts the nature and number of errors produced in speech, but cannot account for the *time* taken to produce spoken words. Thus, it is somewhat limited in focus.

Anticipation and perseveration errors

Dell et al. (1997) developed spreading-activation theory, arguing that most speech errors belong to two categories:

(1) *Anticipatory*: Sounds or words are spoken too early (e.g., "cuff of coffee" instead of "cup of coffee").

(2) *Perseverated*: Sounds or words are spoken too late (e.g., "beef needle" instead of "beef noodle").

The key assumption is that expert speakers are better than non-expert speakers at planning ahead when speaking, and so a higher proportion of their speech errors should be anticipatory. Dell et al. (1997, p. 140) expressed this point as follows: "Practice enhances the activation of the present and future at the expense of the past. So, as performance gets better, perseverations become relatively less common." In other words, the activation levels of sounds and words that have already been spoken are little affected by practice. However, the increasing activation levels of present and future sounds and words increasingly prevent the past from intruding into present speech.

Dell et al. (1997) gave participants extensive practice at saying several tongue twisters (e.g., five frantic fat frogs; thirty-three throbbing thumbs). As the participants developed expertise at this task, the number of errors went down. However, the key finding was that (as predicted) the proportion of anticipatory errors increased.

Levelt's theoretical approach

Levelt et al. (1999) put forward a computational model called WEAVER++ (Word-form Encoding by Activation and VERification), which was based in part on the theoretical ideas of Levelt (1989). It shows how word production proceeds from meaning (lexical concepts and lemmas or abstract words) to sound. Levelt et al. (1999, p. 2) referred to "the major rift" between a word's meaning and its sound, and argued that crossing this rift is of major importance in speech production. The early stages of spoken word production involve deciding which word is to be produced, and the later stages involve working out the details of its word form, phonological representation, and pronunciation. Levelt et al. (1999) argued that *lemma selection* or selection of an abstract word is *completed* before phonological information about the word is accessed. This is an important part of their serial processing model.

Experimental evidence

Lexicalisation is "the process in speech production whereby we turn the thoughts underlying words into sounds: we translate a semantic representation (the meaning) of a content word into its phonological representation or form (its sound)" (Harley, 1995, p. 253). According to Levelt et al. (1999), lexicalisation is an important process that occurs when the lemma or abstract word is translated into its word form.

The "tip-of-the-tongue" state supports the views of Levelt et al. (1999). We have all had the experience of having a concept or idea in mind, but searching in vain for the right word to describe it. This frustrating situation defines the tip-of-the-tongue state. Brown and McNeill (1966) stated that a participant in this state "would appear to be in a mild torment, something like the brink of a sneeze" (Brown & McNeill, 1966, p. 325). They presented their participants with dictionary definitions of rare words, and asked them to identify the words defined. For example, "a navigational instrument used in measuring angular distances, especially the altitude of the sun, moon and stars at sea" defines the word "sextant". The tip-of-the-tongue state occurs when the lemma or abstract word has been activated, but the actual word cannot be accessed.

It has been suggested that the tip-of-the-tongue state is more likely to occur for words sounding like other words, on the basis that these other words block or inhibit retrieval of the word being sought. In fact, Harley and Brown (1998) found exactly the opposite. Words sounding unlike nearly all other words (e.g., nectar, vineyard) were much more prone to the tip-of-the-tongue state than were words sounding like several other words (e.g., litter, pawn), perhaps because their unusual phonological forms make them especially difficult to retrieve.

As we have seen, Levelt et al. (1999) argued in their serial processing model that phonological information about a word is only accessed *after* the abstract word or lemma selection is completed. In contrast, some theorists (e.g., Dell et al., 1997) have argued that phonological processing can start before word selection is completed; in other words, the two stages are *not* totally independent of each other. Theoretical approaches based on this assumption are often termed cascade models.

How can we test these models? According to the cascade model, phonological processing can start before lemma selection is completed, whereas this is impossible on the alternative model. Suppose that participants were presented with pictures having a dominant name (e.g., rocket) and a non-dominant name (e.g., missile). They are given the task of naming the picture as rapidly as possible. The stage of lemma selection typically produces the dominant name (e.g., rocket). According to the serial processing model, there should be very little phonological processing of the non-dominant name (e.g., missile). According to the cascade model, however, this is not necessarily the case.

Peterson and Savoy (1998) used the task described above. What did they find? "We obtained clear evidence for phonological activation of both dominant and secondary picture names during early moments of picture lexicalisation. Thus, in contrast to the serial model's [e.g., Levelt's] central claim, it appears that multiple lexical candidates do undergo phonological encoding . . . we reject the serial processing view and argue, instead, that the cascade model provides the best account" (Peterson & Savoy, 1998, p. 552).

How did Levelt et al. (1999) respond to these findings? They pointed out that multiple phonological encodings have *only* been found for synonyms. Levelt et al. (1999) concluded that the findings of Peterson and Savoy (1998) represented only a minor embarrassment for their model.

Speech disorders

The cognitive neuropsychological approach to speech production is of importance. However, the syndromes or labels attached to patients having difficulties with speech production often have little meaning. This is perhaps especially the case with Broca's or non-fluent aphasia and Wernicke's or fluent aphasia (both of which are discussed later), which do not form coherent syndromes. In spite of these problems, it is useful for purposes of communication to refer to the major syndromes that have been identified.

Anomia

Some patients suffer from *anomia*, which is an impaired ability to name objects. There are two main reasons why such patients might have difficulties in naming (Levelt et al., 1999). First, there could be a problem in lemma selection (thinking of the appropriate word concept), in which case errors in naming would be similar in meaning to the correct word. Second, there could be a problem in finding the appropriate phonological form of the word after the correct lemma has been selected.

A case of anomia involving a semantic impairment (deficient lemma selection) was reported by Howard and Orchard-Lisle (1984). The patient, J.C.U., had good object recognition and reasonable comprehension. However, she was very poor at naming the objects shown in pictures unless given the first phoneme or sound as a cue. If the cue was the first phoneme of a word closely related to the object shown in the picture, then J.C.U. would often be misled into producing the wrong answer. This wrong answer she accepted as correct 76% of the time. In contrast, if she produced a name very different in meaning to the object depicted, she rejected it 86% of the time. J.C.U. had access to some semantic information, but this was often insufficient to specify precisely what it was she was looking at.

Kay and Ellis (1987) studied a patient, E.S.T., who had problems with retrieving the phonological forms of words. His performance on a range of tasks was so good that it seemed that he had no significant impairment to his semantic system, and thus no real problem with lemma or abstract word selection. However, he had a very definite anomia, as can be seen from this attempt to describe a picture (Kay & Ellis, 1987):

> Er . . . two children, one girl one male . . . the . . . the girl, they're in a . . . and their, their mother was behind them in in, they're in the kitchen . . . the boy is trying to get . . . a . . . er, a part of a cooking . . . jar . . . He's standing on . . . the lad, the boy is standing on a . . . standing on a . . . standing on a . . . I'm calling it a seat.

E.S.T.'s speech is reasonably grammatical, and his greatest problem lies in finding words other than very common ones. What are we to make of E.S.T.'s anomia? Kay and Ellis (1987) argued that his condition resembles in greatly magnified form the "tip-of-the-tongue" state we all experience from time to time. However, it is mostly relatively rare words that cause us problems, whereas E.S.T. has problems with all but the most common words.

Agrammatism

According to most theories of speech production, there are rather separate stages of working out the syntax or grammatical structure of utterances and producing the content words to fit that grammatical structure (e.g., Dell, 1986). Thus, there should be some brain-damaged patients who can find the appropriate words, but cannot order them grammatically. Such patients are said to suffer from *agrammatism* or non-fluent aphasia. Patients with agrammatism also produce short sentences lacking function words and word endings.

Saffran, Schwartz, and Marin (1980a, b) studied patients suffering from grammatical impairments. For example, one patient was asked to describe a picture of a woman kissing a man, and produced the following: "The kiss . . . the lady kissed . . . the lady is . . . the lady and the man and the lady . . . kissing." In addition, Saffran et al. found that agrammatic aphasics had great difficulty in putting the two nouns in the correct order when asked to describe pictures containing two living creatures in interaction.

Do the syntactic deficiencies of agrammatic aphasics extend to language comprehension? They do in some (but not all) cases. Berndt, Mitchum, and Haendiges (1996) did a meta-analysis of studies of comprehension of active and passive sentences by agrammatic aphasics. Their findings led to two conclusions:

(1) Agrammatic aphasics do not necessarily have major problems with language comprehension.

(2) "[S]election of patients for study on the basis of features of aphasic sentence production does not assure a homogeneous [similar] grouping of patients" (Berndt et al., 1996, p. 298).

Jargon aphasia

Agrammatic aphasics possess reasonable ability to find the words they want to say, but cannot produce grammatically correct sentences. It would be expected theoretically that there should be patients who speak fairly grammatically but have great difficulty in finding the right words. In general terms, this is the case with patients suffering from *jargon aphasia* or fluent aphasia. This is a condition in which the word-finding problems are so great that patients often produce neologisms or made-up words (see below).

Ellis, Miller, and Sin (1983) studied a jargon aphasic, R.D. He provided the following description of a picture of a scout camp (the words he tried to say are in parentheses): "A b-boy is swi'ing (SWINGING) on the bank with his hand (FEET) in the stringt (STREAM). A table with orstrum (SAUCEPAN?) and . . . I don't know . . . and a three-legged stroe (STOOL) and a strane (PAIL)—table, table . . . near the water." R.D., in common with most jargon aphasics, produced more neologisms or invented words when the word he wanted was not a common one.

Most jargon aphasics are largely unaware of the fact that they are producing neologisms and so do not try to correct them. In the case of R.D., this may well have been linked to the fact that he could not understand spoken material even though he could understand written material. However, there are considerable individual differences among jargon aphasics. Maher, Rothi, and Heilman (1994) studied A.S., a jargon aphasic who had reasonable auditory word comprehension. A.S. was better at detecting his own speech errors when listening to someone else speaking than when listening to his own voice. This suggested to Maher et al. (1994) that A.S. was in a state of denial about his own speech errors.

Evaluation

Cognitive neuropsychological evidence has provided support for major theories of speech production. Findings from anomic patients indicate the value of two-stage theories of lexicalisation. Agrammatic aphasics and jargon aphasics provide evidence for separate stages of syntactic planning and content-word retrieval in speech production. What we have here is a *double dissociation*, which is a particularly powerful kind of evidence that two different sets of processes are involved. This double dissociation is consistent with theories such as those of Dell and of Levelt et al.

Cognitive neuroscience

Are different language functions localised in specific areas of the brain? Several attempts to answer that question have been made over the past 140 years or so. Most of these attempts have been rather inconclusive, but the development of various brain-scanning techniques has led to advances in our understanding of the localisation of language functions. In this section, we will consider only a small fraction of the relevant evidence.

Non-fluent aphasia

Paul Broca studied a patient, Leborgne, who suffered from great problems with speech production but seemed to understand what was said to him. Postmortem examination of this patient and of other patients with similar speech problems suggested to Broca that damage to certain parts of the left hemisphere of the brain was responsible for the deficient speech. The so-called Broca's area consists mainly of "posterior aspects of the third frontal convolution and adjacent inferior aspects of the precentral gyrus" (Caplan, 1994, p. 1035). Patients with Broca's aphasia are now known as non-fluent aphasics or agrammatic aphasics (see above).

Matters are more complex than was assumed by Broca. Willmes and Poeck (1993) found that only 59% of patients with non-fluent aphasia had lesions or damage in Broca's area, and 35% of patients with lesions involving Broca's area had non-fluent aphasia. Dronkers (1996) reported that only 10 out of 22 patients with lesions in Broca's area were suffering from non-fluent aphasia. In addition, all of the patients with non-fluent aphasia had damage to the insular cortex, which does not form part of Broca's area.

PET studies on normal individuals indicate that Broca's area is involved in speech production. Wise et al. (1991) gave their participants the task of silent generation of verbs as uses for a noun. This task produced activation of Broca's area in the left hemisphere. Chertkow et al. (1993) used the task of silent picture naming, and observed activation of Broca's area. However, as Howard (1997, p. 294) pointed out, "Activation of Broca's area seems less frequently found in tasks involving overt speech production, possibly because activation in this region is masked by the bilateral activation of the adjacent articulatory motor cortex."

Fluent aphasia

Carl Wernicke studied patients who had great problems in understanding spoken language, but who could speak fluently although not very meaningfully. Postmortem examination led Wernicke to identify damage to part of the left hemisphere of the brain as responsible for the comprehension problems of these patients. Wernicke's area consists of the "posterior half of the first temporal gyrus and possibly adjacent cortex" (Caplan, 1994, p. 1035). The disorder used to be known as Wernicke's aphasia, but is now known as fluent aphasia or jargon aphasia (see above).

De Bleser (1988) studied six very clear cases of fluent aphasia, seven very clear cases of non-fluent aphasia, and 33 additional aphasic patients. The sites of brain damage were assessed by means of computer tomography (CT) scans, which allowed the patients to be put into three groups: (1) damage to frontal areas including Broca's area; (2) damage to temporo-parietal areas including Wernicke's area; and (3) large lesions including both Broca's and Wernicke's areas. Four of the six patients with fluent aphasia had damage only to Wernicke's area, but the other two had lesions in Broca's area as well as in Wernicke's area. Of the seven non-fluent aphasic patients, four had damage to Broca's area, but the others had damage to Wernicke's area.

Willmes and Poeck (1993) also used CT scans. They found that 90% of patients with fluent aphasia had lesions in Wernicke's area. However, only 48% of patients with damage in Wernicke's area had fluent aphasia.

PET studies have provided clearer evidence of the involvement of Wernicke's area in speech comprehension. For example, Howard et al. (1992) compared two conditions in which the participants either repeated real words or listened to reversed words and said the same word to each stimulus. As predicted, there was greater activation of Wernicke's area in the former condition.

Evaluation

Why is there more evidence for localisation of language functions in brain-scanning (e.g., PET) studies on normals than in studies of brain-damaged patients? We can readily observe individual differences in localisation with brain-damaged patients, but similar individual differences are less apparent when information about brain activation is averaged across many people. As Howard (1997, p. 298) pointed out, "While studies of motor and sensory processes produce changes in rCBF [regional cerebral blood flow] across a group of subjects of up to 30% in specific locations, language studies typically find significant changes of only 5–10%. This is exactly the pattern which one would predict if sensory and motor processes show very consistent localisation across subjects, while there is a great deal of variability of language functions."

What conclusions about speech production can we draw from the findings of cognitive neuroscience? Howard (1997, p. 288) suggested the following answer to that question: "Language functions, while localised in individual subjects, are not consistently localised in different individuals . . . higher cortical functions such as language may have a certain amount of freedom in the areas of cortex devoted to them."

Language and thought

The major language processes discussed in this chapter and the two previous ones raise the issue of the relationship between language and thought. For example, speaking and writing are both activities in which thinking about what one wants to say or write (the intended message) is translated into language. More generally, language is the medium that we use most often to communicate our thoughts to other people.

The best-known theory about the interrelationship between language and thought was put forward by Benjamin Lee Whorf (1956). He was a fire prevention officer for an insurance company, but he spent his spare time working in linguistics. According to his hypothesis of linguistic relativity (known as the *Whorfian hypothesis*), language determines or influences thinking. It is useful to distinguish between the strong and the weak form of this hypothesis (Hunt & Agnoli, 1991). According to the strong hypothesis, language *determines* thinking, implying that some thoughts expressible in one language cannot be expressed in a second language. This is the issue of *translatability*: Can all sentences in one language be translated accurately into sentences in a second language? There is reasonable evidence for translatability, and thus there is little support for the strong hypothesis.

According to the weak form of the Whorfian hypothesis, language *influences* thought. This is a more reasonable hypothesis, and has been tested in studies concerned with the effects of language on memory and perception.

Casual inspection of the world's languages indicates there are significant differences among them. For example, the Hanuxoo people in the Philippines have 92 different names for different varieties of rice, and there are hundreds of camel-related words in Arabic. It is possible that these differences among languages influence thought. A more plausible explanation is that different environmental conditions affect the things people think about, and this in turn affects their linguistic usage. Thus, these differences occur because thought affects language.

Different languages affect our thinking.

Memory, perception, and language

There has been a fair amount of research concerned with possible cultural differences in memory for colours. Lenneberg and Roberts

(1956) found that Zuni speakers made more errors than English speakers in recognising yellows and oranges, presumably because there is only one word in the Zuni language to refer to yellows and oranges. Although the findings of Lenneberg and Roberts suggested that language affects memory, later studies brought this conclusion into doubt.

Heider (1972) used the fact that there are 11 basic colour words in English, and each of these words has one generally agreed best or focal colour. English speakers find it easier to remember focal than non-focal colours, and Heider wondered whether the same would be true of the Dani. The Dani are a Stone Age agricultural people living in Indonesian New Guinea, and their language has only two basic colour terms: "mola" for bright, warm hues, and "mili" for dark, cold hues. Heider (1972) found that the Dani and Americans both showed better recognition memory for focal colours. However, the overall memory performance of the Dani was much worse than that of Americans, perhaps because of the limited colour terms available to the Dani.

The research of Heider and others on memory for colours suggests that the similarities among cultures are far more pronounced than the dissimilarities. This is in spite of the fact that there are considerable differences from one language to the next in the terms available to describe colours. However, numerous languages have words for the same 11 focal colours, and work on the physiology of colour vision (DeValois & Jacobs, 1968) suggests that these colours are processed specially by the visual system.

Other research suggests that language can affect memory for colours. In a study by Schooler and Engstler-Schooler (1990), participants were shown colour chips that were not focal colours, and were or were not asked to label them. Those asked to label the colours did worse than the non-labellers on recognition memory, suggesting that colour memory was distorted by language in the form of labelling.

Language can also affect perceptual processes. Miyawaki et al. (1975) compared English and Japanese speakers with respect to their perception of sounds varying between a pure /l/ and a pure /r/. English speakers made a sharp perceptual distinction between similar sounds on either side of the categorical boundary between "l"and "r"; this is known as *categorical speech perception*. No such perceptual distinction was made by Japanese speakers, presumably because there is no distinction between /l/ and /r/ in the Japanese language.

Research on the effects of language on colour perception was reported by Davies et al. (1998), who compared speakers of English and of Setswana, a language spoken in Botswana. They decided which of three colours was least like the other two, and there were crucial trials on which any linguistic influences should have led the two groups to make different choices. The findings were as follows: "Our data show a striking similarity between language groups in their choice of similarities and differences among colours . . . in addition, there are small, but reliable differences between the two samples associated with linguistic differences" (Davies et al., 1998, p. 14).

Similar findings were reported by Davies (1998). Speakers of English, Setswana, and Russian sorted 65 colours into between 2 and 12 groups on the basis of perceptual similarity. English has 11 basic colour terms, Setswana has 5, and Russian has 12, and it was thought that these differences might influence performance. However, "The most striking feature of the results was the marked similarity of the groups chosen across the three language samples" (Davies, 1998, p. 433). In addition, there were minor influences of language. For example, Setswana has only one word to describe green and blue, and Setswana speakers were more likely than English and Russian speakers to group blue and green colours together.

In sum, language has less impact on cognition than was assumed by Whorf. However, language exerts modest influences on some perceptual and memorial processes, and so a weak form of the Whorfian hypothesis is tenable.

Cognitive approach

Hunt and Agnoli (1991) put forward a cognitive account of the Whorfian hypothesis. The essence of their position was as follows (1991, p. 379):

> Different languages lend themselves to the transmission of different types of messages. People consider the costs of computation when they reason about a topic. The language that they use will partly determine those costs. In this sense, language does influence cognition.

Thus, any given language makes it easy to think in some ways and hard to think in other ways, and this is why thinking is influenced by language.

An interesting demonstration of how language can influence thinking was provided by Hoffman, Lau, and Johnson (1986). Bilingual

English–Chinese speakers read descriptions of individuals, and were later asked to provide free interpretations of the individuals described. The descriptions conformed to either Chinese or English stereotypes of personality. For example, there is a stereotype of the artistic type in English, consisting of a mixture of artistic skills, moody and intense temperament, and bohemian lifestyle, but this stereotype does not exist in Chinese. Bilinguals thinking in Chinese made use of Chinese stereotypes in their free impressions, whereas bilinguals thinking in English used English stereotypes. Thus, the kinds of inferences we draw can be much influenced by the language in which we are thinking.

More evidence consistent with Hunt and Agnoli (1991) was reported by Pederson et al. (1998). They pointed out that space can be coded in either a *relative* system (e.g., left, right, up, down) or an *absolute* system (e.g., north; south). Pederson et al. (1998) gave speakers of 13 languages a non-linguistic spatial reasoning task which could be solved using either a relative or an absolute system. The key finding was that participants' choice of system was determined largely by the dominant system of spatial coding in their native language, presumably because it was easier for them to do this.

Evaluation

Hunt and Agnoli (1991) have provided a plausible cognitive account of the Whorfian hypothesis, and much evidence is consistent with their account. Most of the evidence supporting this cognitive theory (e.g., Hoffman et al., 1986; Pederson et al., 1998) has used tasks that give the participants *flexibility* in the approach they adopt, and so provide scope for language to influence performance. What is lacking so far is a systematic programme of research to establish clearly that language influences thought in the ways specified by Hunt and Agnoli (1991). More specifically, Hunt and Agnoli (1991) emphasised the importance of computational costs, but these costs have rarely been assessed directly.

Social and cultural factors

Several theorists have argued that there are important differences in language use between members of different groups (e.g., middle-class vs. working-class children), and it has been claimed that these differences may lead to group differences in thinking ability. Two of the major theories in this area were proposed by Basil Bernstein and William Labov.

Bernstein

Bernstein (1973) argued that a child's use of language is determined in part by the social environment in which he or she grows up. He distinguished between two language codes or patterns of speech: the restricted code and the elaborated code. The *restricted code* is relatively concrete and descriptive, and consists of short sentences. It is also characterised by *implicitness*, meaning that it is hard to understand unless one knows the context in which it is used. In contrast, the *elaborated code* is more grammatically complex and abstract. It is characterised by *explicitness*, meaning that it can be understood without information about the context.

Bernstein (1973, p. 203) gave the following examples of the two codes based on descriptions of four pictures showing (1) boys playing football; (2) the ball going through the window of a house; (3) a woman looking out of the window; and (4) the children retreating:

- *Restricted code*: "They're playing football and he kicks it and it goes through there it breaks the window and they're looking at it and he comes out and shouts at them because they've broken it so they run away and then she looks out and she tells them off."
- *Elaborated code*: "Three boys are playing football and one boy kicks the ball and it goes through the window the ball breaks the window and the boys are looking at it and a man comes out and shouts at them because they've broken the window so they run away and then that lady looks out of her window and she tells the boys off."

Bernstein (1973) argued that middle-class children generally use the elaborated code, whereas working-class children use the restricted code. He claimed that many middle-class children can use both codes, whereas most working-class children are limited to the restricted code. It might seem as if the lack of an elaborated language code would limit the thinking of working-class children. However, Bernstein claimed that class differences in the use of language do not extend to basic language competence or understanding of language. As a result, users of the restricted code are not necessarily at a disadvantage.

Evidence

Evidence that working-class children may have restricted language development was reported by Bernstein (1961). Middle-class and working-class boys obtaining high scores for non-verbal intelligence (e.g., spatial and mathematical ability) were compared on verbal intelligence based on the use of language. The middle-class boys performed equally well on both kinds of intelligence, whereas the working-class boys obtained lower scores for verbal intelligence. Bernstein argued the discrepancy between verbal and non-verbal intelligence showed by the working-class boys was due to their reliance on the restricted language code.

Hess and Shipman (1965) studied American mothers and their 4-year-old children. Middle-class mothers used language interactively to discuss issues with their children via questions and answers. In contrast, working-class mothers used language to give orders to their children, and there was less exchange of ideas. These differences between middle-class and working-class mothers may well have influenced the language development of their offspring.

Tizard and Hughes (1984) addressed the issue of the explicitness–implicitness of language used by mothers when talking to their daughters. Tizard and Hughes did *not* find the differences across social classes that would have been expected on Bernstein's theory. Instead, they found that mothers of all social classes were often implicit in talking to their daughters, but became explicit when they felt that it was important to communicate a precise message.

Evaluation

There is evidence for the distinction between the elaborated and restricted codes, but Bernstein's views are oversimplified. There are probably several codes, with the elaborated and restricted codes representing the extremes. At the very least, it is likely that many people use a mixture of the two codes in their everyday speech. Bernstein assumed that the elaborated code is superior to the restricted code. In fact, as Harley (1995) pointed out, "[It] is far from obvious that the working class dialect is impoverished compared to the middle class dialect: it is just different" (p. 348). Thus, research in this area suggests that language differences between middle-class and working-class children probably have little or no effect on their ability to think effectively.

Labov

Labov (1972) carried out a series of studies into the use of black English vernacular or dialect by young black people living in the ghetto areas of Harlem, New York. At that time, it was generally argued that the relatively poor school performance of many black children was attributable to their limited command of language. As Durkin (1995, p. 244) pointed out, "Previous work . . . had led some researchers to the conclusion that black speakers were linguistically disadvantaged, speaking an impoverished form of English which did not equip them well for the conceptual demands of the educational system. Indeed, black children often appeared to investigators to be distressingly inarticulate." Thus, it was assumed that the thinking and cognitive abilities of black people were limited because of the language they had learned.

Labov (1972) disagreed with the above conclusions. According to him, most of the differences between black English vernacular and standard English are relatively trivial. For example, consider the distinction between the standard English sentence, "He doesn't know anything", and the black English, "He don't know nothing." The two sentences express the same meaning, and the grammatical complexity of the two sentences is equivalent.

Labov (1972) reported additional evidence of the complexity of black English. A 15-year-old black adolescent called Larry was asked to assume that there was a God, and to decide whether He would be black or white: "He'd be white, man . . . 'Cause the average whitey out here got everything, you dig? And the nigger ain't got shit, y'know?"

Labov (1972, p. 113) pointed out that it can be hard to assess someone's language abilities because of the *observer paradox*: "To obtain the data most important for linguistic theory, we have to observe how people speak when they are not being observed." What had generally happened in previous research was that the language competence of black American participants had been assessed by white interviewers. When Labov (1972) used black interviewers, he found a considerable increase in the linguistic fluency of his participants. Speakers of black English also appeared much more fluent when they were talking in an informal setting about topics that greatly interested them than when they were talking in the school environment about uninteresting matters.

Labov (1972) concluded that black English was of comparable complexity and sophistication to standard English, a view that is increasingly accepted. However, his conclusion was regarded as controversial in the early 1970s. As Labov (1972, p. 240) noted, "Teachers . . . are being taught to hear every natural utterance of the [black] child as evidence of his mental inferiority. As linguists, we are unanimous in condemning this view as bad observation, bad theory, and bad practice."

Evaluation

Labov's argument that black English differs much less from standard English than has traditionally assumed to be the case is strongly supported by the evidence. He was also correct to point out the limitations of previous research, in which insufficient attention had been paid to issues such as the observer paradox. However, it remains unclear whether there are any important differences in thinking ability between speakers of black and standard English that are attributable to the particular dialect they speak.

Summary: Language comprehension and production

- *Discourse processing*: There is an important distinction between bridging and elaborative inferences, with the simplest form of bridging inference being involved in anaphora. According to the minimalist hypothesis, relatively few inferences are drawn automatically. In addition, strategic or goal-directed inferences may also be drawn. According to the constructionist approach, numerous automatic inferences are drawn in order to facilitate full comprehension. According to search-after-meaning theory, readers engage in a search after meaning based on the reader goal, coherence, and explanation assumptions. The evidence is most consistent with the search-after-meaning theory.

- *Story processing*: Story memory resembles a précis. It has been claimed that the structure of all stories is consistent with a story grammar, but there is no agreement on its main features. According to Kintsch's construction–integration model, three levels of text representation are formed: surface, propositional, and situational. The evidence supports this hypothesis, but a situational representation is sometimes not formed because of limited processing capacity. There may be other levels of representation (e.g., the genre level). According to the event-indexing model, readers monitor five aspects or indexes of the evolving situational model. The five aspects are regarded as independent within the model, but they actually interact with each other.

- *Speech production*: Speakers take full account of the common ground they share with the listener only when they have adequate processing time. According to Dell's spreading-activation theory, four levels of representation are involved in speech production: semantic, syntactic, morphological, and phonological. Insertion rules select the items for inclusion in the representation at each level on the basis of the level of activation of the competing items. Speech errors occur when an incorrect item has a higher level of activation than the correct item. Spreading-activation theory does not predict the time taken to produce spoken words. According to Levelt's WEAVER++ model, abstract word or lemma selection is completed before phonological information about the word is accessed. The model is supported by research on the tip-of-the-tongue state, but is limited in that it has little to say about sentence production or speech errors.

- *Speech disorders*: Some patients with anomia have problems in thinking of the appropriate word concept, whereas others have difficulties in finding the appropriate phonological word form. Patients with agrammatism can find the appropriate words, but cannot order them grammatically. In contrast, patients with jargon aphasia speak fairly grammatically but cannot find the right words. Evidence from agrammatic aphasics and jargon aphasics supports the notion that there are separate stages of syntactic planning and content-word retrieval in speech production.

- *Cognitive neuroscience*: Neuroimaging studies with normals indicate that Broca's area is often involved in speech production. In contrast, PET studies suggest that Wernicke's area is often involved in speech comprehension. However, it has generally proved difficult to obtain strong evidence for localisation of function in brain-scanning studies, perhaps because there are individual differences in the brain areas primarily involved in speech comprehension and production.

- *Language and thought*: According to the weak form of the Whorfian hypothesis, language influences thought. In support, there is evidence that language can affect perceptual processes and memory for colours. Hunt and Agnoli (1991) put forward a cognitive account of the

Whorfian hypothesis, according to which any given language makes it easier to think in some ways than in others. This theory has been supported on tasks giving participants flexibility in their approach. Bernstein argued that working-class children have access only to a restricted language code characterised by implicitness. In contrast, middle-class children have access to an elaborated code characterised by explictness. The evidence indicates that Bernstein's views are oversimplified, and it is not clear that the restricted code is impoverished. Labov argued that black English is as complex as standard English, and that speakers of black English are as fluent as speakers of standard English when talking about topics of interest to them. In general, different dialects or ways of speaking are comparable in complexity and sophistication and seem to have little or no effect on thinking ability.

Essay questions

(1) What processes are involved in inference drawing?
(2) Describe and evaluate theoretical approaches to story processing.
(3) Describe some of the main speech errors. How can these errors be accounted for?
(4) What has been learned about speech production from the study of brain-damaged patients?
(5) Discuss some of the relationships between thought and language.

Further reading

Garrod, S., & Pickering, M.J. (1999). *Language processing*. Hove, UK. Psychology Press. Several chapters in this book provide good accounts of areas covered in this chapter.

Graesser, A.C., Millis, R.A., & Zwaan, R.A. (1997). Discourse comprehension. *Annual Review of Psychology, 48*, 163–189. There is a detailed account of the main processes involved in discourse comprehension in this chapter.

Harley, T.A. (1995). *The psychology of language: From data to theory*. Hove, UK: Psychology Press. Chapter 8 in this book provides a very clear introduction to the topic of speech production. The relevant cognitive neuropsychological evidence is also considered.

Problem solving and decision making 9

Introduction

This chapter and the next are concerned with some of the higher-level cognitive processes involved in thinking. For convenience, these two chapters have been organised mainly in terms of the type of task that is given to the participants. Thus, this chapter is divided into sections on problem solving, decision making, and judgement, and Chapter 10 focuses on deductive and inductive reasoning. It is important to bear in mind that we use the same cognitive system to deal with all of these types of task. As a consequence, some of the distinctions among different forms of thinking may well turn out to be rather arbitrary and to camouflage underlying similarities in cognitive processes.

Problem solving

The obvious starting point for this section on problem solving is to consider the definition of a "problem". According to Duncker (1945, p. 1), "a problem arises when a living organism has a goal but does not know how this goal is to be reached." A similar definition was offered by Mayer (1990, p. 284), who argued that problem solving is "cognitive processing directed at transforming a given situation into a goal situation when no obvious method of solution is available to the problem solver."

The above definitions suggest that there are three major aspects to problem solving. First, it is purposeful, in the sense that it is goal directed. Second, it requires the use of cognitive processes rather than automatic processes. Third, a problem only exists when someone lacks the relevant knowledge to produce an immediate solution. Thus, a situation that is a problem for most people (e.g., a mathematical calculation) may not be so for someone with real expertise (e.g., a professional mathematician).

There is an important distinction between well-defined problems and ill-defined problems. Well-defined problems are ones in which all of the major aspects of the problem are clearly specified; these include the initial state or situation, the range of possible moves or strategies, and the goal or solution. The goal is well specified in the sense that it is clear when the goal has been reached. For example, a maze is a well-defined problem, in which escape from it (or reaching the centre as in the Hampton Court maze) is the goal.

In contrast, ill-defined problems can be underspecified in several ways. For example, suppose you have locked your keys inside your car. What you would like to do is to get into your car without causing any damage to it. However, it may seem that the only feasible way of getting into your car is by smashing a window. It may be very hard to know whether this is the best solution to the problem.

Most of the problems that we face in our everyday lives are ill-defined problems. In contrast, psychologists have focused mainly on well-defined problems. Why have they done this? One important reason is because well-defined problems have a best strategy for their solution. As a result, it is usually easy to identify the errors and deficiencies in the strategies adopted by human problem solvers.

Gestalt approach

Some of the earliest research on problem solving was carried out by Thorndike (1898). He placed hungry cats in closed cages within sight of a dish of food outside the cages. The cage doors could be opened when a pole inside the cage was hit. Initially, the cats thrashed about and clawed the sides of the cages. However, after some time, the cat hit the pole inside the cage and opened the door. On repeated trials, the cats gradually seemed to learn what was required of them. Eventually they would hit the pole almost immediately, and so gain access to the food. Thorndike (1898) was not impressed by the performance of these cats, referring to their apparently almost random behaviour as *trial-and-error learning*.

There was a reaction against this view of problem solving by a group of German psychologists known as the Gestaltists during the 1920s and 1930s. The Gestaltists argued that there was more to animal problem solving than trial and error. They also argued that Thorndike's problem situation was unfair, in the sense that there was a purely arbitrary relationship between the cats' behaviour (hitting the pole) and the desired consequence (the opening of the cage door).

One of the key differences between Thorndike's approach and that of the Gestaltists is captured in the distinction between reproductive and productive problem solving. *Reproductive problem solving* involves the re-use of previous experiences, and was the focus of Thorndike's research. In contrast, *productive problem solving* involves a novel restructuring of the problem. It is more complex than reproductive problem solving, but the Gestaltists argued that several species are capable of this higher-level form of problem solving.

Insight

Köhler (1925) carried out a series of experiments to show that animals can engage in productive problem solving. In one of Köhler's studies, an ape was inside a cage, and could only reach a banana outside the cage by joining two sticks together. The ape seemed lost at first. However, it then seemed to realise how to solve the problem, and rapidly joined the sticks together. According to Köhler, the ape had restructured the problem. By so doing, it had shown *insight*, which is often accompanied by the "ah-ha experience".

There was at least one potential problem with Köhler's claimed demonstrations of insight in apes. The apes had spent the early months of their lives in the wild, and so they could have acquired useful information about sticks and how they can be combined. Birch (1945) found in later research that apes raised in captivity showed little evidence of the kind of insightful problem solving observed by Köhler (1925).

It is now time to consider studies on problem solving in humans. Maier (1931) carried out a famous study of restructuring in which people were given the "pendulum problem". The participants were brought into a room containing various objects (e.g., poles, pliers, extension cords), plus two strings hanging from the ceiling (see Figure 9.1). The task was to tie together the two strings hanging from the ceiling. Unfortunately, the strings were too far apart for the participants to reach one string while holding the other. The most "insightful" but rarely produced solution was the pendulum solution. This involved taking the pliers, tying them to one of the strings, and then making the string swing like a pendulum. In this way, it was possible to hold one string and to catch the other on its upswing.

Maier (1931) also found that it was possible to facilitate problem restructuring or insight by having the experimenter apparently accidentally brush against the string to set it swinging. Soon after this was done, the participants tended to produce the pendulum solution,

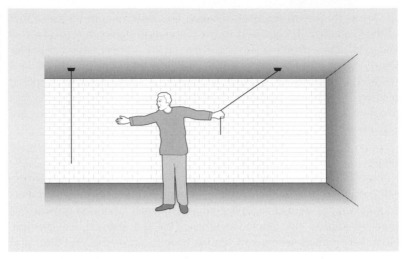

Figure 9.1. The two-string problem, in which it is not possible to reach one string while holding the other.

even though few reported that they had noticed the experimenter brush against the string. This finding is sometimes known as the unconscious cue effect.

In spite of its fame, Maier's (1931) study was carried out in a fairly slipshod way. Of particular importance, the unconscious cue effect does not seem to have been replicated (J. Evans, pers. comm.). However, there is evidence for a conscious cue effect. Battersby et al. (1953) found that the experimenter could greatly speed up solution times on the pendulum problem by highlighting objects that might be relevant to the problem.

There has been much controversy on the issue of whether insight involves special processes (as was claimed by the Gestaltists), and is thus quite different from normal problem solving (see Gilhooly, 1996). Relevant findings were reported by Metcalfe and Weibe (1987). They recorded participants' feelings of "warmth" (closeness to solution) while engaged in solving insight and non-insight problems. There was a progressive increase in warmth during non-insight problems. With insight problems, in contrast, the warmth ratings remained at the same low level until suddenly increasing dramatically when the solution was reached. These findings are consistent with the notion that insight is somewhat special, and occurs in an all-or-none fashion.

Functional fixedness

Past experience usually benefits our ability to solve problems. However, Duncker (1945) argued that this is by no means always the case.

He studied *functional fixedness*, in which problems are not solved because we assume on the basis of past experience that any given object only has a limited number of uses. He carried out a study in which the participants were given a candle, a box of nails, and several other objects. Their task was to attach the candle to a wall by a table, so that it did not drip onto the table below.

How did the participants approach the above problem? Most of them tried to nail the candle directly to the wall or to glue it to the wall by melting it. Only a few participants decided to use the inside of the nail-box as a candle holder, and then nail it to the wall. According to Duncker, most of the participants were "fixated" on the box's function as a container rather than as a platform. More correct solutions were produced when the nail-box was empty at the start of the experiment, presumably because that made the box appear less like a container.

Duncker (1945) assumed that functional fixedness occurred in his study because of the participants' past experience with boxes. However, he had no evidence on this point. Luchins (1942) adopted the superior approach of controlling participants' relevant past experience by providing it within the experiment itself. He used water-jar problems involving three water jars of varying capacity. The participant's task was to imagine pouring water from one jar to another in order to finish up with a specified amount of water in one of the jars.

The most striking finding obtained by Luchins can be illustrated by considering one of his studies in detail. One problem was as follows: Jar A can hold 28 quarts of water, Jar B 76 quarts, and Jar C 3 quarts. The task is to end up with exactly 25 quarts in one of the jars. I am sure all the readers of this book can work out the answer: Jar A is filled, and then Jar C is filled from it, leaving 25 quarts in Jar A. Ninety-five per cent of participants who had previously been given similar problems solved it. Other participants were trained on a series of problems, all of which had the same complex three-jar solution. Of these participants, only 36% managed to solve this relatively simple problem. These findings led Luchins (1942, p. 15) to the following conclusion: "Einstellung—habituation—creates a mechanised state of mind, a blind attitude towards problems; one does not look at the problem on its own merits but is led by a mechanical application of a used method."

Evaluation

The Gestaltists made several notable contributions to our understanding of problem solving. First, they showed that problem solving could involve productive processes as well as reproductive ones. Second, they showed that past experience could disrupt (rather than benefit) current problem solving with their demonstrations of functional fixedness. This proved that at least some problems could not be solved by simply making use of well-learned responses. Third, their research revealed the importance of restructuring, and provided suggestive evidence in favour of insight.

On the negative side, many of the concepts used by the Gestaltists (e.g., "insight", "restructuring") are rather vague and hard to measure. In addition, they did not clarify the processes underlying insight. Finally, many of their studies were poorly controlled, and it has sometimes been hard to replicate the findings obtained by the Gestaltists.

Post-Gestalt approach

There have been various recent attempts to incorporate key aspects of the Gestalt approach into an information-processing theory of problem solving. We will consider the theory proposed by Ohlsson (1992). According to Ohlsson (1992, p. 4), "insight occurs in the context of an impasse [block], which is unmerited in the sense that the thinker is, in fact, competent to solve the problem." The key assumptions of Ohlsson's theory are as follows:

- The way in which a problem is currently represented or structured in the problem-solver's mind serves as a memory probe to retrieve related knowledge from long-term memory in the form of operators or possible actions.
- The retrieval process is based on spreading activation among concepts or items of knowledge in long-term memory (see Chapter 8).
- An impasse or block occurs when the way in which the problem is represented does not permit retrieval of the operators needed to solve the problem.
- The impasse is broken when the problem representation is changed, thus permitting the problem solver to access the necessary knowledge in long-term memory.
- Changing the representation of a problem can occur in various ways:
  (1) Elaboration or addition of new information about the problem.
  (2) Constraint relaxation, in which inhibitions on what is regarded as permissible are removed.

(3) Re-encoding, in which some aspect of the problem representation is re-interpreted (e.g., a pair of pliers is re-interpreted as a weight in the pendulum problem).

● Insight occurs when an impasse is broken, and the retrieved knowledge operators are sufficient to solve the problem. Insight is complete when the operators lead to solution in one step; otherwise, it is partial and more time consuming.

Evidence

There is a reasonable support for the general approach adopted by Ohlsson (1992). Yaniv and Meyer (1987) found that the initial efforts of their participants to access relevant stored information were often unsuccessful. However, these unsuccessful efforts produced spreading activation to other concepts stored in long-term memory. As a result, the participants were more likely to recognise relevant information when it was presented to them.

Knoblich et al. (1999) showed the importance of constraints in reducing the likelihood of insight. They presented their participants with problems such as those shown in Figure 9.2. As you can see, you would need to know all about roman numerals in order to solve the problems! The task was always to move a *single* stick to produce a true statement in place of the initial false one. Some problems (Type A) only required changing two of the values in the equation (e.g., VI = VII + I becomes VII = VI + I). In contrast, other problems (Type B problems) involve a more fundamental change in the representation of the equation (e.g., IV = III – I becomes IV – III = I). Knoblich et al. (1999) argued that it would be much harder for participants to relax the normal constraints of arithmetic (and thus to show insight) for

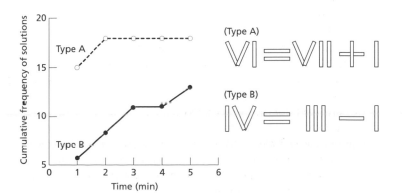

Figure 9.2. Two of the matchstick problems used by Knoblich et al. (1999), and the cumulative solution rates produced to these types of problems in their study. Copyright © 1999 by the American Psychological Association. Reprinted with permission.

Type A problems than for Type B ones. That was precisely what they found (see Figure 9.2).

Evaluation

Ohlsson's view that insight occurs when there is restructuring of a problem leading to a rapid solution is a useful one. It follows that insight is *not* involved on problems where only one problem representation is used from the start of the problem until its solution. In general terms, as Gilhooly (1996, p. 56) pointed out, "Ohlsson's approach is a very promising marriage of Gestalt concerns and information-processing approaches to problem solving." One limitation of Ohlsson's approach is that individual differences have been relatively neglected. It is highly probable that individuals of high intelligence and/or relevant expertise would find it easier to change the representation of a problem.

Computational approach: Newell and Simon

Allen Newell and Herb Simon (1972) argued that it is possible to produce systematic computer simulations of human problem solving. They achieved this with their General Problem Solver, which has been extremely influential. Their starting assumptions were that information processing is serial, that people possess limited short-term memory capacity, and that they can retrieve relevant information from long-term memory.

Newell and Simon (1972) started their research by asking people to solve problems, and to think aloud while they were working on those problems. They then used these verbal reports as the basis for deciding what general strategy tended to be used on each problem. Finally, Newell and Simon (1972) specified the problem-solving strategy in sufficient detail for it to be programmed in their General Problem Solver.

Newell and Simon (1972) felt it was important to develop a theoretical approach relevant to several kinds of problem rather than to just one. Accordingly, they applied the General Problem Solver to 11 rather different problems (e.g., letter-series completions, missionaries and cannibals, the Tower of Hanoi). The General Problem Solver could solve all of the problems, but it did not always do so in the same way as people.

Newell and Simon (1972) argued that many problems can be represented as a problem space. This problem space consists of the initial state of the problem, the goal state, all of the possible mental operators (e.g., moves) that can be applied to any state to change it into a different state, and all of the intermediate states of the problem. From this perspective, the process of problem solving involves a sequence of different knowledge states. These knowledge states intervene between the initial state and the goal state, with mental operators producing the shift from one knowledge state to the next.

The above notions can be illustrated by considering the Tower of Hanoi problem. The initial state of the problem consists of three discs piled in decreasing size on the first of three pegs. When all of the discs are piled in the same order on the last peg, the goal state has been reached. The rules specify that only one disc can be moved at a time, and that a larger disc cannot be placed on top of a smaller disc. These rules restrict the possible mental operators on each move. For example, there are only two possible first moves: place the smallest disc on the middle or last peg.

How do people select mental operators or moves as they proceed through a problem? According to Newell and Simon (1972), the complexity of most problems means that we rely heavily on *heuristics* or rules of thumb. Heuristics can be contrasted with *algorithms*, which are generally complex methods or procedures that are guaranteed to lead to problem solution. The most important of the various heuristic methods is *means–ends analysis*, which consists of the following steps:

- Note the difference between the current state of the problem and the goal state.
- Form a sub-goal that will reduce the difference between the current and goals states.
- Select a mental operator that will permit attainment of the sub-goal.

The way in which means–ends analysis is used can be illustrated with the Tower of Hanoi problem. A reasonable sub-goal in the early stages of the problem is to try to place the largest disc on the last peg. If a situation arises in which the largest disc must be placed on either the middle or the last peg, then means–ends analysis will lead to that disc being placed on the last peg.

Evidence

Thomas (1974) argued that people should experience difficulties in solving a problem at those points at which it is necessary to make a move that temporarily *increases* the distance between the current state and the goal state. He used a variant of the missionaries and cannibals problem based on hobbits and orcs. In the standard form of this problem, three missionaries and three cannibals need to be transported across a river in a boat that can hold only two people. The number of cannibals on either bank of the river must never exceed the number of missionaries, because then the cannibals would eat the missionaries. One move involves transferring one cannibal and one missionary back to the starting point, and thus seems to be moving away from the solution. It was precisely at this point that the participants experienced severe difficulties. However, General Problem Solver did *not* find this move especially difficult.

Thomas (1974) also obtained evidence that participants set up sub-goals. He found that they would often carry out a block of several moves at increasing speed, followed by a long pause before embarking on another rapid sequence of moves. This suggested that participants were dividing the problem up into three or four major sub-goals.

Simon and Reed (1976) studied a more complex version of the missionaries and cannibals problem that involved five missionaries and five cannibals. It can be solved in 11 moves, but on average participants take 30 moves to solve it. There was evidence that the participants initially adopted a *balancing strategy*, in which they simply tried to make sure that there were equal numbers of missionaries and cannibals on each side of the river. This strategy has the advantage that it avoids illegal moves, but it is insufficient on its own to produce a solution to the problem. After a while, the participants shifted to the *means–ends strategy*, in which the focus was on moving more people to the goal side of the river. Finally, the participants used an *anti-looping heuristic* designed to avoid any moves that reversed the immediately preceding move.

Simon and Reed (1976) argued that it was very important for the participants to move from the balancing strategy to the means–ends strategy. Accordingly, they carried out another experiment in which some of the participants were given the hint that they should work to reach a state in which three cannibals were on the goal side of the river on their own without a boat. It was expected that this hint would discourage the use of the balancing strategy and promote the use of the means–ends strategy. The participants given the hint (sub-goal condition) shifted strategies after about four moves on average, compared to 15 moves for the control participants who were not given the hint. The sub-goal participants solved the problem much faster than the controls (see Figure 9.3).

Anzai and Simon (1979) studied the effects of learning on problem-solving performance with a single participant having four successive

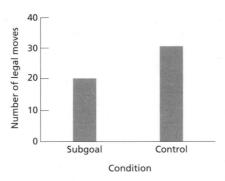

Figure 9.3. The mean number of legal moves made by subjects in the subgoal and control conditions of Simon and Reed (1976).

attempts to solve a five-disc version of the Tower of Hanoi. This participant became progressively more efficient at solving the problem. Initially, he seemed to explore the problem space without much planning of moves. His performance was guided by avoidance of certain states rather than moves towards definite goal/sub-goal states. According to Anzai and Simon (1979), he was using general, domain-independent strategies such as a loop-avoidance strategy (avoid returning to previous states of the problem), and a heuristic strategy of preferring shorter over longer sequences to reach a goal. These general strategies allowed the participant to learn better sequences of moves on subsequent attempts. In sum, the participant moved from general, domain-independent strategies to specific, domain-specific strategies.

Evaluation

The Newell and Simon approach generally works well with well-defined problems in which the initial state, the goal state, and the permissible moves are all clearly specified. It is especially impressive that the general approach has been found of value across a wide range of such problems. In addition, the theory allows us to specify the shortest sequence of moves from the initial state to the goal state, so that we see exactly how an individual participant's performance deviates from this ideal solution. Finally, the theoretical approach is consistent with our knowledge of human information processing. For example, we have limited working memory capacity, and that helps to explain why we typically make use of heuristics or rules of thumb rather than algorithms. Furthermore, the General Problem Solver captures some of the ways in which humans set up and achieve goals and sub-goals during problem solving.

Greeno (1974) used a version of the missionaries and cannibals problem, and found that there were significant differences between the approach taken by the General Problem Solver and by human participants. The General Problem Solver is better than humans at remembering what has happened so far on a problem. However, it is inferior to humans at planning future moves, in that it focuses on only a single move whereas humans often plan small sequences of moves.

The main limitation of the computational approach is that most problems in everyday life are ill defined, and so very different from the problems studied by Newell and Simon. The problems used by Newell and Simon were ones for which the participants had little relevant specific knowledge, thus causing them to rely on rather general strategies such as means–ends analysis. Solving the ill-defined problems of real life typically depends much more on possessing relevant specific knowledge and expertise. Another difference is that all of the information needed to solve the problems was provided by Newell and Simon. In contrast, with most everyday problems, we typically have to search for additional information before being in a position to try to solve them.

Expertise

Most of the traditional research on problem solving made use of "knowledge-lean" problems, meaning that no special training or knowledge is required to solve them. In contrast, studies on expertise have typically used "knowledge-rich" problems, in that they require the use of much knowledge beyond that presented in the problem itself. One reason for studying "knowledge-rich" problems is that they resemble the problems of everyday life more closely than do "knowledge-lean" problems. Another reason for studying expertise is that comparisons between the performance of experts and novices are likely to tell us much about the processes involved in problem solving.

Chess expertise

Why are some people much better than others at playing chess? The obvious answer is given in the following anecdote from Solso (1994): "Several years ago the late Bill Chase gave a talk on experts in which he promised to tell the audience what it would take to become a grand master chess player. His answer: 'Practice.' After the talk, I asked Chase how much practice. 'Did I forget to say how much?' he asked quizzically. 'Ten thousand hours.'"

What benefits occur as a result of practice? One major benefit is that expert chess players have much more detailed information about chess positions stored in long-term memory, and this allows them to relate the position in the current game to previous games. This notion was first tested by De Groot (1965), and then more thoroughly by Chase and Simon (1973).

Chase and Simon (1973) argued that chess players asked to memorise board positions would break them down into about seven chunks or units. Their key assumption was that the chunks formed by expert players contain more information than those of other players, because they can bring more chess knowledge to bear on the memory task. They asked three chess players to look at the position of the pieces on one board, and to reconstruct that board position on a second board with the first board still visible. Chase and Simon (1973) calculated the size of the chunks being formed by taking account of the number of pieces placed on the second board after each glance at the first board. The most expert player (a master) had chunks averaging 2.5 pieces, whereas the novice had chunks averaging only 1.9 pieces. Recent evidence from Gobet and Simon (1996) suggests that Chase and Simon (1973) underestimated the chunk size of masters.

It would be foolish to assume that the *only* advantage that chess experts have over novices is that they have stored information about tens of thousands of chess pieces. That would be like arguing that the only advantage that Shakespeare had over other writers was that he had a larger vocabulary! Holding and Reynolds (1982) asked chess players to think of the best move from various random board positions, chosen so that even expert players would not be able to make use of their detailed stored knowledge of board positions. The expert players produced moves of superior quality to those of non-expert players, suggesting that they possessed better strategic processing skills.

Template theory

Various theories of chess expertise have been produced in recent years (see Ericsson & Lehmann, 1996, for a review). One of the most influential of these approaches is template theory (Gobet & Simon, 1996). According to this theory, outstanding chess players owe much of their success to the relevant knowledge they have stored in memory. Much of this knowledge is in the form of templates, which are schematic structures that are more general than actual board positions. Each template consists of a core (fixed information concerning about 12 chess pieces) and slots (variable information about other pieces). Templates are complex data structures, and it may take hours to learn each one. When a template is retrieved from long-term memory during a game of chess, it can serve to suggest the next move and a plan of action.

According to template theory, outstanding players owe their excellence mostly to their superior template-based knowledge of chess. This knowledge can be accessed rapidly, and allows them to narrow down the possible moves that they need to consider. This approach can be contrasted with that of Holding and Reynolds (1982), who emphasised the importance of strategic thinking and considering numerous possible moves. These theories can be tested by comparing the performance of an outstanding player when playing a single opponent and when playing simultaneously against up to eight opponents with very little time to make each move. According to template theory, the greatly reduced time to search for future moves in the multiple-opponent situation should not have much effect on an outstanding player's performance. Precisely this was found by Gobet and Simon (1996, p. 52) in the chess games of Gary Kasparov: "The rated skill of a top-level grand master is only slightly lower when he is playing simultaneously against a half-dozen grand-master opponents than under tournament conditions that allow much more time for each move."

Gobet and Simon (1996) discussed the reports that grand masters give of their strategy when playing simultaneous matches. They generally make standard or familiar moves until they detect some weakness in an opponent's position. Knowledge that they possess then suggests ways of exploiting this weakness. Such reports suggest that grand masters rely heavily on template-based knowledge to make their moves. They then rely on detecting moves by their opponents that are inconsistent with stored templates to alert them to weaknesses in their opponents' positions.

Lassiter (2000) argued that Gobet and Simon (1996) had de-emphasised the part played by searching for future moves in chess-playing expertise. He pointed out that Kasparov's playing strength was reduced by about 100 Elo points (half a standard deviation) when he was engaged in simultaneous chess rather than playing a single opponent. This reduction is most plausibly attributed to reduced opportunities to search for, and to evaluate, future moves.

Lassiter (2000) also discussed matches in which expert players have competed against chess-playing computers. When the game must be completed in 25 minutes, computers gain about 100 Elo points relative to their human opponents. More strikingly, computers gain 200 or more Elo points when the game is limited to 5 minutes. What do these findings mean? According to Lassiter (2000, p. 172), "The tendency for chess-playing computers to become relatively stronger at shorter time controls is most likely due to the fact that a human's ability to engage in search-evaluation is more hampered by increasingly higher time constraints than is a computer's."

Evaluation

It is clear that outstanding chess players possess a number of different kinds of expertise. These can be subdivided into routine and adaptive expertise (Hatano & Inagaki, 1986). Routine expertise is involved when someone can solve familiar problems in a rapid and efficient way. This is the kind of expertise involved when chess players make use of standard board-position knowledge. Adaptive expertise is involved when a board position is relatively unknown, and so the chess player has to develop strategies for evaluating the situation and deciding what to do next. Early research (e.g., De Groot, 1965; Chase & Simon, 1973) focused on routine expertise, whereas Holding and Reynolds (1982) emphasised the importance of evaluation and of adaptive expertise. In some ways, the templates emphasised within template theory provide the knowledge needed to demonstrate both kinds of expertise.

Anderson's ACT theory

Anderson (e.g., 1983, 1993, 1996) has produced a series of models designed to account for the development of expertise. All of these models are based on a rather similar cognitive architecture known as the Adaptive Control of Thought (ACT), and so they are called ACTE, ACT*, and ACT-R. At the heart of this approach there are three interconnected systems (see Figure 9.4):

- *Declarative memory*: This consists of a semantic network of interconnected concepts (see Chapter 6).
- *Production memory*: This involves procedural knowledge (e.g., if someone hits you, then you hit them; see Chapter 6).
- *Working memory*: This contains information that is currently active (see Chapter 5).

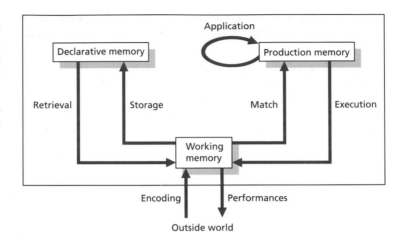

Figure 9.4.
Schematic diagram of
the major components
and interlinking
processes used in
Anderson's (1983,
1993) ACT models.
Reprinted by
permission of the
author.

Application

Declarative memory

Production memory

Retrieval   Storage   Match   Execution

Working
memory

Encoding   Performances

Outside world

There are important differences between declarative and procedural knowledge. Declarative knowledge is stored in *chunks* or small
packets of knowledge, and is consciously accessible. It can be used
across a wide range of situations. For example, suppose that you have
acquired a considerable amount of declarative knowledge about
attention. You can use this information in a very flexible way in a
seminar group, in an essay, or in an examination essay. In contrast, it
is often not possible to gain conscious access to procedural knowledge, which is used automatically whenever a production rule
matches the current contents of working memory. The use of procedural knowledge is tied to specific situations (e.g., we only use
procedural knowledge about subtraction when given a suitable
mathematical problem), which makes it less flexible.

Anderson's crucial assumption is that skill acquisition typically
involves knowledge compilation. What happens with *knowledge
compilation* is that there is a progressive shift from the use of declarative knowledge to the use of procedural knowledge, and linked with
this is an increase in automaticity. A clear example of knowledge
compilation is the development of touch-typing skills. Typing speed
increases greatly with practice, so that a fairly skilled typist can make
one keystroke every 60 ms. However, what is crucial is that the *nature*
as well as the *speed* of the processes involved change with practice.
As Fitts and Posner (1967) pointed out, typists initially rely on rules
of which they are consciously aware (e.g., move the index finger
of the left hand to the right to type the letter g). These rules are
stored in what we would now call declarative memory. Eventually,
typing becomes fast, accurate, and automatic, and depends only on

procedural memory. For example, I have typed over three million words in my life, but find it very hard to tell anyone where any given letter is on the keyboard!

What processes are involved in knowledge compilation? First, there is *proceduralisation*, which involves the creation of specific procedural rules to reduce or eliminate the necessity to search through long-term memory during skilled performance. For example, as a result of proceduralisation, typists do not need to ask themselves where the letters are on the keyboard. Second, there is *composition*, which improves performance by reducing a repeated sequence of actions to a more efficient single sequence.

Evaluation

On the positive side, Anderson's ACT approach has been applied with reasonable success to several kinds of skill acquisition. These include the learning of geometry, computer text editing, and computer programming (see Eysenck & Keane, 2000). However, the ACT approach is most applicable to the development of expertise that is routine in nature and requires unvarying procedures (e.g., touch-typing). It is of less relevance when flexibility of approach is important. Thus, for example, the ACT model has little to say about expertise that is creative and/or adaptive, such as that necessary for the construction of scientific theories or dealing with changing circumstances.

Decision making

As Gilhooly (1996) pointed out, there are clear similarities between decision making and problem solving. Decision making requires an element of problem solving, in that individuals are typically trying to make the best possible choice from a range of options. Problem solving requires some decision making, because it is generally necessary to decide which strategy to adopt in order to solve the problem. What, then, are the crucial differences between decision making and problem solving? According to Gilhooly (1996, p. 174), "In problem solving the focus is on selecting among possible actions, whereas in decision making the options are presented and subjects choose among them without the load of option-generation." In what follows, we will consider some of the main areas of research in decision making.

Risky decisions

Some of the decisions that we make in everyday life are risky, whereas others can be regarded as risk free. The key difference is that there is some uncertainty about the consequences of risky decision making, whereas in risk-free decision making there is no such uncertainty.

According to normative decision theory, a completely rational decision maker would make decisions to maximise expected value. Suppose you are asked to decide whether an unbiased coin will come down heads or tails. You are required to bet £1 on the outcome, and will gain £1 if you correctly call heads or £2 if you correctly call tails. The expected value of calling heads is £0.0; you have a 0.50 probability of losing £1 and a 0.50 probability of gaining £1, which averages out at no gain or loss. In contrast, calling tails has an expected value of 50 pence per throw: you have a 0.50 probability of losing £1, and a 0.50 probability of gaining £2, which averages out at a gain of 50 pence per throw.

The situation with most risky decision making is more complex than has been indicated so far for two reasons. First, the objective probabilities of different outcomes are often not known, and so we must rely on subjective probabilities based on our belief in the likelihood of each outcome. Second, and more important, we need to distinguish between the objective and subjective value of any outcome. Even in the very simple coin-tossing example, it is likely that the subjective value of gaining 50 pence on average by calling tails is greater for someone who is very poor than for someone who is extremely wealthy. Individual differences in subjective value are clearer with more complex situations. When deciding whether to take a highly paid job with no job security, or a less well paid job with complete job security, some people would attach more value to the financial rewards than to job security, whereas others would do the opposite.

Kahneman and Tversky (1984) developed some of the ideas we have been discussing. According to them, risky decisions are made in the context of the individual's current situation, and depend very much on whether the decision making concerns possible gains or losses of money. They proposed a value function relating value to gains and losses (see Figure 9.5). One of the major implications of this value function is that people are much more sensitive to potential losses than to potential gains. Supporting evidence has come from studies of a phenomenon known as *loss aversion*. Kahneman and

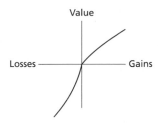

Figure 9.5. A hypothetical value function. From Kahneman and Tversky (1984). Copyright 1984 by the American Psychological Association. Reprinted with permission.

Value

Losses ——————————— Gains

Tversky (1984) found that most of their participants refused to bet when they were offered $20 if a tossed coin came up heads and a loss of $10 if it came up tails. This showed clear sensitivity to loss, because the bet provides an average expected gain of $5 per toss.

However, Kahneman and Tversky (1984) also found evidence that people engage in *risk seeking* to try to avoid losses. They offered their participants the choice between a sure loss of $800 or an 85% probability of losing $1000 with a 15% probability of not incurring any loss. Most of the participants decided to take a chance on avoiding loss, in spite of the fact that they increased the average expected loss from $800 to $850 by engaging in such risk seeking.

As would be expected from the value function, people behave rather differently when a decision has to be made between a sure gain or a risky but potentially greater gain. Kahneman and Tversky (1984) discovered that most people preferred a sure gain of $800 to an 85% probability of gaining $1000 and a 15% probability of gaining nothing. This is known as *risk aversion*, and occurs in spite of the fact that the expected value of the risky decision is greater than that of the sure gain ($850 versus $800, respectively).

Framing effects

Risky decision making is often influenced by irrelevant aspects of the situation, such as the precise way in which an issue is presented. This phenomenon is known as *framing*. Some framing effects can be accounted for in terms of loss aversion. For example, Tversky and Kahneman (1981) studied framing effects in the Asian disease problem. The participants were told that there was likely to be an outbreak of an Asian disease in the United States, and it was expected to kill 600 people. Two programmes of action had been proposed: Programme A would allow 200 people to be saved; Programme B would have a 1/3 probability that all 600 people would be saved, and a 2/3 probability that none of the 600 would be saved. When the choices were expressed in this form (with an emphasis on the number of lives saved), 72% of the participants favoured Programme A. This occurred even though the two programmes (if implemented several times) would on average both lead to the saving of 200 lives. This illustrates the phenomenon of risk aversion when the focus is on gains.

Tversky and Kahneman (1981) also used the Asian disease problem in a negatively framed version. In this version, the participants were told that Programme A would lead to 400 dying, whereas Programme B carried a 1/3 probability that nobody would die, and a 2/3 probability that 600 people would die. The problem is actually the same as in the positively framed version, but there was a marked difference in the participants' decisions. With the negatively framed version, 78% of the participants chose Programme B. In other words, they showed risk-seeking behaviour when the focus was on losses.

Wang (1996) showed that considerations of fairness can influence decision making in the Asian disease problem. In one study, Wang (1996) used various versions of the problem, in which the total number of people in the patient group varied between 6 and 600. He obtained the same framing effect as Tversky and Kahneman (1981) when the group size was 600, but there was no framing effect when the size of the patient group was 6 or 60. With the smaller patient groups, there was a clear overall preference for the option in which there was a 1/3 probability that nobody would die, and a 2/3 probability that everyone would die. Why was this? The participants preferred this option because they were concerned about fairness and about giving everyone an equal chance to survive, and these concerns were greater in a small-group context than in a large-group context.

Wang (1996) obtained more dramatic evidence of the importance of fairness in a further study. The participants had to choose between definite survival of two-thirds of the patients (deterministic option) or a 1/3 probability of all the patients surviving and a 2/3 probability of none surviving (probabilistic option). The patient group consisted of 3, 6, or 600 patients unknown to the participants, or 6 patients who were close relatives. On average, the deterministic option would lead to survival of twice as many patients as the probabilistic option. However, the probabilistic option has the advantage of seeming to be fairer. The decision as to which option was preferred was greatly influenced by group size and by the relationship between the group members and the participants (see Figure 9.6). Presumably the increased percentage of participants choosing the probabilistic option

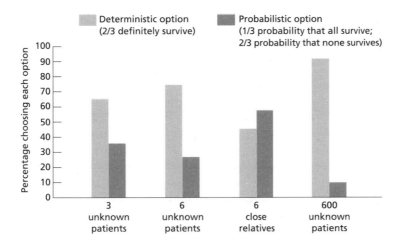

Figure 9.6. Choice of option (deterministic vs. probabilistic) as a function of number of patients and type of patient (unknown vs. close relatives). Data from Wang (1996).

with small group size (especially for relatives) occurred because the social context and psychological factors relating to fairness were regarded as more important in those conditions. Thus, the apparently "irrational" behaviour of the participants can be understood if we take the social context into account.

Dominance

Framing effects are inconsistent with a purely rational approach such as normative decision theory, because the way in which a problem is presented does not affect the underlying probabilities or values of the various outcomes. There are other findings that also reveal deficiencies in normative decision theory. For example, a clear prediction from normative decision theory is that individuals should adhere to the *dominance principle*. According to this principle, "if Option A is at least as good as Option B in all respects and better than B in at least one aspect, then A should be preferred to B" (Gilhooly, 1996, p. 178). As we will see, the dominance principle is violated in some circumstances.

Kahneman and Tversky (1984) asked their participants to make two separate decisions. The first decision involved choosing between:

(A)   a sure gain of $240
(B)   a 25% probability of gaining $1,000 and a 75% probability of gaining nothing.

The second decision involved choosing between:

(C)   a sure loss of $750

(D)   a 76% probability of losing $1,000 and a 25% probability of losing nothing.

According to the dominance principle, the participants should have chosen B and C over A and D. Options B and C together offer a 25% probability of gaining $250 and a 75% probability of losing $750, whereas options A and D together offer a 25% probability of gaining $240 and a 75% probability of losing $760. In fact, 73% of the participants chose A and D, whereas only 3% chose B and C. Kahneman and Tversky (1984) explained this breakdown of the dominance principle along similar lines to other findings that we have discussed: The participants showed risk aversion in the domain of gains and risk seeking in the domain of losses.

Anticipated regret

In order to understand risky decision making fully, we need to consider the emotional and social factors associated with different decisions. The influence of these factors can be seen in a study by Ritov and Baron (1990). Their participants were asked to assume that their child had 10 chances in 10,000 of dying from flu during an epidemic if he or she was not vaccinated. They were told that the vaccine was certain to prevent the child from catching flu, but had potentially fatal side effects. The participants had to indicate the maximum death rate from the vaccine itself that they were willing to tolerate in order to have their child vaccinated. Ritov and Baron (1990) found that the average maximum acceptable risk was five deaths per 10,000. This is puzzling, because it means that people would choose not to have their child vaccinated when the likelihood of the vaccine causing death was much lower than the death rate from the disease against which the vaccine protects!

What was going on in the study by Ritov and Baron (1990)? The participants argued that they would feel more responsible for the death of their child if it resulted from their own actions rather than from their inaction. This is an example of *omission bias*, in which individuals prefer inaction to action. An important factor in omission bias is anticipated regret, with the level of anticipated regret often being greater when an unwanted outcome has been caused by an individual's own actions. Omission bias and anticipated regret influence many real-life decisions, including those involving choices between consumer products, sexual practices, and medical decisions (see Mellers, Schwartz, & Cooke, 1998).

Evaluation

The evidence suggests that people often fail to behave as predicted by normative decision theory. In other words, their decisions tend not to be "rational" in the sense of maximising expected value. Some of the strongest evidence against this theory comes from studies on framing effects and violations of the dominance principle. A common theme running through much of this research is that people are more willing to take risks to avoid losses than to increase gains.

What is needed is more research into the factors that lead to apparently "irrational" decision making. Social factors are important, as is shown by the phenomenon of omission bias and by the research of Wang (1996). As Mellers et al. (1998, p. 450) argued, "Early metaphors for decision makers posited human beings as intuitive scientists, statisticians, and economists . . . Depending on the situation, people may be better understood as intuitive politicians who balance pressures from competing constituencies, intuitive prosecutors who demand accountability, or intuitive theologians who protect sacred values from contamination."

Why have psychologists typically de-emphasised the role of social and political factors in decision making in spite of their importance in everyday life? According to Tetlock (1991, p. 453), "Subjects in laboratory studies of cognitive processes rarely feel accountable to others for the positions they take. They function in a social vacuum (or as close an approximation as can be achieved) in which they do not need to worry about the interpersonal consequences of their conduct."

More research is needed into individual differences. Some people are much more willing than others to engage in risky decision making, but these individual differences have rarely been studied. An exception was a study by Lopes (1987), who used a short questionnaire to identify risk-averse and risk-seeking participants. According to Lopes (1987, pp. 274–275), "Risk-averse people appear to be motivated by a desire for *security*, whereas risk-seeking people appear to be motivated by a desire for *potential* . . . Risk-averse people look more at the downside and risk seekers more at the upside." The participants had to choose between various lotteries having 100 tickets, all of which had an expected value of about $100. The lotteries varied in terms of risk: At one extreme, all 100 tickets were guaranteed to produce $100; at the other extreme, 31 of the tickets produced nothing and 6 tickets produced over $300. As predicted, the risk-averse participants tended to avoid the riskier lotteries, but that was not the case for the risk-seeking ones (see Figure 9.7).

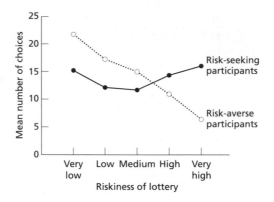

Figure 9.7. Mean riskiness of lottery chosen by risk-seeking and by risk-averse participants. Based on data in Lopes (1987).

Judgement research

We often change our opinion of the likelihood of something being the case in the light of new information or evidence. For example, suppose that you are 90% confident that someone has lied to you. However, their version of events is subsequently confirmed by another person, and this leads you to believe that there is only a 60% probability that you have been lied to. Everyday life is full of cases in which the strength of our belief is increased or decreased by fresh information.

The Rev. Thomas Bayes provided a more precise way of thinking about such cases. He produced a mathematical formula that allows us to combine probabilities in order to work out the impact of new evidence on a pre-existing probability. More specifically, Bayes focused on situations in which there are two possible beliefs or hypotheses (e.g., X is lying vs. X is not lying), and he showed how new information or data can change the probabilities of the two hypotheses.

According to Bayes' theorem, we need to take account of the relative probabilities of the two hypotheses *before* the data are obtained (these are known as the prior odds). We also need to calculate the relative probabilities of obtaining the data under each hypothesis (these are known as the posterior odds). Bayesian methods evaluate the probability of observing the data, D, if hypothesis A is correct, written $p(D/H_A)$, and if hypothesis B is correct, written $p(D/H_B)$. Bayes' theorem itself can be expressed in the form of an odds ratio as follows:

$$\frac{p(H_A/D)}{p(H_B/D)} = \frac{p(H_A)}{p(H_B)} \times \frac{p(D/H_A)}{p(D/H_B)}$$

The above formula may look intimidating, but it is not really so. What we have on the left side of the equation are the relative probabilities of hypotheses A and B in the light of the new data; these are the probabilities we want to work out. On the right side of the equation, we have the prior odds of each hypothesis being correct *before* the data were collected multiplied by the posterior odds based on the probability of the data given each hypothesis.

We can clarify what is involved in Bayes' theorem by taking a concrete example. We will consider the taxi-cab problem used by Tversky and Kahneman (1980). In this problem, a taxi-cab was involved in a hit-and-run accident one night. Of the taxi-cabs in the city, 85% belong to the Green company and 15% to the Blue company. An eyewitness identified the cab as a Blue cab. However, when her ability to identify cabs under appropriate visibility conditions was tested, she was wrong 20% of the time. The participants had to decide the probability that the cab involved in the accident was Blue.

We will refer to the hypothesis that the cab was Blue as H_A and the hypothesis that it was Green as H_B. The prior probability for H_A is .15, and for H_B it is .85, because 15% of the cabs are blue and 85% are green. The probability of the eyewitness identifying the cab as Blue when it was Blue, $p(D/H_A)$, is .80. Finally, the probability of the eyewitness saying that the cab was Blue when it was Green, $p(D/H_B)$ is .20. We then enter these values in the formula:

$$\frac{.15}{.85} \times \frac{.80}{.20} = \frac{.12}{.17}$$

That means that the odds ratio is 12:17. In other words, there is a 41% (12/29) probability that the taxi-cab was Blue compared to a 59% (17/29) probability that it was Green.

Neglecting base rates

So far we have considered the answer that the participants in Tversky and Kahneman's (1980) study *should* have given to the taxi-cab problem. In fact, most of them focused on the evidence of the eyewitness, and claimed that there was an 80% probability that the taxi was Blue. This is a long way from the correct answer of 41%. This discrepancy can easily be explained. The participants tended to ignore the prior odds or the *base-rate information*, which was defined

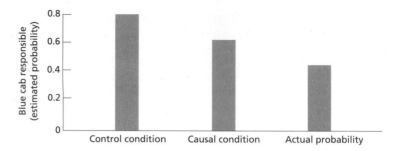

Figure 9.8. Estimated probability in the taxi-cab problem that a Blue cab was responsible for the accident in causal and control conditions. Data from Tversky and Kahneman (1980).

by Koehler (1996, p. 16) as "the relative frequency with which an event occurs or an attribute is present in the population." In this case, the base-rate information was that 85% of the taxi-cabs in the city were Green and 15% were Blue. The base-rate information tips the balance in favour of the taxi-cab involved in the accident being Green in spite of the fact that the eyewitness said that it was Blue.

Could we change the taxi-cab problem so that people would take account of the base-rate information? Tversky and Kahneman (1980) reworded the problem to emphasise that Green cabs were responsible for 85% of cab accidents in the city. This rewording drew a clear *causal* relationship between the accident record of a cab company and the likelihood of it being responsible for any given accident. The participants who were given the reworded version of the problem indicated on average that there was about a 60% probability that the cab responsible for the accident was Blue. Thus, base-rate information was partially taken into account (see Figure 9.8).

There have been numerous other studies designed to study the conditions in which base-rate information is used. We will consider in some detail the related studies of Casscells, Schoenberger, and Graboys (1978) and of Cosmides and Tooby (1996). The problem used by Casscells et al. (1978) was as follows:

> If a test to detect a disease whose prevalence is 1/1000 has a false positive rate of 5%, what is the chance that a person found to have a positive result actually has the disease, assuming that you know nothing about the person's symptoms or signs?

You may want to pit your wits against the members of staff and students at Harvard Medical School who were asked this problem. What happened was that 45% of them ignored the base-rate information, and so produced the wrong answer of 95%. The correct answer (which is 2%) was given by only 18% of the participants. Why is 2% the right answer? According to the base-rate information, 999 people out of 1000 do not suffer from the disease. The fact that the false positive rate is 5% means that 50 out of every 1000 people tested would give a misleading positive finding. As a result, 50 times as many people give a false positive result as give a true positive result (the one person in 1000 who actually has the disease), and so there is only a 2% chance that a person testing positive has the disease.

Cosmides and Tooby (1996) expressed the problem in a rather different way emphasising the *frequencies* of individuals in the various categories relevant to the problem:

> One out of 1000 Americans has disease X. A test has been developed to detect when a person has disease X. Every time the test is given to a person who has the disease, the test comes out positive. But sometimes the test also comes out positive when it is given to a person who is completely healthy. Specifically, out of every 1000 people who are perfectly healthy, 50 of them test positive for the disease. Imagine that we have assembled a random sample of 1000 Americans. They were selected by a lottery. Those who conducted the lottery had no information about the health status of any of these people. How many people who test positive for the disease will actually have the disease? (___ out of ___).

Cosmides and Tooby (1996) found that 76% of the participants produced the correct answer when the problem was presented in frequency terms. This compared with 12% who were correct when the original form of the problem was used. What do these findings mean? Gigerenzer (1993) argued that thinking in frequencies occurs earlier in development (and appeared earlier in evolution) than thinking in probabilities or percentages. However, Johnson-Laird et al. (1999, p. 81) suggested a simpler account: "It is crucial to show that the difference between frequencies and probabilities transcends mere difficulties in calculation and that difficulties with problems about unique events are not attributable merely to difficulties in numerical calculation."

Evaluation

Koehler (1996, p. 1) reviewed findings on use of base-rate information, and concluded that this literature "does not support the conventional wisdom that people routinely ignore base rates. Quite the contrary, the literature shows that base rates are almost always used and that their degree of use depends on task structure and representation." There is reasonable support for that viewpoint. However, what is of more practical importance is the extent to which people use base-rate information in everyday life. As Koehler (1996, p. 14) admitted, "When base rates in the natural environment are ambiguous, unreliable, or unstable, simple normative rules for their use do not exist. In such cases, the diagnostic value of base rates may be substantially less than that associated with many laboratory experiments." There are often several competing base rates in the real world. Suppose you want to calculate the probability that a particular professional golfer will score under 70 in her next round on a given course. What is the relevant base rate? Is it her previous scores on that course during her career, or her general level of performance that season, or her performance over her entire career, or the average performance of other professionals on that course?

Bergus et al. (1995) obtained evidence suggesting that doctors often fail to make effective use of base-rate information. Doctors were presented with the case history of a man who reported a 1-hour episode of weakness in the right arm and leg. Some of the doctors were informed initially that he had had treatment for lung cancer, whereas the others were only told this near the end of the experiment. All the doctors were then told that the patient had been given a CAT scan, which had not revealed any abnormality. They were asked to estimate the probability that the correct diagnosis was brain cancer due to cancer spreading from the lungs. The actual probability using the appropriate base-rate information is 93%. The doctors who had just learned of the lung cancer produced an average probability estimate of 79%, compared to only 11% for those doctors who had been given that information initially. Thus, the doctors were especially likely to neglect information relevant to base rate if it had been provided some time previously.

Representativeness heuristic

Why do we fail to make proper use of base-rate information? According to Tversky and Kahneman, we often use a simple heuristic or rule of thumb known as the *representativeness heuristic*. When people use this heuristic, "events that are representative or typical of a class are assigned a high probability of occurrence. If an event is highly similar to most of the others in a population or class of events, then it is considered representative" (Kellogg, 1995, p. 385). The representativeness heuristic is studied in situations in which people are asked to judge the probability that an object or event A belongs to a class or process B. Suppose you are given the description of an individual, and are asked to estimate the probability that he or she has a certain occupation. What you would probably do is to estimate the probability in terms of the *similarity* between that individual's description and your stereotype of the occupation in question.

Kahneman and Tversky (1973) studied people's use of the representativeness heuristic. Their participants were given a description such as the following: "Jack is a 45-year-old man. He is married and has four children. He is generally conservative, careful, and ambitious. He shows no interest in political and social issues and spends most of his free time on his many hobbies which include home carpentry, sailing, and mathematical puzzles" (Kahneman & Tversky, 1973, p. 241). The participants had to decide the probability that Jack was an engineer or a lawyer. They were all told that the description had been selected at random from a total of 100 descriptions. Half of the participants were told there were descriptions of 70 engineers and 30 lawyers, whereas the other half were told there were descriptions of 70 lawyers and 30 engineers.

What did Kahneman and Tversky (1973) find? The participants decided on average that there was a .90 probability that Jack was an engineer, and they did so regardless of whether most of the 100 descriptions were of lawyers or of engineers. In other words, the participants did not take account of the base-rate information (i.e., the 70:30 split of the 100 descriptions).

The representativeness heuristic is used in a more striking way to produce the *conjunction fallacy*. This is the mistaken belief that the conjunction or combination of two events (A and B) is more likely than one of the two events. Tversky and Kahneman (1983) obtained evidence of the conjunction fallacy. Their participants were presented with the following description:

> Linda is 31 years old, single, outspoken, and very bright. She majored in philosophy. As a student, she was deeply concerned with issues of discrimination and social justice, and also participated in anti-nuclear demonstrations.

They were then asked to rank order eight possible categories in terms of the probability that Linda belonged to each one. Three of the categories were bank teller, feminist, and feminist bank teller. The

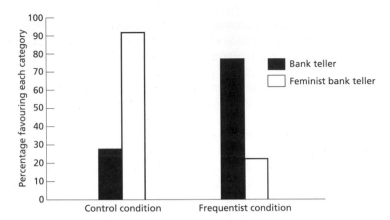

Figure 9.9.
Performance on the
Linda problem in the
frequentist and control
conditions. Data from
Fiedler (1988).

great majority of the participants ranked feminist bank teller as more probable than either bank teller or feminist. This is incorrect, because all feminist bank tellers belong to the larger categories of bank tellers and feminists!

Fiedler (1988) compared performance on the original version of the Linda problem with that on a frequency version, in which the participants had to indicate how many of 100 people fitting Linda's description were bank tellers, and how many were bank tellers and active feminists. The percentage of participants showing the conjunction fallacy dropped from 91% with the original version to 22% with the frequency version (see Figure 9.9).

Availability heuristic

Tversky and Kahneman (1974) studied another heuristic or rule of thumb. This was the *availability heuristic*, and it involves estimating the frequencies of events on the basis of how easy or difficult it is to retrieve relevant information from long-term memory. Tversky and Kahneman (1974) asked their participants the following question:

> If a word of three letters is sampled at random from an English text, is it more likely that the word starts with "r" or has "r" as its third letter?

Most of the participants argued that a word starting with "r" was more likely to be picked out at random than a word with "r" as its third letter. In fact, there are more words with "r" as the third letter. However, words starting with "r" can be retrieved more easily from memory (i.e., they are more available) than words with "r" as their third letter. That is why the participants made the wrong decision.

Tversky and Kahneman (1983) reported a more striking case in which use of the availability heuristic led to error. Their participants rated the frequency of seven-letter words ending in "ing" and "_n_" out of 2000 words taken from a novel. Most of them claimed that there would be many more words ending in "ing". This claim resulted from use of the availability heuristic. However, it is entirely wrong, because all words ending in "ing" also end in "_n_"!

Use of the availability heuristic often produces errors in everyday life. Lichtenstein et al. (1978) asked people to judge the relative likelihood of different causes of death. Those causes of death that often attract considerable publicity (e.g., murder) were judged to be more likely than those that do not (e.g., suicide), even when the opposite is actually the case.

People do *not* always use the availability heuristic in order to judge the frequency of events. For example, Brown (1995) presented category–exemplar pairs (e.g., Country–France), with each category being presented several times. The category name was always accompanied by the same exemplar (same context) or a different exemplar (different context). The task was to decide how frequently each category name had been presented. In the different-context condition, about 60% of the participants reported using the availability heuristic. However, almost 70% of the participants in the same-context condition did not seem to have used any clear strategy.

Support theory

Tversky and Koehler (1994) put forward a support theory of subjective probability, which can be seen in part as extending the notion of an availability heuristic. The crucial assumption of the theory is that any given event will appear more or less likely depending on the way it is described. Thus, we need to distinguish between events themselves and the descriptions of those events. For example, you would almost certainly assume that the probability that you will die on your next summer holiday is extremely low. However, it might seem somewhat more likely if you were asked the following question: "What is the probability that you will die on your next summer holiday from a disease, a sudden heart attack, an earthquake, terrorist activity, a civil war, a car accident, a plane crash, or from any other cause?"

Why would the subjective probability of death on holiday be greater in the second case that the first? According to support theory, a more explicit description of an event will typically be regarded as having greater subjective probability than the same event described in less explicit terms. There are two main reasons lying behind this theoretical assumption:

(1) An explicit description may draw attention to aspects of the event that are not obvious in the non-explicit description.
(2) Memory limitations may mean that people do not remember all of the relevant information if it is not supplied.

Most of the evidence is consistent with support theory (see Tversky & Koehler, 1994). Perhaps surprisingly, the finding that subjective probability is higher for an event when it is explicitly described has been obtained even with experts who could presumably fill in all the missing details of a non-explicit description from their own knowledge and experience. For example, Redelmeier et al. (1995) presented doctors at Stanford University with a description of a woman suffering from abdominal pain. Half of the doctors estimated the probabilities of two specified diagnoses (gastroenteritis and ectopic pregnancy) and of a residual category of everything else. The remaining doctors estimated the probabilities of each of five specified diagnoses (two of which were gastoenteritis and ectopic pregnancy) and of a residual category of everything else. The former group of doctors produced a mean subjective probability of .50 for the residual category. The appropriate comparison figure for the latter group consists of the three additional diagnoses (excluding gastro-enteritis and ectopic pregnancy) plus the residual category. The mean subjective probability was .69, indicating that subjective probabilities are higher for explicit descriptions even for experts.

Evaluation

There is convincing evidence that people make use of various heuristics or rules of thumb in numerous situations, and that they often show a partial or complete neglect of base-rate information even when it is appropriate to use such information. However, several criticisms have been made of the theoretical approach put forward by Kahneman and Tversky. First, as Gigerenzer (1996) pointed out, Kahneman and Tversky have failed to provide process models that specify in detail when and how the various heuristics are used. Thus, interesting phenomena are described rather than explained.

Second, Gigerenzer (1996) pointed out that some of the errors of judgement made by the participants in the various studies occurred simply because they misunderstood parts of the problem presented to them. For example, it has been found in various studies on the Linda problem that between 20% and 50% of participants interpret, "Linda is a bank teller", as implying that she is not active in the feminist movement (see Gigerenzer, 1996). Thus, the conjunction fallacy can be obtained for reasons other than use of the representativeness heuristic.

Third, most of the problems used by Kahneman and Tversky were expressed in terms of probabilities, and typically led to error-prone judgements. However, as we have seen, people sometimes make more accurate judgements when the information is represented by frequencies rather than by probabilities (e.g., Fiedler, 1988; Cosmides & Tooby, 1996). Why does this happen? A speculative answer was provided by Gigerenzer and Hoffrage (1999). They emphasised the notion of natural sampling, which is "the process of encountering instances in a population sequentially" (Gigerenzer & Hoffrage, 1999, p. 425). Natural sampling is what generally happens in everyday life, and it allows us to work out the frequencies of different kinds of events. According to Gigerenzer and Hoffrange (1999, p. 430), "Humans seem to be developmentally and evolutionarily prepared to handle natural frequencies. In contrast, many of us go through a considerable amount of mental agony to learn to think in terms of fractions, percentages, and other forms of normalised counts."

The views of Gigerenzer and Hoffrage (1999) have not gone unchallenged. For example, Johnson-Laird et al. (1999) argued that people often infer the probabilities of events by constructing mental models (see Chapter 10). According to their theoretical position, it is often easier to construct the appropriate mental models when the information is given in the form of frequencies rather than probabilities.

Summary: Problem solving and decision making

- *Problem solving*: Psychologists typically study well-defined problems, but most everyday problems are ill defined. Gestalt psychologists emphasised productive problem solving based on a novel restructuring of the problem and insight. Insight can be thwarted by functional fixedness. Many of the concepts used by the Gestalt theorists are vague and hard to measure. Newell and Simon produced computer simulations of human problem solving based on heuristic methods such as means–ends analysis. The problems they used were ones for which the participants had little relevant specific knowledge, which is quite unlike most real-life problems.

- *Expertise*: Expertise is studied using "knowledge-rich" problems rather than the "knowledge-lean" problems typically found in problem-solving studies. Expert chess players possess much more knowledge of board positions than do non-expert players, and they also have superior strategic processing skills. According to template theory, chess players make use of templates. These are schematic structures containing abstract information about board positions and general plans. Expert chess players possess routine and adaptive expertise. According to Anderson's ACT model, skill acquisition involves three interconnected systems: declarative memory, procedural memory, and working memory. The key assumption of the model is that skill acquisition involves a progressive shift from the use of declarative knowledge to that of procedural knowledge by means of proceduralisation and composition. The ACT approach is more applicable to the development of routine expertise than adaptive expertise.

- *Decision making*: The notion that decision makers are more sensitive to potential losses than to potential gains receives support from the phenomenon of loss aversion. Framing effects and breakdowns of the dominance principle provide evidence against normative decision theory. More generally, decision makers are often influenced by emotional, social, and political factors, and this can give the appearance of "irrational" decision making. For example, a key reason for omission bias is that the level of anticipated regret is greater when an unwanted outcome is caused by an individual's own actions.

- *Judgement research*: We often fail to make full use of base-rate information when deciding on the likelihood of an event, in part because of reliance on the representativeness heuristic. The conjunction fallacy illustrates use of the representativeness heuristic, but sometimes occurs because of misunderstanding of the problem. Another heuristic often used in judgement research is the availability heuristic. According to support theory, any given event will appear more likely when it is described in explicit terms, because this draws attention to aspects of the event that are less obvious in non-explicit descriptions. What is lacking in most of the research is an attempt to provide process models specifying in detail when and how the various heuristics are used.

Essay questions

(1) Describe and evaluate the Gestaltist approach to problem solving.
(2) How does chess-playing expertise develop?
(3) Why has the approach to problem solving proposed by Newell and Simon been so influential?
(4) What factors are involved in risky decision making?
(5) Why do we often make errors when judging the probabilities of events?

Further reading

Eysenck, M.W., & Keane, M.T. (2000). *Cognitive psychology: A student's handbook* (4th ed.). Hove, UK: Psychology Press. The relevant chapters in this book contain more detailed accounts of the topics discussed here.

Gilhooly, K.J. (1996). *Thinking: Directed, undirected and creative.* London: Academic Press. Chapters 2 and 8 of this book provide useful coverage of the main topics discussed in this chapter.

Gilhooly, K.J., & Hoffman, R. (Eds.) (1998). *Expert thinking.* Hove, UK: Psychology Press. This edited book contains a useful collection of recent articles dealing with expertise.

Goldstein, W.M., & Hogarth, R.M. (1997). *Research on judgment and decision making: Currents, connections, and controversies.* Cambridge, UK: Cambridge University Press. This edited book contains a number of thought-provoking chapters on decision making and judgement.

Reasoning 10

Introduction

Research on reasoning can be regarded as falling within the area of problem solving (see Chapter 9), because people trying to solve a reasoning task have a definite goal and the solution is not obvious. However, problem solving and reasoning are typically treated separately. Why is this? Reasoning problems differ from other kinds of problems in that they often owe their origins to systems of formal logic. However, there are clear overlaps between the two areas. For example, cognitive tasks that involve *analogical thinking* (detecting important similarities between two things) are sometimes discussed under analogical reasoning and sometimes under analogical problem solving. Of particular importance, the fact that some reasoning problems can be solved by the application of the rules of logic does not necessarily mean that that is the way in which people normally solve them.

It is customary to distinguish between deductive reasoning and inductive reasoning. *Deductive reasoning* allows us to draw conclusions that are certain provided that other statements are assumed to be true. For example, if we assume that Tom is taller than Dick, and Dick is taller than Harry, the conclusion that Tom is taller than Harry is necessarily true. In contrast, *inductive reasoning* involves drawing general conclusions from specific information, but the conclusions are *not* necessarily true. For example, dozens of experiments may all provide support for a given theory, and this may lead us to conclude that the theory is correct. However, we cannot rule out the possibility that future experiments may show that the theory is incorrect.

Waltz et al. (1999) argued that all forms of reasoning involve what they referred to as *relational integration*, in which the relations between objects and events are manipulated and combined. For example, consider a type of deductive reasoning known as transitive inference.

Figure 10.1.
Accuracy on the test of
transitive inference (a)
and matrices test (b) for
each group of
participants. Results
are shown for patients
with prefrontal damage
(solid lines), patients
with anterior temporal
damage (dotted lines),
and normal control
subjects (dashed lines).
From Waltz et al.
(1999) with permission
from Blackwell
Publishers.

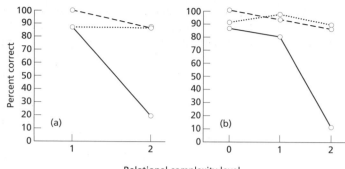

Relational complexity level

Here is an example of a transitive inference problem requiring only modest relational integration: Tom taller than William; William taller than Richard. The following transitive inference problem involves more complex relational integration: Bert taller than Matthew; Fred taller than Bert.

According to Waltz et al. (1999), the prefrontal region of the brain is of crucial importance in relational integration, and thus in all forms of reasoning. They tested groups of patients with prefrontal damage and patients with anterior temporal lobe damage, with both groups having similar IQs within the normal range. The two groups performed comparably on the simple version of the transitive inference task discussed above, but the prefrontal patients were at a massive disadvantage on the more complex version (see Figure 10.1).

Waltz et al. (1999) also tested the same groups of patients on a test of inductive reasoning involving matrix problems, in which the appropriate stimulus to complete each pattern had to be selected. The extent to which relational integration was necessary for problem solution was manipulated. The pattern of findings was the same as with deductive reasoning: The two groups performed comparably when little relational integration was required, but the prefrontal patients were dramatically worse than the anterior temporal patients when the task required substantial relational integration. Waltz et al. (1999, p. 122) concluded as follows: "Our findings indicate that the human prefrontal cortex plays an essential role in relational reasoning—specifically, in the integration of multiple relations."

The involvement of the prefrontal cortex, and especially the dorsolateral prefrontal cortex, in reasoning has also been shown in neuroimaging studies. Baker, Dolan, and Frith (1996) obtained PET scans while normal individuals performed a transitive inference task. There was increased activation in the dorsolateral prefrontal cortex and other areas during task performance. Probhakaran et al. (1997) assessed functional MRI in normals during performance of the Raven's Progressive Matrices Test, which involves pattern completion tasks resembling those used by Waltz et al. (1999). Activation levels were highest in the dorsolateral prefrontal cortex and other associated areas.

Waltz et al. (1999) related the above findings to work on the central executive of the working memory system (see Chapter 5). It has often been suggested that the prefrontal cortex plays an important role in the functioning of the central executive, although that view has been regarded as an oversimplification (see Baddeley, Emslie, Kolodny, & Duncan, 1998). If we put the various ideas and evidence together, it is tempting to conclude that relational reasoning may be one of the main functions of the central executive system.

Analogical reasoning

Many problems can be solved by making use of analogical reasoning, in which the solver notices some important similarities between the current problem and some problem solved in the past. Analogical reasoning has proved important in the history of science. Examples include the computer model of human information processing, the billiard-ball model of gases, and the hydraulic model of the blood circulation system. Historically, analogical reasoning or thinking was often studied by presenting problems having the form "A is to B as C is to D" (e.g., "north is to south as top is to bottom"). The participants were either given the task of deciding whether the analogy was correct, or the final (D) term was missing and had to be supplied. Such analogical reasoning tasks are important in part because performance on them correlates highly with IQ. For example, Spearman (1927) reported a correlation of +.8 between performance on analogical reasoning and IQ.

In everyday life, we generally have to search through long-term memory in order to find a suitable analogy to a current problem. Most recent studies of analogical thinking have been more realistic than earlier ones in that there has been more need for participants to retrieve analogical information from memory. According to Hummel and Holyoak (1997), two of the major processes involved in analogical thinking are access and mapping. Access involves retrieval of a familiar analogue or other information from long-term memory when presented with a novel problem. Mapping involves discovering which elements of the novel problem correspond to elements in the stored analogue. Research in this area, to which we now turn, has focused on some of the factors determining the likelihood that people will draw appropriate analogies.

Evidence

Gick and Holyoak (1980) used Duncker's radiation problem, in which a patient with a malignant tumour in his stomach can only be saved by a special kind of ray. The problem is that a ray of sufficient strength to destroy the tumour will also destroy the healthy tissue, whereas a ray that is not strong enough to harm healthy tissue will be too weak to destroy the tumour.

When this was the only problem that was presented, only about 10% of the participants were able to solve this problem. The answer is to direct several low-intensity rays at the tumour from different directions. Other participants were given three stories to memorise, one of which was conceptually related to the radiation problem. This story was about a general capturing a fortress by having his army converge at the same time on the fortress along several different roads. When the participants were told that one of the three stories might be relevant to solving the radiation problem, about 80% of them solved it (see Figure 10.2). When the hint was not offered, however, only about 40% of those given the stories to memorise solved the problem (see Figure 10.2). Thus, the fact that relevant information is stored in long-term memory is no guarantee that it will be used.

Why did most participants in the Gick and Holyoak (1980) study fail to make spontaneous use of the relevant story they had memorised? Keane (1987) hypothesised that it might be because of the numerous superficial differences between the story and the problem. He tested this prediction by presenting participants with either a semantically close story (about a surgeon using rays on a cancer) or a semantically remote story (the general-and-fortress story). They were given this story during a lecture, and were then asked to take part in an experiment several days later. Of those participants who had been given the close analogy, 88% spontaneously retrieved it when given the radiation problem. In contrast, only 12% of those who had been given the remote analogy spontaneously retrieved it.

Needham and Begg (1991) also addressed the issue of how to increase the likelihood that participants would use analogical thinking when appropriate. Initially, they presented their participants with

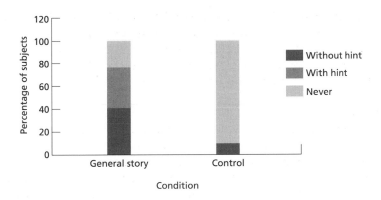

Figure 10.2. Some of the results from Gick and Holyoak (1980, Experiment 4) showing the percentage of subjects who solved the radiation problem when they were given an analogy (general-story condition) or were just asked to solve the problem (control condition). Note that just under half of the subjects in the general-story condition had to be given a hint to use the story analogue before they solved the problem.

a series of training problems. Some of them were instructed to adopt a problem-oriented approach towards the problems, in which they focused on understanding the solution to each problem. Other participants were instructed to take a memory-oriented approach, in which they focused on remembering the problems. After that, the participants were given several further test problems related to the original problems. The participants who had adopted the problem-oriented approach solved 90% of the test problems, whereas those who had adopted the memory-oriented approach solved only 69% of them. Thus, understanding is much more important than memory in producing effective analogical reasoning.

Some recent research has been designed to identify those parts of the brain most involved in analogical thinking. For example, Wharton et al. (1998) obtained PET scans from participants while they solved proportional analogy problems with geometrical shapes. Their findings indicated that analogical mapping is localised in the left prefrontal cortex and left inferior parietal cortex. Some of the functions of working memory also seem to occur in the prefrontal cortex (see Chapter 5). It is probable that the working memory system is involved in analogical thinking, a notion which forms part of the theory we are about to discuss.

Theory: LISA

One of the most influential theories of analogical reasoning was put forward by Hummel and Holyoak (1997). They proposed a connectionist model embodied in a computer simulation called LISA (Learning and Inference with Schemas and Analogies). A key assumption incorporated into LISA is that there are fundamental differences between analogical access and mapping. Access involves retrieval competiton among several stored analogues in long-term memory, because only a small number can become accessible to consciousness after any given retrieval attempt. In contrast, mapping typically involves comparing features of only a single stored analogue against those of the current problem or analogue within working memory. Thus, people's ability to engage in analogical thinking is constrained by the limited capacity of working memory.

One of the main distinguishing features of LISA is that the initial processes involved in mapping occur in a relatively automatic way without the intervention of conscious processes and strategies. According to Hummel and Holyoak (1997, p. 438), "Unlike virtually all current analogy models in which mapping is treated as an explicit comparison between analogs, . . . mapping is a much more implicit process in which the recipient [stored analogue] reacts to semantic patterns created by the driver [current problem]."

Evidence

One of the greatest strengths of LISA is that it is able to simulate many of the phenomena that have been found in research on analogical thinking. For example, Hummel and Holyoak (1997) discussed a study that was designed to see whether access to stored analogues is competitive. The participants were presented with a series of analogue sentences. These were followed by various cue sentences, with the participants instructed to write down any sentences of which they were reminded. The key manipulation was whether the initial set of sentences contained one or two sentences related to each cue sentence. According to the theory, there is competition at retrieval among analogue sentences, and so access to any given analogue sentence should be poorer where there were two related sentences. As predicted, access was less successful with two related sentences than with one (26% vs. 33%, respectively). A LISA computer simulation of this experiment produced the same pattern of results.

Another prediction following from LISA is the existence of a phenomenon known as pragmatic centrality, which applies to situations in which the mappings between the current problem and past analogues are ambiguous. The phenomenon refers to the tendency to select those features of previous analogues that seem important in the context of the current problem. For example, Spellman and Holyoak (1996) reported a study in which participants read two science-fiction stories about countries on two planets. They then made judgements

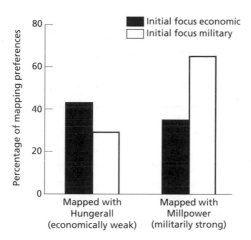

Figure 10.3.
Preferred mapping for
Barebrute with
Hungerall or Millpower
as a function of initial
focus (economic vs.
military). Based on data
in Spellman and
Holyoak (1996).

about individual countries on the basis of either military or economic relationships. After that, they answered mapping questions concerning which countries on one planet corresponded most closely to those on the other. For example, Barebrute on Planet 1 resembled Hungerall on Planet 2 in being economically weak, and it resembled Millpower on Planet 2 in being militarily strong.

According to the notion of pragmatic centrality, the mapping decisions should have been determined by whether the focus of the initial judgements was military or economic. That was precisely what Spellman and Holyoak (1996) found (see Figure 10.3). LISA produced a similar pattern of results when given the same task to perform (Hummel & Holyoak, 1997).

Evaluation

We have a reasonable understanding of the factors determining whether or not people are likely to use relevant past knowledge on analogical thinking tasks. We also have theories (such as LISA), which identify some of the main processes involved in analogical access and mapping. A noteworthy feature of LISA is that it is based on realistic assumptions about the limited capacity of working memory and the processes involved in memory retrieval. However, LISA does not provide a detailed account of all the processes involved in analogical reasoning. As Hummel and Holyoak (1997, p. 457) admitted, "In our simulations we used very informal semantic representations. More realistic applications of the model will require careful attention to difficult issues in meaning representation."

In spite of much progress, analogical reasoning as studied in the laboratory typically differs from analogical reasoning in everyday life. In the laboratory, analogical problems can usually be solved with complete success simply by making use of an appropriate analogy provided earlier in the experiment. In everyday life, in contrast, matters are often much more complex, because the fit or match between previous knowledge and the current problem is nearly always imprecise. In scientific research, analogies often have a great initial impact on thinking, but doubts grow as the implications of the analogy are explored systematically. For example, there are some significant similarities between human cognition and computer functioning, but it is also clear that there are many important differences.

There is another limitation with most studies on analogical reasoning (e.g., Gick & Holyoak, 1980). As Mackintosh (1998, p. 309) pointed out, "What is missing from these experimental studies on the use of analogy in problem solving is any attempt to explain the individual differences they reveal. A significant minority of students see the analogy between the surgeon–tumour and general–fortress problems without any hint . . . we do not know whether these differences would be related to differences in IQ test scores."

Deductive reasoning

Researchers have studied various types of deductive reasoning. However, we will focus on two forms of deductive reasoning that have been studied in great detail: conditional reasoning and syllogistic reasoning. After we have discussed the relevant research, theoretical explanations of the findings will be considered.

Conditional reasoning

Conditional reasoning has been studied in order to decide whether human reasoning is logical. It has its origins in what is known as the propositional calculus, in which logical operators such as "not"; "as . . . if"; "not", "if" and "only if" are included in propositions. Consider, for example, the following problem in conditional reasoning:

Premises
If it is raining, then Fred gets wet
It is raining.

Conclusion
Fred gets wet.

This conclusion is valid. It illustrates one of the most important rules of inference, known as *modus ponens*: "If A, then B", and also given A, we can validly infer B.

Another major rule of inference is *modus tollens*: from the premise, "If A, then B", and the premise, "B is false", the conclusion "A is false" necessarily follows. This rule of inference is shown in the following example:

Premises
If it is raining, then Fred gets wet.
Fred does not get wet.

Conclusion
It is not raining.

People consistently perform much better with modus ponens than with modus tollens. Evans (1989) reviewed the literature, and concluded that very few errors are made with modus ponens, but the error rate often exceeds 30% with modus tollens.

Two other inferences are worth considering at this stage. The first is called *affirmation of the consequent*, and the second is called *denial of the antecedent*. Here is an example of affirmation of the consequent:

Premises
If it is raining, then Fred gets wet.
Fred gets wet.

Conclusion
Therefore, it is raining.

Here is an example of denial of the antecedent:

Premises
If it is raining, then Fred gets wet.
It is not raining.

Conclusion
Therefore, Fred does not get wet.

Do you think the above conclusions are valid? Many people argue that they are, but in fact they are invalid. In the first example (affirmation of the consequent), it does not necessarily have to be raining in order for Fred to get wet: He might have jumped into a swimming pool or someone might have turned a hose on him. In the second example (denial of the antecedent), Fred might still get wet via a swimming pool or garden hose. Evans, Clibbens, and Rood (1995) found that 21% of participants drew the invalid affirmation of the consequent inference when the problem was presented in abstract form. The invalid denial of the antecedent inference was drawn by over 60% of participants when the problem was in abstract form.

Wason selection task

A task that has proved especially useful in shedding light on human reasoning was invented about 30 years ago by the British psychologist Peter Wason. It is generally known as the Wason selection task after its inventor. In the standard version of this task, there are four cards lying on a table. Each card has a letter on one side and a number on the other. The participant is told that there is a rule that applies to the four cards (e.g., "If there is an R on one side of the card, then there is a 2 on the other side of the card"). The task is to select only those cards that would need to be turned over in order to decide whether or not the rule is correct.

In one of the most used versions of this selection task, the four cards have the following symbols visible: R, G, 2, and 7 (see Figure 10.4), and the rule is the example just given. What answer would you give to this problem? Most people select either the R card or the R and 2 cards. If you did the same, then you got the answer wrong. The starting point for solving the problem is to recognise that what needs to be done is to see whether any of the cards fail to obey the rule. From this perspective, the 2 card is irrelevant. If there is an R on the other side of it, then all this tells us is that the rule might be true. If there is any other letter on the other side, then we have also discovered nothing at all about the validity of the rule.

In fact, the correct answer is to select the cards with R and 7 on them, an answer that is selected by only about 5% of university students. The 7 is necessary because it would definitely disprove the rule if it had an R on the other side. There are striking similarities between Wason's selection task and syllogistic reasoning. The selection of the 7 card follows from the modus tollens rule of inference: From the premises "If there is an R on one side of the card,

Figure 10.4. Rule: If there is an R on one side of the card, then there is a 2 on the other.

then there is a 2 on the other side" and "The 7 card does not have a 2 on it", it follows logically that the 7 card should not have an R on the other side. If it does, then the premise specifying the rule must be incorrect. Thus, incorrect performance on the Wason selection task is due in part to the general difficulty that people have with making the modus tollens inference.

Several researchers have argued that the abstract nature of the task makes it hard to solve. Wason and Shapiro (1971) used four cards (Manchester, Leeds, car, and train) and the rule, "Every time I go to Manchester I travel by car". The task was to select only those cards that need to be turned over to prove or disprove the rule. The correct answer that the Manchester and train cards need to be turned over was given by 62% of the participants, against only 12% when the Wason selection task was given in its abstract form.

The findings of Wason and Shapiro (1971) suggest that the use of concrete and meaningful material facilitates performance on the Wason task. However, Griggs and Cox (1982) used the same tasks as Wason and Shapiro with American students in Florida. They failed to find a greater success rate for the meaningful task, presumably because most American students have no direct experience of Manchester or Leeds, and have probably never heard of these cities.

Theoretical perspectives

An interesting theoretical approach to the Wason selection task was put forward by Cosmides (1989). According to her social contract theory, humans during the course of evolution have developed cognitive strategies in order to detect those who cheat. A social contract is based on the agreement that someone will only receive a benefit (e.g., travelling by train) when they have paid the appropriate cost (e.g., bought a ticket). People possess a "cheat-detecting algorithm" (computational procedure) allowing them to identify cases of cheating (e.g., travelling by train without having bought a ticket).

What is the relevance of social contract theory to the Wason selection task? Cheaters are rule breakers, and successful performance on the selection task requires participants to think about falsifying the rule rather than confirming its correctness. Thus, performance on the Wason selection task should be better when the task focuses on cheating than when it does not.

Gigerenzer and Hug (1992) tested social contract theory. One of the tasks they used was based on the following rule of the Kulumae tribe: "If a man eats cassava root, then he must have a tattoo on his face." Married men are identified in the Kulumae tribe by having a tattoo on their faces. The four cards used in the selection task were "has a tattoo"; "has no tattoo"; "eats cassava root"; and "eats molo nuts". In the cheating version of the task, the cassava root was described as a rare aphrodisiac. The participants were told that the rule was designed to ration the rare cassava root for married men, and so prevent premarital sex. In the non-cheating version of the task, the instructions told the participants to adopt the perspective of an anthropologist.

The findings of Gigerenzer and Hug (1992) provided clear support for social contract theory. Between 80% and 90% of the participants turned over the correct cards with cheating versions of the Wason task, compared to only 40% when the task was presented in a non-cheating version. Liberman and Klar (1996, p. 147) noted that the rule to be tested was described more clearly in cheating versions of the task, but concluded that, "The cheating situation is usually an efficient way to produce interpretation of the task situation that coincides with formal logic."

Oaksford and Chater (1994), Oaksford (1997), and Chater and Oaksford (1999) favoured a different approach known as the optimal data selection or information gain model. According to this model, people's reasoning on the Wason selection task (and other reasoning tasks) may be inductive rather than deductive. In essence, the reasoning processes they use on the selection task may be effective and useful in everyday life, and serve the purpose of maximising the amount of information gain.

Oaksford (1997) gave the example of testing the rule, "All swans are white". The application of formal logic would indicate that people should try to find swans and non-white birds. However, there is a problem with formal logic when applied to the real world in this way: only a few birds are swans, and only a few birds are white, and so the pursuit of non-white swans may take up enormous amounts of time and effort. In these circumstances, it may well make more sense to look for white birds in order to see whether they are swans.

At an abstract level, we can regard the rule on the Wason selection task as being of the following form: "If a card has p on one side, then it has q on the other side." According to the information gain model, this rule or hypothesis is tested against the alternative hypothesis that p and q are unrelated to each other. In order to do this most effectively, it is very important to take account of the probabilities of p and q. This assumption was tested by Kirby (1994), who varied the probability of p from practically nothing (.001) all the way up to .90. As predicted, the participants were more likely to select the not-q card and less likely to select the q card as the probability of p increased. This is an appropriate shift if the goal is to maximise information gain from each choice.

Evaluation

There is reasonable support for social contract theory and the information gain model. In addition, the information-gain model offers the prospect of uniting reasoning research with research on judgement and decision making. However, both approaches are limited in some ways. So far as social contract theory is concerned, some participants provide the right answer on the Wason selection task even when the form of the problem does not relate in any way to a social contract. Thus, other factors need to be considered. More generally, the theory has little or no relevance to most other kinds of reasoning task.

One of the limitations of the information gain model was identified clearly by Johnson-Laird (1999, p. 127): "[It] accounts for many phenomena, but there is, as yet, no corresponding theory of the mental processes underlying performance. Naive individuals are unlikely to be explicitly calculating, say, the expected gain in information from selecting a card." Another limitation is that the model has been tested mainly by considering its ability to account for existing findings. As yet, there have been few attempts to test novel predictions of the model.

Syllogistic reasoning

Syllogistic reasoning has been studied for over 2000 years. A syllogism consists of two premises or statements followed by a conclusion. What is involved in syllogistic reasoning is to decide whether the conclusion is valid in the light of the premises. It is important to note that the validity (or otherwise) of the conclusion depends *only* on whether it follows logically from the premises. Thus, the validity of the conclusion in the real world is irrelevant. Consider the following example:

Premises
All children are obedient.
Juliet and William are children.

Conclusion
Therefore, Juliet and William are obedient.

The conclusion follows logically from the premises. Thus, it is valid regardless of your views about the obedience of children.

The premises in the above example are both universal affirmative premises having the form "All A are B". However, the premises in syllogistic reasoning can have various other forms: particular affirmative premises ("Some A are B"); universal negative premises ("No A are B"); and particular negative premises ("Some A are not B").

Biases

People often make errors in syllogistic reasoning. One of the reasons is because of the existence of various biases. For example, there is the *belief bias*, in which people accept believable conclusions and reject unbelievable conclusions irrespective of the logical validity or invalidity of those conclusions. For example, Oakhill, Garnham, and Johnson-Laird (1990) presented syllogisms such as the following:

All of the Frenchmen are wine drinkers.
Some of the wine drinkers are gourmets.
Therefore, some of the Frenchmen are gourmets.

The conclusion is very believable, and is endorsed by many people. However, the conclusion is actually invalid and does not follow logically from the premises.

Another factor in producing poor performance on reasoning tasks is the *atmosphere effect* (Woodworth & Sells, 1935), in which the form of the premises of a syllogism influences our expectations about the form of the conclusion. For example, if both premises include the word "all", then we expect the conclusion to include it as well. There is modest support for the atmosphere effect (see Gilhooly, 1996), but it predicts far more errors than actually occur.

Another factor leading to poor performance is *conversion error*, in which a statement in one form is mistakenly converted into a statement with a different form. As Chapman and Chapman (1959) found, participants often assume that "All As are Bs" means that "All Bs are As", and that "Some As are not Bs" means that "Some Bs are not As". Ceraso and Provitera (1971) tried to prevent conversion errors from occurring by spelling out the premises more unambiguously (e.g., "All As are Bs" was stated as "All As are Bs, but some Bs are not As"). As predicted, this produced a substantial improvement in performance.

Begg and Denny (1969) pointed out that there is not much difference between the atmosphere effect and conversion errors. On the basis of the available evidence, they suggested a revised version of the atmosphere effect based on two principles:

(1) If at least one premise is negative, then the conclusion is negative; otherwise, it is positive.
(2) If at least one premise is particular (some), then the conclusion will be particular; otherwise, it is universal (all).

Evaluation

The problem with accounts focusing on biases and errors is that they provide a *description* rather than an *explanation* of what is happening. For example, a proper explanation would explain *why* reasoning is affected by the believability of the conclusion, and *why* people convert statements and are influenced by the "atmosphere" created by the premises. Something else that is lacking is an account of how it is that some individuals manage to avoid biases and errors in their syllogistic reasoning.

Theories of deductive reasoning

We have seen that people are prone to making errors across a wide range of reasoning tasks. Several theories of reasoning have been put forward to account for these errors, but here we will focus on only two of the major ones. First, there are abstract-rule theories (e.g., Braine, 1994, 1998), according to which people are basically logical, but can be led into error if they misunderstand the reasoning task. Second, there is the mental model approach (e.g., Johnson-Laird, 1983, 1999), according to which people form mental models or representations of the premises, and use these mental models to draw conclusions.

Abstract-rule theories

According to abstract-rule theories, people make use of a mental logic when confronted by a reasoning task. Invalid inferences are made because people misunderstand or misrepresent the reasoning task. However, what is critically important is that, after their initial mis-understanding, people engage in a logical reasoning process.

We will focus on the abstract-rule theory originally proposed by Braine (1978), and subsequently developed and extended by various theorists (e.g., Braine, Reiser, & Rumain, 1984; Braine, 1994, 1998). According to the theory, people comprehend the premises of an argument. After that, they turn them into abstract rules (e.g., a modus ponens rule) from which they make inferences.

Braine et al. (1984) argued that there are three main reasons why people make errors in reasoning:

(1) *Comprehension errors*: The premises of a reasoning problem are interpreted incorrectly (e.g., conversion error).
(2) *Heuristic inadequacy*: The participant's reasoning programme fails to locate the correct line of reasoning.
(3) *Processing errors*: The participant may fail to attend fully to the task in hand or may suffer from memory overload.

Evidence

We can see how this theory works in practice by considering its account of a reasoning error known as affirmation of the consequent. Earlier in the chapter, we considered an example of this error, in which it is mistakenly assumed that the premises, "If it is raining, then Fred gets wet" and "Fred gets wet", lead to the valid conclusion that "Therefore, it is raining". According to Braine et al. (1984), this error occurs because of a conversion error: "If it is raining, then Fred gets wet" is interpreted to mean, "If Fred gets wet, then it has been raining". Why should this be so? According to Braine et al. (1984), we assume that other people will provide us with the information we need to know. If someone says, "If it is raining, then Fred gets wet", it is reasonable to assume that rain is the only event likely to make Fred wet.

Braine et al. (1984) obtained evidence to support their theory. For example, they tried to prevent participants from misinterpreting the premises in affirmation of the consequent syllogisms by providing an additional, clarifying premise:

Premises
If it is raining, then Fred gets wet.
If it is snowing, then Fred gets wet.
Fred gets wet

Conclusion
?

Participants were much more likely to argue correctly that there is no valid conclusion when the additional premise was used.

According to Braine et al. (1984) people have a mental rule corresponding to modus ponens. Thus, syllogisms based on modus ponens are easy to handle, and pose no comprehension problems. However, Byrne (1989) showed that this is not always true. She presented syllogisms of the following type with the starred premise either present or absent:

Premises
If she has an essay to write, then she will study late in the library.
*If the library stays open, then she will study late in the library.
She has an essay to write.

Conclusion
?

The participants were much less likely to draw the valid modus ponens conclusion (e.g., "She will study late in the library") when the additional (starred) premise was presented; this is known as a context effect. This effect shows that the processes involved in reasoning can be more complex (and less logical) than is assumed by the theory.

Evaluation

The abstract-rule approach has proved reasonably successful in accounting for experimental findings. It is especially impressive that this has been achieved with only relatively few reasoning rules. However, the approach has various limitations. First, the comprehension component of the model is underspecified, and so it is not always clear what predictions should be made from the model. Second, the abstract-rule approach has mainly been applied to propositional reasoning, and so it is not known whether it can be applied successfully to other forms of reasoning. Thus, there are concerns about the generality of the theory. Third, the theory does not provide an adequate account of context effects, such as the one reported by Byrne (1989).

Mental models

One of the most influential approaches to deductive reasoning is the mental model theory of Johnson-Laird (e.g., 1983, 1999). According to Johnson-Laird (1999, p. 130), "Reasoning is just the continuation of comprehension by other means." This view has important implications, because we do not normally use logical processes when trying to understand a sentence. It follows that we should stop arguing that thinking is logical when it succeeds and illogical when it fails. Instead, we should argue that successful thinking results from the use of appropriate mental models and unsuccessful thinking occurs when we make use of inappropriate mental models.

What is a *mental model*? According to Johnson-Laird (1999, p. 116), "Each mental model represents a *possibility*, and its structure and content capture what is common to the different ways in which the possibility might occur." That definition may obscure rather than clarify, so we will consider a concrete example:

Premises
The lamp is on the right of the pad.
The book is on the left of the pad.
The clock is in front of the book.
The vase is in front of the lamp.

Conclusion
The clock is to the left of the vase.

According to Johnson-Laird (1983), people use the information contained in the premises to construct a mental model like this:

> book   pad   lamp
> clock   vase

It is easy to see that the conclusion that the clock is to the left of the vase follows from the mental model. The fact that we cannot construct a mental model that is consistent with the premises but inconsistent with the conclusion indicates that it is valid.

It is tempting (but wrong) to assume that mental models always give rise to images. Sometimes they do, but there are numerous exceptions. For example, negation can be represented in a mental model but cannot be visualised.

It is assumed that the construction of mental models involves the limited processing resources of working memory (see Chapter 5). It follows from this assumption that people should find it harder to reason accurately when a problem requires the construction of several mental models rather than just one. A more specific prediction follows from another assumption of the model known as the principle of truth: "Individuals minimise the load on working memory by tending to construct mental models that represent explicitly only what is true, and not what is false" (Johnson-Laird, 1999, p. 116). It follows that people will make more errors in reasoning when a problem requires the representation of what is false.

Evidence

The notion that people's ability to construct mental models is constrained by the limited capacity of working memory was tested by Johnson-Laird (1983). He asked his participants to indicate what conclusions followed validly from sets of premises. The demands on working memory were varied by manipulating the number of mental models consistent with the premises. Seventy-eight per cent of participants drew the valid conclusion when the premises only allowed the generation of one mental model. This figure dropped to 29% when two mental models were possible, and to 13% with three mental models.

According to the theory, it takes time to construct a mental model. It follows that reasoning problems requiring the generation of several mental models would take longer than those requiring the generation of only one model. Bell and Johnson-Laird (1998) tested this

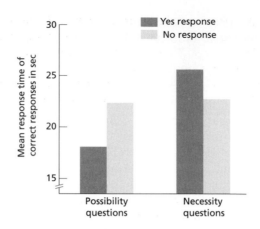

Figure 10.5. Mean response times (in sec.) for correct responses (yes and no) to possibility and necessity questions. Based on data in Bell and Johnson-Laird (1998).

prediction. They argued that a single mental model can establish that something is possible, but all models must be constructed to show that something is not possible. In contrast, all mental models must be constructed to show that something is necessary, but one model can show that something is not necessary. Bell and Johnson-Laird (1998) used reasoning problems consisting of premises followed by a question about a possibility (e.g., "Can Betsy be in the game?") or a question about a necessity (e.g., "Must Betsy be in the game?").

According to the theory, the participants should have responded faster to *possibility* questions when the correct answer was "Yes" rather than "No". However, they should have responded faster to *necessity* questions when the answer was "No" rather than "Yes". That is precisely what they found (see Figure 10.5).

Johnson-Laird et al. (1999) discussed the principle of truth, according to which most mental models represent what is true and ignore what is false. It follows from this principle that most people would make systematic and predictable errors when given a reasoning problem requiring active consideration of falsity. This prediction was tested by Johnson-Laird and Goldvarg (1997). The participants were presented with the following problem:

Only one of the following premises is true about a particular hand of cards:

(1) There is a king in the hand or there is an ace, or both.
(2) There is a queen in the hand or there is an ace, or both.
(3) There is a jack in the hand or there is a 10, or both.

Is it possible that there is an ace in the hand?

What do you think is the correct answer? Johnson-Laird and Goldvarg (1997) found that 99% of their participants gave the answer "Yes", which is amazingly high given that the correct answer is "No". According to Johnson-Laird and Goldvarg (1997), what the participants did was to form mental models of the premises. Thus, for example, the first premise generates the following mental models:

King

      Ace

King   Ace

These mental models suggest that an ace is possible, as do the mental models formed from the second premise. However, this is the wrong answer, because it ignores issues of falsity revolving around the fact that only *one* of the premises is true. If there were an ace in the hand, then premises (1) and (2) would both be true, which is inconsistent with the requirement that only one premise is true. Thus, the participants' over-emphasis on the principle of truth caused nearly all of them to produce faulty reasoning. According to Johnson-Laird (1999), the faulty reasoning shown on this problem cannot be predicted within the abstract-rule approach.

Evaluation

The mental model theory has a number of significant strengths. First, it provides an account of reasoning performance across a very wide range of problems including (but not limited to) conditional reasoning and syllogistic reasoning. Second, most of the predictions of the theory have been confirmed experimentally. Third, the notion that reasoning involves very similar processes to normal comprehension is a powerful one, and a convincing alternative to the view that we possess a mental logic. It is an important notion, because it suggests that the artificial problems used in most studies on reasoning may be less detached from everyday life than might appear to be the case. Fourth, the exceptionally poor reasoning performance found by Johnson-Laird and Goldvarg (1997) was predicted by the mental model theory, but is hard to account for on abstract rule theories.

The mental model approach possesses several limitations. First, the processes involved in forming mental models are underspecified. Johnson-Laird and Byrne (1991) argued that people make use of background knowledge when forming mental models. However, the theory does not spell out how we decide whether any given piece of information should, or should not, be included in a mental model.

Second, the number of mental models that people will construct when solving a reasoning problem is often hard to work out (Bonatti, 1994). However, Johnson-Laird and Savary (1996) produced a computer program, which is claimed to generate automatically the appropriate number of mental models for every set of premises.

Third, the theory de-emphasises individual differences. Consider a study by Sternberg and Weil (1980). They used syllogistic reasoning problems of the following type: Tom is taller than Dick; Harry is taller than Tom; Who is the tallest? Some participants used a mental model strategy based on imagery or spatial relationships, others used a deduction rule strategy based on verbal or linguistic processing, and a majority used a mixture of both strategies. Such varied use of strategies cannot readily be accommodated by the mental model approach.

Fourth, O'Brien, Braine, and Yang (1994) claimed to have disproved the mental model approach. They argued that the approach predicts that deductions depending on numerous models should be very difficult to make. However, they identified cases in which the prediction was falsified. One problem they used was as follows:

If O or K or R or C, then X
If E or F or G or H, then Y
K
F

What follows? All the participants gave the correct answer of X and Y, in spite of the fact that there are about 58 mental models that can be formed for this problem, with up to 15 needing to be considered at the same time.

Johnson-Laird, Bryne, and Schaeken (1994) countered by pointing out that the participants would not generate dozens of unnecessary mental models on a problem like this. However, O'Brien et al. (1994) have identified a weakness in the mental model approach, because it is very hard to know precisely how many mental models the participants did create.

Inductive reasoning

As we saw earlier in the chapter, inductive reasoning involves making a generalised conclusion from premises that refer to particular instances. One of the key features of inductive reasoning is that the conclusions of inductively valid arguments are probably (but not necessarily) true. Consider, for example, the premise, "Every relevant experiment has found that learning depends on reward or reinforcement." We might use that information to draw the general conclusion, "Learning always depends on reward or reinforcement." This conclusion may seem reasonable. However, it is possible that future experiments might reveal that there are circumstances in which learning can occur in the absence of reward.

Hypothesis testing: Relational rule

An inductive reasoning task that has attracted much interest was devised by Peter Wason (1960). He told his participants that the three numbers 2 4 6 conformed to a simple relational rule. Their task was to generate sets of three numbers, and to provide reasons for each choice. After each choice, the experimenter indicated whether or not the set of numbers conformed to the rule the experimenter had in mind. The task was simply to discover the nature of the rule. The rule was apparently very simple: "Three numbers in ascending order of magnitude." However, it took most participants a long time to produce the rule, and only 21% of them were correct with their first attempt to state the rule.

Why was performance so poor on Wason's relational rule problem? According to Wason (1960), the participants showed *confirmation bias*, meaning that they tried to generate sets of numbers that would confirm their original hypothesis. For example, participants whose original hypothesis or rule was that the second number is twice the first, and the third number is three times the first number tended to generate sets of numbers consistent with that hypothesis (e.g., 6 12 18; 50 100 150). It was this confirmation bias and failure to try hypothesis disconfirmation that prevented the participants from replacing their initial hypothesis, which was too narrow and specific, with the correct general rule.

Tweney et al. (1980) found a way of reducing people's reliance on confirmation bias with the relational rule problem. Their participants were told that the experimenter had two rules in mind, and it was their task to identify these rules. One of these rules generated DAX triples, whereas the other rule generated MED triples. They were also told that 2 4 6 was a DAX triple. Whenever the participants generated a set of three numbers, they were informed whether the set fitted the DAX rule or the MED rule. The correct answer was that the DAX rule was any three numbers in ascending order, and the MED rule covered any other set of numbers.

What did Tweney et al. (1980) find? Over 50% of the participants produced the correct answer on their first attempt. The reason for this high level of success was that the participants did not have to focus on disconfirmation of hypotheses. They could identify the DAX rule by confirming the MED rule, and so they did not have to try to disconfirm the DAX rule.

Evaluation

Wason (1968) argued that there were important similarities between the behaviour of participants on his task and that of scientists engaged in testing a hypothesis. More specifically, he claimed that scientists generally design experiments to confirm an existing hypothesis. He then went on to argue that this is not a good strategy, because scientific hypotheses cannot be confirmed conclusively. Karl Popper (1972), the philosopher of science, proposed that the distinguishing characteristic of a scientific theory is falsifiability, meaning that such a theory can potentially be falsified or disconfirmed.

Klayman and Ha (1987) argued that the participants in Wason's studies were trying to produce positive tests of their hypotheses rather than trying to confirm their hypotheses as Wason had claimed. Positive tests involve seeing whether sets of numbers consistent with their hypothesis conform or fail to conform to the relational rule. In contrast, negative tests involve seeing whether sets of numbers inconsistent with their hypothesis conform to the relational rule. Klayman and Ha (1987) showed that the positive test strategy can be more effective than the negative test strategy. For example, it is more likely to produce falsifying results when relatively few number sequences match the relational rule. However, in the unusual conditions used by Wason (1968), numerous number sequences match the rule, and so negative testing is needed in order to produce falsifying results.

Hypothesis testing: Simulated research environments

Mynatt, Doherty, and Tweney (1977) decided to investigate some of the issues raised by Wason's (1968) research in a set-up designed to simulate a real research environment. The participants were presented with computer-generated displays containing several shapes varying in brightness. There was a particle that could be fired across the screen, and which was stopped when it came close to some objects but not others. The participants' task was to think of a hypothesis to explain the behaviour of the particle. The correct hypothesis was that the particle was stopped when it came close to dim objects. However, the participants' initial experience of the task led most of them to form the hypothesis that object shape played a part in determining whether the particle stopped.

The key part of the Mynatt et al. (1977) study was to see which of two environments the participants chose following their initial experience:

(1) An environment in which their observations would probably confirm their initial incorrect hypothesis.
(2) An environment in which other hypotheses could be tested.

Mynatt et al. (1977) found that their participants tended to choose the first environment, thus providing evidence for a confirmation bias. However, those participants who obtained information that falsified their original hypothesis tended to reject it rather than stubbornly sticking to it.

Dunbar (1993) also made use of a simulated research environment. The participants were given the difficult task of providing an explanation for the ways in which genes are controlled by other genes using a computer-based molecular genetics laboratory. The difficulty of the task can be seen in the fact that solving this problem in real life had led to the award of the Nobel prize! The participants were led to focus on the hypothesis that the gene control was by activation, whereas it was actually by inhibition.

Dunbar (1993) found that those participants who simply tried to find data consistent with their activation hypothesis failed to solve the problem. In contrast, the 20% of the participants who did solve the problem set themselves the goal of trying to explain the discrepant findings. According to the participants' own reports, most of them started with the general hypothesis that activation was the key controlling process. They then applied this hypothesis in specific ways, focusing on one gene after another as the potential activator. It was typically only when all the various specific activation hypotheses had been disconfirmed that some participants focused on explaining the data that did not fit the general activation hypothesis.

How closely do the findings in simulated research environments resemble those in real research environments? Mitroff (1974) studied the attitudes of geologists who were involved in the Apollo space programme as experts in lunar geology. They devoted most of their time to trying to confirm rather than falsify their hypotheses, but they were not opposed to the notion of falsifying the hypotheses of other scientists. Their focus on confirmation rather than falsification resembles that found in participants in simulated research environments. However, the real scientists seemed more reluctant than the participants in simulated research studies to abandon their hypotheses. There are probably two main reasons for this. First, the real scientists emphasised the value of commitment to a given position as a motivating factor. Second, real scientists are more likely than participants in an experiment to attribute contrary findings to deficiencies in the measuring instruments.

How flawed is human reasoning?

We have seen in this chapter that people often make mistakes when trying to solve problems in deductive or inductive reasoning. However, there seems to be something paradoxical about these findings. As Evans and Over (1997, p. 403) pointed out, "The human species is the most intelligent on earth and has the most remarkable cognitive abilities . . . Our abilities in thinking and problem solving have allowed us to adapt the environment to suit ourselves." In view of our intelligence and abilities, how is it that we often fail miserably to solve reasoning and other problems in the laboratory?

Evans and Over (1997) answered the above question by distinguishing between two types of rationality: $rationality_1$ and $rationality_2$. According to Evans and Over (1997, p. 403), people have personal rationality or $rationality_1$ "when they are generally successful in achieving their basic goals, to do with keeping themselves alive, finding their way in the world, and communicating with each other." This form of rationality depends on an implicit cognitive system operating at an unconscious level. It is our possession of $rationality_1$ that permits us to cope successfully with everyday life.

In contrast, people display impersonal rationality or $rationality_2$ when "they act with good reasons sanctioned by a normative theory such as formal logic or probability theory" (Evans & Over, 1997, p. 403). This form of rationality depends on an explicit cognitive system operating at a conscious level; it also differs from $rationality_1$ in that it allows us to think in a hypothetical way about the future. Laboratory research has focused on $rationality_2$, which can be error prone even when $rationality_1$ is not.

How useful is the distinction between rationality₁ and rationality₂? According to Johnson-Laird (1999, p. 112), "The strong point of the dichotomy [division into two parts] is that it makes sense of both competence and incompetence in life and the laboratory. Its weakness is that it may accommodate too much." Another problem is that Evans and Over (1997) have described two forms of rationality, but have not provided an explanatory account of human rationality.

Oaksford (1997) also argued that people's reasoning powers are more rational than might initially appear to be the case. He pointed out that there are important differences between reasoning in the real world and in the laboratory. People often have to make decisions on the basis of very incomplete information, but this is not typically the case in laboratory studies. There are other situations in the real world in which people are exposed to a considerable amount of redundant or unnecessary information, and this is also not true of most laboratory studies. As a result, people have developed reasoning strategies that work reasonably well in everyday life, but may not do so in the laboratory. As Oaksford (1997, p. 260) argued, "Many of the errors and biases seen in people's reasoning are likely to be the result of importing their everyday probabilistic strategies into the lab."

Johnson-Laird's mental model theory is an example of an approach based on the assumption that processes used in everyday life are applied to laboratory reasoning problems. More specifically, it is assumed that the processes typically involved in language comprehension are used on reasoning problems, and that these processes often fail to provide a complete representation of such problems. The success of this theoretical approach suggests that people often import their everyday thinking and reasoning strategies into the laboratory.

Summary: Reasoning

- *Introduction*: Deductive reasoning allows us to draw definite conclusions provided that other statements are assumed to be true, whereas the conclusions drawn in inductive reasoning are not necessarily true. Evidence from brain-damaged patients and from neuroimaging studies on normal individuals indicates that the prefrontal cortex (especially the dorsolateral region) is of major importance in all forms of reasoning. The prefrontal cortex is important in relational integration, which is crucial to reasoning, and may be a prime function of the central executive component of the working memory system.

- *Analogical reasoning*: Performance on analogical reasoning tasks often correlates highly with IQ. People are less likely to use analogical thinking when there are superficial differences between the current problem and relevant information in long-term memory. LISA is a computer simulation that emphasises the processes involved in analogical access and mapping, and which can produce most of the main phenomena of analogical reasoning. The use of analogies in the laboratory typically allows problems to be solved with complete success, whereas in everyday life matters are usually more complex.

- *Deductive reasoning*: Many errors are made in conditional reasoning, especially on the Wason selection task. According to social contract theory, performance on the Wason task should be better when it focuses on cheating than when it does not. According to the optimal data selection model, people's apparently faulty reasoning on the Wason task may actually be effective and useful in everyday life. There is some evidence that people try to maximise the information gain from each choice. Syllogistic reasoning is often faulty because of belief bias and conversion errors. However, accounts focusing on biases and errors provide a description rather than an explanation.

- *Theories of deductive reasoning*: According to abstract-rule theories, people use a mental logic when dealing with a reasoning task. Invalid inferences occur when people misunderstand or misrepresent a reasoning task. According to the mental model theory, reasoning uses very similar processes to those involved in language comprehension. People construct mental models of the premises of a reasoning task, and then they use these mental models to decide whether the conclusion is valid or invalid. There are two main reasons why the full set of possible mental models is often not formed: (1) the construction of mental models involves the limited processing resources of working memory; and (2) there is a tendency to construct mental models that represent what is true but not what is false. There is evidence supporting both theories. However, the mental model approach accounts for performance

on a wider range of reasoning problems, and it successfully predicts the exceptionally poor performance found
when falsity needs to be considered.

- *Inductive reasoning*: Wason devised an inductive reasoning
task based on a simple relational rule. Performance was
surprisingly poor on this task, and Wason argued that this
was due to a confirmation bias. He also argued that
scientists often mistakenly use the same bias in their
research. There is evidence that participants use a positive
test strategy rather than confirmation bias, and that a
positive test strategy is often more effective than a negative test strategy. Findings resembling those with Wason's
relational rule task have been obtained in simulated
research environments, and there is evidence that real
scientists focus on confirmation rather than falsification of
hypotheses.

- *How flawed is human reasoning?*: There is an apparent
contradiction between our ability to deal effectively with
our everyday environment, and our failure to perform
well on many laboratory reasoning tasks. One possible
explanation is that there are two types of rationality:
personal rationality or rationality$_1$, which permits us to
cope successfully with everyday life; and impersonal
rationality or rationality$_2$, which is based on some form of
logic, and which is required on most laboratory reasoning
problems. An alternative position, exemplified by the
mental model approach, is that people use their everyday
thinking and reasoning strategies when confronted by
reasoning problems in the laboratory.

Essay questions

(1) What factors determine how analogical thinking is used to
solve problems?
(2) Why is performance generally so poor on the Wason selection
task?
(3) "The mental model approach provides a complete account of
deductive reasoning." Discuss.
(4) What is the relational rule problem? Why do most people take
so long to solve this problem?

Further reading

Eysenck, M.W., & Keane, M.T. (2000). *Cognitive psychology: A student's handbook* (4th ed.). Hove, UK: Psychology Press. Nearly all the topics discussed in this chapter are discussed more fully in this book.

Gilhooly, K.J. (1996). *Thinking: Directed, undirected and creative*. London: Academic Press. Several of the topics dealt with in this chapter are discussed in an accessible way in this book.

Johnson-Laird, P.N. (1999). Deductive reasoning. *Annual Review of Psychology, 50*, 109–135. This article contains a good account of major theoretical approaches to deductive reasoning.

Glossary

accommodation: adjustment in the shape of the lens of the eye when focusing on objects; cue used in depth perception

achromatopsia: a brain-damaged condition in which there is little or no colour perception, but form and motion perception are sometimes intact

action slips: actions that are not carried out as intended

affordances: the potential uses of an object, which Gibson claimed are directly perceived

agrammatism: a condition in which speech productions lack grammatical structure and many function words and word endings are omitted

akinetopsia: a brain-damaged condition in which objects in motion cannot be perceived, whereas stationary objects are perceived fairly normally

alexia: a condition in which there are great problems with reading even though speech is understood

algorithms: methods or procedures that will definitely solve a problem; see Heuristics

Alzheimer's disease: a disease involving progressive dementia or loss of mental powers

amnesia: a condition produced by brain damage in which there are major problems with long-term memory

analogical thinking: a form of thinking that involves the detection of similarities between the current problem and previous problems

anaphora: the use of a pronoun or noun to represent some previously mentioned noun or noun phrase

anomia: a condition in which the patient has great difficulty in naming objects

anterograde amnesia: reduced ability to remember information acquired after the onset of amnesia

apperceptive agnosia: a form of visual agnosia in which there is impaired perceptual analysis of familiar objects

articulatory loop: see Phonological loop, which is the revised name for the articulatory loop

associative agnosia: a form of visual agnosia in which perceptual processing is fairly normal but there is an impaired ability to derive the meaning of objects

atmosphere effect: the tendency to accept a conclusion if its form is consistent with the form of the premises (e.g., use of the word "all")

auditory phonological agnosia: a condition in which there is poor perception of unfamiliar words and non-words, but not familiar words

availability heuristic: a rule of thumb based on estimating event frequencies from ease of retrieval of relevant information

back-propagation: a learning mechanism in connectionist networks, in which the actual outputs of the system are compared against the correct outputs

Balint's syndrome: a brain-damaged condition in which some patients find it hard to shift visual attention

base-rate information: the relative frequency of an event within a population

belief bias: the tendency to decide whether the conclusion of a syllogism is valid on the basis of whether or not it is believable

binocular cues: cues to depth that require both eyes to be used together

binocular disparity: the slightly different images of a visual scene that are present in the retinas of the two eyes

blindsight: the ability to respond appropriately to visual stimuli in the absence of conscious vision in patients with damage to the primary visual cortex

bottom-up processing: processing that is determined directly by an external stimulus rather than by an individual's knowledge and expectations

bridging inferences: inferences which are drawn to increase the coherence between the current and preceding parts of a text

categorical speech perception: classification of ambiguous speech sounds as representing specific phonemes in an all-or-none way

category-specific agnosia: a condition in which there is selective impairment in recognition of objects belonging to a certain category or categories

central executive: a modality-free, limited capacity, component of working memory

centre of moment: the reference point in the upper body around which the shoulders and hips swing

chromatic adaptation: reduced sensitivity to light of a given colour after lengthy exposure

chunks: a stored unit formed from integrating smaller pieces of information

co-articulation: slight distortion in speech when the production of one speech segment is influenced by the production of the previous speech segment

cognitive neuropsychology: an approach to cognitive psychology based on the study of brain-damaged patients

cognitive neuroscience: an approach to cognitive psychology based on the use of various techniques (e.g., brain scans) to study the brain directly

cognitive science: an approach to cognitive psychology based on the construction of computational models

colour constancy: the tendency for any given object to be perceived as having the same colour under widely varying viewing conditions

composition: the process in the ACT model that eliminates unnecessary production rules in skill acquisition

confirmation bias: memory that is distorted by being influenced by the individual's expectations rather than what actually happened; in reasoning, it refers to a greater focus on evidence that confirms one's hypothesis than on disconfirming evidence

conjunction fallacy: the mistaken belief that it is more likely that two events will occur in combination than that one of the events will occur

connectionist networks: they consist of elementary units or nodes that are connected together; each network has various structures or layers (e.g., input, intermediate or hidden, output)

convergence: a cue to depth based on the fact that the eye turn inwards more when focusing on an object that is very close

conversion error: a mistake in syllogistic reasoning occurring because a statement is invalidly converted from one form into another

covert attention: a shift in the focus of attention in the absence of an eye movement

critical period hypothesis: the assumption that language learning depends on biological maturation, and is easier to accomplish prior to puberty

cue-dependent forgetting: forgetting that occurs because of the lack of a suitable retrieval cue; see Trace-dependent forgetting

dark adaptation: the progressive increase in visual sensitivity in darkness following exposure to light

declarative memory: a form of memory resembling explicit memory and based on relationships among different kinds of information; see Procedural memory

deductive reasoning: a process of thought producing valid conclusions that are necessarily true given that their premises are true

deep dyslexia: a condition in which reading of unfamiliar words is impaired, and there are semantic reading errors (e.g., reading "missile" as "rocket")

deep dysphasia: a condition involving poor ability to repeat spoken non-words and semantic errors in repeating spoken words

dichotic listening task: a task in which pairs of auditorily presented items are presented one to each ear, followed by recall of all items

discourse: connected text or speech

divided attention: an experimental situation in which participants try to perform two tasks at the same time; see Dual-task studies

dominance principle: in decision making, the notion that the better of two similar options will be preferred

double dissociation: the finding that some individuals (often brain damaged) do well on task A and poorly on task B, whereas others show the opposite pattern

dual-task studies: studies in which participants perform two tasks together; see Divided attention

dysexecutive syndrome: a condition in which damage to the frontal lobes causes impairments to the central executive component of working memory

echoic store: a sensory store in the auditory modality that can hold information for about 2 seconds

ecological validity: the extent to which the findings of laboratory studies are applicable to everyday settings

elaborated code: a complex, abstract, and context-free form of language production

elaborative inferences: inferences that add details to a text that is being read

elaborative rehearsal: rehearsal in which there is deeper or more semantic analysis of the learning material; see Maintenance rehearsal

encoding specificity principle: the notion that remembering depends on the amount of overlap between the information in the memory trace and the information in the retrieval environment

event-related potentials (ERPs): regularities produced in the brain-wave or electroencephalograph record produced by repeated presentations of stimuli

experimental cognitive psychology: an approach to cognitive psychology in which experiments on normals are carried out, mostly under laboratory conditions

explicit memory: memory that depends on conscious recollection; see Implicit memory

extinction: a disorder of visual attention in which a stimulus presented to the neglected side of the visual field is not detected when another stimulus is presented at the same time

extrinsic context: context which does not affect the meaning of to-be-remembered information; see Intrinsic context

face inversion effect: the finding that faces that are inverted (turned upside down) are harder to recognise than faces viewed in their normal orientation

figure–ground organisation: the perception of a scene as consisting of an object or figure standing out from a less distinct background or ground

flashbulb memories: vivid and detailed memories of dramatic events

focus of expansion: this is the point towards which someone who is in motion is moving; it is the only part of the visual field that does not appear to move

focused attention: an experimental situation in which participants try to attend to only one source of stimulation while ignoring other stimuli

framing: the influence of irrelevant aspects of a situation on decision making

free recall: a form of memory test in which the participants retrieve the to-be-remembered items in any order

functional fixedness: a limitation in problem solving in which participants focus only on likely functions or uses of objects while ignoring other, more unusual, uses

grammatical morphemes: modifiers (e.g., prefixes, suffixes, prepositions) that modify meaning

habituation: the gradual reduction in the amount of attention paid to a stimulus that is presented repeatedly

heuristics: rules of thumb or approximate methods that are used in problem solving; see Algorithms

holophrastic period: a stage of speech development in which infants produce meaningful one-word utterances

iconic store: a sensory store in the visual modality that can hold information for about half a second

implicit learning: learning complex information without the ability to provide conscious recollection of what has been learned

implicit memory: memory that does not depend on conscious recollection; see Explicit memory

inductive reasoning: a form of reasoning in which a generalised conclusion is drawn from specific information

inner scribe: according to Logie, the part of the visuo-spatial sketchpad which deals with spatial and movement information

insight: the sudden restructuring of a problem to produce a solution

integrative agnosia: impaired object recognition due to problems in integrating or combining elements of objects

interposition: a cue to depth based on a closer object hiding part of a more distant one

intrinsic context: context that influences the meaning of to-be-remembered information; see Extrinsic context

isomorphism: the Gestalt notion that the perception of an object involves brain activity that is organised spatially in the same way as the object itself

jargon aphasia: a brain-damaged condition in which speech is reasonably correct grammatically, but there are great problems in finding the right words

knowledge compilation: the shift from knowledge stored in declarative memory to knowledge in procedural memory during skill acquisition

Korsakoff's syndrome: severe memory problems with long-term memory (amnesia) produced by chronic alcoholism

language acquisition device: an innate knowledge of grammatical structure

lateral inhibition: the tendency of receptor cells to inhibit each other; it forms the basis of simultaneous contrast

lemma selection: selection of an abstract word at an early stage of speech production

lexical access: processes involved in entering the lexicon

lexical decision task: a task in which participants have to decide whether letter strings form words

lexicalisation: the process of translating the meaning of a word into its sound representation during speech production

lexicon: the range of knowledge possessed about words, including their meaning, spelling, pronunciation, and grammatical roles

linear perspective: a cue to depth based on the convergence of parallel lines in two-dimensional representations

linguistic universals: features that are common to virtually every language

loss aversion: the tendency to be more sensitive to potential losses than to potential gains

Mach bands: illusory stripes in which the brighter of two adjacent columns appears brighter than it actually is, whereas the darker column appears darker than it is

magnetic resonance imaging (MRI and fMRI): a technique based on the detection of magnetic changes within the brain; MRI provides information about the structure of the brain, and fMRI provides information about brain activity and processes

magneto-encephalography (MEG): a non-invasive brain-scanning technique based on recording the magnetic fields generated by brain activity

maintenance rehearsal: rehearsal in which analyses previously performed are repeated; see Elaborative rehearsal

means–ends analysis: an approach to problem solving in which the difference between the current position and the goal position is reduced

mental model: a representation of a possible state of affairs; used especially with reference to Deductive reasoning

meta-analysis: statistical analyses based on combining data from numerous studies on a given issue

microspectrophotometry: a technique which allows measurement of the amount of light absorbed at various wavelengths by individual cone receptors

modules: independent or separate processors within the cognitive system

monocular cues: cues to depth that can be used with one eye, but can also be used with both eyes

motherese: the short, simple sentences used by mothers when talking to their young children

motion parallax: a cue to depth based on the tendency of images of closer objects to move faster across the retina than do images of more distant objects

naming task: a task in which words have to be spoken as rapidly as possible

negative afterimage: the illusory perception of the complementary colour to the one that has just been fixated for several seconds (e.g., green is the complementary colour to red)

negative priming: slowed processing of a stimulus when it was used as a distracting stimulus on the previous trial

oculomotor cues: kinaesthetic cues to depth based on sensations produced by muscular contraction of the muscles around the eye

omission bias: the tendency to prefer inaction over action when engaged in decision making

operant conditioning: a form of learning in which rewarded responses are produced more frequently and punished responses are produced less frequently

optic aphasia: a condition in which there is a severe impairment in the ability to name visually presented objects even though their use can be mimed

optic array: the structured pattern of light falling on the retina

optic ataxia: a condition in which there are problems with making visually guided limb movements

optic flow pattern: the structured pattern of light intensity created when there is movement of the observer and/or aspects of the environment

orthography: information about the spellings of words

over-regularisation: using a grammatical rule in situations in which it does not apply

parallel processing: two or more cognitive processes occurring at the same time; see Serial processing

pattern recognition: identification or classification of visually presented two- and three-dimensional objects

phonemes: basic speech sounds conveying meaning

phonemic restoration effect: the finding that listeners are unaware that a phoneme has been deleted from an auditorily presented sentence

phonological dyslexia: a condition in which familiar words can be read but there is impaired ability to read unfamiliar words and non-words

phonological loop: a component of working memory, in which speech-based information is held and subvocal articulation occurs

phonology: information about the sounds of words and parts of words

positron emission tomography: a brain-scanning technique that possesses reasonable spatial resolution but poor temporal resolution

primacy effect: the finding that free recall for the first few items in a word list is better than for items in the middle of the list

primal sketch: the initial representation formed during perceptual processing; it contains information about basic features such as edges and contours

proactive interference: disruption of memory by previous learning, often of similar material; see Retroactive interference

proceduralisation: the processes involved in converting declarative knowledge into procedural knowledge

procedural memory: a form of memory resembling implicit memory, and based on specific information; see Declarative memory

productive problem solving: problem solving in which the problem is restructured in some way; see Reproductive problem solving

prosodic cues: features of spoken language such as stress and intonation

prosopagnosia: a condition caused by brain damage in which the patient cannot recognise familiar faces but can recognise familiar objects

psychological refractory period: the slowing of response to the second of two stimuli when they are presented close together in time

pure word deafness: a condition in which there is severely impaired speech perception combined with good speech production, reading, writing, and perception of non-speech sounds

rationalisation: in Bartlett's theory, the tendency for story recall to be distorted to conform to the cultural conventions of the rememberer

recency effect: the finding that recall is much higher for the last few list items in immediate free recall than for other items

repetition priming: more efficient processing of a stimulus when it has been presented and processed previously

representativeness heuristic: the assumption that representative or typical members of a category are encountered most frequently

repression: motivated forgetting of traumatic or other threatening events

repressors: normal individuals who are low in trait anxiety and high in defensiveness

reproductive problem solving: problem solving in which previous experience is used directly to solve a current problem; see Productive problem solving

resonance: the process of automatic pick-up of visual information from the environment in Gibson's theory

restricted code: a relatively concrete and context-bound form of language production; see Elaborated code

retrieval failure: forgetting that is due to an inability to gain access to stored information

retroactive interference: disruption of memory by learning of other material during the retention interval; see Proactive interference

retrograde amnesia: impaired memory for events occurring before the onset of amnesia

risk aversion: a tendency to avoid risk, which is especially likely to be found when people are considering possible gains

risk seeking: a tendency to seek out risk, which is especially likely to be found when people are considering possible losses

saccades: rapid, jerky eye movements

schemas: integrated chunks of knowledge stored in long-term memory; alternatively, within theories of attention, organised plans serve to influence action

semantic priming effect: the finding that word identification is facilitated when there is priming by a semantically related word

sensory buffer: it contains information for a short period of time before it is processed

serial processing: processing in which one process is completed before the next process starts; see Parallel processing

shadowing task: a task in which there are two auditory messages, and one of them has to be shadowed or repeated back aloud

shape constancy: objects are perceived to have a given shape regardless of the angle from which they are viewed

shaping: a version of operant conditioning in which responses need to become closer and closer to the correct response in order to be rewarded

short-term store: a memory store of very limited capacity that holds information for a few seconds

simultanagnosia: a condition in which only one object at a time can be seen

simultaneous contrast: a tendency to exaggerate the difference in lightness between two adjacent areas

sinusoidal gratings: patterns of alternating dark and light bars in which there are gradual intensity changes between bars

size constancy: objects are perceived to have a given size regardless of the size of the retinal image

source amnesia: retention of a fact combined with an inability to remember where or how the fact was learned

specific language impairment: a condition in children in which language ability is far below non-verbal intelligence

stereopsis: a cue to depth based on binocular disparity

story grammar: a set of rules permitting the structure of any story to be generated

Stroop effect: interference effect created when the colours in which words are printed have to be named rapidly, and the words are themselves conflicting colour names

subliminal perception: perceptual processes occurring below the level of conscious awareness

surface dyslexia: a condition in which regular words can be read but there is impaired ability to read irregular words

telegraphic period: a stage of language development in which children's speech is abbreviated like a telegram

3-D model representation: a representation formed during perceptual processing; it is independent of the viewer's viewpoint

top-down processing: processing that is affected by an individual's knowledge and expectations; see Bottom-up processing

trace-dependent forgetting: forgetting due to decay or loss of memory traces

transformational grammar: grammatical rules that guide transforming basic statements into negative statements, questions, and so on

trial-and-error learning: a type of problem solving in which the solution is reached by producing fairly random responses rather than by a process of thought

2½-D sketch: a viewer-centred representation formed during perceptual processing; it includes information about depth and orientation

unilateral neglect: a condition produced by brain damage in which stimuli presented to one side of space are not responded to

visual agnosia: an impairment of visual object recognition in brain-damaged individuals who possess basic visual abilities and reasonable knowledge about objects

visual cache: according to Logie, the part of the visuo-spatial sketchpad which stores information about visual form and colour

visual search: a task in which a target item presented together with distractor items must be detected as rapidly as possible

visuospatial sketchpad: a component of working memory that is involved in visual and spatial processing of information

weapon focus: a phenomenon in which eyewitnesses attend closely to the criminal's weapon and so are unable to recall other information about the criminal and the environment

Whorfian hypothesis: the notion that language determines or influences the ways in which we think

word meaning deafness: a condition in which heard words can be repeated even though their meaning is often not understood

word superiority effect: the phenomenon that a letter is easier to detect when embedded in a word than a non-word

working memory: according to Baddeley, a system consisting of three components: central executive, phonological loop, and visuospatial sketchpad; also used more generally to refer to a general-purpose limited capacity system by other theorists

References

Abramov, I., & Gordon, J. (1994). Colour appearance: On seeing red, or yellow, or green, or blue. *Annual Review of Psychology, 45*, 451–485.

Aggleton, J.P., & Brown, M.W. (1999). Episodic memory, amnesia, and the hippocampal–anterior thalamic axis. *Behavioral and Brain Sciences, 22*, 425–489.

Aglioti, S., Goodale, M.A., & DeSouza, J.F.X. (1995). Size-contrast illusions deceive the eye but not the hand. *Current Biology, 5*, 679–685.

Allbritton, D.W., McKoon, G., & Ratcliff, R. (1996). Reliability of prosodic cues for resolving syntactic ambiguity. *Journal of Experimental Psychology: Learning, Memory, and Cognition, 22*, 714–735.

Allen, B.P., & Lindsay, D.S. (1998). Amalgamations of memories: Intrusion of information from one event into reports of another. *Applied Cognitive Psychology, 12*, 277–285.

Allport, D.A. (1989). Visual attention. In M.I. Posner (Ed.), *Foundations of cognitive science*. Cambridge, MA: MIT Press.

Allport, D.A., Antonis, B., & Reynolds, P. (1972). On the division of attention: A disproof of the single channel hypothesis. *Quarterly Journal of Experimental Psychology, 24*, 225–235.

Allport, G.W., & Pettigrew, T.F. (1957). Cultural influences on the perception of movement: The trapezoidal illusion among Zulus. *Journal of Abnormal and Social Psychology, 55*, 104–113.

Anderson, J.R. (1983). *The architecture of cognition*. Cambridge, MA: Harvard University Press.

Anderson, J.R. (1993). *Rules of the mind*. Hillsdale, NJ: Lawrence Erlbaum Associates Inc.

Anderson, J.R. (1996). ACT: A simple theory of cognition. *American Psychologist, 51*, 355–365.

Anderson, R.C., & Pichert, J.W. (1978). Recall of previously unrecallable information following a shift in perspective. *Journal of Verbal Learning & Verbal Behavior, 17*, 1–12.

Anderson, S.J., Holliday, I.E., Singh, K.D., & Harding, G.F.A. (1996). Localization and functional analysis of human cortical area V5 using magneto-encephalography. *Proceedings of the Royal Society London B, 263*, 423–431.

Andrews, B., Brewin, C.R., Ochera, J., Morton, J., Bekerian, D.A., Davies, G.M., & Mollon, P. (1999). The timing, triggers and qualities of recovered memories in therapy. *British Journal of Psychiatry, 175*, 141–146.

Annis, R.C., & Frost, B. (1973). Human visual ecology and orientation anisotropies in acuity. *Science, 182*, 729–741.

Anzai, Y., & Simon, H.A. (1979). The theory of learning by doing. *Psychological Review, 86*, 124–180.

Arterberry, M., Yonas, A., & Bensen, A.S. (1989). Self-produced locomotion and the development of responsiveness to linear perspective and texture gradients. *Developmental Psychology, 25*, 976–982.

Ashley, W.R., Harper, R.S., & Runyon,

D.L. (1951). The perceived size of coins in normal and hypnotically induced economic states. *American Journal of Psychology, 64*, 564–572.

Atkinson, J., & Braddick, O. (1981). *Acuity, contrast sensitivity, and accommodation in infancy*. New York: Academic Press.

Atkinson, R.C., & Shiffrin, R.M. (1968). Human memory: A proposed system and its control processes. In K.W. Spence & J.T. Spence (Eds.), *The psychology of learning and motivation* (Vol. 2). London: Academic Press.

Atkinson, R.L., Atkinson, R.C., Smith, E.E., & Bem, D.J. (1993). *Introduction to psychology* (11th. ed.). New York: Harcourt Brace.

Auerbach, S.H., Allard, T., Naeser, M., Alexander, M.P., & Albert, M.L. (1982). Pure word deafness: An analysis of a case with bilateral lesions and a defect at the prephonemic level. *Brain, 105*, 271–300.

Baars, B.J., Motley, M.T., & MacKay, D.G. (1975). Output editing for lexical status from artificially elicited slips of the tongue. *Journal of Verbal Learning and Verbal Behavior, 14*, 382–391.

Baddeley, A.D. (1982). Domains of recollection. *Psychological Review, 89*, 708–729.

Baddeley, A.D. (1986). *Working memory*. Oxford: Oxford University Press.

Baddeley, A.D. (1990). *Human memory: Theory and practice*. Hove, UK: Psychology Press.

Baddeley, A.D. (1996). Exploring the central executive. *Quarterly Journal of Experimental Psychology, 49A*, 5–28.

Baddeley, A.D. (1997). *Human memory: Theory and practice* (rev. ed.). Hove, UK: Psychology Press.

Baddeley, A.D., Emslie, H., Kolodny, J., & Duncan, J. (1998). Random generation and the executive control of working memory. *Quarterly Journal of Experimental Psychology, 51A*, 819–852.

Baddeley, A.D., Gathercole, S., & Papagno, C. (1998). The phonological loop as a language learning device. *Psychological Review, 105*, 158–173.

Baddeley, A.D., Thomson, N., & Buchanan, M. (1975). Word length and the structure of short-term memory. *Journal of Verbal Learning and Verbal Behavior, 14*, 575–589.

Baddeley, A.D., & Hitch, G.J. (1974). Working memory. In G.H. Bower (Ed.), *The psychology of learning and motivation* (Vol. 8). London: Academic Press.

Baddeley, A.D., & Lieberman, K. (1980). Spatial working memory. In R.S. Nickerson (Ed.), *Attention & performance* (Vol. VIII). Hillsdale, NJ: Lawrence Erlbaum Associates Inc.

Baker, S.C., Dolan, R.J., & Frith, C.D. (1996). The functional anatomy of logic: A PET study of inferential reasoning. *Neuroimage, 3*, S218.

Balota, D.A., Paul, S., & Spieler, D. (1999). Attentional control of lexical processing pathways during word recognition and reading. In S. Garrod & M.J. Pickering (Eds.), *Language processing*. Hove, UK: Psychology Press.

Banich, M.T. (1997). *Neuropsychology: The neural bases of mental function*. New York: Houghton Mifflin.

Banks, M.S., Aslin, R.N., & Letson, R.D. (1975). Sensitive periods for the development of human binocular vision. *Science, 190*, 675–677.

Bartlett, F.C. (1932). *Remembering*. Cambridge: Cambridge University Press.

Battersby, W.S., Teuber, H.L., & Bender, M.B. (1953). Problem solving behavior in men with frontal or occipital brain injuries. *Journal of Psychology, 35*, 329–351.

Bauer, R.M. (1993). Agnosia. In K.M. Heilman, & E. Valenstein (Eds.), *Clinical Neuropsychology*. New York: Oxford University Press.

Bauer, R.M., & Verfaellie, M. (1988). Electrodermal recognition of familiar but not unfamiliar faces in prosopagnosia. *Brain and Cognition, 8,* 240–252.

Baylis, G.C., & Driver, J. (1992). Visual parsing and response competition: The effects of grouping. *Perception and Psychophysics, 51,* 145–162.

Beales, S.A., & Parkin, A.J. (1984). Context and facial memory: The influence of different processing strategies. *Human Learning: Journal of Practical Research and Applications, 3,* 257–264.

Beauvois, M.-F., & Dérouesné, J. (1979). Phonological alexia: Three dissociations. *Journal of Neurology, Neurosurgery, and Psychiatry, 42,* 1115–1124.

Beauvois, M.-F., Dérouesné, J., & Bastard, V. (1980). *Auditory parallel to phonological alexia.* Paper presented at the Third European Conference of the International Neuropsychological Society, Chianciano, Italy, June.

Beckers, G., & Zeki, S. (1995). The consequences of inactivating areas V1 and V5 on visual motion perception. *Brain, 118,* 49–60.

Begg, I., & Denny, J.P. (1969). Empirical reconciliation of atmosphere and conversion interpretations of syllogistic reasoning errors. *Journal of Experimental Psychology, 81,* 351–354.

Behrmann, M., Moscovitch, M., & Winocur, G. (1994). Intact visual imagery and impaired visual perception in a patient with visual agnosia. *Journal of Experimental Psychology: Human Perception and Performance, 20,* 1068–1087.

Behrmann, M., Nelson, J., & Sekuler, E.B. (1998). Visual complexity in letter-by-letter reading: "Pure" alexia is not pure. *Neuropsychologia, 36,* 1115–1132.

Behrmann, M., & Tipper, S.P. (1999). Attention accesses multiple reference frames: Evidence from visual neglect. *Journal of Experimental Psychology:*

Human Perception and Performance, 25, 83–101.

Bell, V.A., & Johnson-Laird, P.N. (1998). A model theory of modal reasoning. *Cognitive Science, 22,* 25–51.

Bergus, G.R., Chapman, G.B., Fjerde, C., & Elstein, A.S. (1995). Clinical reasoning about new symptoms despite preexisting disease: Sources of error and order defects. *Family Medicine, 27,* 314–320.

Berko, J. (1958). The child's learning of English morphology. *Word, 14,* 150–177.

Berndt, R.S., Mitchum, C.C., & Haendiges, A.N. (1996). Comprehension of reversible sentences in "aggrammatism": A meta-analysis. *Cognition, 58,* 289–308.

Bernstein, B. (1961). Social structure, language, and learning. *Educational Research, 3,* 163–176.

Bernstein, B. (1973). *Class, codes and control.* London: Paladin.

Berry, D.C., & Broadbent, D.E. (1984). On the relationship between task performance and associated verbalisable knowledge. *Quarterly Journal of Experimental Psychology, 36A,* 209–231.

Bertamini, M., Yang, T.L., & Proffitt, D.R. (1998). Relative size perception at a distance is best at eye level. *Perception and Psychophysics, 60,* 673–682.

Beschin, N., Cocchini, G., Della Sala, S., & Logie, R.H. (1997). What the eye perceives, the brain ignores: A case of pure unilateral representational neglect. *Cortex, 33,* 3–26.

Bickerton, D. (1984). The language bioprogram hypothesis. *Behavioral and Brain Sciences, 7,* 173–221.

Biederman, I. (1987). Recognition-by-components: A theory of human image understanding. *Psychological Review, 94,* 115–147.

Biederman, I. (1990). Higher-level vision. In D.N. Osherson, S. Kosslyn, & J. Hollerbach (Eds.), *An invitation to* cognitive science: Visual cognition and action. Cambridge, MA: MIT Press.

Biederman, I., & Gerhardstein, P.C. (1993). Recognising depth-rotated objects: Evidence for 3-D viewpoint invariance. *Journal of Experimental Psychology: Human Perception and Performance, 19,* 1162–1182.

Biederman, I., & Ju, G. (1988). Surface versus edge-based determinants of visual recognition. *Cognitive Psychology, 20,* 38–64.

Biederman, I., Ju, G., & Clapper, J. (1985). *The perception of partial objects.* Unpublished manuscript, State University of New York at Buffalo.

Birch, H.G. (1945). The relationship of previous experience to insightful problem solving. *Journal of Comparative Psychology, 38,* 267–383.

Bishop, D.V.M. (1997). *Uncommon understanding: Development and disorders of language comprehension in children.* Hove, UK: Psychology Press.

Bishop, D.V.M., North, T., & Donlan, C. (1996). Nonword repetition as a behavioural marker for inherited language impairment: Evidence from a twin study. *Journal of Child Psychology and Psychiatry, 37,* 391–403.

Bisiach, E., & Luzzatti, C. (1978). Unilateral neglect of representational space. *Cortex, 14,* 129–133.

Bjork, R.A., & Whitten, W.B. (1974). Recency-sensitive retrieval processes in long-term free recall. *Cognitive Psychology, 6,* 173–189.

Blakemore, C., & Cooper, G.G. (1970). Development of the brain depends on the visual environment. *Nature, 228,* 477–478.

Bock, K., & Huitema, J. (1999). Language production. In S. Garrod & M.J. Pickering (Eds.), *Language processing.* Hove, UK: Psychology Press.

Bohannon, J.N. (1988). Flashbulb memories for the Space Shuttle disaster: A tale of two theories. *Cognition, 29,* 179–196.

Bohannon, J.N., & Warren-Leubecker, A. (1989). Theoretical approaches to language acquisition. In J.B. Gleason (Ed.), *The development of language.* Columbus, OH: Merrill.

Bonatti, L. (1994). Propositional reasoning by model? *Psychological Review, 101,* 725–733.

Boomer, D. (1965). Hesitation and grammatical encoding. *Language and Speech, 8,* 145–158.

Bourke, P.A., Duncan, J., & Nimmo-Smith, I. (1996). A general factor involved in dual-task performance decrement. *Quarterly Journal of Experimental Psychology, 49A,* 525–545.

Bouton, M.E., Nelson, J.B., & Rosas, J.M. (1999). Stimulus generalisation, context change, and forgetting. *Psychological Bulletin, 125,* 171–186.

Bower, G.H., Black, J.B., & Turner, T.J. (1979). Scripts in memory for text. *Cognitive Psychology, 11,* 177–220.

Bower, G.H., Thompson-Schill, S., & Tulving, E. (1994). Reducing retroactive interference: An interference analysis. *Journal of Experimental Psychology: Learning, Memory and Cognition, 20,* 51–66.

Bower, T.G.R., Broughton, J.M., & Moore, M.K. (1970). The co-ordination of visual and tactual input in infants. *Perception & Psychophysics, 8,* 51–53.

Braine, M.D.S. (1963). The ontogeny of English phrase structure: The first phase. *Language, 39,* 1–13.

Braine, M.D.S. (1978). On the relation between the natural logic of reasoning and standard logic. *Psychological Review, 85,* 1–21.

Braine, M.D.S. (1994). Mental logic and how to discover it. In J. Macnamara & G.E. Reyes (Eds.), *The logical foundations of cognition.* Oxford: Oxford University Press.

Braine, M.D.S. (1998). Steps towards a

mental predicate logic. In M.D.S. Braine & D.P. O'Brien (Eds.), *Mental logic*. Mahwah, NJ: Lawrence Erlbaum Associates Inc.

Braine, M.D.S., Reiser, B.J., & Rumain, B. (1984). Some empirical justification for a theory of natural propositional logic. *The psychology of learning and motivation* (Vol. 18). New York: Academic Press.

Bramwell, D.I., & Hurlbert, A.C. (1996). Measurements of colour constancy by using a forced-choice matching technique. *Perception, 25*, 229–241.

Bransford, J.D. (1979). *Human cognition: Learning, understanding and remembering*. Belmont, CA: Wadsworth.

Bransford, J.D., Barclay, J.R., & Franks, J.J. (1972). Sentence memory: A constructive versus interpretive approach. *Cognitive Psychology, 3*, 193–209.

Bransford, J.D., Franks, J.J., Morris, C.D., & Stein, B.S. (1979). Some general constraints on learning and memory research. In L.S. Cermak & F.I.M. Craik (Eds.), *Levels of processing in human memory*. Hillsdale, NJ: Lawrence Erlbaum Associates Inc.

Bransford, J.D., & Johnson, M.K. (1972). Contextual prerequisites for understanding. *Journal of Verbal Learning & Verbal Behavior, 11*, 717–726.

Brewin, C.R., Andrews, B., & Gotlib, I.H. (1993). Psychopathology and early experience: A reappraisal of retrospective reports. *Psychological Bulletin, 113*, 82–98.

Broadbent, D.E. (1958). *Perception and communication*. Oxford: Pergamon.

Broadbent, D.E. (1982). Task combination and selective intake of information. *Acta Psychologia, 50*, 253–290.

Brown, N.R. (1995). Estimation strategies and the judgement of event frequency. *Journal of Experimental Psychology: Learning, Memory, & Cognition, 21*, 1539–1553.

Brown, R. (1973). *A first language: The early stages*. London: George Allen & Unwin.

Brown, R., Caxden, C., & Bellugi, U. (1969). The child's grammar from I to III. In J.P. Hill (Ed.), *Minnesota symposium on child psychology* (Vol. 2). Minneapolis, MI: University of Minnesota Press.

Brown, R., & Kulik, J. (1977). Flashbulb memories. *Cognition, 5*, 73–99.

Brown, R., & McNeill, D. (1966). The "tip of the tongue" phenomenon. *Journal of Verbal Learning and Verbal Behavior, 5*, 325–337.

Bruce, V. (1982). Changing faces: Visual and non-visual coding processes in face recognition. *British Journal of Psychology, 73*, 105–116.

Bruce, V., Green, P.R., & Georgeson, M.A. (1996). *Visual perception: Physiology, psychology, and ecology* (3rd ed.). Hove, UK: Psychology Press.

Bruce, V., & Valentine, T. (1986). Semantic priming of familiar faces. *Quarterly Journal of Experimental Psychology, 38A*, 125–150.

Bruce, V., & Valentine, T. (1988). When a nod's as good as a wink: The role of dynamic information in face recognition. In M. Gruneberg, P. Morris, & R. Sykes (Eds.), *Practical aspects of memory: Current research and issues* (Vol. 1). Chichester, UK: John Wiley.

Bruce, V., & Young, A.W. (1986). Understanding face recognition. *British Journal of Psychology, 77*, 305–327.

Bruner, J.S. (1957). On perceptual readiness. *Psychological Review, 64*, 123–152.

Bruner, J.S., & Goodman, C.D. (1947). Value and need as organising factors in perception. *Journal of Abnormal & Social Psychology, 42*, 33–44.

Bruner, J.S., Postman, L., & Rodrigues, J. (1951). Expectations and the perception of colour. *American Journal of Psychology, 64*, 216–227.

Bruno, N., & Cutting, J.E. (1988). Minimodularity and the perception of layout. *Journal of Experimental Psychology: General, 117*, 161–170.

Bub, D., Cancelliere, A., & Kertesz, A. (1985). Whole-word and analytic translation of spelling to sound in a nonsemantic reader. In K.E. Patterson, J.C. Marshall, & M. Coltheart (Eds.), *Surface dyslexia: Neuropsychological and cognitive studies of phonological reading.* Hove, UK: Lawrence Erlbaum Associates Ltd.

Burgess, P.W., & Shallice, T. (1996). Bizarre responses, rule detection and frontal lobe lesion. *Cortex, 32*, 241–260.

Burton, A.M., & Bruce, V. (1993). Naming faces and naming names: Exploring an interactive activation model of person recognition. *Memory, 1*, 457–480.

Burton, A.M., Young, A.W., Bruce, V., Johnston, R.A., & Ellis, A.W. (1991). Understanding covert recognition. *Cognition, 39*, 129–166.

Butler, B.E. (1974). The limits of selective attention in tachistoscopic recognition. *Canadian Journal of Psychology, 28*, 199–213.

Butters, N., & Cermak, L.S. (1980). *Alcoholic Korsakoff's syndrome: An information-processing approach.* London: Academic Press.

Butterworth, G.E., & Cicchetti, D. (1978). Visual calibration of posture in normal and Down's syndrome infants. *Perception, 5*, 155–160.

Byrne, R.M.J. (1989). Suppressing valid inferences with conditionals. *Cognition, 31*, 61–63.

Campbell, F.W., & Robson, J.G. (1968). Application of Fourier analysis to the visibility of gratings. *Journal of Physiology, 197*, 551–566.

Campos, J.J., Hiatt, S., Ramsay, D., Henderson, C., & Svejda, M. (1978). The emergence of fear on the visual cliff. In M. Lewis & L.A. Rosenblum (Eds.), *The development of affect.* New York: Plenum Press.

Caplan, D. (1994). Language and the brain. In M.A. Gernsbacher (Ed.), *Handbook of psycholinguistics.* San Diego, CA: Academic Press.

Carey, D.P., Harvey, M., & Milner, A.D. (1996). Visuomotor sensitivity for shape and orientation in a patient with visual form agnosia. *Neuropsychologia, 34*, 329–338.

Carey, D.P., & Milner, A.D. (1994). Casting one's net too widely? *Behavioral and Brain Sciences, 17*, 65–66.

Casscells, W., Schoenberger, A., & Graboys, T.B. (1978). Interpretation by physicians of clinical laboratory results. *New England Journal of Medicine, 299*, 999–1001.

Cavanaugh, P., Tyler, C.W., & Favreau, O.E. (1984). Perceived velocity of moving chromatic gratings. *Journal of the Optical Society of America A, 1*, 893–899.

Ceci, S.J. (1995). False beliefs: some developmental and clinical considerations. In D.L. Schacter (Ed.), *Memory Distortions.* Cambridge, MA: Harvard University Press.

Ceraso, J., & Provitera, A. (1971). Sources of error in syllogistic reasoning. *Cognitive Psychology, 2*, 400–410.

Cermak, L.S., Talbot, N., Chandler, K., & Wolbarst, L.R. (1985). The perceptual priming phenomenon in amnesia. *Neuropsychologia, 23*, 615–622.

Challis, B.H., & Brodbeck, D.R. (1992). Level of processing affects priming in word fragment completion. *Journal of Experimental Psychology: Human Perception & Performance, 11*, 317–328.

Chapman, J.L., & Chapman, J.P. (1959). Atmosphere effect re-examined. *Journal of Experimental Psychology, 58*, 220–226.

Chase, W.G., & Simon, H.A. (1973). Perception in chess. *Cognitive Psychology, 4*, 55–81.

Chater, N. (1997). Simplicity and the mind. *The Psychologist, 10*, 495–498.

Chater, N., & Oaksford, M. (1999).

Information gain and decision-theoretic approaches to data selection: Response to Klauer (1999). *Psychological Review, 106*, 223–227.

Cheesman, J., & Merikle, P.M. (1984). Priming with and without awareness. *Perception and Psychophysics, 36*, 387–395.

Cheesman, J., & Merikle, P.M. (1985). Word recognition and consciousness. In D. Besner, T.G. Waller, & G.E. McKinnon (Eds.), *Reading research: Advances in theory and in practice.* New York: Academic Press.

Cheng, P.W. (1985). Restructuring versus automaticity: Alternative accounts of skills acquisition. *Psychological Review, 92*, 414–423.

Cherry, E.C. (1953). Some experiments on the recognition of speech with one and two ears. *Journal of the Acoustical Society of America, 25*, 975–979.

Chertkow, H., Bub, D., Evans, E., Meyer, S., & Marrett, S. (1993). Neural correlates of picture processing studied with positron emission tomography. *Brain and Language, 44*, 460.

Chomsky, N. (1959). Review of Skinner's "Verbal behaviour". *Language, 35*, 26–58.

Chomsky, N. (1965). *Aspects of the theory of syntax.* Cambridge, MA: MIT Press.

Chomsky, N. (1980). *Rules and representations.* Oxford: Blackwell.

Chomsky, N. (1986). *Knowledge of language: Its nature, origin, and use.* New York: Praeger.

Churchland, P.S., & Sejnowski, T.J. (1991). Perspectives on cognitive neuroscience. In R.G. Lister & H.J. Weingartner (Eds.), *Perspectives on cognitive neuroscience.* Oxford: Oxford University Press.

Cicerone, C.M., & Nerger, J.L. (1989). The relative number of long-wavelength-sensitive to middle-wave-length-sensitive cones in the human fovea centralis. *Vision Research, 29*, 115–128.

Clark, H.H., & Carlson, T.B. (1981).

Context for comprehension. In J. Long & A. Baddeley (Eds.), *Attention and performance* (Vol. IX). Hillsdale, NJ: Lawrence Erlbaum Associates Inc.

Clifton, C., & Ferreira, F. (1987). Discourse structure and anaphora: Some experimental results. In M. Coltheart (Ed.), *Attention and performance* (Vol. XII). Hove, UK: Lawrence Erlbaum Associates Ltd.

Cohen, G. (1990). Why is it difficult to put names to faces? *British Journal of Psychology, 81*, 287–297.

Cohen, N.J., Poldrack, R.A., & Eichenbaum, H. (1997). Memory for items and memory for relations in the procedural/declarative memory framework. *Memory, 5*, 131–178.

Cohen, N.J., & Squire, L.R. (1980). Preserved learning and retention of pattern-analysing skill in amnesia using perceptual learning. *Cortex, 17*, 273–278.

Cohen, N.J., Ramzy, C., Hut, Z., Tomaso, H., Strupp, J., Erhard, P., Anderson, P., & Ugurbil, K. (1994). Hippocampal activation in fMRI evoked by demand for declarative memory-based bindings of multiple streams of information. *Society for Neuroscience Abstracts, 20*, 1290.

Cole, R.A., Rudnisky, A.I., Zue, V.W., & Reddy, W. (1980). Speech as patterns on paper. In R.A. Cole (Ed.), *Perception and production of fluent speech.* Hillsdale, NJ: Lawrence Erlbaum Associates Inc.

Coltheart, M. (1983). Ecological necessity of iconic memory. *Behavioral & Brain Sciences, 6*, 17–18.

Coltheart, M., Curtis, B., Atkins, P., & Haller, M. (1993). Models of reading aloud: Dual-route and parallel-distributed-processing approaches. *Psychological Review, 100*, 589–608.

Connine, C.M., Blasko, P.J., & Titone, D. (1993). Do the beginnings of spoken words have a special status in auditory word recognition? *Journal of Memory and Language, 32*, 193–210.

Conway, M.A., Anderson, S.J., Larsen, S.F., Donnelly, C.M., McDaniel, M.A., McClelland, A.G.R., & Rawles, R.E. (1994). The formation of flashbulb memories. *Memory & Cognition*, 22, 326–343.

Coren, S., & Girgus, J.S. (1972). Visual spatial illusions: Many explanations. *Science*, 179, 503–504.

Cosmides, L. (1989). The logic of social exchange: Has natural selection shaped how humans reason? Studies with the Wason selection task. *Cognition*, 31, 187–276.

Cosmides, L., & Tooby, J. (1996). Are humans good intuitive statisticians after all? Rethinking some conclusions from the literature on judgement under uncertainty. *Cognition*, 58, 1–73.

Craik, F.I.M. (1973). A "levels of analysis" view of memory. In P. Pliner, L. Krames, & T.M. Alloway (Eds.), *Communication and affect: Language and thought*. London: Academic Press.

Craik, F.I.M., & Lockhart, R.S. (1972). Levels of processing: A framework for memory research. *Journal of Verbal Language & Verbal Behavior*, 11, 671–684.

Craik, F.I.M., & Tulving, E. (1975). Depth of processing and the retention of words in episodic memory. *Journal of Experimental Psychology: General*, 104, 268–294.

Curran, T., & Schacter, D.L. (1997). Implicit memory: What must theories of memory explain? *Memory*, 5, 37–47.

Curtiss, S. (1977). *Genie: A psycholinguistic study of a modern-day "wild child"*. London: Academic Press.

Cutler, A., Mehler, J., Norris, D., & Segui, J. (1987). Phonemic identification and the lexicon. *Cognitive Psychology*, 19, 141–177.

Cutting, J.E. (1978). Generation of synthetic male and female walkers through manipulation of a biomechanical invariant. *Perception*, 7, 393–405.

Cutting, J.E., Proffitt, D.R., & Kozlowski, L.T. (1978). A biomechanical invariant for gait perception. *Journal of Experimental Psychology: Human Perception and Performance*, 4, 357–372.

Daneman, M., & Carpenter, P.A. (1980). Individual differences in working memory and reading. *Journal of Verbal Learning & Verbal Behavior*, 19, 450–466.

Dannemiller, J.L., & Stephens, B.R. (1988). A critical test of infant pattern preference models. *Child Development*, 59, 210–216.

Dartnall, H.J.A., Bowmaker, J.K., & Mollon, J.D. (1983). Human visual pigments: Microspectrophotometric results from the eyes of seven persons. *Proceedings of the Royal Society of London Series B 220*, 115–130.

Darwin, C.J., Turvey, M.T., & Crowder, R.G. (1972). An auditory analogue of the Sperling partial report procedure: Evidence for brief auditory storage. *Cognitive Psychology*, 3, 255–267.

Davidoff, J., & Warrington, E.K. (1999). Apperceptive agnosia: A deficit of perceptual categorisation of objects. In G.W. Humphreys (Ed.), *Case studies in the neuropsychology of vision*. Hove, UK: Psychology Press.

Davidson, D. (1994). Recognition and recall of irrelevant and interruptive atypical actions in script-based stories. *Journal of Memory and Language*, 33, 757–775.

Davies, G.M., & Logie, R.H. (1998). *Memory in everyday life*. Amsterdam: Elsevier.

Davies, I.R.L. (1998). A study of colour grouping in three languages: A test of the linguistic relativity hypothesis. *British Journal of Psychology*, 89, 433–452.

Davies, I.R.L., Sowden, P.T., Jerrett, D.T., Jerrett, T., & Corbett, G.G. (1998). A cross-cultural study of English and Setswana speakers on a colour triads task: A test of the Sapir-Whorf hypothesis. *British Journal of Psychology*, 89, 1–15.

Daw, N.W. (1995). *Visual development*. New York: Plenum.

De Bleser, R. (1988). Localisation of aphasia: Science or fiction? In G. Denese, C. Semenza, & P. Bisiacchi (Eds.), *Perspectives on cognitive neuropsychology*. Hove, UK: Lawrence Erlbaum Associates Ltd.

De Boysson-Bardies, B., Sagart, L., & Durand, C. (1984). Discernible differences in the babbling of infants according to target language. *Journal of Child Language, 11*, 1–16.

De Groot, A.D. (1965). *Thought and choice in chess*. The Hague: Mouton.

De Haan, E.H.F., Young, A.W., & Newcombe, F. (1991). A dissociation between the sense of familiarity and access to semantic information concerning familiar people. *European Journal of Cognitive Psychology, 3*, 51–67.

Delk, J.L., & Fillenbaum, S. (1965). Differences in perceived colour as a function of characteristic colour. *American Journal of Psychology, 78*, 290–293.

Dell, G.S. (1986). A spreading-activation theory of retrieval in sentence production. *Psychological Review, 93*, 283–321.

Dell, G.S., Burger, L.K., & Svec, W.R. (1997). Language production and serial order: A functional analysis and a model. *Psychological Review, 104*, 123–147.

Dell, G.S., & O'Seaghdha, P.G. (1991). Mediated and convergent lexical priming in language production: A comment on Levelt et al. (1991). *Psychological Review, 98*, 604–614.

DeLucia, P.R., & Hochberg, J. (1991). Geometrical illusions in solid objects under ordinary viewing conditions. *Perception & Psychophysics, 50*, 547–554.

Deregowski, J., Muldrow, E.S., & Muldrow, W.F. (1972). Pictorial recognition in a remote Ethiopian population. *Perception, 1*, 417–425.

Deutsch, J.A., & Deutsch, D. (1963). Attention: Some theoretical considerations. *Psychological Review, 70*, 80–90.

Deutsch, J.A., & Deutsch, D. (1967). Comments on "Selective attention: Perception or response?" *Quarterly Journal of Experimental Psychology, 19*, 362–363.

DeValois, R.I., & DeValois, K.K. (1975). Neural coding of colour. In E.C. Carterette & M.P. Friedman (Eds.), *Handbook of perception* (Vol. 5). New York: Academic Press.

DeValois, R.L., & Jacobs, F.H. (1968). Primate colour vision. *Science, 162*, 533–540.

de Villiers, J.G., & de Villiers, P.A. (1973). A cross-sectional study of the acquisition of grammatic morphemes in child speech. *Journal of Psycholinguistic Research, 2*, 267–278.

Di Pellegrino, G., & De Renzi, E. (1995). An experimental investigation on the nature of extinction. *Neuropsychologia, 33*, 153–170.

Dobelle, W.H., Mladejovsky, M.G., & Girvin, J.P. (1974). Artificial vision for the blind: Electrical stimulation of visual cortex offers hope for a functional prosthesis. *Science, 183*, 440–444.

Dodson, C. & Reisberg, D. (1991). Indirect testing of eyewitness memory: The (non) effect of misinformation. *Bulletin of the Psychonomic Society, 29*, 333–336.

Dosher, B.A., & Corbett, A.T. (1982). Instrument inferences and verb schemata. *Memory & Cognition, 10*, 531–539.

Driver, J. (1998). The neuropsychology of spatial attention. In H. Pashler (Ed.), *Attention*. Hove, UK: Psychology Press.

Driver, J., & Baylis, G.C. (1989). Movement and visual attention: The spotlight metaphor breaks down. *Journal of Experimental Psychology: Human Perception and Performance, 15*, 448–456.

Driver, J., & Tipper, S.P. (1989). On the nonselectivity of "selective seeing": Contrast between interference and priming in selective attention. *Journal of Experimental Psychology: Human Perception and Performance, 15*, 304–314.

Dronkers, N. (1996). A new brain region for coordinating speech articulation. *Nature, 384*, 159–161.

Duhamel, J.-R., Colby, C.L., & Goldberg, M.E. (1992). The updating of the representation of visual space in parietal cortex by intended eye movements. *Science, 255*, 90–92.

Dunbar, K. (1993). Concept discovery in a scientific domain. *Cognitive Science, 17*, 397–434.

Duncan, J. (1979). Divided attention: The whole is more than the sum of its parts. *Journal of Experimental Psychology: Human Perception, 5*, 216–228.

Duncker, K. (1945). On problem solving. *Psychological Monographs, 58* (Whole No. 270).

Durkin, K. (1995). *Developmental social psychology: From infancy to old age.* Oxford: Blackwell.

Ebbinghaus, H. (1885/1913). *Uber das Gedåchtnis.* Leipzig: Dunker (translated by H. Ruyer and C.E. Bussenius). New York: Teacher College, Columbus University.

Ehrlich, S.F., & Rayner, K. (1981). Contextual effects on word perception and eye movements during reading. *Journal of Verbal Learning and Verbal Behavior, 20*, 641–655.

Ellis, A.W. (1993). *Reading, writing, and dyslexia: A cognitive analysis* (2nd ed.). Hove, UK: Lawrence Erlbaum Associates Ltd.

Ellis, A.W., Miller, D., & Sin, G. (1983). Wernicke's aphasia and normal language processing: A case study in cognitive neuropsychology. *Cognition, 15*, 111–144.

Ellis, A.W., & Young, A.W. (1988). *Human cognitive neuropsychology.* Hove, UK: Lawrence Erlbaum Associates Ltd.

Ellis, R., & Humphreys, G. (1999). *Connectionist psychology: A text with readings.* Hove, UK: Psychology Press.

Ericsson, K.A., & Lehmann, A.C. (1996). Expert and exceptional performance: Evidence of maximal adaptation to task constraints. *Annual Review of Psychology, 47*, 273–305.

Eriksen, C.W., & St. James, J.D. (1986). Visual attention within and around the field of focal attention: A zoom lens model. *Perception and Psychophysics, 40*, 225–240.

Eslinger, P.J., & Damasio, A.R. (1985). Severe disturbance of higher cognition after bilateral frontal lobe ablation: Patient EVR. *Neurology, 35*, 1731–1741.

Evans, J.St.B.T. (1989). *Bias in human reasoning.* Hove, UK: Lawrence Erlbaum Associates Ltd.

Evans, J.St.B.T., Clibbens, J., & Rood, B. (1995). Bias in conditional inference: Implications for mental models and mental logic. *Quarterly Journal of Experimental Psychology, 48A*, 644–670.

Evans, J.St.B.T., & Over, D.E. (1997). Are people rational? Yes, no, and sometimes. *The Psychologist, 10*, 403–406.

Eysenck, M.W. (1997). *Anxiety and cognition: A unified theory.* Hove, UK: Psychology Press.

Eysenck, M.W. (2000). Tele-interview, *European Psychologist, 5*, 108–110.

Eysenck, M.W., & Keane, M.T. (2000). *Cognitive psychology: A student's handbook* (4th ed.). Hove, UK: Psychology Press.

Fantz, R.L. (1961). The origin of form perception. *Scientific American, 204*, 66–72.

Farah, M.J. (1990). *Visual agnosia: Disorders of object recognition and what they tell us about normal vision.* Cambridge, MA: MIT Press.

Farah, M.J. (1994). Specialisation within

visual object recognition: Clues from prosopagnosia and alexia. In M.J. Farah & G. Ratcliff (Eds.), *The neuropsychology of high-level vision: Collected tutorial essays*. Hillsdale, NJ: Lawrence Erlbaum Associates Inc.

Farah, M.J. (1999). Relations among the agnosias. In G.W. Humphreys (Ed.), *Case studies in the neuropsychology of vision*. Hove, UK: Psychology Press.

Farah, M.J., & Wallace, M.A. (1992). Semantically-bounded anomia: Implications for the neural implementation of naming. *Neuropsychologia, 30*, 609–621.

ffytche, D.H., Guy, C., & Zeki, S. (1995). The parallel visual motion inputs into areas V1 and V5 of the human cerebral cortex. *Brain, 118*, 1375–1394.

Fiedler, K. (1988). The dependence of the conjunction fallacy on subtle linguistic factors. *Psychological Research, 50*, 123–129.

Finkenauer, C., Luminet, O., Gisle, L., El-Ahmadi, A., & van der Linden, M. (1998). Flashbulb memories and the underlying mechanisms of their formation: Toward an emotional-integrative model. *Memory & Cognition, 26*, 516–531.

Fischler, I., Rundus, D., & Atkinson, R.C. (1970). Effects of overt rehearsal procedures on free recall. *Psychonomic Science, 19*, 249–250.

Fitts, P.M., & Posner, M.I. (1967). *Human performance*. Englewood Cliffs, NJ: Prentice-Hall.

Fodor, J.A., & Pylyshyn, Z.W. (1981). How direct is visual perception? Some reflections on Gibson's "ecological approach". *Cognition, 9*, 139–196.

Forde, E.M.E. (1999). Category-specific recognition impairments for living and nonliving things. In G.W. Humphreys (Ed.), *Case studies in the neuropsychology of vision*. Hove, UK: Psychology Press.

Forde, E.M.E., Francis, D., Riddoch, M.J., Rumian, R.I., & Humphreys, G.W. (1997). On the links between visual knowledge and naming: A single case study of a patient with a category-specific impairment for living things. *Cognitive Neuropsychology, 14*, 403–458.

Fox, R., & McDaniel, C. (1982). The perception of biological motion by human infants. *Science, 218*, 486–487.

Francolini, C.N., & Egeth, H.E. (1980). On the non-automaticity of automatic activation: Evidence of selective seeing. *Perception and Psychophysics, 27*, 331–342.

Franklin, S., Turner, J., Ralph, M.A.L., Morris, J., & Bailey, P.J. (1996). A distinctive case of word meaning deafness? *Cognitive Neuropsychology, 13*, 1139–1162.

Franz, V.H., Gegenfurter, K.R., Bülthoff, H.H., & Fahle, M. (2000). Grasping visual illusions: No evidence for a dissociation between perception and action. *Psychological Science, 11*, 20–25.

Frauenfelder, U.H., Segui, J., & Dijkstra, T. (1990). Lexical effects in phonemic processing: Facilitatory or inhibitory? *Journal of Experimental Psychology: Human Perception and Performance, 16*, 77–91.

Frazier, L., & Rayner, K. (1982). Making and correcting errors during sentence comprehension: Eye movements in the analysis of structurally ambiguous sentences. *Cognitive Psychology, 14*, 178–210.

Freud, S. (1915). Repression. In *Freud's collected papers* (Vol. IV). London: Hogarth.

Freud, S. (1943). *A general introduction to psychoanalysis*. New York: Garden City.

Fromkin, V.A. (1993). Speech production. In J.B. Gleason & N.B. Ratner (Eds.), *Psycholinguistics*. Orlando, FL: Harcourt Brace.

Frost, R. (1998). Toward a strong phonological theory of visual word recognition: True issues and false trails. *Psychological Bulletin, 123*, 71–99.

Fruzzetti, A.E., Toland, K., Teller, S.A., & Loftus, E.F. (1992). Memory and eyewitness testimony. In M. Gruneberg & P. Morris (Eds.), *Aspects of memory: The practical aspects*. London: Routledge.

Fujii, T., Rukatsu, R., Watabe, S., Ohnura, A., Teramura, K., Kimura, I., Saso, S., & Kogure, K. (1990). Auditory sound agnosia without aphasia following a right temporal lobe lesion. *Cortex, 26*, 263–268.

Funnell, E., & De Mornay Davies, P. (1996). JBR: A reassessment of concept familiarity and a category-specific disorder for living things. *Neurocase, 2*, 461–474.

Gabrieli, J.D.E. (1998). Cognitive neuroscience of human memory. *Annual Review of Psychology, 49*, 87–115.

Gabrieli, J.D.E., Cohen, N.J., & Corkin, S. (1988). The impaired learning of semantic knowledge following bilateral medial temporal-lobe resection. *Brain, 7*, 157–177.

Gabrieli, J.D.E., Desmond, J.E., Demb, J.B., Wagner, A.D., Stone, M.V., Vaidya, C.J., & Glover, G.H. (1996). Functional magnetic resonance imaging of semantic memory processes in the frontal lobes. *Psychological Science, 7*, 278–283.

Garrett, M.F. (1975). The analysis of sentence production. In G.H. Bower (Ed.), *The psychology of learning and motivation* (Vol. 9). San Diego, CA: Academic Press.

Garrett, M.F. (1976). Syntactic processes in sentence production. In R.J. Wales & E. Walker (Eds.), *New approaches to language mechanisms*. Amsterdam: North-Holland.

Garrett, M.F. (1980). Levels of processing in sentence production. In B. Butterworth (Ed.), *Language production: Vol. 1. Speech and talk*. San Diego, CA: Academic Press.

Garrod, S., & Pickering, M.J. (1999). *Language processing*. Hove, UK: Psychology Press.

Gathercole, S.E., & Baddeley, A.D. (1989). Evaluation of the role of phonological STM in the development of vocabulary in children: A longitudinal study. *Journal of Memory and Language, 28*, 200–213.

Gathercole, S.E., & Baddley, A.D. (1990). Phonological memory deficits in language disordered children: Is there a causal connection? *Journal of Memory and Language, 29*, 336–360.

Gauld, A., & Stephenson, G.M. (1967). Some experiments relating to Bartlett's theory of remembering. *British Journal of Psychology, 58*, 39–50.

Gazzaniga, M.S., Ivry, R.B., & Mangun, G.R. (1998). *Cognitive neuroscience: The biology of the mind*. New York: W.W. Norton.

Georgopoulos, A.P. (1997). Voluntary movement: Computational principles and neural mechanisms. In M.D. Rugg (Ed.), *Cognitive neuroscience*. Hove, UK: Psychology Press.

Gibson, E.J., & Walk, R.D. (1960). The visual cliff. *Scientific American, 202*, 64–71.

Gibson, J.J. (1950). *The perception of the visual world*. Boston: Houghton Mifflin.

Gibson, J.J. (1966). *The senses considered as perceptual systems*. Boston: Houghton Mifflin.

Gibson, J.J. (1979). *The ecological approach to visual perception*. Boston: Houghton Mifflin.

Gick, M.L., & Holyoak, K.J. (1980). Analogical problem solving. *Cognitive Psychology, 12*, 306–355.

Gigerenzer, G. (1993). The bounded rationality of probabilistic mental models. In K.I. Manktelow, & D.E. Over (Eds.), *Rationality. Psychological and philosophical perspectives*. London: Routledge.

Gigerenzer, G. (1996). On narrow norms and vague heuristics: A reply to

Kahneman and Tversky (1996). *Psychological Review, 103*, 592–596.

Gigerenzer, G., & Hoffrage, U. (1999). Overcoming difficulties in Bayesian reasoning: A reply to Lewis and Keren (1999) and Mellers and McGraw (1999). *Psychological Review, 106*, 425–430.

Gigerenzer, G., & Hug, K. (1992). Domain-specific reasoning: Social contracts, cheating and perspective change. *Cognition, 43*, 127–171.

Gilhooly, K.J. (1996). *Thinking: Directed, undirected and creative* (3rd ed.). London: Academic Press.

Gilhooly, K.L., & Hoffman, R. (1998). *Expert thinking*. Hove, UK: Psychology Press.

Glanzer, M., & Cunitz, A.R. (1966). Two storage mechanisms in free recall. *Journal of Verbal Learning & Verbal Behavior, 5*, 351–360.

Glenberg, A.M. (1987). Temporal context and recency: In D.S. Gorfein & R.R. Hoffman (Eds.), *Memory and learning: The Ebbinghaus centennial conference*. Hillsdale, NJ: Lawrence Erlbaum Associates Inc.

Glenberg, A.M., Meyer, M., & Linden, K. (1987). Mental models contribute to foregrounding during text comprehension. *Journal of Memory and Language, 26*, 69–83.

Glenberg, A.M., Smith, S.M., & Green, C. (1977). Type I rehearsal: Maintenance and more. *Journal of Verbal Learning & Verbal Behavior, 16*, 339–352.

Glushko, R.J. (1979). The organisation and activation of orthographic knowledge in reading aloud. *Journal of Experimental Psychology: Human Perception and Performance, 5*, 674–691.

Gobet, F., & Simon, H.A. (1996). The roles of recognition processes and look-ahead search in time-constrained expert problem solving. *Psychological Science, 7*, 52–55.

Godden, D.R., & Baddeley, A.D. (1975). Context-dependent memory in two natural environments: On land and under water. *British Journal of Psychology, 66*, 325–331.

Godden, D.R., & Baddeley, A.D. (1980). When does context influence recognition memory? *British Journal of Psychology, 71*, 99–104.

Goldstein, E.B. (1996). *Sensation and perception* (4th ed.). New York: Brooks/Cole.

Gomulicki, B.R. (1956). Recall as an abstractive process. *Acta Psychologica, 12*, 77–94.

Goodale, M.A., & Humphrey, G.K. (1998). The objects of action and perception. *Cognition, 67*, 181–207.

Goodale, M.A., Milner, A.D., Jakobson, L.S., & Carey, D.P. (1991). A neurological dissociation between perceiving objects and grasping them. *Nature, 349*, 154–156.

Gopnik, M. (1990). Feature blindness: A case study. *Language Acquisition, 1*, 139–164.

Gopnik, M. (1994). The perceptual processing hypothesis revisited. In J. Matthews (Ed.), *Linguistic aspects of familial language impairment*. Montreal, Canada: McGill University.

Gordon, I.E. (1989). *Theories of visual perception*. Chichester, UK: Wiley.

Graesser, A.C., Millis, K.K., & Zwaan, R.A. (1997). Discourse comprehension. *Annual Review of Psychology, 48*, 163–189.

Graesser, A.C., Singer, M., & Trabasso, T. (1994). Constructing inferences during narrative text comprehension. *Psychological Review, 101*, 371–395.

Graf, P., & Schacter, D.L. (1985). Implicit and explicit memory for new associations in normal and amnesic subjects. *Journal of Experimental Psychology: Learning, Memory, and Cognition, 11*, 501–518.

Graf, P., Squire, L.R., & Mandler, G. (1984). The information that amnesic patients do not forget. *Journal of Experimental*

Psychology: Learning, Memory, and Cognition, 10, 164–178.

Grafton, S., Hazeltine, E., & Ivry, R. (1995). Functional mapping of sequence learning in normal humans. *Journal of Cognitive Neuroscience, 7,* 497–510.

Gray, J.A., & Wedderburn, A.A. (1960). Grouping strategies with simultaneous stimuli. *Quarterly Journal of Experimental Psychology, 12,* 180–184.

Green, K.P., Kuhl, P.K., Meltzoff, A.N., & Stevens, E.B. (1991). Integrating speech information across talkers, gender, and sensory modality: Female faces and male voices in the McGurk effect. *Perception and Psychophysics, 50,* 524–536.

Greenberg, J.H. (1963). Some universals of grammar with particular reference to the order of meaningful elements. In J.H. Greenberg (Ed.), *Universals of language.* Cambridge, MA: MIT Press.

Greeno, J.G. (1974). Hobbits and orcs: Acquisition of a sequential concept. *Cognitive Psychology, 6,* 270–292.

Greeno, J.G. (1994). Gibson's affordances. *Psychological Review, 101,* 336–342.

Greenwald, A.G. (1992). New Look 3: Unconscious cognition reclaimed. *American Psychologist, 47,* 766–779.

Gregor, A.J., & McPherson, D.A. (1965). A study of susceptibility to geometrical illusion among cultural subgroups of Australian aborigines. *Psychology in Africa, 11,* 1–13.

Gregory, R.L. (1970). *The intelligent eye.* New York: McGraw-Hill.

Gregory, R.L. (1972). Seeing as thinking. *Times Literary Supplement,* 23 June.

Gregory, R.L. (1980). Perceptions as hypotheses. *Philosophical Transactions of the Royal Society of London, Series B, 290,* 181–197.

Gregory, R.L. (1996). Twenty-five years after *The Intelligent Eye. The Psychologist, 9,* 452–455.

Grice, H.P. (1967). Logic and conversation. In P. Cole & J.L. Morgan (Eds.), *Studies in syntax* (Vol. III). New York: Seminar Press.

Griggs, R.A., & Cox, J.R. (1982). The elusive thematic-materials effect in Wason's selection task. *British Journal of Psychology, 73,* 407–420.

Groeger, J.A. (1997). *Memory and remembering.* Harlow, UK: Addison Wesley Longman.

Grudin, J.T. (1983). Error patterns in novice and skilled transcription typing. In W.E. Cooper (Ed.), *Cognitive aspects of skilled typewriting.* New York: Springer.

Gunther, H., Gfoerer, S., & Weiss, L. (1984). Inflection, frequency, and the word superiority effect. *Psychological Research, 46,* 261–281.

Haber, R.N. (1983). The impending demise of the icon: A critique of the concept of iconic storage in visual information processing. *Behavioral & Brain Sciences, 6,* 1–11.

Haberlandt, K. (1999). *Human memory: Exploration and applications.* Boston: Allyn & Bacon.

Hampson, P.J. (1989). Aspects of attention and cognitive science. *Irish Journal of Psychology, 10,* 261–275.

Harley, T. (1984). A critique of top-down independent levels models of speech production: Evidence from non-plan-internal speech errors. *Cognitive Science, 8,* 191–219.

Harley, T.A. (1995). *The psychology of language: From data to theory.* Hove, UK: Psychology Press.

Harley, T.A., & Brown, H.E. (1998). What causes a tip-of-the-tongue state? Evidence for lexical neighbourhood effects in speech production. *British Journal of Psychology, 89,* 151–174.

Harris, M., Jones, D., Brookes, S., & Grant, J. (1986). Relations between the non-verbal context of maternal speech and rate of language development. *British Journal of Developmental Psychology, 4,* 261–268.

Harvey, L.O., Roberts, J.O., & Gervais, M.J.

(1983). The spatial frequency basis of internal representations. In H.G. Geissler, H.F.J.M. Buffart, E.L.J. Leeuwenberg, & V. Sarris (Eds.), *Physiology of the ear*. New York: Raven Press.

Hatano, G., & Inagaki, K. (1986). Two courses of expertise. In H. Stevenson, H. Azuma, & K. Hatuka (Eds.), *Child development in Japan*. San Francisco: Freeman.

Hay, J.F., & Jacoby, L.L. (1996). Separating habit and recollection: Memory slips, process dissociations, and probability matching. *Journal of Experimental Psychology: Learning, Memory, and Cognition, 22*, 1323–1335.

Hayward, W.G., & Williams, P. (2000). Viewpoint dependence and object discriminability. *Psychological Science, 11*, 7–12.

Heather, N. (1976). *Radical perspectives in psychology*. London: Methuen.

Heider, E. (1972). Universals in colour naming and memory. *Journal of Experimental Psychology, 93*, 10–20.

Helmholtz, H. von (1866). *Treatise on physiological optics* (Vol. III). New York: Dover (translation published 1962).

Hering, E. (1878). *Zur Lehre vom Lichtsinn*. Vienna: Gerold.

Hess, R.D., & Shipman, V. (1965) Early experience and the socialisation of cognitive modes in children. *Child Development, 36*, 860–886.

Heywood, C.A., Cowey, A., & Newcombe, F. (1994). On the role of parvocellular P and magnocellular M pathways in cerebral achromatopsia. *Brain, 117*, 245–254.

Hirst, W., Spelke, E.S., Reaves, C.C., Caharack, G., & Neisser, U. (1980). Dividing attention without alternation or automaticity. *Journal of Experimental Psychology: General, 109*, 98–117.

Hoffman, C., Lau, I., & Johnson, D.R. (1986). The linguistic relativity of person cognition. *Journal of Personality and Social Psychology, 51*, 1097–1105.

Holding, D.H., & Reynolds, J.R. (1982). Recall or evaluation of chess positions as determinants of chess skill. *Memory & Cognition, 10*, 237–242.

Holender, D. (1986). Semantic activation without conscious identification in dichotic listening, parafoveal vision, and visual masking: A survey and appraisal. *Behavioral and Brain Sciences, 9*, 1–66.

Holway, A.F., & Boring, E.G. (1941). Determinants of apparent visual size with distance variant. *American Journal of Psychology, 54*, 21–37.

Horton, W.S., & Keysar, B. (1996). When do speakers take into account common ground? *Cognition, 59*, 91–117.

Howard, D. (1997). Language in the human brain. In M.D. Rugg (Ed.), *Cognitive neuroscience*. Hove, UK: Psychology Press.

Howard, D.V., & Howard, J.H. (1992). Adult age differences in the rate of learning serial patterns: Evidence from direct and indirect tests. *Psychology and Aging, 7*, 232–241.

Howard, D., & Orchard-Lisle, V. (1984). On the origin of semantic errors in naming: Evidence from the case of a global aphasic. *Cognitive Neuropsychology, 1*, 163–190.

Howard, D., Patterson, K.E., Wise, R.J.S., Brown, W.D., Friston, K., Weiller, C., & Frackowiak, R.S.J. (1992). The cortical localisation of the lexicons: Positron emission tomography evidence. *Brain, 115*, 1769–1782.

Hubel, D.H., & Wiesel, T.N. (1962). Receptive fields, binocular interaction, and functional architecture in the cat's visual cortex. *Journal of Physiology, 160*, 106–154.

Hubel, D.H., & Wiesel, T.N. (1979). Brain mechanisms of vision. *Scientific American, 241*, 150–163.

Hummel, J.E., & Holyoak, K.J. (1997).

Distributed representations of structure: A theory of analogical access and mapping. *Psychological Review, 104,* 427–466.

Humphreys, G.W. (1999). Integrative agnosia. In G.W. Humphreys (Ed.), *Case studies in the neuropsychology of vision.* Hove, UK: Psychology Press.

Humphreys, G.W., & Bruce, V. (1989). *Visual cognition: Computational, experimental and neuropsychological perspectives.* Hove, UK: Psychology Press.

Humphreys, G.W., Lamote, C., & Lloyd-Jones, T.J. (1995). An interactive activation approach to object processing: Effects of structural similarity, name frequency and task in normality and pathology. *Memory, 3,* 535–586.

Humphreys, G.W., & Riddoch, M.J. (1984). Routes to object constancy: Implications from neurological impairments of object constancy. *Quarterly Journal of Experimental Psychology, 36A,* 385–415.

Humphreys, G.W., & Riddoch, M.J. (1985). Author corrections to "Routes to object constancy". *Quarterly Journal of Experimental Psychology, 37A,* 493–495.

Humphreys, G.W., & Riddoch, M.J. (1987). *To see but not to see: A case study of visual agnosia.* Hove, UK: Psychology Press.

Humphreys, G.W., & Riddoch, M.J. (1993). Interactions between object and space systems revealed through neuropsychology. In D.E. Meyer & S.M. Kornblum (Eds.), *Attention and performance* (Vol. XIV). London: MIT Press.

Humphreys, G.W., Riddoch, M.J., & Quinlan, P.T. (1988). Cascade processes in picture identification. *Cognitive Neuropsychology, 5,* 67–103.

Humphreys, G.W., Riddoch, M.J., Quinlan, P.T., Price, C.J., & Donnelly, N. (1992). Parallel pattern processing in visual agnosia. *Canadian Journal of Psychology, 46,* 377–416.

Hunt, E., & Agnoli, F. (1991). The Whorfian hypothesis: A cognitive psychological perspective. *Psychological Review, 98,* 377–389.

Hurvich, L.M. (1981). *Colour vision.* Sunderland, MA: Sinauer.

Hyde, T.S. & Jenkins, J.J. (1973). Recall for words as a function of semantic, graphic, and syntactic orienting tasks. *Journal of Verbal Learning & Verbal Behavior, 12,* 471–480.

Ittelson, W.H. (1951). Size as a cue to distance: Static localisation. *American Journal of Psychology, 64,* 54–67.

Ittelson, W.H. (1952). *The Ames demonstration in perception.* New York: Hafner.

Jakobsson, T., Bergstrøm, S.S., Gustafsson, K.A., & Fedorovskaya, E. (1997). Ambiguities in colour constancy and shape from shading. *Perception, 26,* 531–541.

Janowsky, J.S., Shimamura, A.P., & Squire, L.R. (1989). Source memory impairment in patients with frontal lobe lesions. *Neuropsychologia, 27,* 1043–1056.

Johansson, G. (1975). Visual motion perception. *Scientific American, 232,* 76–89.

Johnson, M.H., Dziurawiec, S., Ellis, H., & Morton, J. (1991). Newborns' preferential tracking of face-like stimuli and its subsequent decline. *Cognition, 40,* 1–19.

Johnson, M.K., Hashtroudi, S., & Lindsay, D.S. (1993). Source monitoring. *Psychological Bulletin, 114,* 3–28.

Johnson-Laird, P.N. (1983). *Mental models.* Cambridge: Cambridge University Press.

Johnson-Laird, P.N. (1999). Deductive reasoning. *Annual Review of Psychology, 50,* 109–135.

Johnson-Laird, P.N., & Byrne, R.M.J. (1991). *Deduction.* Hillsdale, NJ: Lawrence Erlbaum Associates Inc.

Johnson-Laird, P.N., Byrne, R.M.J., & Schaeken, W. (1994). Why models rather than rules give a better account of propositional reasoning: A reply to Bonatti and to O'Brien, Braine and Yang. *Psychological Review, 101,* 734–739.

Johnson-Laird, P.N., & Goldvarg, Y. (1997). How to make the impossible seem possible. In *Proceedings of the 19th Annual Conference of the Cognitive Science Society.* Mahwah, NJ: Lawrence Erlbaum Associates Inc.

Johnson-Laird, P.N., Legrenzi, P., Girotto, V., Legrenzi, M.S., & Caverni, J.-P. (1999). Naive probability: A mental model theory of extensional reasoning. *Psychological Review, 106,* 62–88.

Johnson-Laird, P.N., & Savary, F. (1996). Illusionary inferences about probabilities. *Acta Psychologia, 93,* 69–90.

Joseph, J.E., & Proffitt, D. (1996). Semantic versus perceptual influences of colour in object recognition. *Journal of Experimental Psychology: Learning, Memory and Cognition, 22,* 407–429.

Juola, J.F., Bowhuis, D.G., Cooper, E.E., & Warner, C.B. (1991). Control of attention around the fovea. *Journal of Experimental Psychology: Human Perception and Performance, 15,* 315–330.

Kahneman, D. (1973). *Attention and effort.* Englewood Cliffs, NJ: Prentice-Hall.

Kahneman, D., & Henik, A. (1979). Perceptual organisation and attention. In M. Kubovy & J.R. Pomerantz (Eds.), *Perceptual organisation.* Hillsdale, NJ: Lawrence Erlbaum Associates Inc.

Kahneman, D., Tursky, B., Shapiro, D., & Crider, A. (1969). Pupillary, heart rate and skin resistance changes during a mental task. *Journal of Experimental Psychology, 79,* 161–167.

Kahneman, D., & Tversky, A. (1973). On the psychology of prediction. *Psychological Review, 80,* 237–251.

Kahneman, D., & Tversky, A. (1984). Choices, values and frames. *American Psychologist, 39,* 341–350.

Kaneko, H., & Uchikawa, K. (1997). Perceived angular and linear size: The role of binocular disparity and visual surround. *Perception, 26,* 17–27.

Kanizsa, G. (1976). Subjective contours. *Scientific American, 234,* 48–52.

Kanwisher, N., McDermott, J., & Chun, M.M. (1997). The fusiform face area: A module in human extrastriate cortex specialised for face perception. *Journal of Neuroscience, 9,* 605–610.

Kay, J., & Ellis, A.W. (1987). A cognitive neuropsychological case study of anomia: Implications for psychological models of word retrieval. *Brain, 110,* 613–629.

Kay, J., & Marcel, A.J. (1981). One process, not two in reading aloud: Lexical analogies do the work of nonlexical rules. *Quarterly Journal of Experimental Psychology, 33A,* 397–414.

Keane, M.T. (1987). On retrieving analogues when solving problems. *Quarterly Journal of Experimental Psychology, 39A,* 29–41.

Kellman, P.J. (1996). The origins of object perception. In R. Gelman & T.K.-F. Au (Eds.), *Perceptual and cognitive development.* New York: Academic Press.

Kellogg, R.T. (1995). *Cognitive psychology.* Thousand Oaks, CA: Sage.

Kenealy, P.M. (1997). Mood-state-dependent retrieval: The effects of induced mood on memory reconsidered. *Quarterly Journal of Experimental Psychology, 50A,* 290–317.

Kilpatrick, F.P., & Ittelson, W.H. (1953). The size–distance invariance hypothesis. *Psychological Review, 60,* 223–231.

Kimchi, R. (1992). Primacy of wholistic processing and global/local paradigm: A critical review. *Psychological Bulletin, 112,* 24–38.

Kinchla, R.A., & Wolfe, J.M. (1979). The order of visual processing: "Top-down", "bottom-up", or "middle-out". *Perception & Psychophysics, 25,* 225–231.

Kintsch, W. (1988). The role of knowledge in discourse comprehension: A construction-integration model. *Psychological Review, 95,* 163–182.

Kintsch, W. (1992). A cognitive architecture for comprehension. In H.L. Pick, P. van den Broek, & D.C. Knill (Eds.), *Cognition: Conceptual and methodological issues.* Washington, DC: American Psychological Association.

Kintsch, W. (1994). The psychology of discourse processing. In M.A. Gernsbacher (Ed.), *Handbook of psycholinguistics.* London: Academic Press.

Kintsch, W., Welsch, D., Schmalhofer, F., & Zimny, S. (1990). Sentence memory: A theoretical analysis. *Journal of Memory and Language, 29,* 133–159.

Kirby, K.N. (1994). Probabilities and utilities of fictional outcomes in Wason's four-card selection task. *Cognition, 51,* 1–28.

Klayman, J., & Ha, Y.-W. (1987). Confirmation, disconfirmation and information in hypothesis testing. *Psychological Review, 94,* 211–228.

Knoblich, G., Ohlsson, S., Haider, H., & Rhenius, D. (1999). Constraint relaxation and chunk decomposition in insight. *Journal of Experimental Psychology: Learning, Memory, & Cognition, 25,* 1534–1555.

Knowlton, B.J., Ramus, S.J., & Squire, L.R. (1992). Intact artificial grammar learning in amnesia: Dissociation of abstract knowledge and memory for specific instances. *Psychological Science, 3,* 172–179.

Koehler, J.J. (1996). The base rate fallacy reconsidered: Descriptive, normative, and methodological challenges. *Behavioral and Brain Sciences, 19,* 1–17.

Koffka, K. (1935). *Principles of Gestalt psychology.* New York: Harcourt Brace.

Köhler, W. (1925). *The mentality of apes.* New York: Harcourt Brace & World.

Köhler, S., & Moscovitch, M. (1997). Unconscious visual processing in neuropsychological syndromes: A survey of the literature and evaluation of models of consciousness. In M.D. Rugg (Ed.), *Cognitive neuroscience.* Hove, UK: Psychology Press.

Koriat, A., & Goldsmith, M. (1996). Memory metaphors and the real-life/laboratory controversy: Correspondence versus storehouse conceptions of memory. *Behavioral and Brain Sciences, 19,* 167–188.

Kroll, N.E., Knight, R.T., Metcalfe, J., Wolf, E.S., & Tulving, E. (1996). Cohesion failure as a source of memory illusions. *Journal of Memory and Language, 35,* 176–196.

Kunnapas, T.M. (1968). Distance perception as a function of available visual cues. *Journal of Experimental Psychology, 77,* 523–529.

Kvavilashvili, L., & Ellis, J. (1996). Let's forget the everyday/laboratory controversy. *Behavioral and Brain Sciences, 19,* 199–200.

Kvavilashvili, L., & Ellis, J. (in press). Ecological validity and twenty years of real-life/laboratory controversy in memory research: A critical review.

LaBerge, D. (1983). The spatial extent of attention to letters and words. *Journal of Experimental Psychology: Human Perception and Performance, 9,* 371–379.

Labov, W. (1972). *Language in the inner city: Studies in Black English vernacular.* Philadelphia: Falmer Press.

Lachman, R., Lachman, J.L., & Butterfield, E.C. (1979). *Cognitive psychology and information processing.* Hillsdale, NJ: Lawrence Erlbaum Associates Inc.

Land, E.H. (1977). The retinex theory of colour vision. *Scientific American, 237,* 108–128.

Land, E.H. (1986). Recent advances in retinex theory. *Vision Research, 26,* 7–21.

Larsen, A., & Bundesen, C. (1992). The efficiency of holistic template matching in the recognition of unconstrained handwritten digits. *Psychological Research, 54,* 187–193.

Larsen, A., & Bundesen, C. (1996). A template-matching pandemonium recognises unconstrained handwritten characters with high accuracy. *Memory & Cognition, 24,* 136–143.

Lashley, K.S., Chow, K.L., & Semmes, J. (1951). An examination of the electrical field theory of cerebral integration. *Psychological Review, 58,* 123–136.

Lassiter, G.D. (2000). The relative contributions of recognition and search-evaluation processes to high-level chess performance: Comment on Gobet and Simon. *Psychological Science, 11,* 172–173.

Lea, W.A. (1973). An approach to syntactic recognition without phonemics. *IEEE Transactions on Audio and Electroacoustics, AU-21,* 249–258.

Lee, D.N. (1980). Visuo-motor coordination in space-time. In G.E. Stelmach & J. Requin (Eds.), *Tutorials in motor behaviour.* Amsterdam: North-Holland.

Lenneberg, E.H. (1967). *The biological foundations of language.* New York: Wiley.

Lenneberg, E.H., & Roberts, J.M. (1956). *The language of experience, memoir 13.* Indiana: University of Indiana, Publications in Anthropology and Linguistics.

Levelt, W.J.M. (1989). *Speaking: From intention to articulation.* Cambridge, MA: MIT Press.

Levelt, W.J.M., Roelofs, A., & Meyer, A.S. (1999). A theory of lexical access in speech production. *Behavioral and Brain Sciences, 22,* 1–38.

Liberman, N., & Klar, Y. (1996). Hypothesis testing in Wason's selection task: social exchange cheating detection or task understanding. *Cognition, 58,* 127–156.

Lichten, W., & Lurie, S. (1950). A new technique for the study of perceived size. *American Journal of Psychology, 63,* 280–282.

Lichtenstein, S., Slovic, P., Fischhoff, B., Layman, M., & Combs, J. (1978). Judged frequency of lethal events. *Journal of Experimental Psychology: Human Learning and Memory, 4,* 551–578.

Lief, H., & Fetkewicz, J. (1995). Retractors of false memories: The evolution of pseudo-memories. *The Journal of Psychiatry & Law, 23,* 411–436.

Lindsay, R.C.L., Lea, J.A., Nosworthy, G.J., Fulford, J.A., Hector, J., LeVan, V., & Seabrook, C. (1991). Biased lineups: Sequential presentation reduces the problem. *Journal of Applied Psychology, 76,* 741–745.

Lindsay, R.C.L., & Wells, G.L. (1980). What price justice? Exploring the relationship of lineup fairness to identification accuracy. *Law & Human Behavior, 4,* 303–314.

Lockhart, R.S., & Craik, F.I.M. (1990). Levels of processing: A retrospective commentary on a framework for memory research. *Canadian Journal of Psychology, 44,* 87–112.

Loftus, E.F. (1979). *Eyewitness testimony.* Cambridge, MA: Harvard University Press.

Loftus, E.F. (1992). When a lie becomes memory's truth: Memory distortion after exposure to misinformation. *Current Directions in Psychological Science, 1,* 121–123.

Loftus, E.F., Loftus, G., & Messo, J. (1987). Some facts about "weapon focus". *Law and Human Behavior, 11,* 5–62.

Loftus, E.F., & Palmer, J.C. (1974). Reconstruction of automobile destruction: An example of the interaction between language and memory. *Journal of Verbal Learning & Verbal Behavior, 13,* 585–589.

Logan, G.D. (1988). Toward an instance theory of automatisation. *Psychological Review, 95*, 492–527.

Logie, R.H. (1995). *Visuo-spatial working memory*. Hove, UK: Psychology Press.

Logie, R.H. (1999). State of the art: Working memory. *The Psychologist, 12*, 174–178.

Lopes, L.L. (1987). Between hope and fear: The psychology of risk. In L. Berkowitz (Ed.), *Advances in experimental social psychology* (Vol. 20). San Diego: Academic Press.

Lucas, M. (1999). Context effects in lexical access: A meta-analysis. *Memory & Cognition, 27*, 385–398.

Luchins, A.S. (1942). Mechanisation in problem solving: The effect of Einstellung. *Psychological Monographs, 54*, 248.

Luck, S.J. (1998). Neurophysiology of selective attention. In H. Pashler (Ed.), *Attention*. Hove, UK: Psychology Press.

Lueck, C.J., Zeki, S., Friston, K.J., Deiber, M.-P., Cope, P., Cunningham, V.J., Lammertsma, A.A., Kennard, C., & Frackowiak, R.S.J. (1989). The colour centre in the cerebral cortex of man. *Nature, 340*, 386–389.

Mackintosh, N.J. (1998). *IQ and human intelligence*. Oxford: Oxford University Press.

Maclay, H., & Osgood, C.E. (1959). Hesitation phenomena in spontaneous English speech. *Word, 15*, 19–44.

MacLeod, C., & Hagan, R. (1992). Individual differences in the selective processing of threatening information, and emotional responses to a stressful life event. *Behaviour Research and Therapy, 30*, 151–161.

Macleod, C., & Rutherford, E.M. (1992). Anxiety and the selective processing of emotional information: Mediating roles of awareness, trait and state variables, and personal relevance of stimulus materials. *Behaviour Research and Therapy, 30*, 479–491.

Madison, P. (1956). Freud's repression concept: A survey and attempted clarification. *International Journal of Psychoanalysis, 37*, 75–81.

Maher, L.M., Rothi, L.J.G., & Heilman, K.M. (1994). Lack of error awareness in an aphasic patient with relatively preserved auditory comprehension. *Brain and Language, 46*, 402–418.

Maier, N.R.F. (1931). Reasoning in humans. II: The solution of a problem and its appearance in consciousness. *Journal of Comparative Psychology, 12*, 181–194.

Malone, D.R., Morris, H.H., Kay, M.C., & Levin, H.S. (1982). Prosopagnosia: A double dissociation between the recognition of familiar and unfamiliar faces. *Journal of Neurology, Neurosurgery, and Psychiatry, 45*, 820–822.

Marcel, A.J. (1983). Conscious and unconscious perception: Experiments on visual masking and word recognition. *Cognitive Psychology, 15*, 197–237.

Marr, D. (1982). *Vision: A computational investigation into the human representation and processing of visual information*. San Francisco: W.H. Freeman.

Marr, D., & and Nishihara, K. (1978). Representation and recognition of the spatial organisation of three-dimensional shapes. *Philosophical Transactions of the Royal Society, Series B*, 269–294.

Marshall, J.C., & Halligan, P.W. (1988). Blindsight and insight in visuo-spatial neglect. *Nature, 336*, 766–767.

Marshall, J.C., & Halligan, P.W. (1994). The yin and yang of visuo-spatial neglect: A case study. *Neuropsychologia, 32*, 1037.

Marshall, J.C., & Newcombe, F. (1973). Patterns of paralexia: A psycholinguistic approach. *Journal of Psycholinguistic Research, 2*, 175–199.

Marslen-Wilson, W.D. (1990). Activation, competition, and frequency in lexical access. In G.T.M. Altmann (Ed.),

Cognitive models of speech processing: Psycholinguistics and computational perspectives. Cambridge, MA: MIT Press.

Marslen-Wilson, W.D., Moss, H.E., & van Halen, S. (1996). Perceptual distance and competition in lexical access. *Journal of Experimental Psychology: Human Perception and Performance, 22,* 1376–1392.

Marslen-Wilson, W.D., & Tyler, L.K. (1980). The temporal structure of spoken language understanding. *Cognition, 8,* 1–71.

Marslen-Wilson, W.D., & Warren, P. (1994). Levels of perceptual representation and process in lexical access: Words, phonemes and features. *Psychological Review, 101,* 653–675.

Martin-Loeches, M., Schweinberger, S.R., & Sommer, W. (1997). The phonological loop model of working memory: An ERP study of irrelevant speech and phonological similarity effects. *Memory & Cognition, 25,* 471–483.

Massaro, D.W. (1989). Testing between TRACE and the fuzzy logical model of speech perception. *Cognitive Psychology, 21,* 398–421.

Massaro, D.W. (1994). Psychological aspects of speech perception: Implications for research and theory. In M.A. Gernsbacher (Ed.), *Handbook of psycholinguistics*. San Diego: Academic Press.

Mather, G., & Murdoch, L. (1994). Gender discrimination in biological motion displays based on dynamic cues. *Proceedings of the Royal Society of London, B,* 273–279.

Matlin, M.W., & Foley, H.J. (1997). *Sensation and perception* (4th ed.). Bostyn: Allyn & Bacon.

Mayer, R.E. (1990). Problem solving. In M.W. Eysenck (Ed.), *The Blackwell dictionary of cognitive psychology*. Oxford: Blackwell.

McBride, D.M., & Dosher, B.A. (1999).

Forgetting rates are comparable in conscious and automatic memory: A process-dissociation study. *Journal of Experimental Psychology: Learning, Memory and Cognition, 25,* 583–607.

McCarthy, R., & Warrington, E.K. (1984). A two-route model of speech production. *Brain, 107,* 463–485.

McClelland, J.L. (1991). Stochastic interactive processes and the effect of context on perception. *Cognitive Psychology, 23,* 1–44.

McClelland, J.L. (1993). The GRAIN model: A framework for modelling the dynamics of information processing. In D.E. Meyer & S. Kornblum (Eds.), *Attention and performance* (Vol. XIV). Hillsdale, NJ: Lawrence Erlbaum Associates Inc.

McClelland, J.L., & Elman, J.L. (1986). The TRACE model of speech perception. *Cognitive Psychology, 18,* 1–86.

McClelland, J.L., & Mozer, M.C. (1986). Perceptual interactions in two-word displays: Familiarity and similarity effects. *Journal of Experimental Psychology: Human Perception and Performance, 12,* 18–35.

McClelland, J.L., & Rumelhart, D.E. (1981). An interactive activation model of context effects in letter perception. Part 1. An account of basic findings. *Psychological Review, 88,* 375–407.

McGlinchey-Berroth, R., Milber, W.P., Verfaellie, M., Alexander, M., & Kilduff, P.T. (1993). Semantic processing in the neglected visual field: Evidence from a lexical decision task. *Cognitive Neuropsychology, 10,* 79–108.

McGurk, H., & MacDonald, J. (1976). Hearing lips and seeing voices. *Nature, 264,* 746–748.

McKoon, G., & Ratcliff, R. (1986). Inferences about predictable events. *Journal of Experimental Psychology: Learning, Memory, and Cognition, 12,* 82–91.

McKoon, G., & Ratcliff, R. (1992). Inference

during reading. *Psychological Review, 99*, 440–466.

McLeod, P. (1977). A dual-task response modality effect: Support for multiprocessor models of attention. *Quarterly Journal of Experimental Psychology, 29*, 651–667.

McNamara, D.S., Kintsch, E., Songer, N.B., & Kintsch, W. (1995). Text coherence, background knowledge and levels of understanding in learning from text. *Cognitive Instruction, 3*, 455–468.

McNeill, D. (1970). *The acquisition of language: The study of developmental linguistics.* New York: Harper & Row.

Meadows, S. (1986). *Understanding child development.* London: Routledge.

Mellers, B.A., Schwartz, A., & Cooke, A.D.J. (1998). Judgement and decision making. *Annual Review of Psychology, 49*, 447–477.

Merzenich, M.M., Jenkins, W.M., Johnston, P., Schreiner, C., Miller, S.L., & Tallal, P. (1996). Temporal processing deficits of language-learning impaired children ameliorated by training. *Science, 271*, 77–81.

Metcalfe, J., & Weibe, D. (1987). Intuition in insight and noninsight problem solving. *Memory & Cognition, 15*, 238–246.

Meyer, B.J.F., & McConkie, G.W. (1973). What is recalled after hearing a passage? *Journal of Educational Psychology, 65*, 109–117.

Meyer, D.E., & Schvaneveldt, R.W. (1971). Facilitation in recognising pairs of words: Evidence of a dependence between retrieval operations. *Journal of Experimental Psychology, 90*, 227–234.

Miller, G.A. (1956). The magic number seven, plus or minus two: Some limits on our capacity for information processing. *Psychological Review, 63*, 81–93.

Miller, G.A., & Nicely, P. (1955). An analysis of perceptual confusions among some English consonants. *Journal of the Acoustical Society of America, 27*, 338–352.

Milner, A.D., & Goodale, M.A. (1995). *The visual brain in action.* Oxford: Oxford University Press.

Milner, A.D., & Goodale, M.A. (1998). The visual brain in action. *Psyche, 4*, 1–14.

Mitroff, I.I. (1974). *The subjective side of science.* Amsterdam: Elsevier.

Miyawaki, K., Strange, W., Verbrugge, R., Liberman, A.M., Jenkins, J.J., & Furjima, O. (1975). An effect of linguistic experience. The discrimination of [r] and [l] by native speakers of Japanese and English. *Perception and Psychophysics, 18*, 331–340.

Moray, N. (1959). Attention in dichotic listening: Affective cues and the influence of instructions. *Quarterly Journal of Experimental Psychology, 11*, 56–60.

Morris, C.D., Bransford, J.D., & Franks, J.J. (1977). Levels of processing versus transfer appropriate processing. *Journal of Verbal Learning & Verbal Behavior, 16*, 519–533.

Moscovitch, M., Winocur, G., & Behrmann, M. (1997). What is special about face recognition? Nineteen experiments on a person with visual object agnosia and dyslexia but normal face recognition. *Journal of Cognitive Neuroscience, 9*, 555–604.

Moss, H.E., & Gaskell, M.G. (1999). Lexical semantic processing during speech comprehension. In S. Garrod & M.J. Pickering (Eds.), *Language processing.* Hove, UK: Psychology Press.

Muter, P. (1978). Recognition failure of recallable words in semantic memory. *Memory and Cognition, 6*, 9–12.

Myers, L.B., & Brewin, C.R. (1994). Recall of early experiences and the repressive coping style. *Journal of Abnormal Psychology, 103*, 288–292.

Mynatt, C.R., Doherty, M.E., & Tweney, R.D. (1977). Confirmation bias in a simulated research environment: An experimental study of scientific inference. *Quarterly Journal of Experimental Psychology, 29,* 85–95.

Navon, D. (1977). Forest before trees: The precedence of global features in visual perception. *Cognitive Psychology, 9,* 353–383.

Needham, D., & Begg, I. (1991). Problem-oriented training promotes spontaneous analogical transfer: Memory-oriented training promotes memory for training. *Memory & Cognition, 19,* 543–557.

Neely, J.H. (1977). Semantic priming and retrieval from lexical memory: Roles of inhibitionless spreading activation and limited capacity attention. *Journal of Experimental Psychology: General, 106,* 226–254.

Neisser, U. (1964). Visual search. *Scientific American, 210,* 94–102.

Neisser, U. (1967). *Cognitive psychology.* New York: Appleton-Century-Crofts.

Neisser, U. (1996). Remembering as doing. *Behavioral and Brain Sciences, 19,* 203–204.

Neisser, U., & Becklen, R. (1975). Selective looking: Attending to visually specified events. *Cognitive Psychology, 7,* 480–494.

Nelson, K. (1973). Structure and strategy in learning to talk. *Monographs of the Society for Research in Child Development, 38* (serial no. 149).

Newell, A., & Simon, H.A. (1972). *Human problem solving.* Englewood Cliffs, NJ: Prentice-Hall.

Norman, D.A., & Bobrow, D.G. (1975). On date-limited and resource-limited processes. *Cognitive Psychology, 7,* 44–64.

Norman, D.A., & Shallice, T. (1986). Attention to action: Willed and automatic control of behaviour. In R.J. Davidson, G.E. Schwartz, & D. Shapiro (Eds.), *The design of everyday things.* New York: Doubleday.

Oakhill, J., Garnham, A., & Johnson-Laird, P.N. (1990). Belief bias effects in syllogistic reasoning. In K.J. Gilhooly, R.H. Logie, & G. Erdos (Eds.), *Lines of thinking* (Vol. 1). New York: Wiley.

Oaksford, M. (1997). Thinking and the rational analysis of human reasoning. *The Psychologist, 10,* 257–260.

Oaksford, M., & Chater, N. (1994). A rational analysis of the selection task as optimal data selection. *Psychological Review, 101,* 608–631.

O'Brien, D.P., Braine, M.D.S., & Yang, Y. (1994). Propositional reasoning by mental models? Simple to refute in principle and practice. *Psychological Review, 101,* 711–724.

O'Brien, E.J., Shank, D.M., Myers, J.L., & Rayner, K. (1988). Elaborative inferences during reading: Do they occur on-line? *Journal of Experimental Psychology: Learning, Memory, and Cognition, 14,* 410–420.

Ohlsson, S. (1992). Information processing explanations of insight and related phenomena. In M.T. Keane & K.J. Gilhooly (Eds.), *Advances in the psychology of thinking.* London: Harvester Wheatsheaf.

Okada, S., Hanada, M., Hattori, H., & Shoyama, T. (1963). A case of pure word deafness. *Studia Phonologica, 3,* 58–65.

Palmer, S.E. (1975). The effects of contextual scenes on the identification of objects. *Memory and Cognition, 3,* 519–526.

Papagno, C., Valentine, T., & Baddeley, A.D. (1991). Phonological short-term memory and foreign-language learning. *Journal of Memory and Language, 30,* 331–347.

Parkin, A.J. (1996). *Explorations in cognitive neuropsychology.* Oxford: Blackwell.

Parkin, A.J., & Williamson, P. (1986). Cerebral lateralisation at different stages of facial processing. *Cortex, 26,* 23–42.

Pashler, H. (1990). Do response modality effects support multiprocessor models of divided attention? *Journal of Experimental Psychology: Human Perception and Performance, 16,* 826–842.

Pashler, H. (1998). *Attention.* Hove, UK: Psychology Press.

Patterson, K.E., & Baddeley, A.D. (1977). When face recognition fails. *Journal of Experimental Psychology: Human Learning and Memory, 3,* 406–417.

Pederson, E., Danziger, E., Wilkins, D., Levinson, S., Kita, S., & Senft, G. (1998). Semantic typology and spatial conceptualisation. *Language, 74,* 557–589.

Perenin, M.-T., & Vighetto, A. (1988). Optic ataxia: A specific disruption in visuomotor mechanisms. 1. Different aspects of the deficit in reaching for objects. *Brain, 111,* 643–674.

Perfect, T.J., & Hollins, T.S. (1996). Predictive feeling of knowing judgements and postdictive confidence judgements in eyewitness memory and general knowledge. *Applied Cognitive Psychology, 10,* 371–382.

Peterson, R.R., & Savoy, P. (1998). Lexical selection and phonological encoding during language production: Evidence for cascaded processing. *Journal of Experimental Psychology: Learning, Memory, and Cognition, 24,* 539–557.

Pinel, J.P.J. (1997). *Biopsychology* (3rd ed.). Boston: Allyn & Bacon.

Pinker, S. (1984). *Language learnability and language development.* Cambridge, MA: Harvard University Press.

Plaut, D.C., McClelland, J.L., Seidenberg, M.S., & Patterson, K. (1996). Understanding normal and impaired word reading: Computational principles in quasi-regular domains. *Psychological Review, 103,* 56–115.

Plaut, D.C., & Shallice, T. (1993). Deep dyslexia: A case study of connectionist neuropsychology. *Cognitive Neuropsychology, 10,* 377–500.

Plunkett, K., & Marchman, V.A. (1991). U-shaped learning and frequency effects in a multi-layered perception. *Cognition, 38,* 43–102.

Pomerantz, J.R., & Garner, W.R. (1973). Stimulus configuration in selective attention tasks. *Perception & Psychophysics, 14,* 157–188.

Popper, K.R. (1972). *Objective knowledge.* Oxford: Oxford University Press.

Posner, M.I. (1980). Orienting of attention: The VIIth Sir Frederic Bartlett lecture. *Quarterly Journal of Experimental Psychology, 32A,* 3–25.

Posner, M.I., & Petersen, S.E. (1990). The attention system of the human brain. *Annual Review of Neuroscience, 13,* 25–42.

Posner, M.I., Rafal, R.D., Choate, L.S., & Vaughan, J. (1985). Inhibition of return: Neural basis and function. *Cognitive Neuropsychology, 2,* 211–228.

Posner, M.I., Walker, J.A., Friedrich, F.J., & Rafal, R.D. (1984). Effects of parietal lobe injury on covert orienting of visual attention. *Journal of Neuroscience, 4,* 1863–1874.

Pratkanis, A.R., & Aronson, E. (1992). *Age of propaganda: The everyday use and abuse of persuasion.* New York: W.H. Freeman.

Probhakaran, V., Smith, J.A.L., Desmond, J.E., Glover, G., & Gabrieli, J.D.E. (1997). Neural substrates of fluid reasoning: An fMRI study of neocortical activation during performance of the Raven's Progressive Matrices Test. *Cognitive Psychology, 33,* 43–63.

Protopapas, A. (1999). Connectionist modeling of speech perception. *Psychological Bulletin, 125,* 410–436.

Quinlan, P.T., & Wilton, R.N. (1998). Grouping by proximity or similarity? Competition between the Gestalt principles in vision. *Perception, 27,* 417–430.

Quinn, J.G., & McConnell, J. (1996). Irrelevant pictures in visual working memory. *Quarterly Journal of Experimental Psychology, 49A,* 200–215.

Rafal, R., Smith, J., Krantz, A., Cohen, A., & Brennan, C. (1990). Extrageniculate vision in hemianopic humans: Saccade inhibition by signals in the blind field. *Science, 250*, 118–121.

Rafal, R.D., & Posner, M.I. (1987). Deficits in human visual spatial attention following thalamic lesions. *Proceedings of the National Academy of Science, 84*, 7349–7353.

Rayner, K., Inhoff, A.W., Morrison, R.E., Slowiaczek, M.L., & Bertera, J.H. (1981). Masking of foveal and parafoveal vision during eye fixations in reading. *Journal of Experimental Psychology: Human Perception and Performance, 18*, 163–172.

Rayner, K., & Pollatsek, A. (1989). *The psychology of reading*. London: Prentice Hall.

Rayner, K., & Sereno, S.C. (1994). Eye movements in reading: Psycholinguistic studies. In M.A. Gernsbacher (Eds.), *Handbook of psycholinguistics*. New York: Academic Press.

Reason, J.T. (1979). Actions not as planned: The price of automatisation. In G. Underwood & R. Stevens (Eds.), *Aspects of consciousness: Vol. 1. Psychological issues*. London: Academic Press.

Reason, J.T. (1992). Cognitive underspecification: Its variety and consequences. In B.J. Baars (Ed.), *Experimental slips and human error: Exploring the architecture of volition*. New York: Plenum Press.

Reber, A.S. (1993). *Implicit learning and tacit knowledge*. Oxford: Oxford University Press.

Redelmeier, D., Koehler, D.J., Liberman, V., & Tversky, A. (1995). Probability judgment in medicine: Discounting unspecified alternatives. *Medical Decision Making, 15*, 227–230.

Reed, J.M., & Squire, L.R. (1998). Retrograde amnesia for facts and events: Findings from four new cases. *Journal of Neuroscience, 18*, 3943–3954.

Reicher, G.M. (1969). Perceptual recognition as a function of

meaningfulness of stimulus material. *Journal of Experimental Psychology, 81*, 274–280.

Reichle, E.D., Pollatsek, A., Fisher, D.L., & Rayner, K. (1998). Toward a model of eye movement control in reading. *Psychological Review, 105*, 125–157.

Reitman, J.S. (1971). Mechanisms of forgetting in short-term memory. *Cognitive Psychology 2*, 185–195.

Restle, F. (1979). Coding theory of the perception of motion configuration. *Psychological Review, 86*, 1–24.

Ritov, I., & Baron, J. (1990). Reluctance to vaccinate: Omission bias and ambiguity. *Journal of Behavioral Decision Making, 3*, 263–277.

Robbins, T.W., Anderson, E.J., Barker, D.R., Bradley, A.C., Fearnyhough, C., Henson, R., Hudson, S.R., & Baddeley, A. (1996). Working memory in chess. *Memory & Cognition, 24*, 83–93.

Robertson, I.H., Manly, T., Andrade, J., Baddeley, B.T., & Yiend, J. (1997). "Oops!" Performance correlates of everyday attentional failures in traumatic brain injured and normal subjects. *Neuropsychologia, 35*, 747–758.

Rock, I., & Palmer, S. (1990). The legacy of Gestalt psychology. *Scientific American*, December, 48–61.

Rubin, D.C., & Wenzel, A.E. (1996). One hundred years of forgetting: A quantitative description of retention. *Psychological Bulletin, 103*, 734–760.

Rudge, P., & Warrington, E.K. (1991). Selective impairment of memory and visual perception in splenial tumours. *Brain, 114*, 349–360.

Rumelhart, D.E., & Ortony, A. (1977). The representation of knowledge in memory. In R.C. Anderson, R.J. Spiro, & W.E. Montague (Eds.), *Schooling and the acquisition of knowledge*. Hillsdale, NJ: Lawrence Erlbaum Associates Inc.

Rumiati, R.I., Humphreys, G.W., Riddoch, J.M., & Bateman, A. (1994). Visual object agnosia without prosopagnosia or alexia: Evidence for hierarchical theories of visual recognition. In V. Bruce & G.W. Humphreys (Eds.), *Object and face recognition*. Hove, UK: Lawrence Erlbaum Associates Ltd.

Rundus, D., & Atkinson, R.C. (1970). Rehearsal processes in free recall, a procedure for direct observation. *Journal of Verbal Learning and Verbal Behavior, 9*, 99–105.

Runeson, S., & Frykholm, G. (1983). Kinematic specifications of dynamics as an informational basis for person-and-action perception: Expectation, gender recognition, and deceptive intention. *Journal of Experimental Psychology: General, 112*, 585–615.

Rylander, G. (1939). Personality changes after operations on the frontal lobes. *Acta Psychiatrica Neurologica* (Supplement No. 30).

Ryle, G. (1949). *The concept of mind*. London: Hutchinson.

Saffran, E.M., Schwartz, M.F., & Marin, O.S.M. (1980a). Evidence from aphasia: Isolating the components of a production model. In B. Butterword (Ed.), *Language production* (Vol. 1). London: Academic Press.

Saffran, E.M., Schwartz, M.F., & Marin, O.S.M. (1980b). The word order problem in agrammatism: II. Production. *Brain and Language, 10*, 249–262.

Samuel, A.G. (1981). Phonemic restoration: Insights from a new methodology. *Journal of Experimental Psychology: General, 110*, 474–494.

Samuel, A.G. (1990). Using perceptual-restoration effects to explore the architecture of perception. In G.T.M. Altmann (Ed.), *Cognitive models of speech processing*. Cambridge, MA: MIT Press.

Sanocki, T., Bowyer, K.W., Heath, M.D., & Sarkar, S. (1998). Are edges sufficient for object recognition? *Journal of Experimental Psychology: Human Perception and Performance, 24*, 340–349.

Savelsbergh, G.J.P., Pijpers, J.R., & van Santvoord, A.A.M. (1993). The visual guidance of catching. *Experimental Brain Research, 93*, 148–156.

Schacter, D.L. (1987). Implicit memory: History and current status. *Journal of Experimental Psychology: Learning, Memory, and Cognition, 13*, 501–518.

Schacter, D.L., Alpert, N.M., Savage, C.R., Rauch, S.L., & Albert, M.S. (1996). Conscious recollection and the human hippocampal formation: Evidence from positron emission tomography. *Proceedings of the National Academy of Science, USA, 93*, 321–325.

Schacter, D.L., & Church, B.A. (1995). Implicit memory in amnesic patients: When is auditory priming spared? *Journal of the International Neuropsychological Society, 1*, 434–442.

Schacter, D.L., Church, B.A., & Bolton, E. (1995). Implicit memory in amnesic patients: Impairment of voice-specific impairment priming. *Psychological Science, 6*, 20–25.

Schafer, R., & Murphy, G. (1943). The role of autism in visual figure–ground relationship. *Journal of Experimental Psychology, 32*, 335–343.

Schank, R.C., & Abelson, R.P. (1977). *Scripts, plans, goals and understanding*. Hillsdale, NJ: Lawrence Erlbaum Associates Inc.

Schiffman, H.R. (1967). Size estimations of familiar objects under informative and reduced conditions of viewing. *American Journal of Psychology, 80*, 229–235.

Schneider, W., & Shiffrin, R.M. (1977). Controlled and automatic human information processing: 1. Detection, search, and attention. *Psychological Review, 84*, 1–66.

Schooler, J.W., & Engstler-Schooler, T.Y. (1990). Verbal overshadowing of visual memories: Some things are better left unsaid. *Cognitive Psychology, 22*, 36–71.

Schwartz, M.F., Saffran, E.M., & Marin,

O.S.M. (1980). Fractionating the reading process in dementia: Evidence for word-specific print-to-sound associations. In M. Coltheart, K.E. Patterson, & J.C. Marshall (Eds.), *Deep dyslexia*. London: Routledge & Kegan Paul.

Searcy, J.H., & Bartlett, J.C. (1996). Inversion and processing of component and spatial-relational information in faces. *Journal of Experimental Psychology: Human Perception and Performance, 22,* 904–915.

Segal, S.J., & Fusella, V. (1970). Influence of imaged pictures and sounds on detection of visual and auditory signals. *Journal of Experimental Psychology, 83,* 458–464.

Segall, M.H., Campbell, D.T., & Herskovits, M.J. (1963). Cultural differences in the perception of geometrical illusions. *Science, 139,* 769–771.

Seger, C.A. (1994). Implicit learning. *Psychological Bulletin, 115,* 163–196.

Seidenberg, M.S., Waters, G.S., Barnes, M.A., & Tanenhaus, M. (1984). When does irregular spelling or pronunciation influence word recognition? *Journal of Verbal Learning and Verbal Behavior, 23,* 383–404.

Sekuler, R., & Blake, R. (1994). *Perception* (3rd ed.). New York: McGraw-Hill.

Selfridge, O.G. (1959). Pandemonium: A paradigm for learning. In *The mechanisms of thought processes*. London: HMSO.

Sellen, A.J., & Norman, D.A. (1992). The psychology of slips. In B.J. Baars (Ed.), *Experimental slips and human error: Exploring the architecture of volition*. New York: Plenum Press.

Shaffer, D.R. (1993). *Developmental psychology: Childhood and adolescence* (3rd ed.). Pacific Grove, CA: Brooks/Cole.

Shaffer, L.H. (1975). Multiple attention in continuous verbal tasks. In P.M.A.

Rabbitt & S. Dornic (Eds.), *Attention and performance* (Vol. V). London: Academic Press.

Shah, P., & Miyake, A. (1996). The separability of working memory resources for spatial thinking and language processing: An individual difference approach. *Journal of Experimental Psychology: General, 125,* 4–27.

Shah, P., & Miyake, A. (1999). Models of working memory: An introduction. In A. Miyake & P. Shah (Eds.), *Models of working memory: Mechanisms of active maintenance and executive control*. New York: Cambridge University Press.

Shallice, T., & Burgess, P. (1996). The domain of supervisory processes and temporal organisation of behaviour. *Philosophical Transactions of the Royal Society of London, B, 351,* 1405–1412.

Shallice, T., & Warrington, E.K. (1970). The association between long-term retention of meaningful sounds and verbal material. *Neuropsychologia, 12,* 553–555.

Shallice, T., & Warrington, E.K. (1974). The association between long-term retention of meaningful sounds and verbal material.

Shanks, D.R., & St. John, M.F. (1994). Characteristics of dissociable human learning systems. *Behavioral and Brain Sciences, 17,* 367–394.

Shatz, M., & Gelman, R. (1973). The development of communication skills: Modifications in the speech of young children as a function of the listener. *Monographs of the Society for Research in Child Development, No. 38.*

Sheridan, J., & Humphreys, G.W. (1993). A verbal-semantic category-specific deficit. *Cognitive Neuropsychology, 10,* 143–184.

Shiffrin, R.M., & Schneider, W. (1977). Controlled and automatic human information processing: II. Perceptual learning, automatic attending, and a general theory. *Psychological Review, 84,* 127–190.

Shipp, S., de Jong, B.M., Zihl, J., Frackowiak, R.S.J., & Zeki, S. (1994). The brain activity related to residual activity in a patient with bilateral lesions of V5. *Brain, 117,* 1023–1038.

Simon, H.A. (1974). How big is a chunk? *Science, 183,* 482–488.

Simon, H.A., & Reed, S.K. (1976). Modelling strategy shifts on a problem solving task. *Cognitive Psychology, 8,* 86–97.

Siqueland, E.R., & DeLucia, C.A. (1969). Visual reinforcement of non-nutritive sucking in human infants. *Science, 165,* 1144–1146.

Skinner, B.F. (1957). *Verbal behaviour.* New York: Appleton-Century-Crofts.

Slamecka, N.J. (1966). Differentiation versus unlearning of verbal associations. *Journal of Experimental Psychology, 71,* 822–828.

Slater, A. (1990). Perceptual development. In M.W. Eysenck (Ed.), *The Blackwell dictionary of cognitive psychology.* Oxford: Blackwell.

Slater, A. (1996). The organisation of visual perception in early infancy. In F. Vital-Durand, J. Atkinson, & O. Braddick (Eds.), *Infant vision.* Oxford: Oxford University Press.

Slater, A., Matock, A., & Brown, E. (1990). Size constancy at birth: Newborn infants' responses to retinal and real size. *Journal of Experimental Child Psychology, 49,* 314–322.

Slater, A., & Morison, V. (1985). Shape constancy and slant perception at birth. *Perception, 14,* 337–344.

Smith, P.K., Cowie, H., & Blades, M. (1998). *Understanding children's Development* (3rd ed.). Oxford: Blackwell.

Smith, D.E., & Hochberg, J.E. (1954). The effect of "punishment" (electric shock) on figure–ground perception. *Journal of Psychology, 38,* 83–87.

Smith, E.E., & Jonides, J. (1997). Working memory: A view from neuroimaging. *Cognitive Psychology, 33,* 5–42.

Smyth, M.M., Morris, P.E., Levy, P., & Ellis, A.W. (1987). *Cognition in action.* Hove, UK: Lawrence Erlbaum Associates Ltd.

Solso, R.L. (1994). *Cognition and the visual arts.* Cambridge, MA: MIT Press.

Spearman, C. (1927). *The abilities of man.* London: Macmillan.

Spelke, E.S., Breinlinger, K., Jacobson, K., & Phillips, A. (1993). Gestalt relations and object perception: A developmental study. *Vision Research, 22,* 531–544.

Spelke, E.S., Hirst, W.C., & Neisser, U. (1976). Skills of divided attention. *Cognition, 4,* 215–230.

Spellman, B.A., & Holyoak, K.J. (1996). Pragmatics in analogical mapping. *Cognitive Psychology, 31,* 307–346.

Sperling, G. (1960). The information available in brief visual presentations. *Psychological Monographs, 74* (Whole No. 498), 1–29.

Squire, L.R., & Frambach, M. (1990). Cognitive skill learning in amnesia. *Psychobiology, 18,* 109–117.

Stemberger, J.P. (1982). The nature of segments in the lexicon: Evidence from speech errors. *Lingua, 56,* 235–259.

Sternberg, R.J. (1990). *Metaphors of mind: Conceptions of the nature of intelligence.* New York: Cambridge University Press.

Sternberg, R.J., & Gardner, M.K. (1983). Unities in inductive reasoning. *Journal of Experimental Psychology: General, 112,* 80–116.

Sternberg, R.J., & Weil, E.M. (1980). An aptitude X strategy interaction in linear syllogistic reasoning. *Journal of Educational Psychology, 72,* 226–239.

Stewart, F., Parkin, A.J., & Hunkin, N.M. (1992). Naming impairments following recovery from herpes-simplex encephalitis: Category specific? *Quarterly Journal of Experimental Psychology, 44A,* 261–284.

Stroop, J.R. (1935). Studies of interference in serial verbal reactions. *Journal of Experimental Psychology, 18,* 643–662.

Styles, E.A. (1997). *The psychology of attention.* Hove, UK: Psychology Press.

Sulin, R.A., & Dooling, D.J. (1974). Intrusion of a thematic idea in retention of prose. *Journal of Experimental Psychology, 103,* 255–262.

Sullivan, L. (1976). Selective attention and secondary message analysis: A reconsideration of Broadbent's filter model of selective attention. *Quarterly Journal of Experimental Psychology, 28,* 167–178.

Tallal, P. (1976). Rapid auditory processing in normal and disordered language development. *Journal of Speech and Hearing Research, 19,* 561–571.

Tallal, P. (1990). Fine-grained discrimination deficits in language-learning impaired children are specific neither to the auditory modality nor to speech perception. *Journal of Speech and Hearing Research, 33,* 616 621.

Tallal, P., Miller, S.L., Bedi, G., Byma, G., Wang, X., Najarajan, S.S., Schreiner, C., Jenkins, W.M., & Merzenich, M.M. (1996). Language comprehension in language-learning impaired children improved with acoustically modified speech. *Science, 271,* 81–84.

Tarr, M.J., & Bülthoff, H.H. (1995). Is human object recognition better described by geon structural descriptions or by multiple views? Comment on Biederman and Gerhardstein (1993). *Journal of Experimental Psychology: Human Perception and Performance, 21,* 1494–1505.

Tarr, M.J., & Bülthoff, H.H. (1998). Image-based object recognition in man, monkey and machine. *Cognition, 67,* 1–20.

Teller, D.Y. (1997). First glances: The vision of infants. *Investigative Opththalmology & Visual Science, 38,* 2183–2203.

Tetlock, P.E. (1991). An alternative metaphor in the study of judgement and choice: People as politicians. *Theory and Psychology, 1,* 451–475.

Thomas, J.C. (1974). An analysis of behaviour in the hobbits–orcs problem. *Cognitive Psychology, 6,* 257–269.

Thorndike, E.L. (1898). Animal intelligence: An experimental study of the associative processes in animals. *The Psychological Review Monograph Supplements, 2,* No. 4 (Whole No. 8).

Thorndyke, P.W. (1977). Cognitive structures in comprehension and memory of narrative discourse. *Cognitive Psychology, 9,* 77–110.

Tizard, B., & Hughes, M. (1984). *Young children learning.* London: Fontana.

Treisman, A.M. (1964). Verbal cues, language, and meaning in selective attention. *American Journal of Psychology, 77,* 206–219.

Treisman, A.M. (1988). Features and objects: The fourteenth Bartlett memorial lecture. *Quarterly Journal of Experimental Psychology, 40A,* 201–237.

Treisman, A.M. (1992). Spreading suppression or feature integration? A reply to Duncan and Humphreys (1992). *Journal of Experimental Psychology: Human Perception and Performance, 18,* 589–593.

Treisman, A.M., & Davies, A. (1973). Divided attention to ear and eye. In S. Kornblum (Ed.), *Attention and performance* (Vol. IV). London: Academic Press.

Treisman, A.M., & Geffen, G. (1967). Selective attention: Perception or response? *Quarterly Journal of Experimental Psychology, 19,* 1–18.

Treisman, A.M., & Gelade, G. (1980). A feature integration theory of attention. *Cognitive Psychology, 12,* 97–136.

Treisman, A.M., & Riley, J.G.A. (1969). Is selective attention selective perception or selective response: A further test.

Journal of Experimental Psychology, 79,
27–34.

Treisman, A.M., & Sato, S. (1990).
Conjunction search revisited. Journal of
Experimental Psychology: Human
Perception and Performance, 16, 459–478.

Treisman, A.M., & Schmidt, H. (1982).
Illusory conjunctions in the perception
of objects. Cognitive Psychology, 14, 107–
141.

Tresilian, J.R. (1994). Two straw men stay
silent when asked about the "direct"
versus "inferential" controversy.
Behavioral and Brain Sciences, 17, 335–
336.

Tresilian, J.R. (1995). Perceptual and
cognitive processes in time-to-contact
estimation: Analysis of prediction-
motion and relative judgement tasks.
Perception and Psychophysics, 57, 231–
245.

Tulving, E. (1972). Episodic and semantic
memory. In E. Tulving & W. Donaldson
(Eds.), Organisation of memory. London:
Academic Press.

Tulving, E. (1974). Cue-dependent
forgetting. American Scientist, 62, 74–82.

Tulving, E. (1979). Relation between
encoding specificity and levels of
processing. In L.S. Cermak & F.I.M.
Craik (Eds.), Levels of processing in
human memory. Hillsdale, NJ: Lawrence
Erlbaum Associates Inc.

Tulving, E., & Psotka, J. (1971). Retroactive
inhibition in free recall: Inaccessibility
of information available in the memory
store. Journal of Experimental Psychology,
87, 116–124.

Tulving, E., & Schacter, D.L. (1990).
Priming and human memory. Science,
247, 301–306.

Tulving, E., Schacter, D.L., & Stark, H.A.
(1982). Priming effects in word-
fragment completion are independent
of recognition memory. Journal of
Experimental Psychology: Learning,
Memory, and Cognition, 17, 595–617.

Tulving, E., & Thomson, D.M. (1973).

Encoding specificity and retrieval
processes in episodic memory.
Psychological Review, 80, 352–373.

Turnbull, C.M. (1961). The forest people.
New York: Simon & Schuster.

Tversky, A., & Kahneman, D. (1974).
Judgement under uncertainty:
Heuristics and biases. Science, 185,
1124–1131.

Tversky, A., & Kahneman, D. (1980).
Causal schemas in judgements under
uncertainty. In M. Fishbein (Ed.),
Progress in social psychology. Hillsdale,
NJ: Lawrence Erlbaum Associates Inc.

Tversky, A., & Kahneman, D. (1981). The
framing of decisions and the
psychology of choice. Science, 211, 453–
458.

Tversky, A., & Kahneman, D. (1983).
Extensional versus intuitive reasoning:
The conjunction fallacy in probability
judgement. Psychological Review, 91,
293–315.

Tversky, A., & Koehler, D.J. (1994).
Support theory: A nonextensional
representation of subjective probability.
Psychological Review, 101, 547–567.

Tweney, R.D., Doherty, M.E., Warner,
W.J., Pliske, D.B., Mynatt, C.R., Gross,
K.A., & Arkkezin, D.L. (1980). Strategies
of rule discovery in an inference task.
Quarterly Journal of Experimental
Psychology, 32, 109–124.

Tzelgov, J., Henik, A., Sneg, R., & Baruch,
O. (1996). Unintentional reading via the
phonological route: The Stroop effect
with cross-script homophones. Journal
of Experimental Psychology: Learning,
Memory, and Cognition, 22, 336–339.

Underwood, B.J. (1957). Interference and
forgetting. Psychological Review, 64, 49–
60.

Underwood, B.J., & Postman, L. (1960).
Extra-experimental sources of
interference in forgetting. Psychological
Review, 67, 73–95.

Underwood, G. (1974). Moray vs. the rest:
The effect of extended shadowing

practice. *Quarterly Journal of Experimental Psychology, 26*, 368–372.

Valdois, S., Carbonnel, S., David, D., Rousset, S., & Pellat, J. (1995). Confrontation of PDP models and dual-route models through the analysis of a case of deep dysphasia. *Cognitive Neuropsychology, 12*, 681–724.

Valentine, T., Brédart, S., Lawson, R., & Ward, G. (1991). What's in a name? Access to information from people's names. *European Journal of Cognitive Psychology, 3*, 147–176.

Vallar, G., & Baddeley, A.D. (1984). Phonological short-term store, phonological processing and sentence comprehension: A neuropsychological case study. *Cognitive Neuropsychology, 1*, 121–141.

Vargha-Khadem, F., Watkins, K., Alcock, K., Fletcher, P., & Passingham, R. (1995). Praxic and nonverbal cognitive deficits in a large family with a genetically transmitted speech and language disorder. *Proceedings of the National Academy of Sciences, 92*, 930–933.

Vargha-Khadem, F., Gadian, D.G., Watkins, K.E., Connelly, A., Van Paesschen, W., & Mishkin, M. (1997). Differential effects of early hippocampal pathology on episodic and semantic memory. *Science, 277*, 376–380.

Vecera, S.P., & Farah, M.J. (1997). Is visual image segmentation a bottom-up or an interactive process? *Perception and Psychophysics, 59*, 1280–1296.

Von Wright, J.M., Anderson, K., & Stenman, U. (1975). Generalisation of conditioned G.S.R.s in dichotic listening. In P.M.A. Rabbitt & S. Dornic (Eds.), *Attention and performance* (Vol. V). London: Academic Press.

Wagner, A.D., Desmond, J.E., Demb, J.B., Glover, G.H., & Gabrieli, J.D.E. (1997). Semantic repetition priming for verbal and pictorial knowledge: A functional MRI study of left inferior prefrontal cortex. *Journal of Cognitive Neuroscience, 9*, 714–726.

Wallach, H. (1948). Brightness constancy and the nature of achromatic colors. *Journal of Experimental Psychology, 38*, 310–324.

Walton, G.E., Bower, N.J.A., & Bower, T.G.R. (1992). Recognition of familiar faces by newborns. *Infant Behavior and Development, 15*, 265–269.

Waltz, J.A., Knowlton, B.J., Holyoak, K.J., Boone, K.B., Mishkin, F.S., Santos, M. de M., Thomas, C.R., & Miller, B.L. (1999). A system for relational reasoning in human prefrontal cortex. *Psychological Science, 10*, 119–125.

Wang, X.T. (1996). Domain-specific rationality in human choices: Violations of utility axioms and social contexts. *Cognition, 60*, 31–63.

Wann, J.P. (1996). Anticipating arrival: Is the tau margin a specious theory? *Journal of Experimental Psychology: Human Perception and Performance, 22*, 1031–1048.

Wann, J.P., & Rushton, S.K. (1995). Grasping the impossible: Stereoscopic virtual balls. In B.G. Bardy, R.J. Bootsma, & Y. Guiard (Eds.), *Studies in perception and action* (Vol. III). Hillsdale, NJ: Lawrence Erlbaum Associates Inc.

Warr, P.B. (1964). The relative importance of proactive interference and degree of learning in retention of paired associate items. *British Journal of Psychology, 55*, 19–30.

Warren, R.M., & Warren, R.P. (1970). Auditory illusions and confusions. *Scientific American, 223*, 30–36.

Warrington, E.K., & James, M. (1988). Visual apperceptive agnosia: A clinico-anatomical study of three cases. *Cortex, 24*, 13–32.

Warrington, E.K., & McCarthy, R.A. (1994). Multiple meaning systems in the brain: A case for visual semantics. *Neuropsychologia, 32*, 1465–1473.

Warrington, E.K., & Shallice, T. (1972). Neuropsychological evidence of visual storage in short-term memory tasks. *Quarterly Journal of Experimental Psychology, 24,* 30–40.

Warrington, E.K., & Shallice, T. (1984). Category-specific semantic impairment. *Brain, 107,* 829–854.

Warrington, E.K., & Taylor, A.M. (1978). Two categorical stages of object recognition. *Perception, 7,* 695–705.

Wason, P.C. (1960). On the failure to eliminate hypotheses in a conceptual task. *Quarterly Journal of Experimental Psychology, 12,* 129–140.

Wason, P.C. (1968). Reasoning about a rule. *Quarterly Journal of Experimental Psychology, 20,* 273–281.

Wason, P.C., & Shapiro, D. (1971). Natural and contrived experience in reasoning problems. *Quarterly Journal of Experimental Psychology, 23,* 63–71.

Watkins, M.J., Watkins, O.C., Craik, F.I.M., & Mazauryk, G. (1973). Effect of non-verbal distraction on short-term storage. *Journal of Experimental Psychology, 101,* 296–300.

Waugh, N.C., & Norman, D.A. (1965). Primary memory. *Psychological Review, 72,* 89–104.

Weinberger, D.A., Schwartz, G.E., & Davidson, J.R. (1979). Low-anxious, high-anxious, and repressive coping styles: Psychometric patterns and behavioural and physiological responses to stress. *Journal of Abnormal Psychology, 88,* 369–380.

Weir, W. (1984). Another look at subliminal "facts". *Advertising Age,* 15 October, 46.

Weiskrantz, L. (1986). *Blindsight: A case study and implications.* Oxford: Oxford University Press.

Weiskrantz, L., Barbur, J.L., & Sahraie, A. (1995). Parameters affecting conscious versus unconscious visual discrimination with damage to the visual cortex V1. *Proceedings of the National Academy of Sciences, USA, 92,* 6122–6126.

Weiskrantz, L., Warrington, E.K., Sanders, M.D., & Marshall, J. (1974). Visual capacity in the hemianopic field following a restricted occipital ablation. *Brain, 97,* 709–728.

Weisstein, N., & Harris, C.S. (1974). Visual detection of line segments: An object-superiority effect. *Science, 186,* 752–755.

Weisstein, N., & Wong, E. (1986). Figure–ground organisation and the spatial and temporal responses of the visual system. In E.C. Schwab & H.C. Nusbaum (Eds.), *Pattern recognition by humans and machines* (Vol. 2). New York: Academic Press.

Welford, A.T. (1952). The psychological refractory period and the timing of high speed performance. *British Journal of Psychology, 43,* 2–19.

Wells, G.L. (1993). What do we know about eye-witness identification? *American Psychologist, 48,* 553–571.

Werker, J.F., & Tees, R.C. (1992). The organisation and reorganisation of human speech perception. *Annual Review of Neuroscience, 15,* 377–402.

Wharton, C.M., Grafman, J., Flitman, S.K., Hansen, E.K., Brauner, J., Marks, A., & Honda, M. (1998). The neuroanatomy of analogical reasoning. In K.J. Holyoak, D. Gentner, & B. Kekinar (Eds.), *Analogy 98.* Sofia, Bulgaria: New University of Bulgaria.

Wheatstone, C. (1838). Contributions to the physiology of vision. Part 1: On some remarkable and hitherto unobserved phenomena of binocular vision. *Philosophical Transactions of the Royal Society of London, 128,* 371–394.

Wheeler, M.A., Stuss, D.T., & Tulving, E. (1997). Toward a theory of episodic memory: The frontal lobes and autonoetic consciousness. *Psychological Bulletin, 121,* 331–354.

Whitlow, S.D., Althoff, R.R., & Cohen, N.J. (1995). Deficit in relational (declarative) memory in amnesia. *Society for Neuroscience Abstracts, 21*, 754.

Whorf, B.L. (1956). *Language, thought, and reality: Selected writings of Benjamin Lee Whorf*. New York: John Wiley.

Wickens, C.D. (1984). Processing resources in attention. In R. Parasuraman & D.R. Davies (Eds.), *Varieties of attention*. London: Academic Press.

Williams, L.M. (1994). Recall of childhood trauma: A prospective study of women's memories of childhood abuse. *Journal of Consulting and Clinical Psychology, 62*, 1167–1176.

Willingham, D.B., & Goedert-Eschmann, K. (1999). The relation between implicit and explicit learning: Evidence for parallel development. *Psychological Science, 10*, 531–534.

Willmes, K., & Poeck, K. (1993). To what extent can aphasic syndromes be localised? *Brain, 116*, 1527–1540.

Wise, R.J.S., Chollet, F., Hadar, U., Friston, K., Hoffner, E., & Frackowiak, R.S.J. (1991). Distribution of cortical neural networks involved in word comprehension and word retrieval. *Brain, 114*, 1803–1817.

Woldorff, M.G., Gallen, C.C., Hampson, S.A., Hillyard, S.A., Pantev, C., Sobel, D., & Bloom, F.E. (1993). Modulation of early sensory processing in human auditory cortex during auditory selective attention. *Proceedings of the National Academy of Sciences, 90*, 8722–8726.

Wolfe, J.M. (1998). Visual search. In H. Pashler (Ed.), *Attention*. Hove, UK: Psychology Press.

Woodworth, R.S., & Schlosberg, H. (1954). *Experimental psychology* (2nd ed.). New York: Holt, Rinehart, & Winston.

Woodworth, R.S., & Sells, S.B. (1935). An atmosphere effect in formal syllogistic reasoning. *Journal of Experimental Psychology, 18*, 451–460.

Wraga, M., Creem, S.H., & Proffitt, D.R. (2000). Perception–action dissociations of a walkable Müller–Lyer configuration. *Psychological Science, 11*, 239–243.

Wright, D.B., & Gaskell, G.D. (1995). Flashbulb memories: Conceptual and methodological issues. *Memory, 3*, 67–80.

Wright, D.B., Gaskell, G.D., & O'Muircheartaigh, C.A. (1998). Flashbulb memory assumptions: Using national surveys to explore cognitive phenomena. *British Journal of Psychology, 89*, 103–121.

Wynn, V.E., & Logie, R.H. (1998). The veracity of long-term memories: Did Bartlett get it right? *Applied Cognitive Psychology, 12*, 1–20.

Yaniv, I., & Meyer, D.E. (1987). Activation and metacognition of inaccessible information. Potential bases for incubation effects in problem solving. *Journal of Experimental Psychology: Learning, Memory, & Cognition, 13*, 187–205.

Yantis, S. (1998). Control of visual attention. In H. Pashler (Ed.), *Attention*. Hove, UK: Psychology Press.

Yonas, A., & Granrud, C.E. (1985). The development of sensitivity to kinetic, binocular and pictorial depth information in human infants. In D. Ingle, D. Lee, & R.M. Jeannerod (Eds.), *Brain mechanisms and spatial vision*. The Hague: Nijhoff.

Young, A.W., & de Haan, E.H.F. (1988). Boundaries of covert recognition in prosopagnosia. *Cognitive Neuropsychology, 5*, 317–336.

Young, A.W., Hay, D.C., & Ellis, A.W. (1985). The faces that launched a thousand slips: Everyday difficulties and errors in recognising people. *British Journal of Psychology, 76*, 495–523.

Young, A.W., McWeeny, K.H., Hay, D.C., & Ellis, A.W. (1986a). Matching familiar and unfamiliar faces on identity and expression. *Psychological Research, 48*, 63–68.

Young, A.W., McWeeny, K.H., Hay, D.C., & Ellis, A.W. (1986b). Naming and categorisation latencies for faces and written names. *Quarterly Journal of Experimental Psychology, 38A*, 297–318.

Young, A.W., Newcombe, F., de Haan, E.H.F., Small, M., & Hay, D.C. (1993). Face perception after brain injury: Selective impairments affecting identity and expression. *Brain, 116*, 941–959.

Zeki, S. (1983). Colour coding in the cerebral cortex: The reaction of cells in monkey visual cortex to wavelengths and colour. *Neuroscience, 9*, 741–756.

Zeki, S. (1992). The visual image in mind and brain. *Scientific American, 267*, 43–50.

Zeki, S. (1993). *A vision of the brain.* Oxford: Blackwell.

Zihl, J., von Cramon, D., & Mai, N. (1983). Selective disturbance of movement vision after bilateral brain damage. *Brain, 106*, 313–340.

Zihl, J., von Cramon, D., Mai, N., & Schmid, C. (1991). Disturbance of movement vision after bilateral posterior brain damage, further evidence and follow up observations. *Brain, 114*, 2235–2252.

Zwaan, R.A. (1994). Effects of genre expectations on text comprehension. *Journal of Experimental Psychology: Learning, Memory and Cognition, 20*, 920–933.

Zwaan, R.A., Langston, M.C., & Graesser, A.C. (1995). The construction of situation models in narrative comprehension: An event-indexing model. *Psychological Science, 6*, 292–297.

Zwaan, R.A., & Radvansky, G.A. (1998). Situation models in language comprehension and memory. *Psychological Bulletin, 123*, 162–185.

Zwaan, R.A., & van Oostendop, U. (1993). Do readers construct spatial representations in naturalistic story comprehension? *Discourse Processes, 16*, 125–143.

Zwitserlood, P. (1989). The locus of the effects of sentential–semantic context in spoken-word processing. *Cognition, 32*, 25–64.

Author index

Griggs, R.A. 361
Groeger, J.A. 223
Gross, K.A. 373, 374
Grudin, J.T. 150
Gunther, H. 264
Gustafsson, K.A. 46
Guy, C. 61

Ha, Y.-W. 374
Haber, R.N. 159
Hadar, U. 302
Haendiges, A.N. 300
Hagan, R. 59
Haider, H. 321
Haller, M. 269
Halligan, P.W. 120, 124
Hampson, P.J. 130
Hampson, S.A. 19
Hanada, M. 252
Hansen, E.K. 355
Harley, T. 239, 251, 269, 284, 295, 297, 309
Harding, G.F.A. 19
Harper, R.S. 28
Harris, C.S. 72
Harris, M. 240
Harvey, L.O. 72
Harvey, M. 34
Hashtroudi, S. 221
Hatano, G. 329
Hattori, H. 252
Hay, D.C. 89, 90
Hay, J.F. 150, 151
Hayward, W.G. 79
Hazeltine, E. 183
Heath, M.D. 77, 78
Heather, N. 5
Hector, J. 223
Heider, E. 305
Heilman, K.M. 301
Helmholtz, Hermann von 41, 48, 63
Henderson, C. 103
Henik, A. 143, 273
Henson, R. 166, 167
Hering, E. 43, 62
Herskovits, M.J. 104, 105
Hess, R.D. 309
Heywood, C.A. 19
Hiatt, S. 103
Hillyard, S.A. 119
Hirst, W.C. 132, 140
Hitch, G.J. 166, 168

Hochberg, J. 38
Hochberg, J.E. 28
Hoffman, C. 306, 307
Hoffner, E. 302
Hoffrage, U. 347
Holding, D.H. 327, 328, 329
Holender, D. 59
Holliday, I.E. 19
Hollins, T.S. 224
Holway, A.F. 55
Holyoak, K.J. 353, 354, 355, 356, 357, 358
Holyoak, K.L. 351, 352, 353
Honda, M. 355
Horton, W.S. 290
Howard, D. 299, 302, 303
Howard, D.V. 183, 184, 187
Howard, J.H. 183, 184, 187
Hubel, D.H. 70, 71
Hudson, S.R. 166, 167
Hug, K. 362
Hughes, M. 309
Hummel, J.E. . 353, 355, 356, 357
Humphrey, G.K. 35
Humphreys, G. 8, 83, 87, 262, 272
Humphreys, G.W. 74, 79, 81, 82, 83, 84–6, 98, 110, 122
Hunkin, N.M. 98
Hunt, E. 304, 306, 307, 312
Hurlbert, A.C. 46
Hurvich, L.M. 44
Hut, Z.212
Hyde, T.S. 177, 178, 180

Inagaki, K. 329
Inhoff, A.W. 259
Ittelson, W.H. 27, 29, 53, 55
Ivry, R.B. 8, 97, 183

Jacobs, F.H. 305
Jacobson, K. 107
Jacoby, L.L. 150, 151
Jakobson, L.S. 34
Jakobsson, T. 46
James, M. 81
James, W. 98
Janowsky, J.S. 202
Jenkins, J.J. 177, 178, 180, 305
Jenkins, W.M. 242
Jerrett, D.T. 306
Jerrett, T. 306

Johansson, G. 50
Johnson, M.H. 102
Johnson, D.R. 306, 307
Johnson, M.H. 102
Johnson, M.K. 215, 216, 221
Johnson-Laird, P.N. 341, 347, 363, 364, 366, 368, 369, 370, 371, 372, 377
Johnston, P. 242
Johnston, R.A. 95
Jones, D. 240
Jonides, J. 169, 172
Joseph, J.E. 76
Ju, G. 76, 77

Kahneman, D. 134, 135, 137, 138, 143, 155, 332–3, 334, 335, 336, 339, 340, 342, 343, 344, 345, 346, 347
Kaneko, H. 57
Kanizsa, G. 52
Kanwisher, N. 94
Kay, J. 267, 299
Kay, M.C. 89, 90
Keane, M.T. 331, 354
Kellman, P.J. 107
Kellogg, R.T. 343
Kenealy, P.M. 197, 198
Kennard, C. 19
Kertesz, A. 267
Keysar, B. 290
Kilduff, P.T. 125, 126
Kilpatrick, F.P. 55
Kimchi, R. 77
Kimura, I. 253
Kinchla, R.A. 69
Kintsch, W. 283, 284–5, 286, 288, 311
Kirby, K.N. 363
Kita, S. 307
Klar, Y. 362
Klayman, J. 374
Knight, R.T. 212
Knoblich, G. 321
Knowlton, B.J. 182, 351, 352, 353
Koehler, D.J. 346
Koehler, J.J. 340, 341, 342
Koffka, K. 20, 21
Kogure, K. 253
Köhler, S. 19, 20, 60
Köhler, W. 317
Kolodny, J. 353

Sanocki, T. 77, 78
Santos, M. de M. 351, 352, 353
Sarkar, S. 77, 78
Saso, S. 253
Sato, S. 128, 129
Savage, C.R. 204
Savary, F. 372
Savelsbergh, G.J.P. 49
Savoy, P. 298, 299
Schacter, D.L. 203, 204, 209, 210, 211, 213
Schaeken, W. 372
Schafer, R. 28
Schank, R.C. 214, 217
Schiffman, H.R. 57
Schlosberg, H. 55
Schmalhofer, F. 285, 286
Schmidt, H. 128
Schneider, W. 143–6, 155
Schoenberger, A. 340
Schooler, J.W. 222, 305
Schreiner, C. 242
Schvaneveldt, R.W. 260
Schwartz, A. 336, 337
Schwartz, G.E. 191
Schwartz, M.F. 268, 300
Schweinberger, S.R. 170
Seabrook, C.223
Searcy, J.H. 92, 93
Segal, S.J. 138, 139
Segall, M.H. 104, 105
Seger, C.A. 181
Segui, J. 249, 250
Seidenberg, M.S. 269, 270, 271, 272, 275, 276
Sejnowski, T.J. 10
Sekuler, E.B. 97
Sekuler, R. 17, 18, 40, 43, 48, 71
Sellen, A.J. 150, 152, 153
Sells, S.B. 365
Semmes, J. 22, 23
Senft, G. 307
Sereno, S.C. 259
Shaffer, D.R. 232, 241
Shaffer, L.H. 133
Shah, P. 175
Shallice, T. 4, 82, 130, 143, 147–8
Shank, D.M. 279
Shanks, D.R. 183, 184, 187
Shapiro, D. 137, 361
Shatz, M. 235, 240
Sheridan, J. 86

Shiffrin, R.M. 143–6, 155, 157, 158, 161, 162, 177
Shimamura, A.P. 202
Shipman, V. 309
Shipp, S. 20
Shoyama, T. 252
Simon, H.A. 161, 322–6, 327, 328, 329, 348
Sin, G. 300
Singer, M. 218, 219, 282
Singh, K.D. 19
Siqueland, E.R. 100
Skinner, B.F. 239, 240, 274
Slamecka, N.J. 196
Slater, A. 104, 109
Slovic, P. 345
Slowiaczek, M.L. 259
Small, M. 90
Smith, D.E. 28
Smith, E.E. 44, 169, 172
Smith, J. 60
Smith, J.A.L. 353
Smith, S.M. 165, 177
Smyth, M.M. 292
Sneg, R. 273
Sobel, D. 119
Solso, R.L. 326
Sommer, W. 170
Sowden, P.T. 306
Spearman, C. 353
Spelke, E.S. 107, 132, 140
Spellman, B.A. 356, 357
Sperling, G. 159, 160
Spieler, D. 256
Squire, L.R. 182, 183, 202, 206, 209, 210
St James, J.D. 122
St John, M.F. 183, 184, 187
Stark, H.A. 203
Stein, B,S. 178
Stemberger, J.P. 292
Stenman, U. 117
Stephens, B.R. 101
Stephenson, G.M. 214
Sternberg, R.J. 372
Stevens, E.B. 246
Stewart, F. 98
Stone, M.V. 180
Strange, W. 305
Stroop, J.R. 260
Strupp, J. 212
Stuss, D.T. 201, 202
Styles, E.A. 119

Sulin, R.A. 215
Sullivan, L. 133
Svec, W.R. 293, 296, 297
Svejda, M. 103

Talbot, N. 207
Tallal, P. 241, 242
Tanenhaus, M. 269
Tarr, M.J. 78
Taylor, A.M. 80
Tees, R.C. 243
Teller, D.Y. 100, 108, 109
Teller, S.A. 225
Termura, K. 253
Tetlock, P.E. 337
Teuber, H.L. 318
Thomas, C.R. 351, 352, 353
Thomas, J.C. 323, 324
Thompson-Schill, S. 194, 195
Thomson, D.M. 157
Thomson, N. 167, 168, 169
Thorndike, E.L. 316, 317
Thorndyke, P.W. 283
Tipper, S.P. 113, 124, 125
Titone, D. 247, 248
Tizard, B. 309
Toland, K. 225
Tomaso, H. 212
Tooby, J. 340, 341, 347
Trabasso, T. 218, 219, 282
Treisman, A.M. 118, 119, 127, 128, 129, 131, 142, 154, 160
Tresilian, J.R. 48, 49
Tulving, E. 157, 178, 194, 195, 196, 197, 198, 199, 200, 201, 202, 203, 204, 208, 212
Turnbull, C.M. 105
Turner, J. 253, 254
Turner, T.J. 218
Tursky, B. 137
Turvey, M.T. 160
Tversky, A. 332–3, 334, 335, 336, 339, 340, 342, 343, 344, 345, 346, 347
Tweney, R.D. 373, 374, 375
Tyler, C.W. 19
Tyler, L.K. 246, 247, 249
Tzelgov, J. 273

Uchikawa, K. 57
Ugurbil, K. 212
Underwood, B.J. 194, 195
Underwood, G. 116

Vaidya, C.J. 180
Valdois, S. 254, 255
Valentine, T. 87, 90, 91, 93, 170
Vallar, G. 168
van Halen, S. 249, 250
Van Paesschen, W. 208
Vargha-Khadem, F. 208, 237
Vaughan, J.121
Vecera, S.P. 24
Verbrugge, R. 305
Verfaellie, M. 94, 125, 126
Vicary, James 58
Vighetto, A. 35
von Cramon, D. 20
von Oostendop, U. 288
von Santvoord, A.A.M. 49
Von Wright, J.M. 117

Wagner, A.D. 180, 204
Walk, R.D. 102
Walker, J.A. 121
Wallace, M.A. 86
Wallach, H. 17
Walton, G.E. 102
Waltz, J.A. 351, 352, 353
Wang, X. 242
Wang, X.T. 334, 335, 337
Wann, J.P. 49
Ward, G. 87, 90
Warner, W.J. 373, 374
Warr, P.B. 1954
Warren, P.247
Warren, R.M. 244, 249
Warren, R.P. 244, 249
Warren-Leubecker, A. 240

Warrington, E.K. 80, 81, 82, 87,
   164, 165, 253
Wason, P.C. 360, 361, 373, 374,
   379
Watabe, S. 253
Waters, G.S. 269
Watkins, K.E. 208, 237
Watkins, M.J. 163
Watkins, O.C. 163
Waugh, N.C. 162
Wedderburn, A.A. 117
Weibe, D. 318
Weil, E.M. 372
Weiller, C. 303
Weinberger, D.A. 191
Weir, W. 58
Weiskrantz, L. 60
Weiss, L. 264
Weisstein, N. 22, 72
Welford, A.T. 139, 140
Wells, G.L. 223
Welsch, D. 285, 286
Wenzel, A.E. 189, 190
Werker, J.F. 243
Wernicke, Carl 302–3
Wharton, C.M. 355
Wheatstone, C. 54
Wheeler, M.A, 201, 202
Whitlow, S.D. 211, 212
Whitten, W.B. 161
Whorf, B.L. 304, 306
Wickens, C.D. 140, 141
Wiesel, T.N. 70, 71
Wilkins,D. 307
Williams, L.M. 192

Williams, P. 79
Williamson, P. 98
Willingham, D.B. 184, 185
Willmes, K. 184, 185
Wilton, R.N. 25, 26
Winocur, G. 83, 94
Wise, R.J.S. 302, 303
Wolbarst, L.R. 207
Woldorff, M.G. 119
Wolf, E.S. 212
Wolfe, J.M. 69, 128, 129, 130
Wong, E. 22
Woodworth, R.S. 55, 365
Wraga, M. 40
Wright, D.B. 227
Wynn, V.E. 216

Yang, T.L. 57
Yang, Y. 372
Yaniv, I. 321
Yantis, S. 122
Yiend, J. 151
Yonas, A. 104, 108
Young, A.W. 87, 88, 89, 90, 91,
   92, 95, 111, 251, 252, 265, 266
Young, T. 41

Zeki, S. 16, 17, 19, 20, 46, 59, 61,
   129
Zihl, J. 20
Zimny, S. 285, 286
Zue, V.W. 262
Zwaan, R.A. 277, 282, 286, 287,
   288, 289
Zwitserlood, P. 248

Subject index

Note: Page references in *italics* refer to Figures

familiar size 53
Farah's two-process model, face recognition and 95–8, *96*
feature integration theory 127–30, *128*
feature theories 68–72
feature-blindness hypothesis 237
figure–ground organisation 21–2
flashbulb memories 220, 225–8
focus of expansion 29
focused attention 113
focused auditory attention 114–19
focused visual attention 119–30
forgetting 162–3
  theories of 189–200
frames 213–14
framing 333–5
free recall 161, *161*
functional fixedness 318–19
functional magnetic resonance imaging (fMRI) 9, 180
functional specialisation theory 16–17

General Problem Solver 322, 324, 325–6
generalisability 5, 219
geons 74–6, *75*
Gestalt theory 107
grammatical morphemes 234
gratings 71
guided search theory 128–9

habituation 109
habituation method 99, 104
heuristics 322
holophrastic period of language development 233
horizontal-vertical illusion 105

iconic store 159–60
identification parades 223
Identikit 92
illusory square 52, *53*
implicit learning 181–5
implicit memory 180, 181, 203–4, 209–10
implicitness 308

incorrect comparison theory 38
inductive reasoning 351, 372–6
  relational rule 373–4
  simulated research environments 374–6
inference drawing 278–82
information criterion 184
information gain model 362, 363
information-processing approach 2–3
informational overlap 199
initial design model of speaking 290
inner scribe 172
insertion rules 294
insight 317–18
instance theory 146–7
integration process 285
integrative agnosia 83–4
interactive activation and competition model of object recognition and naming 84–7, *85*
  modification 90–2
  prosopagnosia and 95
  word identification 262–5
interference theory 193–6
interposition 52
intrinsic context 199
irrelevant speech effect 170
isomorphism 22

jargon aphasia 300–1
judgement research 338–47
  neglecting base rates 339–42
  support theory 345–6

Kanizsa's illusory square 52, *53*
knowledge compilation 330
knowledge-lean problems 326
knowledge-rich problems 326
Kolmogorov complexity theory 25
Korsakoff's syndrome 205

language acquisition 231–42
  critical period hypothesis 238–9
  in deprived children 238–9
  environmental theories 239–41

nativist theories of child language 235–8
  stages of language development 231–5
  early vocalisations 232
  one-word stage 232–3
  telegraphic period 233–4
language acquisition device 235
language bioprogramme hypothesis 236
language, thought and 304–11
  cognitive account 306–7
  memory, perception and language 304–6
  social and cultural factors 307–11
lateral inhibition 17
lemma selection 296
lesioning 86
letter vs word identification 262
levels-of-processing theory 176–81
lexical access 258, 261
lexical bias effect 295
lexical decision task 59, 256
lexicalisation 297–8
lexicon 261
Linda problem 344, *344*
linear perspective 52
linearity problem of speech perception 243
linguistic universals 235–6
lip-reading 245–6
LISA 355–8
long-term memory 5–6, 160–2, 164, 285
  theories of 200–4
loop-avoidance strategy 325
loss aversion 332

Mach bands 17
magnetic resonance imaging (MRI) 9, 19
magneto-encephalography (MEG) 9, 19
magnocellular (M) pathway 15
maintenance rehearsal 176–7
mapping 353, 354
McGurk effect 246
means–ends analysis 323
means–ends strategy 324

memory retrieval 202
mental model theory 368–72, 377
meta-analysis 261–2
microspectrophotometry 41
minimalist hypothesis 279–82
misinformation acceptance 222
modus ponens 359
modus tollens 359
monitoring and adjustment model of speaking 290
monocular cues 52–3
mood-state-dependent retrieval 197
morpheme-exchange errors 292
motherese 240–1
motion parallax 53
movement perception 47–51
Müller–Lyer illusion 36–8, 37, 40, 105
multiple processing resources 140–2, 141
multi-store model of memory 157–65, 158

name recognition units (NRUs) 90
naming task 256
nature–nurture debate 106–8
negative afterimage 43
negative priming 125
non-invariance problem of speech perception 243
nonword repetition 242, 243

object recognition 73–9
    Biederman's recognition-by-components theory 74–9, 75
    Marr's computation approach 73–4, 79
objective threshold 58
object-superiority effect 72
observer paradox 310
oculomotor cues 52, 53–4
omission bias 336
open words 234
operant conditioning 239
opponent-process theory 43–4
optic aphasia 80

optic ataxia 35
optic flow pattern 29–30
optimal data selection 362
orthography 256
outflow theory 48
over-regularisation 234–5

parallel processing 3
parvocellular (P) pathway 15
pattern recognition 65–72
    feature theories 68–72
    template theories 66–8
pendulum problem 317
perception
    indirect vs direct theories 32–3
    reconciliation 34–5
    theoretical integration 32–5
    without awareness 57–61
perceptual categorisation tasks 81–2
perceptual development 98–109
    cross-cultural studies 104–6
    depth perception 102–4
    nature–nurture debate 106–8
    Piaget's approach 108
    preference method: faces 101–2, 109
    shape and size constancy 104
perceptual organisation 20–6
    evaluation 20–1
    Gestalt approach 206–
perceptual span 257
perseveration errors 296
person identity nodes (PINs) 90
phoneme response buffer 251
phonemic restoration effect 244–5
phonological dyslexia 268, 271–2
phonological loop 167–70, 169
phonological similarity effect 170
phonology 232, 256, 272–3
physiological method of perceptual assessment 99
pictorial cues 52
pivot words 234
Ponzo illusion 36, 37, 38

positron emission tomography (PET) 9
posterior odds 338
pragmatics 232
preference method
    face recognition 101–2, 109
    of perceptual assessment 99
Prägnanz, law of 20–1, 21, 24
primacy effect 162
primal sketch 73
prior odds 338
proactive interference 193–6
problem solving 315–26
    computational approach 322–6
    Gestalt approach 316–22
    post-Gestalt approach 320–2
procedural knowledge 330
procedural memory 210–13
proceduralisation 331
production memory 329
productive language 231
productive problem solving 317
programme assembly failures 149
progressive supranuclear palsy 121
propositional net 284
prosodic cues 245, 291
prosodic patterns 245
prosopagnosia 80, 87, 93–4, 94, 97
proximity–similarity conflict 25–6, 25
psychological refractory period 139–40
pure word deafness 252

rationalisation 214
rationality 376–7
Raven's Progressive Matrices Test 353
reader goal assumption 218, 282
reading span task 175
reading, basic processes 255–65
    eye movements 256–7
    E-Z Reader model 257–9
    research methods 256
    word identification 259–65

reading, routes from print to
sound 265–73
  cognitive
    neuropsychological
    approach 265–9
    evaluation of dual-route
    (triple-route) model 269
    grapheme–phoneme
    conversion 267
    lexicon only 268–9
    lexicon plus semantic
    system 267–8
  connectionist approaches
  270–2
  phonological theory 272–3
  search-after-meaning theory
  282
recency effect 161–2
receptive language 231
recognition-by-components
  theory 74–9, 75
recognition point of a word
  246
recovered memories 192–3
red–green deficiency 41–3
regularity of words 270
relational integration 351
relational rule 373–4
relative judgements 223
repetition priming 203, 207
representative heuristic 342–4
representativeness 5, 219
repression 191–3
repressors 191
reproductive problem solving
  317
resonance 30–1
restricted code 308
retina–geniculate–striate
  pathway 14, 15
retinex theory 46–7
retrieval failure 196–200
retroactive interference 193–6
retrograde amnesia 205–6
rhyming recognition test 179
risk aversion 333, 337, 338
risk seeking 333
risky decisions 332–8

saccades 256
schema theories 152–3, 213–19
script-pointer-plus-tag
  hypothesis 214, 217–19

scripts 213–14
search-after meaning theory
  218, 282
semantic categorisation 81
semantic information units
  (SIUs) 90
semantic memory 200–3, 208,
  251
semantic priming effect 260
semantic substitution 292
semantic system 251
semantics 232
sensitivity criterion 184
sensory buffer 115
sensory stores 158–60
serial processing 2
shading 52–3
shadowing task 114
shaping 239
shifting of attention 121
short-term memory 5–6,
  160–2, 164
  in amnesia 207
simplicity 24–5
simultanagnosia 121
sinusoidal gratings 71–2
size constancy 36, 55–7
size–distance invariance
  hypothesis 55–6, 57
skill learning in amnesia 207
sound-exchange errors 292
source amnesia 202
space (depth) perception 52–7,
  102–4
specific language impairment
  241–2
speech disorders 298–301
speech errors 291–3
speech output lexicon 251
speech perception 243–51
  cognitive neuropsychology
  of 251–5
speech production 289–98
  processes in 291–3
  theories 293–8
spillover effect 257
spoonerisms 292–3
spotlight model of focused
  visual attention 122–5
spreading-activation theory
  293–6
standard recognition test 179
stereopsis 54

storage failures 149
story grammar 283–4
story processing 283–9
strategic inferences 279–82
Stroop effect 143, 260, 273, 280,
  281
Stroop task 280, 281
subjective threshold 58
subliminal perception 58–9
subroutine failures 149
superconducting quantum
  interference device (SQUID)
  9
surface dyslexia 267, 271–2
Sustained Attention to
  Response Task 151
syllogistic reasoning 364
syntax 232

task difficulty 133
task similarity 131
tau (T) hypothesis 49
telegraphic period of language
  development 233–4
template theories 66–8
  of chess expertise 327–9
temporal processing
  hypothesis 241
test failures 149
text representation 285
texture 52
texture gradient 52
thought, language and 304–11
3-D model representation 73
time to contact 48–9
tip-of-the-tongue state 297,
  299
top-down processing 2–3, 26,
  244–5
total free cued recall 196, 197,
  197
total free recall 196, 197, 197
Tower of Hanoi problem 322,
  323
TRACE model 246, 248–50
trace-dependent forgetting
  196
transfer-appropriate
  processing theory 179
transformational grammar
  235
transitive inference 351–2, 352
translatability 304

trial-and-error learning 316
two-stage theory of colour
visions 44–5, *44*
21/2–D sketch 73

unattended visual stimuli
125–6
unconscious cue effect 318
unilateral neglect 120, 124, 125

varied mapping 143
verbal working memory test
175
vertical–horizontal illusion 32,
32
*viewpoint-invariant theory 73,
78–9*
vision, development 100–1
visual acuity in infants 100
visual agnosia 34, 79–87, 97
visual attention, disorders of
120–2
  components of 121–2
visual cache 172
visual cliff 102–3, *103*, 109
visual illusions 35–40

visual reinforcement method
  of perceptual assessment
  99–100
visual search 126–8
visual system 13–20
  colour processing 19
  dark adaptation 18
  development 100–1
  edge perception 17–18
  eye movements in reading
    256–7
  motion processing 19–20
  pathways from eye to cortex
    14–15, *15*
  processing in the cortex
    16–17
  simultaneous contrast 17–18
visuospatial scratch (sketch)
  pad 166, 170–3

Wason selection task 360–4
WEAVER++ 296
Wernicke's (fluent) aphasia
  298, 302–3
Whorfian hypothesis 304–5
word-exchange error 292

word-fragment completion
  180
word identification 259–65
  automatic processing 259–60
  context effects 260–2
  letter vs word identification
    262
  interactive activation model
    262–5
word-initial cohort 246
word-length effect 167
word meaning deafness 253–4
word recognition 244–6
  bottom-up and top-down
    processes 244–5
  lip-reading 245–6
  prosodic patterns 245
  theories of 246–50
word superiority effect 262
working memory 166–76, 329

Young–Helmholtz theory of
  colour perception 41–3

zoom-lens model of focused
  visual attention 122–5